Marxism and World Po

This book brings together internationally-distinguished scholars from History, Philosophy, Development Studies, Geography and International Relations (IR) to examine recent developments in Marxist approaches to world politics.

Offering original and stimulating analyses of subjects traditionally at the forefront of Marxist studies of world politics, the collection also considers issues which have yet to be fully explored within a number of disciplines. Examining a wide array of topics ranging from the imperialism-globalization debate, the connections between social structures and foreign relations, the role of identity and imperialist norms in world politics, to the relationship between Marxist and Realist IR Theory, the contributors seek to further theoretical discussions and their implications for emancipatory radical politics. These contributions are structured around two major themes:

- The relationship between capitalist modernity and the states system in explaining the changing patterns of interstate conflict and cooperation;
- The debates within Marxist and IR discourses on the theoretical significance of 'the international', covering topics including uneven and combined development and passive revolution.

An impressive collection that seeks to advance dialogue and research, *Marxism and World Politics* will be of interest to students and scholars of IR, International Political Economy, Political Science and Historical Sociology.

Alexander Anievas is a PhD candidate at the Centre of International Studies, University of Cambridge, UK. He is also currently the managing editor of the *Cambridge Review of International Affairs* and member of the Editorial Board of *Historical Materialism: Research in Critical Marxist Theory*.

Marxism and World Politics

Contesting global capitalism

Edited by Alexander Anievas

Routledge
Taylor & Francis Group

LONDON AND NEW YORK

First published 2010 by Routledge
2 Park Square Milton Park Abingdon Oxon OX14 4RN

Simultaneously published in the USA and Canada
by Routledge
270 Madison Avenue, New York, NY 10016

Routledge is an imprint of the Taylor & Francis Group, an informa business.

Typeset in Times New Roman by Newgen Imaging Systems (P) Ltd.
Printed and bound in Great Britain by CPI Antony Rowe Ltd, Chippenham

British Library Cataloguing in Publication Data
A catalogue record for this book is available from the British Library

Library of Congress Cataloging in Publication Data
Library of Congress Cataloging-in-Publication Data
Marxism and world politics : contesting global capitalism / edited by Alexander Anievas.
p. cm.
Includes bibliographical references and index.
1. Communism. 2. World politics. 3. International relations. I. Anievas, Alexander.
HX73.M385 2009
320.53'2–dc22
2009027628

ISBN 10: 0-415-47802-2 (hbk)
ISBN 10: 0-415-47803-0 (pbk)
ISBN 10: 0-203-86186-8 (ebk)

ISBN 13: 978-0-415-47802-1 (hbk)
ISBN 13: 978-0-415-47803-8 (pbk)
ISBN 13: 978-0-203-86186-8 (ebk)

This volume is dedicated to the memory of Peter Gowan

Contents

Contributors   ix

Origins and Acknowledgements   xi

The renaissance of historical materialism in international relations theory:
an introduction   1

PART I
The geopolitics of capitalist modernity   11

1   Does capitalism need the state system?   13
    ALEX CALLINICOS

2   The changing 'logics' of capitalist competition   27
    BENNO TESCHKE AND HANNES LACHER

3   Western hegemony and transnational capital: a dialectical perspective   42
    KEES VAN DER PIJL

4   Beyond the theory of imperialism: global capitalism and the transnational
    state   61
    WILLIAM I ROBINSON

5   Many capitals, many states: contingency, logic or mediation?   77
    NEIL DAVIDSON

6   Post-Fordist capitalism and imperial power: toward
    a neo-Gramscian view   94
    MARK RUPERT

7   To be or not to be a non-reductionist Marxist: is that the question?   110
    JOHN M HOBSON

8   Industrial development and international political conflict in contemporary
    capitalism   125
    PETER GOWAN

PART II
Marxism and 'the international'   147

9   Uneven and combined development: the social-relational substratum of
    'the international'? An exchange of letters   149
    ALEX CALLINICOS AND JUSTIN ROSENBERG

10 Capitalism, uneven and combined development, and the transhistoric   183
    SAM ASHMAN

11 Approaching 'the international': beyond Political Marxism   197
    JAMIE C ALLINSON AND ALEXANDER ANIEVAS

12 The geopolitics of passive revolution   215
    ADAM DAVID MORTON

13 Politics and the international   231
    SIMON BROMLEY

    References   248
    Index   271

Contributors

Jamie C Allinson is a PhD student at the Political and International Relations Department, University of Edinburgh.

Alexander Anievas is a PhD student at the Centre of International Studies, University of Cambridge.

Sam Ashman is a Senior Researcher at the University of the Witwatersrand in South Africa.

Simon Bromley is a Senior Lecture in Politics and International Studies at the Open University, UK.

Alex Callinicos is Professor of European Studies at Kings College London.

Neil Davidson is Senior Research Fellow at the Department of Geography and Sociology at the University of Strathclyde.

Peter Gowan was Professor of International Relations at London Metropolitan University.

John M Hobson is Professor of Politics and International Relations at the University of Sheffield.

Hannes Lacher is an Assistant Professor in Department of Political Science at York University, Toronto, Canada.

Adam David Morton is Senior Lecturer in the School of Politics and International Relations, University of Nottingham.

William I Robinson is Professor of Sociology at the University of California, Santa Barbara.

Justin Rosenberg is Reader in International Relations at the University of Sussex.

Mark Rupert is Professor of Political Science at the Maxwell School of Citizenship and Public Affairs, Syracuse University.

Benno Teschke is a Senior Lecturer in the Department of International Relations at the University of Sussex.

Kees van der Pijl is Professor of International Relations at the University of Sussex.

Origins and Acknowledgements

A number of the contributions in this book find their origins (in full or part) in two sections put together for the *Cambridge Review of International Affairs* (CRIA) (2007 and 2009). The chapters by Callinicos, Ashman and Lacher and Teschke originally appeared in these sections. The Callinicos-Rosenberg exchange was printed as its own free-standing article in CRIA (2008). Other chapters—such as those by Hobson, van der Pijl, Morton, and Allinson and Anievas—further develop their earlier contributions to the CRIA debates. Robinson's chapter is a revised and updated version of an article first published in *Sociologists without Borders* (issue 2, 2007). The pieces by Rupert, Gowan, and Bromley appear here in printed form for the first time.

This collection would not have been possible had it not been for the patience and hard work of all the contributors whom I thank. Heidi Bagtazo and Lucy Dunn were model editors and I greatly appreciate all their patience and help. I also need to thank, among others, those friends and colleagues whom, however indirectly, contributed to the making of this book: Nana Antwi-Ansorge, Duncan Bell, Charles Jones, Vincent Randazzo, Lisa Smirl, Srdjan Vucetic, Andrew Weck, Luke Williams, and the late Matt Gibney. Moreover, I must express my appreciation to Alena, Alex, Aurora, Chris, Danielle, Isabel, Keith, Renata and Stephanie of the Café (Cambridge) and Passport Café (Budapest), where most of this collection was edited. Special thanks must be given to my dear friends and theoretical sparring partners Jamie Allinson, Josef Ansorge, and Gonzo Pozo-Martin, as well as my PhD supervisor, Tarak Barkawi. Finally, I owe the deepest gratitude to my family, and particularly my mother, father and Uncle Ralph for their endless intellectual and moral support, as well my dear Linda Szilas—for without them none of this would have been possible.

The renaissance of historical materialism in international relations theory

An introduction

Alexander Anievas

Introduction: why Marxism? Why now?

The first years of the twenty-first century have witnessed US-led wars in Iraq and Afghanistan and the worst global economic downturn since the 'Great Depression' of the 1930s. Consequently, the once self-evident 'common sense' truisms of the self-regulating market and the inherently pacifying effects of liberal capitalism have been destabilized once again. After three decades of neoliberal restructuring, the rapidity of such changes in both the financial landscape of contemporary capitalism and its hegemonic ideologies is indeed dramatic. Words not heard uttered in polite discourse are once again on the front pages. Headlines such as 'Capitalism in Crisis' and 'Communism: an alternative to capitalism once again?' decorate the financial pages. Thirty years ago, at the start of the neoliberal phase, it became standard to dismiss such talk as the ravings of 'one of those guys with saliva dribbling out of his mouth who wanders into a cafeteria with a shopping bag, screaming about socialism', as Woody Allen put it in his 1977 Oscar-winning film, *Annie Hall*. Today, neoliberalism may be reaching its limits, and the categories of 'Marxism' and 'socialism' are being recovered.

The resurgence of popular interest in Marx(ism) follows a major efflorescence in historical materialist thinking in the discipline of International Relations (IR). The revival of an intellectual tradition associated with Marx(ism) in IR within just two decades after the demise of the world's first self-identified 'communist' state might seem a rather ironic event. Indeed, for many, the fall of the Soviet bloc had represented a great blow to Marxism and emancipatory socialist projects around the world. While it would be 'faintly absurd' to deny the massive setbacks the disintegration of the far-Left as an 'organized force in the world' has been dealt (Cox 2002, 59), the collapse of the Soviet Union can be viewed as setting the (geo-)political grounds for a certain ideological 'liberation' of Marxist thought and (potentially) socialist praxis. No longer hostage to official Soviet ideology, or an automatic association with it, a space was thereby opened for a creative surge of historical materialist thinking.

This collection seeks to contribute to this recent renaissance of historical materialist thinking on world politics. A central reason for bringing these contributions together is to provide both students and scholars of IR with a single and easily accessible volume laying out some of the major issues and themes within contemporary Marxist IR debates with an aim to further developing these theoretical discussions and their implications for emancipatory socialist politics. What then does it mean to speak of a Marxist approach to international relations? What relevance does Marxism hold for IR theory in particular and analyses of world politics in general? And what conceptual tools might it provide us with in navigating the turbulent waters of contemporary geopolitics?

A Marxist IR?

As the contributions to this collection demonstrate, there is no single 'Marxist' approach to world politics; but rather 'many Marxisms', representing different and contending interpretations of Marx and other key thinkers of the historical materialist canon.[1] This plurality of approaches is, of course, the logical result of any rich and wide-ranging intellectual tradition. What then might be considered the 'guiding threads' of thought uniting such a diversity of Marxist approaches? And what sets Marxism apart from other, more traditional theories of IR such as (neo-)realism or (neo-)liberalism?

Four central tenets of Marxist thought can be identified which, taken together, distinguish it from traditional IR theories. First, Marxist approaches to IR seek to 'de-reify' the seemingly 'natural' or supra-historical structures of world politics. Being committed to the 'ruthless criticism of all that exists' (Marx 1975, 142), historical materialists have sought to uncover the *historical* and *sociological* foundations of world politics and traditional IR categories, such as the 'international system', 'anarchy', 'balance of power', or 'the international' itself. The slogan 'Always historicize!' is 'the one absolute and we can even say "transhistorical" imperative of all dialectical thought' (Jameson 1981, 9). Marxist IR thus works with a radically 'historicist' and social-relational ontology of world politics—one which situates (though in no way necessarily reduces) international relations within the context of capitalist social relations. That people make their own history but not under conditions of their own choosing is the hallmark of any Marxist historicism. From this, naturally flows another central principle of Marxism: Its commitment to a *holistic* methodology in understanding and explaining world politics. This strong conception of 'totality' sets Marxist thought apart from much conventional IR theory.

According to the Hungarian Marxist philosopher, György Lukács, Marx's idea of society as totality was *the* defining component of the historical materialist method. As he put it, 'Marx's dictum: "The relations of production of every society form a whole" is the methodological point of departure and the key to the *historical* understanding of social relations' (Lukács 1972, 9).[2] Marxism thus rejects the analytical slicing of the social world into seemingly discrete spheres to be studied in isolation. It is against any methodological assumption positing bifurcated social realities of opposing spheres as exemplified by Waltzian realism's artifice of the domestic and international or Wendtian constructivism's binary conceptions of the 'material' and 'ideational'. Such dichotomous compartmentalizations of social relations are antithetical to Marx's idea of social structures forming organic, systemic totalities.[3] Extrapolating this holistic conception of the social to the inter-societal, the Marxist anthropologist Eric Wolf writes:

> Concepts like 'nation', 'society', and 'culture' name bits and threaten to turn names into things. Only by understanding these names as bundles of relationships, and by placing them back into the field from which they were abstracted, can we hope to avoid misleading inferences and increase our share of understanding.
>
> (Wolf 1997, 3)

From this holistic perspective of world politics, the key agents and structures are not simply the nation-state units and international systems of (neo-)realist and (neo-)liberal analysis, but also classes, ideological movements, economic market forces, ideas, identities and norms operating at the international and often connected transnational and global levels.

Underlying these methodological moves is a research programme to grasp social phenomenon in their essential relations and not be misled by ephemera. '[A]ll science would be superfluous if the form of appearance [*Erscheinungsform*] of things directly coincided with their essence ... ', Marx (1981, 956) wrote. This basic dictum entails a *critical realist* philosophy of science and constitutes the third key feature of Marxist thought in IR.[4] However, is this emphasis on 'essence' over 'appearance' proof of Marxism's economic reductionism? A common critique of Marxist theory is that it is inherently 'economistic'—that is, reducing all social phenomena to their technical-economic foundations and conceiving all other elements of society as mere epiphenomena (see, for example, Waltz 1979; Kubalkova and Cruickshank 1989; de Goede 2003; cf. Alker and Beirsteker 1984; Bieler and Morton 2008).[5] To paint all Marxist thought with the economism brush is, however, to miss a central point of Marx's *Capital*—itself seen by many as his most economistic work. It is easily overlooked that, as the book's sub-title indicates, Marx's magnum opus was intended as a *critique* of classical bourgeoisie political economy which he viewed as economically reductionist. Hence, Marx's excavation of the human, social-relation substratum of the capitalist production process, so hidden by bourgeois economists, and his formulation of a *social theory of value* lie at the heart of his conception of capitalist modernity. One of the many ironies of Marx's interpreters is how this social theory of value would continually fall foul to the charges of economism.[6]

Finally, historical materialism is not only concerned with explaining world politics as it is, but radically improving it. There is no sharp distinction between theory and praxis for Marxists; the two are necessarily and dialectically related to one another. Marxism thus comes fitted with a particular conception of ethics and politics oriented towards radical, universal human emancipation. This further entails a reflexivity in regards to the role of knowledge and theory itself in concealing the contradictory and conflictual nature of capitalist social relations. Unlike the 'problem solving' theories of the 'neo-neos' (Cox 1986), Marxism is a *critical theory* involving a strong notion of the relationship of scholarship to politics. And, although much decried, the fact that Marxism has a theory of ideology provides it with a very different kind of analytical purchase in times of changing economic paradigms.[7] At the most general level then, these four principles of analysis—historicism, critical realism, methodological holism, theory-praxis nexus—can be said to define a distinctively Marxist approach to world politics.

Themes, debates, and contexts

Contributing to the creative regeneration of Marxist thinking in world politics, this collection seeks to address some crucial issues confronting Marxism and IR theory. Two central, interconnected sets of themes run throughout the following pages: (1) the geopolitics of capitalist modernity, and; (2) the significance of 'the international' (or inter-societal, in its less historically particular form) for Marxist theory. The first cluster of themes concerns the precise relationship between the modern system of sovereign nation-states and global capitalism to understand and explain contemporary patterns of geopolitical cooperation and conflict.

The issue of why there are many states under a global capitalist system invites a number of related questions. Are the connections between capitalism and the states system, as well as the tendencies toward geopolitical rivalry and war, contingently or structurally related? Is there anything *inherent* to capitalism which perpetuates a plurality of territorial states? If so, what mechanism(s) or tendencies might be identified to explain this? And, if not, is it conceivable that in the era of 'globalization' capitalism may be transcending the states system? In other words, has globalizing capital led to a transnationalization of state relations and forms? These questions are the centre of the below contributions by Alex Callinicos, Kees van der Pijl, Hannes Lacher and Benno Teschke, Neil Davidson, William I Robinson and others.

The geopolitics of capitalist modernity

In 'Does Capitalism Need the State System?', Alex Callinicos seeks to demonstrate the necessarily structural relationship between capitalism and a plurality of states, whilst allowing the international system a measure of autonomy in explaining geopolitical rivalry and war. Situating the above questions within the context of recent globalization-imperialism debates, Callinicos theorizes capitalist imperialism as the historical intersection of two analytically distinct, but mutually irreducible, forms of economic and geopolitical competition. This 'two logics' theory of imperialism, sharing much in common with the approach of David Harvey (2003), has been the subject of much recent debate in Marxist circles (see *HM* 2006). This is illustrated in the criticisms made, from very different perspectives, in the chapters by Davidson, Lacher and Teschke, and Robinson.

Taking issue with Callinicos's apparent resuscitation of the classical Marxist theory of imperialism, Lacher and Teschke propose an alternative theoretical framework building on the Political Marxist perspectives of Robert Brenner and Ellen Meikins Wood. This conceives the 'interstate-ness of capitalism' as being structurally internalized into, and thereby constitutive of, capitalist modernity. Thus, rather than subsuming patterns of international relations under the intersection of two 'generic', 'ideal-typified' logics of anarchy and capital, as Lacher and Teschke charge Callinicos's theory, they argue for an 'agency-centred and dialectical approach' which 'reconstruct[s] the real-historical socio-economic and (geo)political conflicts in order to then arrive at the multiple 'logics' of capitalist geopolitical competition and co-operation' (p. 32). Lacher and Teschke's emphasis on an agency-centred and dialectical approach is shared by William Robinson, who also criticizes Callinicos's (and Harvey's) theory of imperialism as falling into the twin pitfalls of reification and 'theoreticism'. In contrast to the 'schizophrenic dualism of economic and political logics', Robinson claims that as capital has globalized, so too has the capitalist state. Arguing that world capitalism has witnessed the emergence of a qualitatively novel transnational stage of development, Robinson thus challenges Marxists to abandon their 'nation-state centric thinking' and move beyond the classical theories of imperialism (p. 74, 68). Robinson makes a case for the emergence of a transnational capitalist class and, with it, a transnational state apparatus formed by the nexus of supra-national organizations such as the WTO, IMF, World Bank, UN and others in conjunction with national states that are themselves experiencing transnationalization.

In a broad overview of recent Marxist IR perspectives, John Hobson questions both the desirability and success of approaches such as those offered by Callinicos and Lacher and Teschke seeking theoretical 'non-reductionism': that is, one aiming to avoid the pitfalls of economically or class-reductionist analyses of world politics. Offering a three-fold typology of non-reductionist strategies employed by contemporary Marxist IR ('relative autonomy', 'two-logics pluralism', and 'collapsed base/superstructuralism'), Hobson suggests that such alterations of Marx's base/superstructure model may be simply 'treating the symptom rather than the cause' (p. 121). From a very different perspective, Neil Davidson also takes issue with both Callinicos's 'two logics' approach and Lacher and Teschke's argument that the states system is 'contingent' to capitalism (the latter subject further explored by Allinson and Anievas). In contradistinction to both, Davidson offers a conception of states forming moments of a 'mediated totality'—a concept attributed to Lukács.

Davidson's approach emphasizes the systemic connection between capitalism and a rivalrous multi-state system through an analysis of capitalism's defining character-istic—competitive accumulation. Dispensing with the afflatus of 'perpetual peace' theses emerging with the age of 'globalization', he explores the myriad 'indirect routes by which economic competition is manifested politically' in the international arena (p. 95): So long as world capitalism continues to exist, so too will war and geopolitical competition. This is a conclusion shared by Peter Gowan in his con-tribution 'Industrial Development and International Political Conflict in Con-temporary Capitalism' (as well as by Callinicos, Ashman, Allinson and Anievas and others). In this, Gowan examines a crucial dimension of industrial competition rela-tively unexplored within Marxist international political economy: that is, the 'logic of increasing returns to scale' and its relationship to interstate rivalry among 'core' capitalisms in the Global North. Focusing on how economies of scale operate in the industrial world economy, Gowan details the 'imperialist character of the organiza-tion of trade rules in the contemporary world economy'. In doing so, he explores the myriad ways in which the capitalisms of the industrial core engage in mercantilist practices, protecting their own markets while securing new ones. Demolishing the myths of 'free trade' capitalism, Gowan demonstrates the 'normless and politicized zone' (p. 136, 140) in which national capitals operate and compete.

Turning to an analysis of a role of US imperial power in the contemporary conjuncture, Mark Rupert offers a neo-Gramscian perspective tracing the contradictory social relations and processes underlying US imperialism in the context of the changing historical structures of global capitalism—specifically the shift from Fordist to post-Fordist globalizing capitalism. Rupert's 'multi-layered account' incorporates economic, political and cultural aspects of these historical structures of capitalism, whilst demonstrating how these structures have interacted with deeply embedded ideas of American Exceptionalism, and the recreation of masculinized forms of militarism in contemporary US popular culture. Thus, Rupert illuminates the multiplicity of factors pushing the contemporary US state/society complex towards an 'imperial exercise of coercive force' (p. 104).

Working from a shared neo-Gramscian perspective, Kees van der Pijl outlines his theory of the 'Lockean Heartland/Contender state' contradiction structuring modern world politics. This conceives capital emerging as an extra-territorial and disciplining social force originating in the Anglo-Saxon 'Lockean Heartland', from which it expanded outwards confronting and (for the most part) successfully subduing later-developing 'contender states'. Van der Pijl conceives this Heartland/Contender state structure as the latest manifestation of the *'contradictory unity of community and humanity'* forming the 'core contradiction' of different historically-limited 'modes of foreign relations'—defined as specific patterns of how 'communities occupying separate spaces and considering each other as outsiders, protect their own occupation and organize exchanges with others' (p. 42, 48). Van der Pijl's rich theoretical exposition culminates in an empirical analysis of the 2007 Bilderberg conference, illustrating the complex interconnections between transnational class agency and geopolitics in the contemporary conjuncture.

Marxism and 'the international'

Van der Pijl's theory of 'modes of foreign relations' points to the more general theoretical standing of foreign (or inter-societal) relations in Marxism: A key theme of Part II of this book. In particular, contributions to this section focus on three issues. The first concerns the potential utility of extending the historical and conceptual reach of Leon Trotsky's idea of uneven and combined development (U&CD) to provide a theorization of 'the international' beyond capitalism. A second, more implicit issue, regards whether inter-societal relations can be conceived as more than a superstructure of any historically specific mode of production. And, if so, the third relates to how one might then conceive the role of the political in the production of social orders and inter-societal relations.

Given the high level of theoretical abstraction debates surrounding 'the international' have proceeded from, some grounding of these issues in their specific historical and political contexts is useful. As with most theoretical advances in Marxist thinking, the genesis of Trotsky's idea of U&CD was a politically strategic innovation: A means of further developing revolutionary socialist praxis within the specific context of early twentieth century Tsarist Russian politics. The fundamental themes of U&CD were formulated, in all but name, in Trotsky's *Results and Prospects* (1906) and *1905* (1907). In these works and others, Trotsky explicitly rejected the 'stagist' theories of development popular among contemporary Marxists—particularly those associated with the Second International. These generally held that within those countries where capitalism had not fully developed, the cause for socialism would necessarily take a back-seat to the primary task of completing the bourgeois revolution. In the case of Tsarist Russia, therefore, the proletariat of the most 'backward' of European capitalisms would be required, by the laws of historical development, to join forces with their national bourgeois in disposing of the absolutist monarchy. Only after making way for the unfettered development of capitalism, which would establish the material preconditions for socialism, could the Russian working class prepare for the coming socialist revolution.

This 'two-stage' strategy of revolution was adhered to by the majority of Russian Marxists at the time. It was based on an 'internalist' schema of social development which, in its crudest forms, held that all societies were destined to repeat the developmental trajectory of the more 'advanced' capitalist countries in the chronological succession of increasingly progressive (that is, technologically advanced) modes of production within each state/society. This took Marx's famous '1859 Preface' to the *Contribution to the Critique of Political Economy* to its logical *reductio ad absurdum*, dogmatically interpreting his declaration that

> [n]o social order is ever destroyed before all the productive forces for which it is sufficient have been developed, and new superior relations of production never replace older ones before the material conditions for their existence have matured within the framework of the old society.
>
> (Marx 1970, 21)

In contrast to the 'state-centrism' of these approaches, Trotsky conceptualized Russian development and its prospects for socialist revolution in its related geopolitical and world-economic contexts. From this perspective, Trotsky formulated an alternative strategy of 'permanent revolution'. This proposed that Russia's minority working class movement could successfully telescope the supposedly compulsory stages of bourgeois democracy and capitalist development into one single 'uninterrupted' or 'permanent' process. How?

In *History of the Russian Revolution* (1930), Trotsky coined the term 'uneven and combined development'. From this idea, Trotsky articulated an explanation of the origins and socialist nature of the 1917 Bolshevik revolution fundamentally based on the *international constitution* of the capitalist system. Despite Russia's relative 'backwardness',[8] military competition (the 'whip of external necessity') with the more advanced Western European states allowed, indeed compelled, the Tsarist ruling classes to adopt the ready-made developmental innovations (technological, political, intellectual, ideological, etc.) of the European powers thereby permitting the 'skipping' of 'a whole series of intermediate historical stages'. As Trotsky famously put it: 'Savages throw away their bows and arrows for rifles all at once without travelling the road which lay between ... ' The resulting social structure formed a 'peculiar combination of different stages in the historic process'—an 'amalgam of archaic with more contemporary forms' (Trotsky 1977, 26–27), 'smash[ing] the limited boundaries of classification' (Trotsky 1998, 77). This 'combined' Russian social formation was characterized by islands of advanced capitalist relations and productive techniques enmeshed, in potentially socially and geopolitically explosive ways, within a sea of feudal relations. The result was the rise of one of the most advanced class-conscious proletariat, joining together with a majority peasant class, capable of over-throwing Tsarist power and leading the world's first socialist revolution.

Trotsky's concept of U&CD has the great virtue of capturing the dialectics of the particular and general—the intertwining and synthesis of different social temporal-ities (the 'simultaneity of the unsimultaneous')—in explaining phenomenon at both structural and conjunctural 'levels' of analysis. Trotsky's analysis was a response, Michael Buroway (1989, 187) suggests, to the emergence of particular anomalies within a Marxist research programme committed to a uni-linear conception of social development: An answer to Lenin's question of why socialist revolutions arose in the 'weakest links in the imperialist chain'. Yet, precisely because Russia remained the 'weakest link', for the socialist revolution to succeed it would need to internationalize itself through the promotion of revolution in the capitalist West. '*Without a more or less rapid victory of the proletariat in the advanced countries*,' Trotsky argued, 'the workers government in Russia will not survive. Left to itself, the Soviet regime must either fall or degenerate' (quoted in Löwy 1981, 72). In the absence of successful revolutions in Western Europe, the very idea (U&CD) formulated to capture the prospects for socialist revolution in Tsarist Russia thereby came to provide a framework to begin an inquiry into its Stalinist degeneration. The precise nature of the resulting social structure of the USSR, and subsequent Soviet bloc states, has been a matter of great dispute among Marxists and others.[9] It is perhaps no exaggeration to say that the questions of what the USSR was and why it failed underlies much of the recent debates on the international within Marxist circles.

It is these strategic, political and historical issues, among many others, which form the background horizon of the contributions to Part II of this collection. The first chapter of this section reproduces a series of letters between Callinicos and Rosenberg on the theoretical status of the international within Marxism and social theory. Debating the promises and potential problems of Rosenberg's extension of Trotsky's U&CD as a 'general abstraction' to capture the 'multilinear and interactive dimension of all sociohistorical development' (p. 155), they touch on a wide array of issues, including: Marx's method of abstraction and its connection to theorizing inter-socie-tal relations, and; the political and intellectual standing of Realism and its relation-ship to Marxist IR, among others. Their exchange forms the focus of Sam Ashman's chapter.

Critiquing Rosenberg's conceptualization of U&CD as a transhistorical phenom-enon, Ashman argues for a necessary limitation of its conceptual reach by illustrating the 'specifically capitalist determinacy of combination and unevenness' (p. 190). Taking Brenner and Wood's analyses of the specificities of capitalist social relations and political forms as her point of departure, Ashman claims that the separation of the economic and the political identified by them as unique to capitalism meet important counter-tendencies re-uniting economics and politics. From this perspec-tive, Ashman argues that U&CD can be usefully employed as a 'mediating level of analysis' in moving from an abstract conception of the capitalist 'mode of production' to the more concrete 'social formation' whilst providing a powerful analytical tool in examining specific societies.

Many of these issues are further taken up by Jamie C Allinson and Alexander Anievas. Like Ashman, they begin with an interrogation of the Political Marxism of Wood and Brenner and its recent influence in Marxist IR. In particular, their chapter focuses on Political Marxism's proposed 'solution' to the dilemmas derivative of Marx's basis/superstructure metaphor through which they explore the larger problematic of 'the international'. In contrast to Ashman, they defend a conception of U&CD as a 'general abstraction', whilst more thoroughly differentiating between what they term the 'simple' and 'full' forms of U&CD in the pre-capitalist and capitalist epochs. In doing so, they argue for the necessary analytical distinction among the concepts of 'diffusion', 'articulation' and 'combination', illustrated through the historical example of European absolutism's pre-capitalist interaction with the Ottoman Empire.

Contributing to these themes, Adam David Morton, in turn, criticizes what he views as the potential pitfalls of Rosenberg's 'transhistorical sociological articulation' of U&CD. Developing an immanent reading of Antonio Gramsci's writings, Morton offers a theorization of 'passive revolution' as expressing the 'political rule of capital'; thereby capturing the internal relation between capitalist modernity and the states system. This idea is further explored through a focus on Gramsci's examination of 'Americanism and Fordism' and an analysis of the contemporary patterns of U&CD constitutive of postcolonial states/societies—both illustrative of different historical forms of passive revolutions.

In the final chapter, Simon Bromley takes up the relatively unexplored question of the relation between the political to the international. Focusing on explaining the 'generic features of political life in the production of social order', Bromley draws on a diversity of political philosophers and social theorists in casting light on why political multiplicity is the defining feature of the international. Approaching the question of what politics is and how political order is accomplished, he identifies and explores three ideal-type forms of achieving political order: 'community governance', 'coercive rule' and 'legitimate authority'. In examining the relations between collective action and territory, he concludes that the fragmentation and division of societies is the result of the specific nature of political order which 'answers a distinctive set of ontological and existential needs on a territorial basis' (p. 251).

The revival of work in contemporary Marxist thinking on world politics, we are thankful to note, extends beyond the scope of any single volume, this one included. We hope, however, that this collection both provides significant insights into recent engagements between Marxism and IR theory, while further pushing these debates forward. Developed openly and critically, Marxism is not a simplistic call to arms or a state ideology but a sophisticated invitation to think. Engagement with its rich intellectual tradition challenges and enriches our understanding of the world, calling for *permanent critique*. If this volume can in part answer that call in the field of IR, it will have served its purpose.

Notes

1. For a recent survey of Marxist IR see Teschke (2008).
2. On Lukács's conception of totality as 'mediated', as opposed to 'expressive', see Davidson's chapter.
3. Whether this notion of social structure as totality should be, however, conceived in the singular or need be broadened to a more general conception of social development, incorporating its inter-societal dimension, is a topic of much debate in the following pages: see, in particular, Callinicos and Rosenberg, Ashman, and Allinson and Anievas.
4. This critical realist approach to philosophy is not to be confused with the *political* realism of IR theory; though, the two may overlap as a number of recent studies on the deeper roots of political realist though have sought to illustrate (see Bell 2008)
5. The classic, and still highly influential, example of such misguided interpretations is Kenneth Waltz's (1979) critique of the so-called 'Hobson-Lenin' theory of imperialism and his subsumption of other (neo-)Marxian approaches to such critique. That 'Waltz's concatenation of Hobson and Lenin confuses fundamental differences in approaches as well as differences of philosophies of social science' remains essentially unacknowledged in 'mainstream' IR (Alker and Biersteker 1984, 133–34).With some qualifications, this criticism holds true to this day. On the issue of economism in this volume see especially Hobson, and also Van der Pijl, and Morton.
6. A point well brought out in Rosenberg (1994), as well as the exchange between Callinicos and Rosenberg below.
7. I'd like to thank Josef Ansorge for reminding me of this crucial point.
8. In using the terms 'backward' or 'backwardness', as Knei-Paz's (1978, 63) claims, 'no moral judgment whatever is intended'.
9. See Van der Linden (2009) for an encyclopedic overview of the Marxist debates.

Part I

The geopolitics of capitalist modernity

1 Does capitalism need the state system?

Alex Callinicos[1]

Introduction

One of the major puzzles in international politics since the end of the Cold War has been whether the collapse of the Soviet Union also marked the effective termination of geopolitics, at least on a global scale.[2] Realists famously answered this question in the negative. Kenneth Waltz, for example, predicted that Germany and Japan would develop into great powers armed with nuclear weapons and that the unipolar structure of global politics produced by the eclipse of the Union of Soviet Socialist Republics (USSR) would prove a passing phenomenon as states started to balance against the United States: 'over time, unbalanced power will be checked by the responses of the weaker who will, rightly or not, feel put upon' (Waltz 1993, 79). Samuel Huntington (1999, 44) argued that 'the formation of an anti-hegemonic coalition ... would ... appear to be a natural phenomenon in a uni-multi-polar world' where the American superpower coexists with regional powers. But, most observers see little real sign of a coalition capable of limiting US primacy. For Huntington, the slowness of significant balancing behaviour to appear is to be accounted for, in part at least, by the greater influence of civilizations, larger cultural unities than the political units of the state system, in a post-ideological world (Huntington 1999, 45–46); for Waltz, it simply reflects the inherent difficulty of determining the precise timing of structural trends: 'Realist theory predicts that balances disrupted will one day be restored. A limitation of the theory, a limitation common to social science theories, is that it cannot say when' (Waltz 2000, 27).

For many, however, these responses represent unsuccessful attempts to rescue a failed research programme. Some offer explanations that seek to show that, granted the realist premise of an anarchic international system in which rational states must seek their own security, balancing is not the necessary outcome of a unipolar structure (for example, see Wohlforth 1999 or Paul 2005). Others posit a transformation in the nature of global politics: one influential thought is that economic globalization has been accompanied by the development of forms of global governance that both impose further restrictions on the sovereignty and capabilities of nation-states than those arising from the changed structure of the world economy and offer states real incentives to cooperate and to pool some of their remaining powers (for example, Held, McGrew, Goldblatt *et al.* 1999).

Similar debates have emerged among Marxist political economists and students of international relations. This chapter seeks to explore these debates and, in the process, to respond to criticisms of my own approach made by Ray Kiely (2006) and Gonzalo Pozo-Martin (2006). I do so by, first, framing the argument in the major controversy dividing Marxists about the nature of contemporary imperialism, second, addressing one particular theoretical anomaly, namely the relationship between the capitalist economic system and the international state system, and, finally, returning to the problem with which we started—the nature and future of contemporary geopolitics. While practitioners of mainstream international relations theory may find the conceptual vocabulary and the specific content of these Marxist debates unfamiliar, they may still discover some benefit from seeing how important problems are approached from a different perspective. Given that I defend the same conclusion as that affirmed by realists—that the end of the Cold War did not terminate geopolitical competition, of necessity I make some points about the relationship between Marxism and realism, though there is much more that could be said on this subject.

The debate on imperialism renewed

It has become a cliché to say that, with the Bush administration's proclamation of a 'long war' against terrorism, imperialism is back with a vengeance. This has coincided with a renaissance of Marxist writing on imperialism. Of course, this is not exactly a coincidence, but the intellectual revival predated George W Bush's entry to the White House. It was the conjuncture of the 1990s—in particular, the combination of the unrivalled hegemony of the US and the proliferating discourse of globalization—that commanded a new focus on imperialism among Marxist theorists (see, for example, Rupert and Smith 2002 for a good range of theoretical perspectives, and, on the conjuncture, Rosenberg 2005). Of course, this return was no simple repetition. Common ground among most contributors to the resulting debates was that the theory of imperialism formulated by Vladimir Lenin (1964) and considerably refined by Nikolai Bukharin (1972) during the First World War was a dead dog (for a rare exception, see Halliday 2002a).

Nevertheless, the Lenin-Bukharin theory can provide a useful framework for contrasting the positions staked out in the current Marxist discussion of imperialism.[3] This theory did two things: (1) it offered an account of the specific phase of capitalist development that Marxists of the time generally agreed had been reached by the beginning of the twentieth century, in which the concentration and centralization of capital had produced what Rudolf Hilferding (1981) called 'organized capitalism' at the national level, culminating (Bukharin affirmed more strongly than Lenin) in the fusion of the state and private capital; and (2) it attempted an explanation of the geopolitical rivalries among the great powers that produced the First World War as a consequence of the economic and territorial competition of the 'state capitalist trusts' that now dominated these states. Given these two claims, it can be understood why both Lenin and Bukharin were so hostile to Karl Kautsky's (1914) theory of ultra-imperialism, which asserted that the process of 'organization' would not stop at the national level but would so integrate capital transnationally as to make war irrational from a capitalist perspective (Callinicos 2002).

This is not the place for a full assessment of the strengths and weaknesses of the Lenin-Bukharin theory (see Callinicos 1987, 79–88; 1991). More to the point, claim (2) can be used as a template for framing contemporary debates. One can identify, broadly speaking, three positions. First, there are those who offer a version of Kautsky's argument. Thus, Michael Hardt, Antonio Negri and William I Robinson all claim that capitalism is now organized both economically and politically along transnational lines: the conclusion straightforwardly follows that geopolitical conflicts among the leading capitalist states are obsolete (Hardt and Negri 2000; 2004; Robinson 2004). The minor premise of this argument is that the interstate system that has provided the structural context of geopolitical rivalries, first in Europe, then globally, for the past few centuries is neither inherently necessary nor any longer required for capitalist relations of production to function optimally. This claim has been very strongly contested, notably by Ellen Wood (2002; 2003), but those who reject it do not share the same view of contemporary imperialism. A second position, argued systematically by Leo Panitch and Sam Gindin, asserts that while capitalism needs the state system, the US has succeeded in constructing since the Second World War an 'informal empire' that effectively subordinates the other leading capitalist states to American hegemony (Panitch and Gindin 2003; 2004; 2005). This argument implies the same conclusion as is affirmed by Hardt, Negri and Robinson: geopolitical competition is obsolete. Neither the crisis of the 1970s, in which Japanese and West German economic competition with the US played a significant causal role, nor the contretemps over the Iraq war, has significantly dented American primacy, according to Panitch and Gindin.

It is probably fair to say that some version of this position is widely supported on the intellectual left: for example, it informs the editorial outlook of the *New Left Review*. It has the merit of consistency with the assertion of American national power under George W Bush (a development highly embarrassing to Hardt and Negri: see Boron 2005), and it certainly captures the asymmetry of power between the US and all other states in the post-Cold War era. Kiely (2006, 208, 212) has put forward a variant on this position that differs from Hardt and Negri in asserting that 'the increased globalization of capital does not mean the erosion of the nation-state or the end of a hierarchical nation-state system', but stresses the benefits that US hegemony offers the other leading capitalist classes: accordingly, 'the most useful classical Marxist theory for understanding current realities is Kautsky's ... theory of ultra-imperialist cooperation between the core capitalist states'.

Both these perspectives are contested by a third group, dubbed 'theorists of the new imperialism' by Kiely (2005, 32–34). They are most prominently represented by David Harvey (2003), but also include Walden Bello (2005), Peter Gowan (1999), Chris Harman (2003), John Rees (2006), Claude Serfati (2004) and myself (2003). Broadly speaking, all these theorists affirm the following:

1 Global capitalism has yet to exit from the era of economic crisis into which it entered in the late 1960s and early 1970s (Brenner 1998; 2002).

2   One important dimension of this crisis is the division of advanced capitalism between three competing centres of economic and political power, the so-called Triad of Western Europe, North America and East Asia.

3   Consequently, despite the real asymmetries of power between the US and the other leading capitalist states, significant conflicts of interest exist among them (and indeed other states such as Russia and China) that are likely, in the context of the continuing 'long downturn', to give rise to geopolitical struggles.[4]

This third school of thought therefore differs from the other two in claiming that geopolitical conflict continues in the post-Cold War era. I have myself expressed this view strongly in debate with Panitch and Gindin (Callinicos 2005c; 2006; Panitch and Gindin 2006). Plainly who is right or wrong about this and other issues is ultimately an empirical and historical question.

What I want to do in this chapter is to clarify some theoretical problems as a way of addressing criticisms that have been made of Harvey's and my views. Perhaps I should preface this with some remarks about where I am coming from. I start from a standpoint that is relatively sympathetic to the Lenin-Bukharin theory but recognizes that the theory's limitations demand criticism, revision, and refinement. Therefore, *pace* some lazy critics, my position is not simply a reaffirmation or defence of the Lenin-Bukharin theory.[5] In contrast, Harvey's analysis in *The New Imperialism* is evidently a development of his own restatement and extension, in a broader 'geo-historical' framework, of Marx's theory of the capitalist mode of production in *The Limits to Capital*—though it should be noted that this earlier work already concludes with an account of how inter-imperialist rivalries and war are one way of resolving crises of over-accumulation (for more on Harvey, see Ashman and Callinicos 2006).

Mention of this analysis brings me to the first point of clarification. It is common in contemporary Marxist debates to pose one of the main questions at issue between the third current of thought and the other two as whether inter-imperialist rivalries persist today. I prefer to formulate this question in more abstract terms as that of the persistence of geopolitical competition, for two reasons. First, though the phrase 'inter-imperialist rivalries' has canonical status in Marxist discussion deriving from the Lenin-Bukharin theory, it has the disadvantage of equating conflicts between states with the polarization of the state system into Great Power blocs that prevailed between (roughly) the 1890s and 1989–91. The implication is that conflicts among states tend to take the form of general war between the Great Powers: the apparent absence of such a tendency today therefore demonstrates the absence altogether of interstate conflict. To avoid such rhetorically effective but question-begging tactics, I prefer to use the more general concept of geopolitical competition, which denotes all conflicts over security, territory, resources and influence among states.[6]

Second, geopolitical competition thus understood characterizes one of the main forms of interaction among units of the state system. This has the merit of reframing the problem in terms of the relationship between capitalism and the state system. Both Weberian historical sociologists, such as Anthony Giddens, Michael Mann and Theda Skocpol, and international relations theorists in one or other realist tradition have reproached Marxists for failing to see the kind of competition specific to interstate systems as a transhistorical phenomenon governed by a logic irreducible to that of class exploitation. Recently some Marxist theorists, notably Hannes Lacher and Benno Teschke, have gone part of the way with these critics. They argue that (1) the modern state system, while not, as Weberians and realists affirm, a transhistorical phenomenon, emerged prior to the predominance of capitalism, in the era of the absolutist states that developed out of the crisis of feudal property relations but which they argue (contrary to earlier Marxist interpretations of absolutism) did not yet represent the transition to capitalism; and (2) consequently the state system has only a contingent connection with capitalism, which could in principle dispense with it, though they differ about whether it is actually doing so (Lacher 2002; 2005; Teschke 2003).

Lacher's and Teschke's argument rests in part on a mistaken view of the development of capitalism (Harman 1989; 2004). But their conclusion (item (2) in the preceding paragraph) is rejected by at least one theorist who shares this view, Ellen Wood (2002). For Wood, even if the modern state system originated prior to capitalism, the sovereign territorial state required capitalist property relations and the separation they effect between the economic and the political for its perfection (see also Rosenberg 1994). Furthermore, the more globally integrated capitalism becomes, the more dependent it is on a system of such states to provide the intensive management of those subject to its domination. Wood's argument can be extended using Mann's (1986; 1993) distinction between the despotic and infrastructural power of states. A state's despotic power is greater the fewer restraints there are on its exercise over its subjects. Its infrastructural power is, by contrast, a function of its capacity actually to regulate the lives of all its subjects. Thus, the rulers of ancient empires had great despotic power, but restricted to a relatively confined territory around the capital; modern states, by contrast, have, thanks to their bureaucratic organization and the extractive capabilities facilitated by capitalist economic relations, very great infrastructural power, which may or may not be exercised despotically. So one might restate Wood's case by saying capitalist domination not only makes possible but actually requires the infrastructural power exercised by the plurality of states making up the modern state system.

There are two difficulties with this argument. The first is that it suffers from what Vivek Chibber (2005, 157) calls 'soft functionalism': in other words, it goes from the needs of capital to the existence of the state system. Second, even if we nevertheless grant that capitalism both facilitates and requires a far more intensive management of populations than earlier modes of production, why should the exercise of this function have to be by a plurality of states (Callinicos 2004b)? Hardt and Negri are perfectly clear that capitalist reproduction needs state capabilities, they just deny that these capabilities are now exercised by sovereign territorial states, as opposed to the transnational political networks binding together different actors—states certainly but also transnational corporations, international institutions, NGOs, etc—that they claim to be constitutive of the new 'imperial sovereignty'. This illustrates one of the more general problems with functionalism, hard or soft, namely that to identify a function that must be performed if certain effects are to be produced does not of itself explain why the performance of that function takes any specific form. Hence, to repeat, granted that the reproduction of capitalist relations depends on the exercise of the kind of state capabilities that Mann describes as infrastructural power, why should the exercise of these capabilities be undertaken by a plurality of states?

But other Marxist approaches that also treat the relationship between capitalism and the state system as necessary seem vulnerable. Both Harvey and I have independently developed very similar conceptions of capitalist imperialism as constituted by the intersection of, respectively, capitalist and territorial logics of power and economic and geopolitical competition. One of the attractions of this approach is that it avoids any attempt to reduce the geopolitical strategies of states to economic interests. Thus for Harvey, '[t]he relation between these two logics should ... be seen as problematic and often contradictory (that is, dialectical) rather than as functional or one-sided' (Harvey 2003, 30). Similarly I argue that:

> the Bush Doctrine can't simply be read off the administration's corporate connections: rather, it represents a more or less coherent project for maintaining and strengthening US hegemony that has, *inter alia*, an economic dimension. ... More generally, throughout the history of modern imperialism, Great Powers have acted for complex mixtures of economic and geopolitical reasons. ... The Marxist theory of imperialism analyses the forms in which geopolitical and economic competition have become interwoven in modern capitalism, but does not seek to collapse these analytically distinct dimensions into one another.
>
> (Callinicos 2003, 105–6)

I commit what might seem to be the vulgarity of quoting myself at length in part because of the misrepresentation of my views persistently committed by Kiely. Thus, he describes my position as 'seeing the Bush administration in terms of its functionality to US capital' (Kiely 2006, 218), an interpretation that is hard to square with the passage I have just cited, let alone with the overall account of the Bush administration's global strategy from which this passage is drawn, *The New Mandarins of American Power*.[7] The real challenge to Harvey's and my position is not that it is economic reductionist, but rather precisely the opposite. Thus, Pozo-Martin (2006, 236) writes:

> two separate logics are posited, and thus it seems perfectly possible to uphold the realist explanation, in the sense that at certain conjunctures, the territorial logic might be seen as taking precedence over the economic one. Might not this lead to an abuse of explanations based on themes like national interests or balance of power? ... Has Marxism not already dealt a strong enough blow to realism, only now to return to its (partial) virtues?

Pozo-Martin cites me as a prime example of this 'ambiguity towards realism': thus an article of mine on Iraq is 'a Marxist explanation that often reads like an excellent realist one' (Pozo-Martin 2006, 236fn12; compare Callinicos 2005b).

This criticism can be reformulated as follows: Harvey's and my conception of imperialism succeeds in incorporating interstate competition only formally within a Marxist framework. By positing two distinct logics or forms of competition—economic and geopolitical—we have surreptitiously embraced the explanatory pluralism of Weber and of historical sociologists such as Mann and Skocpol. To assert that the two logics intersect or interact tells us nothing about the relative causal primacy of one over the other. But without such an assignment of priority, our position is, in effect identical to Mann's conception of the four sources of power (ideological, military, economic and political), or Skocpol's notion of two relatively autonomous and causally equivalent transnational dimensions, the world economy and the interstate system (Mann 1986, Chapter 1; Skocpol 1979). Harvey and I have therefore avoided economic reductionism and an instrumentalist conception of the state, but at a high price since the explanatory pluralism to which we are, in effect, committed licences the kind of reliance on reified concepts of national interest and the like characteristic of realism.[8]

Geopolitical competition and the logic of capital

This charge is serious, but it can be rebutted. Doing so requires a detour into Marx's theory of the capitalist mode of production, incompletely developed in *Capital*. For Karl Marx, capitalist relations of production are constituted by two separations—first, that of labour-power from the means of production, which leads to the sale of labour-power to capital on terms that lead to its exploitation; second, that of the 'many capitals' that jointly control the means of production from one another, and hence their competitive interaction, which places units of production under systematic pressure to maximize profitability and to accumulate. It follows that the characteristic features of the capitalist mode—the exploitation of wage-labour, accumulation and crises—are a consequence of economic mechanisms in which competition plays an indispensable role (for a good recent discussion of competition in *Capital*, see Arthur 2002). From this perspective, the emergence of capitalist imperialism can be seen as a transformation in the nature of the competition constitutive of capitalist production relations.

Geopolitical competition predates capitalism as both the Weberians and Marxists such as Lacher and Teschke insist. Robert Brenner (1983, 37–41) has developed an important analysis of what he calls 'political accumulation'. In pre-capitalist modes of production (paradigmatically feudalism) where neither exploiters nor exploited have any incentive to increase their income by introducing productivity-enhancing technological innovations, the main opportunity that the ruling class has to improve its material situation is through territorial expansion—through lords seizing other lords' estates and peasants. This requires investment in troops and weapons and also the more effective political organization of estates to organize this investment and mobilize the resources necessary to fund it. Feudal relations of production therefore command a dynamic of territorial expansion and state-building. The emergence of the interstate system in late medieval and early modern Europe, therefore, was not simply a consequence of the contingent imperatives of military and political power, as Mann would have it, but arose from what Brenner (1986) calls the 'rules of reproduction' specific to feudal property relations—that is, the strategies that classes of economic actors must, within a given system of property relations, pursue in order to gain access to the means of subsistence.

But—here I go beyond Brenner—the development of capitalist relations of production gives those states where they prevail (first Holland, then England in the early modern period) a selective advantage in the process of interstate competition thanks, in particular, to the spectacular increase in the capacity of these states to finance and organize their activities (see, for example, Brewer 1989). This advantage was evident prior to the development of industrial capitalism, but the 'industrialization of war' in the 19th century (McNeill 1982, Chapters 7 and 8) gave every state an interest in the promotion of capitalist economic relations in order to produce domestically the high technology weapons and transport systems on which military success now depended. Correlatively, there were the trends in the latter part of the 19th century stressed by Bukharin for both an increasing concentration of economic power within national borders and the internationalization of trade and investment. These were driven by the processes of economic competition among capitals (constituted primarily as private firms), but they made individual capitals increasingly dependent on the support of their nation-states for the prosecution of their interests. Thus, both economic and geopolitical rivalries brought about a growing interdependence of state and capital as a result of which the process of interstate competition became subsumed under that between capitals. The moment of imperialism comes, at the end of the 19th century, as this subsumption becomes a historical reality.[9]

I first developed the historical argument hastily sketched out above nearly 20 years ago (Callinicos 2004a, Chapter 4.4; Carling 1992, Part 1). It still seems to me correct, but it requires more precise theoretical grounding, in particular, to clarify the sense in which geopolitical competition can be said to have been subsumed under and therefore become a species of competition between capitals. This requires us to consider the place of the state within Marx's own theoretical discourse in *Capital* and the method that he employs there. Marx originally envisaged that his critique of political economy would be 'divided into 6 books: 1. On Capital. 2. Landed Property. 3. Wage Labour. 4. State. 5. International Trade. 6. World Market' (Marx 1983, 298). Famously, of course, he never finished *Capital*, the first of these six 'books'. Commentators disagree about whether or not he abandoned the larger plan (compare Rosdolsky 1977 and Dussel 2001). My own view is that, as Marx came to write *Capital*, he found himself forced to incorporate much of the material he had intended for Books 2 and 3, on Wage Labour and Landed Property, but that he did not really start whatever he planned for the remaining three 'books', including that on the state. But he did develop a method of theory construction that is relevant to addressing the problem under discussion here.

As is well known, *Capital* is conceived as a multi-levelled theoretical structure in which successive levels represent increasing degrees of complexity: thus Volume I analyzes the creation of value and the extraction of surplus value in the process of production; Volume III, devoted to the capitalist economic system as a whole, traces the distribution of surplus value, first among individual capitals, and then between different kinds of capital (productive, money and commercial) and landed property, processes that give rise to the formation of a general rate of profit and to the differentiation of surplus value into different forms of revenue, namely, entrepreneurial and commercial profit, interest and rent (Mosley 2002). The relationship between different levels is non-deductive: the complexities that are developed in the course of *Capital* are not somehow 'contained' in the concepts developed at the start of the book—the commodity, use-value, value, abstract and concrete labour, etc. Rather, new and more complex determinations are progressively introduced in order to overcome problems that emerged at prior stages in the analysis: these determinations are explained by their place in the overall argument, but each possesses specific properties that are irreducible to those of the determinations posited earlier.[10]

Now this procedure should, in my view, apply to any attempt to develop a Marxist understanding of the state system (one of the many reasons why no one should try to write Marx's missing Book 4 on 'the State' is that, as Colin Barker (1978a) insisted during the state derivation debate of the 1970s, states always exist in the plural). In other words, the state system is to be understood as a distinct determination (or, rather, set of determinations) within the larger enterprise of developing a satisfactory theory of the capitalist mode of production. As I have already noted, each such determination has specific properties irreducible to those of previously introduced determinations. Therefore, the fact, cited by Pozo-Martin as an objection to Harvey's and my conceptualization of imperialism, that in it geopolitical competition has properties different from those of economic competition, is precisely what this method would lead us to expect to be the case. Of course the state system has distinctive properties: if it did not, it could not play an explanatory role. One implication of this point is that there is, necessarily, a realist moment in any Marxist analysis of international relations and conjunctures: in other words, any such analysis must take into account the strategies, calculations and interactions of rival political elites in the state system. But there is no reason why this should lead one to an uncritical reification of the concepts employed by realist theorists such as Waltz and Mearsheimer and critics should identify concrete examples of where Harvey, I, or others of similar outlook have committed this error, rather than issue vague general warnings. More importantly, any Marxist analysis following this approach will be radically distinctive in that it sets the strategies, calculations and interactions of state managers in the context of the crisis tendencies and class conflicts constitutive of capitalism at any stage in its development; it is part of the success of *The New Imperialism* that Harvey in so situating the behaviour of the Bush administration makes an independent contribution to our understanding of the contemporary evolution of capitalism.[11]

It is, however, not enough to posit the state system as a distinct set of determinations within a larger theorization of the capitalist mode. As Jacques Bidet (2000) has shown, as Marx recast his concepts and elaborated his arguments across successive drafts of *Capital*, he became increasingly reliant on citing competitive structures to explain the systemic tendencies that he ascribed to capitalism. To take the most important example, the tendency of the general rate of profit to fall central to Marx's theory of crises depends on the introduction of technological innovations that are introduced by capitals seeking a higher than average rate of profit and then imitated by other capitals, leading to a rise in investment per worker and hence a fall in the return on capital. This kind of argument provides Marx's theory with 'microfoundations' by showing how macro-tendencies become operative thanks to the incentives capitalist relations give individual actors to behave in ways that realize the processes responsible for these tendencies. Any theory of the place of the state system in the capitalist mode must provide such micro-mechanisms. Sam Ashman and I argue that the interrelation of economic and geopolitical competition must be grounded in an account of the rules of reproduction of two groups of actors, capitalists and state managers (Ashman and Callinicos, 2006). This argument builds on the idea, pioneered by Fred Block in the 1970s, that the pursuit of its distinctive interests by each of these groups will draw it into alliance with the other: capitalists need state support for a myriad of reasons, while the relative power of any individual state is dependent on the resources generated by the process of capital accumulation (Block 1987). This idea, which has the great merit of starting from the assumption of a non-identity of interests between capitalists and state managers, seems to us to be capable of fruitful extension to the international arena.[12]

All of this, however, begs the question of the plural character of the state system. Why are there many states? Is it merely a contingent historical fact inherited from the pre-capitalist processes of 'political accumulation'? Or is there anything inherent in capitalism that tends to keep states plural? My answer is that there is: what Leon Trotsky calls the tendency to uneven and combined development. In other words, capitalism tends to unify the globe in a single world system where access to investment and markets is extremely unequally distributed geographically. It is interesting to see the role this plays in Lenin's critique of Kautsky's theory of ultra-imperialism. Lenin concedes that the ultimate formation of a single world monopoly as a result of the progressive organization of capitalism is theoretically conceivable, but argues that to base political analysis on such a possibility is profoundly misleading. International agreements and cartels register the existing correlation of forces among the capitalist powers, but—given that the dynamism of capitalist development is constantly altering the global distribution of power—such arrangements are necessarily temporary and liable to give way to periods of instability in which the new correlation can only be established through the proof of force:

> The only conceivable basis under capitalism for the division of spheres of influence, interests, colonies, etc., is a calculation of the *strength* of those participating, their general economic, financial, military strength, etc. And the strength of these participants in the division does not change to an equal degree, for the *even* development of different undertakings, trusts, branches of industry, or countries is impossible under capitalism. Half a century ago Germany was a miserable insignificant country, if her capitalist strength is compared with that of the Britain of that time; Japan compared with Russia in the same way. Is it 'conceivable' that in ten or twenty years' time the relative strength of the imperialist powers will have remained *un*changed? It is out of the question.
>
> (Lenin 1964, 295)

Underlying this argument is Lenin's view that capitalism is inherently dynamic and also governed by what he calls the law of uneven development. The two are related. Marx's analysis of competition rests on the idea that individual capitals are impelled to maintain or improve their market position by seeking profits higher than the average rate (surplus profits). Monopoly is one source of surplus profits, but much more important is technological innovation that, by increasing productivity, reduces the innovator's costs of production below the sectoral average. It is thus the pursuit of differential profits that is the source of the development of the productive forces responsible for the dynamism of capitalism. It is true that this happens only when innovations are generalized, eliminating the innovator's competitive advantage, and hence the surplus profits (we might see this as the economic kernel of the 'law' of combined development). But this is only the beginning of a new disequilibrating round of innovation driven by the search for differential profits. Uneven development and, what is more, uneven development that both raises productivity and is economically destabilizing is inherent in capitalism. It is this force, Lenin suggests, that constantly subverts the efforts to integrate 'many capitals' into a single entity. Of course, this is an argument restricted to the economic: it would contradict what I have already argued simply to assume that it carries over to the political. All the same, there would seem to be good reason to believe that it *does* carry over: the tendency not simply to uneven development, but to destabilizing shifts in its pattern, would constantly subvert attempts to construct a transnational state.

This argument can be further reinforced by the evidence increasingly thematized by Marxist political economists that the global accumulation process leads not to the evening up of economic differences predicted by neoclassical theory, but rather to the spatial concentration of investment, markets and skilled labour in certain privileged regions of the world economy (Ashman 2006). Success reinforces success: those regions enjoying such concentrations are likely to be able to continue to make the innovations generating surplus profits that will allow them to maintain and even strengthen their lead. Uneven development is thus an inherent tendency of the capitalist mode, not a contingent feature. The extension of the East Asian hub of the Triad to incorporate coastal China does not contradict this analysis, since it leaves unchanged—indeed accentuates—the global picture of uneven development. Harman (1991, 7–10) and Harvey (2003, 101–8) have independently suggested that such dense clusterings of capitalist economic relations provide the territorial base of states, both demanding and providing the resources necessary to support effectively functioning state apparatuses. Of course, all sorts of contingencies, many reflecting a past irreducible to capitalism, others more recent history (consider, for example, the lasting impact of Japanese imperialism in Asia), must explain the specificities of the territorial division of the world into states. Moreover, the formation and fission of national identities no doubt plays its part in producing the intense and exclusive nature of modern territorial sovereignty. Nevertheless, the centrifugal pulls generated by the inherently geographically uneven distribution of resources under capitalism play an irreducible role in keeping the state system plural.[13]

Changing patterns of interstate competition

My argument has proceeded at a high level of theoretical abstraction. This has been unavoidable, given that my aim has been to establish whether, within the Marxist theory of capitalist mode of production, the state system and geopolitical competition are necessary determinations of that mode. Let me conclude, then, with at least a gesture towards how this argument might help to shape empirical research agendas. Capitalist imperialism is best understood, I claim, as the intersection of economic and geopolitical competition. But, since (*per hypothese*) these forms of competition differ in structure and are (immediately at least) supported by the interests of different actors, how they interrelate is historically variable. I have suggested in earlier work that the first and second halves of the twentieth century are significantly different (for example, Callinicos 1991). In the first half, the era of Arno Mayer's (1981, 329) 'Thirty Years' War of the twentieth century' (1914–45), economic and geopolitical competition were mutually reinforcing. Britain, hitherto the closest the state system had to a hegemon, found itself confronted by two powers that challenged both its industrial and its naval supremacy, Germany and the US. The solution it came up with in two world wars was to defeat the former by allying with the latter, but in the process it lost the resources required to sustain any claim to hegemonic status. The second half of the twentieth century was, by contrast, marked by a partial dissociation of economic and geopolitical competition. The new hegemonic power, the US, confronted the Soviet Union geopolitically and ideologically, leading to the polarization of the state system into two rival blocs. But the US was able simultaneously to integrate all the regions of advanced capitalism into a single transnational political and economic space. Within that space, economic competition could occur and, indeed, it became increasingly destabilizing from the late 1960s onwards, but the decline of the weaker of the superpower blocs turned out to be running on a faster clock.[14]

Since the end of the Cold War, the US has been seeking to perpetuate its hegemony by making the transnational space constructed under its leadership after 1945 genuinely global and preventing shifts in economic power from developing into geopolitical challenges. The institutionalized forms of cooperation among the leading capitalist states—the international financial institutions, the G8, NATO, UN, etc.—provide the political frame of this process. Their role and importance, along with the development since the early 1970s of what Peter Gowan (1999) calls the Dollar-Wall Street Regime that provides the key regulating mechanisms of global financial markets, are evidence of Panitch's and Gindin's American 'informal empire'. But the overall pattern of relations among the leading capitalist states is much more complex and contradictory than they suggest.

The kind of Marxist approach I have sought to develop here can make an important contribution to unravelling some of these perplexities. It is much easier, for example, to understand from this perspective the puzzle posed for realists by the failure of anything more than 'soft balancing' against the US to emerge (Pape 2005; Paul 2005). Marxists, like liberal internationalists, are free to recognize the significance of the development since the 1940s of a liberal world economy in providing the leading capitalist states strong incentives to cooperate, rather than to balance against each other. But liberals rely for their economic theory on neoclassical orthodoxy, which conceives a market economy as necessarily a positive-sum game, since it treats equilibrium as by definition a Pareto optimum that no actor has an interest in changing. It is undoubtedly important that positive-sum games are possible, since otherwise hegemons would be unable to provide public goods for all states. But

Marxist political economy does not privilege such outcomes as the default situation: on the contrary, it conceives capitalist economic relations as inherently conflictual, presupposing and generating antagonisms of interest between workers and capitalists and among capitals and unleashing economic crises and self-reinforcing processes of uneven development. This seems a much more plausible perspective on a world economy constituted, as we have seen, by extreme geographical concentrations of economic power than that offered by liberal internationalism. The unfolding rivalries among these concentrations will shape geopolitics in the twenty-first, century. Careful thought and intensive study by many scholars will be required to make sense of how it develops. The Marxist theoretical apparatus to which this chapter has been devoted is not a substitute for this intellectual effort, but it can provide it with some useful tools.

Notes

1 I am grateful to Alex Anievas, Sam Ashman, Colin Barker, Peter Gowan, Oliver Nachtwey, Justin Rosenberg and three anonymous reviewers for their comments on this chapter, and to the participants in the Cambridge International Political Theory Seminar and the London Metropolitan University International Relations Seminar where I presented versions of it.

2 Buzan (2004) offers a suggestive analysis of the changing structure of geopolitics.

3 In a brief, primarily conceptual chapter of this kind, a degree of stylization is appropriate. The Lenin-Bukharin theory was by no means the only perspective on imperialism offered by Marxists during the eras of the Second and Third Internationals: Rosa Luxemburg offered a significantly different explanation whose major premise—the theory of capitalist breakdown developed in *The Accumulation of Capital*—was implicitly rejected by Lenin and explicitly criticized by Bukharin: see Luxemburg and Bukharin (1972).

4 From a realist perspective, of course, asymmetry of power does not exclude geopolitical conflict but may rather produce it if unipolarity provokes balancing against the hegemon, but Marxist and non-Marxist versions of hegemonic stability theory suggest that, so long as the dominant power provides public goods, other states may have an incentive to cooperate: see, for example, Gilpin (1981). The above classification of current debates is not exhaustive. The most important contemporary exponent of World Systems theory, Giovanni Arrighi, spreads himself with brio across all three positions: he certainly rejects Hardt's and Negri's premises but accepts their conclusion (that geopolitical rivalries are obsolete), while further affirming that, while the US is currently hegemonic, its dominance has probably entered its 'terminal crisis'. See, for example, Arrighi (2005a; 2005b). Robert Brenner's position is also, albeit in a different way, inassimilable to this classification, though he would probably not reject the three propositions listed in the text; see Brenner (2006a).

5 Kiely offers an example of this kind of lazy criticism. Thus he charges 'theorists of the new imperialism' with simply repeating Lenin and Bukharin. For example, '[t]he small power imperialism of the Iraqi regime in 1991 is barely mentioned in these accounts as "local" conflicts appear to be completely determined by global (big power) imperialist conflicts. The analysis therefore lacks a convincing account of processes of state formation and development, and primitive accumulation in the periphery' (Kiely 2005, 33). Kiely cites as an instance of this kind of approach a collective work to which I contributed a revised version of Callinicos (1991), which includes in its survey of 'Imperialism after the Cold War' a substantial section devoted to 'The rise of sub-imperialisms in the Third World' that takes Saddam's Iraq as a prime example (Callinicos *et al.* 1994, 45–54). This analysis may be inadequate, but that would be no reason for effectively denying its existence, as Kiely does. His historical criticisms of the Lenin-Bukharin theory (Kiely 2005, 30–34; 2006, 208–10) refer to phenomena long familiar to 'theorists of the new imperialism':

compare Callinicos (1987, 79–88), and Callinicos (1991, 13–26). Many of the substantive points that Kiely makes about the contemporary global political economy are, in my view, also unexceptionable: it is a pity then that he feels obliged to present theoretical differences in such a caricatured and misleading way.

6 Realists such as John Mearsheimer (1994–95; 2001) tend to equate competition between states with security competition, but there is no reason for a Marxist approach that seeks to embed interstate relations within the global accumulation process and consequently to diversify the interests and connections of state managers to make this restrictive assumption.

7 Panitch laid the (equally improbable) charge that Harvey has an instrumentalist conception of the state at the International Marx Congress in Paris in October 2004.

8 Alex Anievas (2005), Robert Brenner (at a conference in London devoted to his work in November 2004) and Sebastian Budgen (on various occasions) make what amount to similar criticisms.

9 For a historical treatment, see Hobsbawm (1987). This process can be seen as an instance of what Alan Carling (1993) calls the 'competitive primacy' of the productive forces, in which interstate competition provides the mechanism through which societies are led to develop the productive forces (in this case by promoting capitalist economic relations).

10 For much more on the nature and difficulties of this procedure, see Callinicos (2001; 2005a). The concept of determination derives ultimately from Hegel, for whom it means what gives something an identity differentiating it from other things. For the purposes of Marx's explanatory strategy, a determination is best understood simply as a social phenomenon constituted by the causal powers that it has different from those constitutive of other social phenomena.

11 Nevertheless, the implication of this position will be that, despite the entirely valid criticisms of realism made notably by Justin Rosenberg (1994), there will be issues on which Marxists and realists will find themselves on the same side—for example, in contesting exaggerated expectations of interstate harmony after the end of the Cold War and criticizing idealist conceptions of the international offered by constructivists such as Alexander Wendt (1999, especially Chapter 3). For an example of an effective realist challenge in both these respects, see Mearsheimer (1994–95).

12 A somewhat analogous conception was also put forward in the 1970s by Claus Offe and Volker Ronge, although they do not posit a symmetrical interdependence between the state and capital: 'The agents of accumulation are not interested in "using" the power of the state, but the state must be interested—for the sake of its own power—in guaranteeing and safeguarding a "healthy" accumulation process upon which its depends' (Offe and Ronge 1982, 250). Brenner (2006) expresses a similar view. Compare Miliband (1983) and Harman (1991), both of which, like Block, argue for the structural interdependence of the state and capital.

13 I am grateful to Gowan for emphasizing the role of collective identity formation. Justin Rosenberg (2006, 2007) has developed an extremely interesting argument for making Trotsky's conception of uneven and combined development the basis of a transhistorical theory of the inter-societal. This argument is perfectly consistent with the one developed here, provided that one acknowledges, as Rosenberg does, the much more imperative way in which societies are subject to combined development under capitalism, which is in turn a consequence of how actors' rules of reproduction come to depend on their access to means of subsistence through the market: see Brenner (1986).

14 Layne (2006) offers an exceptionally interesting treatment of US grand strategy since the 1940s that, while starting from realist assumptions, goes beyond them in identifying a domestic 'multinational liberal coalition' responsible for the pursuit by the American state of global hegemony: here there does seem to be an intriguing convergence between a practitioner of realism associated with the libertarian right and the critical interpretation of US global strategy developed by radical scholars (for example, Kolko 1970 and Williams 1991).

2 The changing 'logics' of capitalist competition

Benno Teschke and Hannes Lacher[1]

Introduction

The history of the discipline of international relations is still largely written as if categories like great powers, anarchy, the balance of power, or international law, ethics and public opinion had been the natural starting points for everyone concerned, in the aftermath of World War I, with the systematic study of international conflict and cooperation, and broadened only much later under the impact of interdependence (or dependency) and globalization. Yet, the origin of the field of international relations (IR) owes much to classical Marxist theories of imperialism, if only because the latter formulated a potentially explosive challenge that had to be defused, given the apparent explanatory power of Marxist imperialism theories, and the potential political implications of the intellectual hegemony of this radical narrative, which linked the contradictions of capitalism in the phase of industrial monopolization and financial organization with the great conflagration that had enveloped Europe and the world after the 'hundred years' peace. The moment of IR's foundation as an independent discipline—in the Anglo-American countries as liberal institutional idealism, in Germany as *Geopolitik* and in Soviet Russia as the study of imperialism—was thus part and parcel of a wider ideological conflict over the course of world politics.

The Western discourse of IR thus constituted itself by exorcizing the question of capitalism from the debate over the origins of major war and the conditions of lasting peace. But if it has become increasingly clear that this exclusion of the epochal implications and conjunctural dynamics of capitalist development has debilitating consequences for our understanding of international processes, it is much less clear that the monumental effort required can be achieved (or even kick-started) by taking us back to Vladimir Lenin, Nikolai Bukharin or Rosa Luxemburg.

Whether—and how far—Alex Callinicos would like to take us down this road remains unclear. Admitting to his sympathy for what he calls the 'Lenin-Bukharin theory' of imperialism, he nevertheless insists on the need for more than a simple 'restatement or defense': a new approach to 'geopolitical competition' that through critique, revision and refinement overcomes the limitations of the original Lenin-Bukharin thesis (Callinicos 2007, 537). There is no doubt that historical materialists need to broaden their engagement with 'the international' beyond the traditional notion of imperialism, and seek to explain 'all conflicts over security, territory, resources, and influence among states' (Callinicos 2007, 538). This welcome broadening becomes a problem, however, when it is turned into a vehicle for the preservation of the substance of the Lenin-Bukharin thesis. For Callinicos asks us to take a stance on the old and, by now, rather stale alternative between inter-imperialist rivalry—in the more generic form of geopolitical competition—and ultra-imperialism in the specific form of Michael Hardt and Antonio Negri's Empire (2000) or William Robinson's 'transnational state' (2004).

Now, we are happy to concede that the idea of a global state formation is hopelessly exaggerated, and that the political sphere of capitalist modernity remains characterized by certain elements of interstate competition. But none of that follows from the monopolization of capital and the fusion of capital and the national state that Lenin and Bukharin considered central to the shift to capitalist imperialism. Indeed, Callinicos's broadening of imperialist rivalry to geopolitical competition militates against the historically specific purposes of the classical Marxist theory of imperialism. For if we can agree that some forms of geopolitical competition, 'soft-balancing' and so on persist today, we might point out with equal justification that such forms of interstate interaction prevailed too in the era of free-trade capitalism (before the turn to monopoly capitalism and classical imperialism, therefore).

Rather than forcing us to agree that we still live in the phase of capitalist imperialism that started in the 1890s, as Callinicos seems to expect, it then becomes clear that we need to develop a more systematic understanding of the geopolitical structuring of capitalist modernity that is not held hostage by old debates.[2] This, in turn requires two clarifications: first, an explication of why there are many states in capitalist modernity; and secondly, how we can conceptualize the very different historical dynamics of capitalist interstate competition and cooperation over the last two centuries. We will suggest that Callinicos ultimately fails to clarify either of these issues, though he provides some fundamental markers that any historical materialist approach to geopolitics would need to incorporate.

Does capitalism need a states system?

The classical Marxist theorists of imperialism have well described the fusion of world-market competition with interstate antagonism. The question that they failed to address satisfactorily was: why? Rooting the drive to imperialism in the shift from competitive to monopoly capitalism, these theorists seemed able to explain why states came to express the competitive interests of their national capitals in military and geopolitical forms. But that was not really an explanation, for it took for granted something that a theory of capitalism cannot simply take as given (however much it is empirically manifest): the national form of the state. If we *assume* the national form of the capitalist state then, yes, we can see how monopoly formation may have led, for example, to increasing rivalry between national states and their capitals for market access.

But, once again, why was/is the capitalist state a national state? Why did capitalist class relations and accumulation strategies find expression in a territorial political framework to begin with? Lenin, as Anthony Brewer (1990, 122) notes, never explained why countries/states should be 'relevant units' in the process of capitalist expansion and David Harvey notes:

> To convert the Marxian insights into a geopolitical framework, Lenin introduced the concept of the state which, to this day, remains the fundamental concept whereby territoriality is expressed. But in so doing, Lenin largely begged the question as to how or why the circulation of capital and the deployment of labor power should be national rather than global in their orientation and why the interests of either capitalists or laborers should or even could be expressed as national interests.
>
> (Harvey 2001, 326)

The contemporary return to imperialism theory runs the danger of replicating these theoretical problems, despite all the efforts of the last three decades to develop a Marxist theory of the state. As Callinicos (following Colin Barker 1978a) points out, these efforts were mostly limited by their failure to start, from the outset, from the exclusive and multiple territoriality of the capitalist state. But Callinicos's (2007, 544) attempt to provide an answer to the question he poses, namely that of the 'plural character of the [capitalist] state system', by referring to the necessarily uneven and combined nature of capitalism, cannot entirely convince. Charging us with a 'mistaken view of the development of capitalism',[3] Callinicos (2007, 538) fails to offer either a theoretical derivation or a historical specification of the conditions under which capitalist class relations took shape, politically, in the form of multiple and competing sovereign states. At best, he explains why the itself unexplained interstate system persists, pointing to the ways in which competition and unequal development between existing states act to prevent the formation of a permanent cooperative or integral structure among them. While this logic of anarchical competition between unevenly developing states may indeed be useful in helping us understand the persistence of exclusive and multiple territorial sovereignties (which is the point of Ellen Wood's (2002) argument), it should be noted that it is very much at odds with the developmental logic outlined by both Lenin and Bukharin (a point to which we shall return later).

So *why* is capitalist modernity's political space fragmented along territorial lines, demarcating sovereign realms each seeking to organize and mobilize capital on the basis of distinct national interests? It should be noted that, in some ways, this conceptual problem is specific to historical materialism (though most historical materialists do not recognize it as such). For Weberians and other methodological pluralists, the issue is relatively unproblematic in that capitalism and territorial sovereignty are regarded as two particular and distinct historical forms of organization of the economic and the political structures of society respectively; as these structures are developing autonomously (though in interaction with each other), there is no theoretical enigma to be found in the fact that an inherently non-territorial system of capitalist market-relations should coexist together with a system of territorial states. While Weberians have developed competing explanations of the supposedly interrelated origins of capitalism, the state and the states system, they are not faced, at the very outset, with a paradox. Indeed, most historical sociologists have highlighted the ways in which militarized interstate competition has fostered capitalist modernization processes, and vice versa.

The issue is more problematic, however, for historical materialists, even when they develop descriptively similar historical accounts. If we start from the notion that historical epochs are defined by particular property relations (or, more traditionally, specific modes of production), then it becomes necessary to explicate the major structures of society in terms of these property relations (or, at least, in terms of their relation to these property relations). In the case of the capitalist epoch, it is clear, for instance, that capitalism cannot be understood, as Weberians do, as simply an economic structure. Capitalism is, in a historical materialist perspective, a mode of societal organization that involves *both* a particular organization of production and exploitation and a particular differentiation between the private and the public—a differentiation that could not hold in pre-capitalist societies as the relations of domination were identical with the relations of exploitation. The public state then appears as a paradoxical entity that assumes an 'abstractly political' character, yet also turns into a central site of struggle over the ongoing institutionalization of social property relations, the organization of capital accumulation and the terms of redistribution—a second-order alienation that becomes highly politicized. More specifically, capitalism facilitates the institutional separation of the relations of rule and surplus appropriation, since the latter can operate in the process of production itself rather than, as in all other class societies, after production by political (coercive and legal) means. This institutional differentiation, however, forms the centre of social conflicts as it is regularly challenged and actively—often violently—reproduced. Capitalism thus generates the appearance of state autonomy, rather than imposing its structural necessity.

The capitalist state, uniquely, appears 'abstractly political', though not in the sense of the 'nightwatchman' state of liberal lore (and it should be noted here that we do not seek to imply that this abstractly political state does not 'intervene' in the economy in manifold ways). Yet, the conflicts over the control of the capitalist state determine the degree to which capitalist property relations, the process of surplus appropriation and the conditions for capital's profitable re-investment are re-politicized or de-politicized (implying that the separation of rule and exploitation is as much apparent as it is real). In a way, it is this regulatory capacity of the state as a site of conflict that does not simply intervene from the outside into an ongoing process of capitalist reproduction, but constitutes its dynamics in a fundamental sense as a socio-political, and not merely economic, relation.[4]

What does this conceptualization of the capitalist state imply for the theorization of the international relations of capitalist modernity? In our perspective, the main implication is that we must return to history in order to reconstruct historical materialist theory. For the critical study of early modern European societies seems to suggest that much of the Marxist narrative (and that of Weberian historical sociologists to boot) has been far too keen on identifying 'capitalist' or 'modern' elements in their efforts to maintain Karl Marx's notion of a more or less system-wide and necessary progression of modes of production (or Max Weber's inexorable rise of Western rationality). The work of Robert Brenner (1985, 1993) and similarly that of Heide Gerstenberger (2006), in contrast, indicate that the class structures, along with systems of rule and material reproduction, of different parts of medieval and early modern Europe followed fundamentally distinctive trajectories, and allows us to recognize the emergence of capitalism as a much more localized and specific phenomenon than either the traditional Marxist or the Weberian strait-jackets would suggest.[5]

One implication of 'Political Marxism' is that the widely shared notion of the simultaneous emergence of capitalism, the sovereign state and the system of territorially organized sovereignties—their co-emergence and co-constitution—appears as historically and theoretically problematic. Indeed, it is not only problematic, but fundamentally implausible. We suggest, therefore, that any attempt to develop a theory of international relations in the capitalist period needs to start from the recognition of the socially spatio-temporally differentiated and geopolitically mediated trajectories of territorial state formations and the emergence of capitalism.[6] And, if this perspective is applied to the historical material, it becomes very apparent that regional developments in Europe (and beyond) were not only highly differentiated, but that a territorially defined geopolitical pluriverse preceded the rise of capitalism and modern sovereignty. It was not the contingent legacy of an untheorizable past or the independent by-product of autonomous military or political sources of power, as Neo-Weberians would want us to believe, but the determinate long-term consequence of centuries of social conflicts over rights of domination and appropriation over land and people amongst pre-capitalist classes. These conflicts stretch right back to the dissolution of the Carolingian Empire and finally crystallized in a primarily dynastic multi-state system. And this inherited territorial pluriverse has profound consequences for conceptualizing the *variable patterns of capitalist international relations*, for it implies that the construction and management of capitalism was from the beginning contained in multiple states whose interactions had to be coordinated one way or the other (on the following see Teschke 2003; 2005; 2006 and Lacher 2002; 2005; 2006).

The best way to conceptualize this history of capitalist international relations is not to stretch the notion of inter-imperialist rivalry beyond breaking-point or to revert to two distinct, competing and separate logics, as Harvey (2003, 29–30) suggests—a Realist 'territorial logic of power', pursued by state managers, and a transnational 'capitalist logic of power', pursued by firms.[7] Rather, the challenge is to show historically what constellation of socio-political forces struggled at any point in time over the control of the state, to establish which social interests prevailed, and to ascertain how the variable resolution of these conflicts shaped variable national and international strategies of accumulation and territorialization within a multi-state system whose anarchic structure and nationally differential development always posed problems of coordination and concertation.[8] In this respect, it is not entirely clear to what degree Callinicos (2007, 543) embraces Harvey's notion of 'two logics' (reformulated as two sets of different 'rules of reproduction'). However, the theoretical ascription of *one* generic rationality of permanent politico-territorial (imperial) accumulation to state-managers seems to us as being as historically unwarranted and fraught with dangers of reification (constituting also an unnecessary relapse into Realist verities) as the ascription of *one* generic rationality of transnational capital accumulation to capitalists. The question is never what state managers or capitalists *ought* to do or *ought* to have done according to an ideal-typified logic, but what they actually did.

This is not to deny that 'the logic of anarchy' and 'the logic of capital' exercise certain pressures, but the ways in which states or firms react to these pressures cannot simply be derived from these 'imperatives', but always depend on a variety of factors—the balance of class forces, the degree of self-organization, the setting of hegemonic discourses, the mobilization of institutions and other sources of power, and so on. And this theoretical premise does not translate into the dissolution of theory or its subsumption under history, but requires an agency-centred and dialectical approach that accords explanatory primacy to the widely varying and fundamentally contested construction and implementation of strategies of territorialization and accumulation by historically situated actors—historically situated within the wider strategic force fields of domestic conflicts over the direction of policy and of the spatio-temporally uneven and geopolitically combined development on a world-scale. This move also requires a modification of Brenner's term 'rules of reproduction' (Brenner 1986) that also stipulates analytically a limited set of strategic options to class-specific reproduction and its replacement by the more flexible and historically open term, 'ways of reproduction'. Thus, rather than abstracting out two separate logics and then trying to reintegrate them historically by tracing their 'intersections' (or by complexifying the analysis through the progressive introduction of other sets of determinations), we suggest proceeding inversely by first reconstructing the real-historical socio-economic and (geo)political conflicts in order to then arrive at the multiple 'logics' of capitalist geopolitical competition and cooperation, if the term 'logics' makes any sense at all. In other words, two theoretical logics will then not generate multiple patterns of capitalist competition, but the historical record of multiple patterns of competition and cooperation will dispense with two theoretical logics. This approach overcomes the dangers inherent in imparting one invariant rationality to state-managers—territorially expansive power-maximization driven by the alleged competitive imperatives of geopolitical anarchy—and another invariant rationality to capitalists—transnational profit maximization driven by the competitive imperatives of the anarchy of the market.

This perspective implies not merely a need to recognize the gradual and protracted nature of the transition from feudalism to capitalism, as Perry Anderson would have it. Anderson contends that while the early modern period did see the rise of capitalist production relations—and in this sense pointed towards modernity—the absolutist state was developed as a bulwark to defend the aristocracy's privileges and incomes in the face of the dissolvent powers of money. In this sense, the early modern state represents a form of political organization that stands between feudalism and capitalism, and only becomes fully part of capitalist modernity through a series of bourgeois revolutions (Anderson 1974b, 19). Nevertheless, for Anderson, the early modern period did witness the gradual separation of politics and economics, and the consignment of the two moments of social life to two separate spheres of society—though on the whole the dynamic of this society remained dominated by the political pole until this, too, was brought under the logic of bourgeois development.

The problem with Anderson's account is that it relies heavily on the notion that the private property rights that emerged in the early modern period were capitalist property rights, and thus constitutive of (at a minimum) a capitalist economy. But what sort of property did in fact emerge in France and other continental European states (those that also pioneered variations of the absolutist state)? To be sure, there was a widespread consolidation of property titles, increasing guarantees in law of possessions, whether movable or immobile. Merchants' wealth and the loans they provided to kings became more secure, although these loans were only forthcoming on the back of extraordinarily high interest rates. And the peasants were able to shed many of the feudal obligations and fees associated with the feudal past. In this way, their control over their plots came to approximate the modern definition of private property.

But was it this type of property that structured the economic dynamic of early modern Europe? In a sense, yes, but only in a very inverted sense. Peasant proprietors did not—and could not—act as capitalists. Their situation made it 'rational' for them to pursue diversification, rather than specialization, to minimize dependency on unpredictable markets for agricultural products, and thus to limit commercialization. And, if peasants were far removed from being capitalists, much the same applies to merchants. The mercantilist policies of absolutist France, it has been suggested, were an indicator precisely of the *lack* of entrepreneurial activity of merchants and industrialists. Under these circumstances, it should never have come as a surprise when Theda Skocpol (1979, 51–67) was quite unable to find either capitalist economic activity, or indeed a capitalist class in pre-revolutionary France.

The point here is not simply that a capitalist dynamic was absent from the absolutist societies of continental Europe. More important is the fact that the consolidation of property rights among the peasants, in particular, was closely related to the emergence of a very different (though still 'private') form of property that had much more (and much more devastating) consequences for the economic, political and geopolitical development of early modern Europe. For once the late-feudal nobility lost its coercive (though legalized) access to the surplus produced by the peasantry, it was forced to turn to the king for alternative forms of income. The French kings had of course played an important role in strengthening peasant proprietorship in their attempts to gain direct access to peasant surplus in the form of taxes. Now, as the *taille* diminished, undermining the very foundations of the aristocratic way of life and feuding, the kings were able to incorporate the nobility into their burgeoning state apparatuses by selling offices to generate income to finance their ever costlier wars in a dynastic system of states that obeyed the pre-capitalist logic of geopolitical competition over people and territory: geopolitical accumulation. Conversely, nobles, bourgeois financiers (and increasingly merchants) found it attractive to invest available means in the income opportunities provided by this state apparatus, buying offices and thus regaining access to peasant surplus.

The consequent dynamic was not simply marked by the absence of capitalism, but by a necessary, if cyclical, pattern of secular economic deterioration which by 1760 had left the absolutist states of early modern Europe far behind the only country in which, arguably, capitalist development *had* taken place in the early modern epoch: England. In France, the socially and economically effective form of property was, as in all pre-capitalist societies, *politically constituted property* (Brenner 1985). The 'tax/office structure' of absolutist states was the expression of a new and distinctive form of political appropriation of surplus, which unlike in feudalism was no longer wielded by individual lords but embedded in networks of patronage, office venality and clientelism that were ultimately concentrated in the state apparatus itself.

This state, quite clearly, was not a capitalist state. It was the centre of a system in which political domination and surplus appropriation were organically fused. It was the apex of a system where both the *social property relations* (a much more useful concept than 'property rights') and the *social relations of sovereignty* were part and parcel of a society in which there was a systematic tendency for wealth to be invested in the means of surplus extraction (offices held as private property, hereditable and with legally enforceable claims to the financial proceeds). As Richard Bonney (1991, 360), a leading scholar of absolutism notes: 'Absolutism can be viewed as a set of arrangements, unique to a particular country, by which the civil power operated to protect private property rights such as those enshrined in public offices and annuities'. In this society, as a result of the absolutist system of property relations, there was very little investment in the means of production, either by merchants and other members of the decidedly non-capitalist bourgeoisie, or by the peasants who in the face of growing exactions were increasingly unable to maintain, much less raise, levels of land and labour productivity.[9] And it was this pre-capitalist state-society relation that came to dominate the specific dynamics of the long defunct 'Westphalian system of states'— the foundational myth of IR.

But if the countries of continental Europe, under different forms of absolutism or other non-capitalist forms of political-economic organization, were not capitalist, they nevertheless pioneered a form of state that continues to influence the organization of political space even today. To be sure, the sovereignty of these states remained personalized and incomplete and riddled by local and corporate particularisms. The territoriality of these states (a form of generalized personal dominion over the inhabitants of a territory) was not the impersonal territoriality of capitalist states in which the relationship between state and its subjects is regulated by the rule of law. But nonetheless, the emergence of these states did mark a change in the organization of social space that—though not constitutive of a 'modern international system' based on sovereignty or territoriality and lasting from 1500 (or 1648) to 1973 (or perhaps even beyond)—helps us to understand why the capitalist epoch that started, if unevenly, at some point in the first half of the 19th century remains structured by a multiplicity of capitalist states. For it was during the absolutist epoch that territoriality received a much sharper definition, as the lord-based 'parcellised sovereignty' of the feudal period was transformed through the demilitarization of the land-based nobility and their absorption into the dynastic state. The territorial particularism of medieval times was thus transformed into the more homogeneous and bounded, if still shifting, territoriality of dynastic kingdoms.

The capitalist transformations of the continental European states took place in response to the dual pressure generated by the comparative fiscal-military advantages of the late 18th century British state and the industrial revolution (and the hegemony built on it). Both resulted from the previous development of a system of agrarian capitalism and the subsequent shift from dynastic to parliamentary sovereignty that facilitated the growing rationalization of the English/British state in the wake of the Glorious Revolution (Teschke 2003, 252–62). In continental Europe, the fiscal-military superiority enjoyed by capitalist Britain undermined absolutism's ability to engage in successful geopolitical competition, exhausted its tax basis and state finances, and sharpened the domestic social conflicts over redistribution, leading to the terminal crises of the 'Old Regimes'. After the turn of the century, the products of British industry challenged not only weak economies, they also threatened to increase immeasurably the gap between available financial resources for military purposes on both sides of the Channel—and thus the internal and external reproduction of the absolutist or post-absolutist state classes on the continent. Capitalist transformation here took the form of a profound and acrimonious crisis within the old ruling classes (reformers versus conservatives), resulting in a series of revolutions from above.

Capitalist 'late development' (for what the European states went through was not just, as Alexander Gerschenkron thought, a process of late industrialization, but a process of becoming capitalist in a situation where a capitalist country already existed), then, was originally designed to increase the geopolitical competitiveness of European states, or more specifically of their ruling classes; yet had the unintended effect of challenging and eventually undermining the social bases of their class power. 'Late development' sought to increase the capacity of these states to maintain their sovereignty, territorial integrity and strategic survival, while the rise of nationalism reinforced the momentum towards territorial consolidation. The double challenge of finding, on the one hand, new ways of making tax bases more productive and systems of taxation more effective and, on the other hand, of rallying the forces of nationalism by granting civil codes that flattened inherited socio-political hierarchies fused in the eras of reform and the consolidation of the 19th century nation-state. The reproduction of the territorial framework established in the early modern period supplied both the motivational source and the institutional framework for the management of capitalist transformation (with an international dimension in the form of the political and geopolitical stabilisation imperfectly secured by the post-Vienna Concert of Europe).

In this sense, the social relations of sovereignty, and even the character of territoriality, underwent a radical transformation—except, of course, that it all took place within the framework of multiple states that continued claiming sovereign authority over territorial realms like in the past. Exclusive sovereignty over territorially demarcated political spaces constitutes the basic configuration of capitalist modernity not because it is in the nature of capitalism—much less in its concept—to generate such a states system. Capitalism requires some form of (geo-)political organization, but it does not require the specific configuration of the geopolitical in which it historically emerged: a system of states. There simply is no straight line from capitalism to any specific geo-territorial matrix or set of international relations. Counterfactually, it is perfectly possible to imagine that had capitalism emerged within an imperial formation—let us say, the Roman Empire—it would not have required its political break-up into multiple territorial units. Capitalism did not develop out of itself the system of territorial states which fragments capitalist world society; inversely, capitalism is structured by an international system because it was born in the context of a pre-existing system of territorial states.

The poverty of Marxist imperialism theory

There are good reasons to treat claims for the transition from national to global statehood with more than a dose of scepticism. While a hesitant and contradictory process of global state formation is an aspect of the current conjuncture, the uneven and combined development of capitalist states under 'anarchical' conditions seems to prevent the necessary consolidation of global state institutions.[10] However, none of this can be derived, as Callinicos seems to suggest, from the Lenin-Bukharin thesis. Indeed, faced with the conceptual choice between inter-imperialist rivalry and ultra-imperialism in today's world, Lenin and Bukharin would be forced, on the basis of their own arguments, to accept the predominance of ultra-imperialism. For what is obscured in this stale debate based on the conjunctural circumstances of the early twentieth century is that neither Lenin nor Bukharin considered inter-imperialist rivalry a possible long-term structural condition of capitalism. Instead, they outlined the spectre of an ultra-imperialist future as the most likely trajectory of capitalist development in the absence of a communist world revolution—something which they both considered inconceivable. A short reconstruction will do, allowing us to debunk some of the myths surrounding the old and new 'imperialism debate'.[11]

Bukharin argued that the result of the early twentieth century internationalization of capital, as opposed to the exchange of goods typical of the world market in the era of free-trade capitalism, was the creation of an 'ever thickening network of international interdependence' (Bukharin 1972, 41–42). World market conditions (world prices and profit rates) came to form the presupposition of all 'national spheres' of capitalism. If this sounds much like the recent claims of globalization theorists, however, Lenin and Bukharin did not see such international interdependence leading to a harmony of interests between states. On the contrary, they argued that '[ca]pital export unusually sharpens the relations between the great powers. Already the struggle for opportunities to invest *capital* ... is always reinforced by military pressure' (Bukharin 1972, 100).

So corresponding to the internationalization of finance capital was a foreign policy which 'reduces itself to the struggle of the Great Powers for the economic and political division of the world' (Lenin 1973, 101). Force is ultimately the arbiter over the relative extent of each state's spheres of influence, colonies and so on. While military violence is not the primary tool of imperialistic statecraft, it can be expected to be employed when an existing balance of world market control and state power changes. Moreover, the necessarily uneven development of capitalist countries makes such shifts inevitable: 'Once the relation of forces is changed, what other solution of the contradictions can be found under capitalism than that of force?' (Lenin 1973, 116; Bukharin 1972, 87).

Thus, the internationalization of economic activity and increasing interstate competition went hand in hand. The reason, as Bukharin especially sought to establish, was that 'the internationalization of economic activity is by no means identical with the process of the internationalization of capital interests' (Bukharin 1972, 61). As they became involved in economic activities beyond their national boundaries, individual capitals found that they have parallel, not identical interests (Bukharin 1972, 62). Internationalization therefore enhances competition between capitals and, in this competition, the relationship with their respective states becomes of great significance. In fact, Bukharin argues, this is increasingly a competition between state-organized blocs of national capitals. The process of monopolization, in this perspective, has turned each national economy into a 'single combined enterprise' organized through finance capital and the nation-state. Crucially, therefore, 'together with the internationalisation of economy and the internationalisation of capital, there is going on a process of "national" intertwining of capital, fraught with the greatest consequences' (Bukharin 1972, 80).

It is on these grounds that Bukharin and Lenin dismiss Karl Kautsky's argument regarding the likelihood of an ultra-imperialist state trust, at least in the medium-term. But there is a twist in this familiar argument that subverts any attempt to apply this argument to the post-war period and the present conjuncture. For Lenin and Bukharin did not just concede that ultra-imperialism is conceivable (as Callinicos suggests). Lenin, in fact argues: 'There is no doubt that the development is going in the direction of a single world trust that will swallow up all enterprises and all states without exception' (Lenin's Foreword to Bukharin 1972). If this sounds more like Hardt and Negri's Empire than Lenin's Imperialism, Lenin saw no real chance of this inherent capitalist developmental logic ever being realized for 'before a single world trust will be reached, ... imperialism will inevitably explode, capitalism will turn into its opposite' (Lenin's Foreword to Bukharin 1972).

A similar logic is set out by Bukharin, who specifies more clearly the conditions under which ultra-imperialism may be realized: 'The great stimulus to the formation of an international state capitalist trust is given by the internationalisation of capital interests. ... Significant as this process may be in itself, it is, however, counteracted by a still stronger tendency of capital towards nationalisation' (Bukharin 1972, 138). However, Bukharin seems to suggest that there are some ways in which the internationalization tendency could prevail: if one capitalist state subordinated all the others.

> But is not the epoch of 'ultra-imperialism' a real possibility after all, can it not be affected by the centralization process? Will not the state capitalist trusts devour one another gradually until there comes into existence an all-embracing power which has conquered all the others? This possibility would be thinkable if we were to look at the social process as a purely mechanical one, without counting the forces that are hostile to imperialism'.
>
> (Bukharin 1972, 142)

Again, therefore, it is not the inexorable logic of 'uneven and combined development', which, according to Bukharin and Lenin, can be expected to maintain both the territorial sovereignty of capitalist statehood, and the dynamic of geopolitical competition. It was only the world revolution that in their perspectives prevents permanent ultra-imperialist concertation and global state formation. But the world revolution never came. Instead, World War II gave rise to something akin to the unipolar capitalist state system (within the bipolar Cold War structure) envisaged by Bukharin. If this is more of a hyper-imperialist structure, its consequences may nevertheless come close to the conditions under which Bukharin saw the emergence of a true ultra-imperialist global capitalist state as possible:

> There is only one case in which we can say with assurance that solidarity of interests is created. This is the case of growing 'participation' and financing, that is, when, due to the common ownership of securities, the class of capitalists of various countries possesses collective property in one and the same object. Here we actually have before us the formation of a golden international.
>
> (Bukharin 1972, 62)

Only if the parallelism (and thus antagonism) of interests were to be replaced by an 'actual unity' of interests could inter-imperialist rivalry be avoided. This would require an internationalization of the 'capital interest' itself.

That something like this has occurred over the last 30 years is precisely the argument of Marxist globalization theorists, who argue that there are crucial differences between the forms of capital export of the age of imperialism, and the current age of globalization; the former saw the internationalization of money capital, while the present is witnessing the internationalization of productive capital leading to an intertwining of capital interests in transnational corporations, joint ventures and the like. As a result, it is argued, no longer do national blocs of capital confront each other, specifying distinctive and competitive national interests. We would suggest that, on the basis of their understanding of the developmental logic of capitalism, Lenin and Bukharin would therefore come closer to Hardt and Negri and Robinson than to Callinicos if they had been able to witness today's world.

Capitalism and geopolitics: one, two or many 'logics'?

This is not to say that we agree with the globalization thesis (should we call it 'Lenin-Bukharin 2'?) any more than we find the original Lenin-Bukharin thesis satisfactory. What stands out most clearly at the end of this chapter is the need for historical materialists to break free from the original debate on imperialism and the narrow framework it imposes on our attempts to understand the present. Broadening the issue of contention to encompass all forms of geopolitical competition, as Callinicos rightly suggests, does not lend new credence to the underpinnings of the Lenin-Bukharin thesis, no matter how modified, nor does it allow us to foreclose the possibility of 'ultra-imperialism'. We need to develop an understanding of different types and patterns of geopolitical competition and cooperation that goes beyond this dichotomy, in order to understand the historical evolution of forms of states and the changing dynamics of interstate competition over the last 200 years.

For even the most cursory glance over the history of capitalist international orders—from the establishment of the liberal trade system of the Pax Britannica and the 'New Imperialism' of Salisbury or Chamberlain, with its oscillation between 'formal' and 'informal empire' via the territorially expansive and economically autarchic *Mitteleuropa* and *Lebensraum* conceptions of German *Geopolitik* and the Japanese project of a 'Greater East-Asian Co-Prosperity Sphere', to the US-sponsored (but multilateral) post-war liberal world order within the Cold War context and contemporary European integration—shows how the historical record exhibits an immense co-variation in the nexus between capitalist states and projects of territorialization.

To negate these historical fluctuations as aberrations from a 'normal' correlation between capitalism and the classical states system would be to reify a structuralist view of an essentially invariant international order. The reality is that capitalist states have adopted different 'strategies of spatialization', ranging from the grant of full juridical independence to subaltern states, via semi-hegemonic projects like the European Union, to systems of outright territorial control in the pursuit of *Lebensraum* or 'formal Empire'. Moreover, the capitalist core countries themselves have structured their relationships to each other and to the world market in historically changing ways. What an understanding of these diverse strategies of spatialization requires is an agency-centred perspective that emphasizes the variable politics and geopolitics of territorialization and de-territorialization. Inter-imperialist rivalry is best understood as but one historically limited variation, which needs to be set in the context of capitalism's crisis tendencies and class struggles in this particular conjuncture.

If we find 'geopolitical competition' at each of the decisive conjunctures of capitalist development, including the period of the 'hundred years' peace, it becomes clear in the light of those substantial differences that we need to go far beyond the development of an abstract theory of geopolitical competition based on the elaboration of two distinctive but intersecting 'logics'. Geopolitical competition after 1945, for instance, was not more of the same, but significantly different, just as the post-1972 and post-1989 periods (and again 9/11) ushered in new dynamics. While geopolitical competition characterizes the entire period of capitalist modernity, the specific dynamics of international competition (and cooperation) underwent conjunctural transformations that have to be set in the context of the variable resolution of specific social and international conflicts in the political and economic organization of capitalist modernity. Where Callinicos does speak to the 'changing structures of international competition', he remains entirely descriptive. While he recognizes the differences in international dynamics after 1945 compared to the period of the two wars and to the period of 'globalization', he provides little guidance as to how to conceptualize and explain these differences.

Furthermore, we should note that far from the notion of inter-imperialist rivalry lending itself to the abstraction of a more general dynamic of capitalist geopolitics, we need to reconsider just how useful those classical Marxist theories of imperialism are for our understanding of the age of inter-imperialist rivalry itself, from the 1890s to 1945. The problems are familiar and include the relative dearth of capital exports to non-industrial markets and the rather mixed pattern of monopolization among the leading capitalist powers. It is, perhaps, finally time not only to debunk the applicability of 'Lenin-Bukharin 1' to the present, but also to recognize that Lenin, Bukharin, Rudolf Hilferding and Luxemburg did not even get their own period right. As we suggested above, any theory of the increasingly prominent role of the state in capitalist competition at the turn of the twentieth century needs to start by not simply taking national states as givens, but by theorizing the national state form and its complex and contradictory internalization into the fabric of capitalist modernity. Finally, we need to reconsider the nature of the underlying dynamic that brought about the shift from relative cooperation to outright military, diplomatic and economic confrontation. According to Callinicos (2007, 541), the defining element of the late 19th century shift to capitalist imperialism was the 'increasing interdependence of state and capital' with the result that 'interstate competition became subsumed under that between capitals'. We would suggest that a reversal of the suggested dynamism might yield a more accurate understanding of this shift: the subsumption of capital under the state and the political mobilization of economic forms of competition.

Finally, Callinicos (2007, 544) answers the question whether there is 'anything inherent in capitalism that tends to keep states plural' in the affirmative, due to its tendency of combined and uneven development that regularly tends to destabilize unifying tendencies—destabilizations based on varying correlations of forces that are ultimately sealed by the proof of force. But to what degree is uneven and combined development inherent to capitalism? If anything, capitalism developed unevenly not because it is in its nature—conceptually, of course (that is, abstracted from history and agency), it should even itself out internationally through world-price formation and the long-term equalization of profit-rates—but because its spatio-temporally differentiated historical origin and expansion was from the first suffused with non-capitalist (and often anti-capitalist) elements that produced and kept reproducing unevenness, manifested in differential strategies of late development and catching-up. In fact, the very notion of uneven and combined development—or socially uneven and geopolitically combined development—is only meaningful due to something that lies outside the pure notion of capitalism, but is constitutive of Leon Trotsky's term: capitalism's progressive historical development and incorporation of non-capitalist regions within and through an antecedent geo-territorial configuration that is not of its making: the states system. And although we may agree that this geopolitical premise, which forced Trotsky to decisively reformulate the notion of capitalist development by adding 'uneven and combined', has historically exerted powerful barriers to the integration of states, it provides no absolute guarantee against its possibility, as the European integration project testifies.

What we therefore suggest is not a return to the 'old masters', nor a partial Harveyan move to Weberian pluralist models to capture the realist imagination and align power politics with Marxist concerns, nor an evolutionary understanding of capitalism's progressive cancellation of state-boundaries, nor even an orthodox reading of Political Marxism, but a constant attentiveness to the rich diversity of socio-politically contested constructions of international relations that time and again seem to escape the 'logics' of pre-conceived concepts.

Notes

1 We would like to thank the four anonymous reviewers for their helpful comments.
2 For a critical survey of Marxist approaches to international relations see Teschke (2008).
3 Ironically, Callinicos's (2007, 540–41) own sketch, of the origin of the interstate system based on Brenner's approach, and his extension of this perspective to the military dynamic of capitalist late-industrialization processes seem perfectly compatible with our own arguments, which we have developed in historical detail in Teschke (1998; 2002; 2003) and Lacher (2002; 2005; 2006).
4 This raises, of course, the question of to what degree there is any definitional coherence to the concept of capitalism itself.
5 It should also be noted that this perspective is not Eurocentric in the sense that it assumes something inherent to the course of European history as a whole—be it either a specific form of European rationality, as Weber believed, or a specific succession and concatenation of forms of socio-political organization stretching back to antiquity, as Perry Anderson suggested. If anything, it is an Anglocentric perspective that does not posit normatively any superiority or greater 'rationality' of England or the English people. Instead, it highlights the specificity of a regional socio-political transformation and the concomitant construction of new forms of economic and political subjectivity that would create consequences of world-historical relevance, but does not presume that it was the inevitable and teleological product of a directional historical evolution.
6 The original research programme of 'Political Marxism' as that of Heide Gerstenberger (2006) paid little attention to the problematique of the states system and international relations. It remained wedded to the comparative method, according insufficient empirical and, especially, theoretical consideration to the effects of international relations on regionally differential development and the general course of history.
7 Wood points to two conflicting readings of the 'two logics' in Harvey. One suggests that unlimited capital accumulation, very functionally, requires a geographically co-extensive sphere of direct politico-territorial control, assuming a compatibility if not identity of interests between state and capital; the other suggests two distinctive, separate and conflicting logics between state-managers and capitalists that might contradict each other (Wood 2006, 11). While the first reading would make sense for the period of inter-imperial rivalry proper (but only here), the latter would lend itself more easily to a wider appreciation of capitalist international relations, but would then militate against Callinicos's attempt to rescue the original Lenin-Bukharin thesis.
8 Brenner (2006a, 84) has recently arrived at a similar conclusion.
9 The predominant revisionist interpretation in the literature on absolutism is now powerfully surveyed and confirmed by Beik (2005).
10 For a critique of the concepts of 'uneven and combined development' and 'the international' as general abstractions see Teschke (2008, 179–80).
11 For a more systematic elaboration of this argument, see Lacher (2008).

3 Western hegemony and transnational capital

A dialectical perspective

Kees van der Pijl[1]

My central claim in this chapter is that the global constellation of political forces and transnational capital do not just relate externally to each other, as their usual designation as 'actors' would suggest. Capital and world politics, I would argue, are *internally* related as emanations of what Richard Ashley (1984) calls a 'deep structure' constitutive of actors (which in the Weberian perspective are seen as autonomous forces). This deep structure is the social exploitation of nature, which occurs within bounds set by definite patterns of social relations. These patterns may be summarized, for consecutive levels of the socialization of nature, as modes of production; but also, in the relations between communities occupying spaces and dealing with each other as outsiders, by what I term *modes of foreign relations* (Van der Pijl 2007). A mode of foreign relations is a specific pattern of how communities occupying separate spaces and considering each other as outsiders, protect their own occupation and organize exchanges with others. Such 'modes' denote the combination of a pattern of social relations with a level of development of the productive forces, at some point becoming a break on that development. Revolution and war, which often accompany a crisis of the old order, then mark the end of an epoch in which the relevant modes were conducive to further development.

In this chapter, I begin by outlining how the English-speaking West—both in terms of military-diplomatic power and as a pivot of global capital flows—has occupied the commanding heights of the global political economy for several centuries, facing, fighting and subduing successive contenders. As I have argued in a range of works, most recently in *Global Rivalries from the Cold War to Iraq* (2006), the transnationalization of a capitalist class is premised on this liberal, originally Anglophone heartland. However, its ability to overcome and dispossess rival state classes appears to be faltering. Following this, I present a methodology for studying global political economy as a combined process of productive and foreign relations (rather than in terms of economic basis and political superstructure). Finally, I go into the role of private policy councils in which a transnational class interest is synthesized and articulated, and illustrate this by analyzing the 2007 Istanbul Bilderberg conference.

The heartland-contender state structure of modern world politics

As a specific political-economic structure, the origins of the English-speaking West go back to the 17th century. At this juncture, Calvinist and other sectarian Christian communities crossed the Atlantic to find a safe haven in North America, whilst their brethren back home fought a protracted civil war that resulted in laying the groundwork for a specific spatial constellation spanning the Atlantic. This structure, which I call (after the ideologue of the Glorious Revolution) the 'Lockean heartland', took another century to fully crystallize from the British Empire. 1776 (American secession) and 1823 (the restoration of English-speaking unity of purpose under the Monroe Doctrine) are among the key dates of the establishment of this heartland. Its defining characteristics include:

a) liberal constitutionalism, constructed around notions of innate individual rights and limitations of monarchical/state prerogative. This allows the constituent societies a considerable measure of self-regulation, enshrined in civil law, under their own sovereign states;

b) identical concepts of private property setting the social conditions for self-sustaining capital accumulation whilst creating a structural free space and similar conditions for capital across the constituent states (resulting in dense capital interpenetration);

c) the notion that state power serves to pursue global liberalism in the sense of creating the spaces for capital to expand transnationally, lay claim to the world's resources, and reproduce the characteristics of the Lockean constellation beyond the original Anglophone West (the particular missionary mindset that accompanies this goes back to the Calvinist quest for a new Jerusalem);

d) the use of force as a means of redistributing spheres-of-influence in the imperialist sense, has been largely suspended within the expanding heartland (on the 'democratic peace' thesis, see Owen 1994);

e) the territoriality that we associate with nationality, has been largely overcome, both between states and within each constituent one (see Van der Pijl 2006, Chapter 1).

Although there remain regionalisms with territorial nationality involved, the original English-speaking heartland (by displacing and largely eliminating the indigenous populations), and since World War II, the EU (by constitutional arrangements) have created a melting-pot of resident and new immigrant communities. The ghettoes and deprived areas they may contain do not usually have secessionist aspirations; where cleavages do have separatist potential (Belgium or Italy, Quebec or Scotland) this is primarily being generated by neoliberal deconstruction of the public sphere and of state redistribution. The West's relative homogeneity gives it a crucial lever in playing on territorial disputes in the rest of the world without the fear of reciprocation.

The proximate structural condition in which both capital and the West crystallized then was the liberal turn that Anglophone society took at the close of the English Civil War. The Glorious Revolution was not just a political settlement; it also concluded the enclosure movement and a number of other aspects of the emerging capitalist economy, taking in its stride the maritime monopoly established by the Navigation Act and other steps taken in previous stages of the transformation contested in the Civil War. By homogenizing the social space, taxation and the use of consolidated public debt, the Civil War upon its conclusion allowed the British state to wage war more effectively than any of its rivals (Padfield 2000, 4; Homer 1963, 149). The transformation of the English-speaking sphere liberated the forces of private initiative under a property guarantee valid for the entire space under its control. Although this would only become fully apparent in the ensuing century, the most powerful of Britain's rivals, or contender states, in their contest with the liberal West typically resorted to an inverse relationship between state and society, between nationality and transnationality. Thus, radically different state/society complexes, to use Robert Cox's (1986) term, came to confront each other on a shifting frontier.

Beginning with France, from the Cardinals-First Ministers and Louis XIV to Napoleon, the contenders set about organizing their social basis from above (with varying degrees of central planning and coercion). Moulding society into forms which had not yet matured within the social body itself they thus 'nationalized' the social space under their control, demarcating it sharply from others. The social transformations which in the epoch from the English Civil War up to the American secession had come about primarily from the social sphere itself, in this way were matched by the contenders. From France to Germany, Japan and Italy in the late 19th century, on to the USSR, and China today, the primary contenders of Western hegemony have been compelled by the greater (and more flexible, adaptable) military and economic power of the expanding West, as well as by the hegemony of its evolving way of life, to shape their societies through varying degrees of state control. The alternative had to be developed 'nationally', even though all the major contenders at some point did organize blocs around themselves. But these were assembled through coercion, never by the free adhesion typical of the expanding heartland. In the end they all were defeated in global wars by which every contender episode is concluded (Thomson 1988)—except in the case of the Soviet Union, which capitulated in a crippling arms race, and with its planned economy in a tailspin.

Capital can only fully develop in the transnational, free space created by the Lockean heartland. Only here the contradictory, and hence dynamic, unity of capital-in-general and particular capitals can come about. Particular capitals are units of mobile wealth ('value'), each run as a legal entity in property terms. In their competitive exploitation of society and nature, however, they 'act out' an inherent, underlying set of common characteristics which the process of competition forces them to recognize—the characteristics of capital-in-general. In that sense we may speak of the operation of a 'total capital' (*Gesamtkapital*). This operation comes about involuntarily, without a unified subject. Only as aggregations of particular capitals unified by outlook on grounds of (some combination of) size, functional role, and/or nationality, as fractions of capital, can there be an approximation of the general capitalist interest (Hickel 1975). Yet such an imagined totality will always be a temporary approximation, undermined by competition and the fluctuating, conjunctural nature of capitalist development. At some point the claim to articulate the overall capitalist interest, indeed the 'general' interest as such, is bound to be exposed as a concept of control that is no longer comprehensive.

A 'capital-in-general/particular capitals' configuration and all that it entails, requires that states refrain from affecting the competitive process (including its interest articulation aspect through private policy planning) other than by generalized support to regulate key class relations and the currency (de Brunhoff 1976), and infrastructural provision. The 'playing field' itself must be 'level'—ideally free from state intervention. That is why capitalist development in this comprehensive sense can only occur in a liberal setting; and why capital originated in the same social context from which emerged the Lockean constitution of the heartland. So when the strategists of the ruling class meet in the boardrooms of large banks and corporations, or in dedicated policy councils such as the World Economic Forum or the Trilateral Commission, they not only seek to hammer out a general interest of capital. They must also provide guidance to the West at large.

In a contender state context, this sequence (free competition, interest aggregation along fractional lines, competitive articulation of a comprehensive class interest) cannot function in this way. There may be 'particular capitals' to various degrees, from actual business firms to officials operating on private account, but the state exerts influence at each stage—'distorting' economic competition, inflecting interest aggregation towards the centre, and formulating the general interest. In other words, the constraints under which capitals operate are set not by capital-in-general as a *Gesamtkapital* as in the West. Rather, they are set by the state, or more precisely, a class in control of the state—the 'state class'. In a contender state there is no property-owning, directive ruling class that can leave companies and the state to a managerial and political cadre trained in the rules of the game, as in the Lockean context. Here, as in most non-Western states, the state itself is the key lever of wealth creation and power, not the self-regulating social sphere. Losing control of it spells the end, not just of a political career, but of one's social position throughout.

The West historically has exerted pressure on contender state societies (as on all others) to submit to capitalist discipline, and consciously probes for partners in the target state willing to be mobilized behind transnational liberalism. Condoleezza Rice on the eve of her appointment as George W Bush's national security adviser saw the main foreign policy job as 'finding peace, security, and opportunities for entrepreneurs in other countries'. Change in China for instance was being driven by 'people who no longer owe their livelihood to government'.[2] Such potential partners of the liberal West should be aided to emancipate from state control—a strategy applied to all prior contenders, albeit with the timing and emphasis in each case depending on the degree of capital penetration and liberalism already achieved. To minimize the cost of defeating and opening up a major contender for capital, the West has typically recruited vassals among the lesser, 'secondary' contenders (the East Asian states were such vassals in the Cold War, see Castells 1998, 277). In fact, each primary contender was a vassal before it rose to primacy on its own—Prussia and Austria against France, the USSR against the Axis powers, China against the USSR. The caveats in presenting such a stylized, apparently mechanical process are self-evident, but however modified in each case there is an element of repetition and structural continuity that deserves to be recognized.

Productive forces and social relations

Marx's historical materialism synthesizes the materialist idea that humanity exists as a force of nature with Hegel's conception of a realm of spiritual development, which is historical in opposition to nature. In Hegel, of course, this was still understood as an emanation of the divine (the World Spirit), but in Marx it becomes a historical force in its own right, what Gramsci calls 'absolute historicism' (Gramsci 1971, 465). Economism, the tendency to reduce society to the economy (capitalism) and to see all other aspects as epiphenomena, was the result of the fact that the development of Marx's legacy, centrally built around *Capital*, by 1900 had shifted to late industrializing contender states—notably, Germany, Austria-Hungary, Italy and Russia. Whilst in the liberal heartland, pragmatist and empiricist mental habits created a general imperviousness to Marxism (or to any other 'systemic' approach not anchored in the free agent and the plainly evident 'fact'), the Marxism developed in the German-speaking and Slavic lands was economistic and deterministic, a fatalism of impending crisis. Socialism would emerge from this crisis either by working class action in the factories and the cities or by parliamentary majority decision. In the Second International, as well as in Soviet Marxism (both in its Stalinist and Trotskyist lines of development), economic determinism with its variable political implications was solidly entrenched.

Ultimately, however, all spheres of social life are encompassed by the methodology of historical materialism in their own right, not just the economy. Indeed, the same array of productive forces allows a community to engage in the transformation of nature through a labour process (in which it differentiates internally) and to engage in foreign relations (in which it deals with those who appear as already different). The naturalization of hierarchy and difference accompany each. In foreign relations, the emergence of states only condenses and formalizes the social and foreign relations within and between communities and societies; it does not add a qualitatively different dimension. The 'state system' in this sense is premised on a reordering of foreign relations across a particular grid, which includes, at some point, the attempt to homogenize the ethnic profile of the society under the state's jurisdiction and, hence, a parallel effort to exteriorize the 'foreign' from it. But as indicated, this itself proceeds through the differentiated structure of the heartland confronted by successive contenders, with secondary contenders as vassals.

Productive and foreign relations thus provide a specific structure to how the productive forces are developed. These relations (and others I do not address separately here) foster that development up to a point, and then become an obstacle to it. Thus the competitive exploitation of labour by capital will initially have a highly dynamic effect in societies organized around relations of personal dependence and used to a slow pace of reproduction; but at some point it becomes more and more difficult to force the growth of the productive forces into the straitjacket of capitalist relations of production. The Internet, one of the most dynamic productive forces today, is unifying large parts of the world's knowledge and information into a single grid, available to everybody with access to it. Although inundating the web with advertising and spawning large fortunes for a handful of pioneers, capital has difficulty imposing market discipline on Internet use in any comprehensive sense. Indeed, the World

Wide Web is evolving into what may be termed a 'global brain' through which humanity thinks collectively (not only of noble and useful causes of course). The campaign against the abortive Multilateral Agreement on Investment—the defining moment in the emergence of the alternative, 'anti'-globalization movement—gained its breadth and strength through widespread use of the Internet (Mabey 1999).

In foreign relations, the conquest of the oceans by political formations on the Atlantic frontier of Western Christianity likewise had a dynamic effect on the development of the productive forces. Shipbuilding and navigational expertise, cartography and astronomy were all fostered through foreign relations (for example, through information obtained by the Portuguese monarchy from experience gained by Chinese ocean-going enterprise) as much as they were specifically linked to commerce (see Van der Pijl 2007, Chapter 4). The productive forces, from stone tools and elementary speech to nuclear technology and the Java computer language, do not at once become available to humanity as a whole, but to specific communities who develop culturally on the basis of their mastery (Shirokogorov 1970, 12; see also Borochov 1972, 137).

The indigenous peoples of the Americas were conquered by Europeans because the latter had horses and iron metallurgy and the former did not (just as Cortés and Pizarro had a level of intellectual sophistication combined with brutality with which they could outwit and subdue the indigenous rulers and their populations in spite of the fact that they had come with only a handful of men). The current effort to deny Iran access to its own uranium enrichment base of which the consequences would certainly be important, but not necessarily more dangerous than its availability to the United States, Britain or Israel, is a reminder that the development of the productive forces is usually not immediately global, but mediated by productive and foreign relations. The same applies to medicines and other products of science ring fenced by intellectual property rights (see May 2000).

Summing up, the productive forces develop in the context of specific sets of relations of production and of foreign relations. Even if at some point it would appear as if capital 'faces' the state from the outside (from Raymond Vernon's thesis in 1973 to globalization arguments about the loss of sovereignty today), in fact we are looking at differential forms of social relations reproducing a common fund of productive forces—the deep structure in which they are both anchored.

Contradictory unity and differential development

In the historical materialist perspective, the productive forces and the social relations in which the exploitation and socialization of nature evolves are related in a contradictory way; they are compatible *and* they are not. From the perspective of formal logic, a contradiction is a meaningless antinomy. But since Hegel, we may look at the contradictory unity as a combination in development, because a contradictory state of affairs can only exist in movement—not just in thought but objectively too (Hegel 1923, 68).

To identify the key contradiction within a specific field, Marx left us an oft-quoted method of abstraction and concretization applied to the economic structure of bourgeois civil society. It starts from the dual nature of the commodity, which is contradictory in itself, as use-value constrained by its simultaneous social form as exchange-value. The constraining, alienating social form given by the relations of production complicates actual use: You don't just eat, but first have to buy your food, earn the money for it, and so on. In the end, there may be plenty to eat but you still go hungry. This inner tension then is amplified and reproduced in more developed forms, such as 'work' being subjected to the need to valorize capital, varieties of daily life selected on grounds of profitability, and so on.

All the qualitative aspects of social existence are thus subjected, hemmed in, by quantitative criteria. The method, however, allows us to deconstruct and then reconstruct social reality through a step-by-step procedure; each contradiction is traced back to a more fundamental one, until we get to a core principle that allows us to see how the complex reality facing us is determined by the modalities of these underlying structures (Marx 1973, 100; see Hegel 1923, 106). As always, what Marx adds is real historicity (Ritsert 1973): How a contradictory process will develop is not preordained, like a Hegelian rationality 'unfolding' from the cell form into an immanent totality. It develops through departures and struggles in which elements that were not originally part of the equation enter into it from the outside as well, such as the original expropriation of the direct producers that precedes the commodity form and actual capital accumulation (Luxemburg 2003).

In foreign relations, I would argue, the core contradiction (and hence, the polarity within which all foreign and international relations evolve) is the *contradictory unity of community and humanity*. Humans constitute a single species, but the social form in which human groups become aware of themselves and the existence of others who are (culturally) different, is that of foreign relations. The singular human substratum thus develops within this contradiction as different and mutually foreign.[3] Tendentially, the contradiction will push towards a breaking point where it must be overcome; 'globalization', the use of terms like humankind, planetary community, etc., all reveal that in our contemporary consciousness this stage is becoming a reality—albeit mortgaged by Western hegemony and imperialism.

Today, the contradiction between the social and the private constitutes the specific form in which the subjection of the productive forces by the relations of production develops. The real economy tends towards a single, world-embracing labour process into which all inputs enter, and which is operated by what Marx (MEW 25, 485–86) called the 'collective worker'. At the same time it is enveloped by a capitalist economy which, through webs of financial transactions, is pumping wealth from that global productive organism on an unprecedented scale (see Merk 2004).

Now, one of the real misconceptions that underlay the twentieth century experiment with state socialism was the assumption that capitalist development drives forward the socialization of labour 'objectively', so that at some point only the capitalist shell has to be removed and we have the finished infrastructure of a socialist society. One key source of this was Lenin's famous piece on state monopoly capitalism, 'The Impending Catastrophe and How to Combat It' of October 1917. In this brief tract, he claimed that state control of the economy for war purposes created 'the complete material preparation for socialism, the threshold of socialism' (Coll. Works 25, 363). This idea resonated in much 1960s and 1970s Soviet Marxist theorizing about 'state monopoly capitalism'; the Programme Commun of French Socialists and Communists was based on it.

However, the contradictory unity of productive forces and relations of production should not be read as productive forces merely adding up positively. As will be clear once we think of work, the form of wage labour has a huge effect on its content, on the people performing it, on products, etc. Indeed, society evolves in increasingly awkward and lopsided ways as a result of the need to satisfy the requirements of 'the markets'. So, even if there are many instances of a global socialization of labour in evidence—and it is possible to think about them in terms of what they could develop into if only the discipline of capital were to be removed—we must recognize that the specific form of capitalist socialization has also worked to exhaust and poison the biosphere, and society as well. People exhausted by capitalist exploitation, Thorstein Veblen argued in 1898, become conservative because this exploitation reduces 'their means of sustenance, ... and consequently their available energy, to such a point as to make them incapable of the effort required for the learning and adoption of new habits of thought' (quoted in Ross 1991, 209). This does not rule out regeneration, but that certainly is not given either.

In terms of foreign relations, the common humanity that we may hope will, at some point, emerge in the course of the drive towards global governance will be likewise a degraded one. War and destruction are obvious causes. But also, if we only think of what happened to 'global justice' (desirable in itself) with its war crimes tribunals ('justice' for Slobodan Milošević who died in his cell, but not for Bill Clinton and Tony Blair who still enjoy celebrity status), or how the societies in which the West pursued 'humanitarian intervention' were left behind, it will be clear that here too a mutilated and exhausted humanity has been created at the receiving end of 'liberation'. Whether in the case of the West imposing global governance on the state system, or capital exploiting society and nature on a world scale, the alienating form distorts the productive forces and impoverishes and degrades its human substratum. Whatever social form will be achieved in the coming crisis of Western hegemony and capitalist discipline, it will have to rebuild this substratum and the exhausted and contaminated biosphere in which it precariously survives today (see Brennan 2000).

The class format of global governance

The global governance projected by the liberal West (which I call imperialist to distinguish it from an equitable, democratic variety) builds on the prior experience with informal, flexible forms of class rule operating behind the formal structures of parliamentary government. They were pioneered in the British Commonwealth and transmitted to the English-speaking world at large and to the European Union (see Jordan 1971). The West's hegemony and coercive power contribute to laying the foundations for an equitable global governance, but are distorting them in the same process. As I have argued elsewhere (Van der Pijl 2006, Chapter 4), the 1970s attempt to create a New International Economic Order through the United Nations, for all its shortcomings was an attempt to build a global governance on the basis of equality. The specific degradations of the social infrastructure of today's world came about in the Western counterrevolution unleashed against this enterprise (see Van der Pijl 2006), as much as they result from two more rounds of rapacious exploitation by globalizing capital.

Now, categories like the 'West', the Lockean heartland of the global political economy, transnational capital, and 'contender state' should not be read as referring to empirical entities. The West is obviously spearheaded by the US and Britain, with the other white English-speaking countries and the EU in flanking roles. The Fortune 500 are a reasonable approximation of world capital, and so on. But as concepts, the 'West' etc. denote postulated structures and relations that have empirical aspects but are not themselves 'facts'. As Peter Bratsis (2006, 21–22) argues, the concept of the 'state' should not be reified into something that exists as such. The state is a unifying category under which we can range a broad set of practical actions and experiences—it is a 'sublime object'. Others have tried to capture this in terms of 'overdetermining' structures which are not themselves present, but appear through a range of other instances which yet derive their coherence from them (Laffey and Dean 2002).

The West, capital, and certainly the hegemonic structure into which they are welded together, are sublime objects in the above sense emanating from the deep structure and relayed through particular complexes of productive and foreign relations. They denote fields of action which in combination reveal a certain orientation and sense of direction. But the actual directive social forces—the ruling classes first of all—are constantly engaged in shaping this orientation and direction; it is not given. It must be elaborated as an ideational constellation, what I call a comprehensive concept of control—a structural constraint supported by a particular configuration of classes and fractions of classes galvanizing themselves behind a common strategic orientation, which then serves as the framework in which everybody defines their 'interests'. As Max Weber famously put it, 'not ideas, but material and ideal interests, directly govern men's conduct. Yet very frequently the world-images that have been created by "ideas" have, like switchmen, determined the tracks along which action has been pushed by the dynamic of interests' (quoted in Seidman 1983, 252).

The social substance of either foreign or productive relations can only be made up of people who act in a particular capacity on these dimensions. They do so under a compulsion they have articulated among themselves and for themselves (a comprehensive concept of control), and seek to impose this as a formula on the rest of society, and via the heartland/contender structure, on other states. Today, the exploitative, energy-intensive Western way of life appears to be reaching the limits of sustainability; just as the pyramids of debt and the fragile webs of global finance are unravelling, and energy resources are running out in spite of the increasingly aggressive attempts by the West to retain control of them (see Klare 2001; Nesvetailova 2007).

In terms of the heartland/contender structure, Russia remains incompletely integrated even after the collapse of the USSR. Its assertion of power in response to Georgia's military action in South Ossetia in August 2008, encouraged by loose promises of NATO membership, marks the end of all illusions for the West that it will be able to set the rules for the global political economy indefinitely. China, with

India rising behind it (and courted as a potential vassal by nuclear concessions on the part of the Bush administration), are already on the horizon as the next contender states. As *New York Times* commentator and champion of neoliberal globalization Thomas Friedman (2006, 2) notes in an article entitled 'Contending with China', this is the real confrontation of the future, much more than 9/11 and even Afghanistan and Iraq.

With the world of high finance in meltdown and the American and even the EU manufacturing base crumbling without a compensating ability for Western capital to participate in the direct exploitation of Chinese, Russian, or Iranian labour, it is hard to see how a Western offensive might come about. In the past, strategies translating domestic mobilization for democracy into forward pressure to open new areas for trade and foreign investment were typically pursued by Democratic presidencies (see Van der Pijl 1984). Thus, the West sought to restructure the relationship between state and society in a contender state to a liberal, Lockean one and dispossess the state class. But in the current circumstances, this would be a very unlikely event as the representatives of the Atlantic class, in council in Istanbul in June 2007, themselves seemed to acknowledge.

The transnational ruling class in council—the Istanbul Bilderberg Conference 2007

Classes are constituted in the context of relations. They are not containers of empirical social groups, but polar positions structuring the fields of productive and foreign relations. These polarities mutate along with the succession and imbrication of modes of production and modes of foreign relations. A contender state class, for example, renews and retains its hold on social development by passive revolution; both to maintain the initiative (associated with its directive role) against its own population, and vis-à-vis the ruling classes of the West. In the process, this works to generate, even in nominally state-socialist formations, the Western-style differentiation between a capitalist class properly speaking and a managerial cadre running the state that is answerable to a ruling class. The former develops, in Gramsci's famous phrase, 'molecularly', as an unintentional effect of the effort to emulate the achievements of the liberal West (Gramsci 1971, 114). Social transformation must remain 'passive' to ensure that the state class is not dispossessed.[4] But as private social forces become more prominent, they may succeed in removing the limits of liberalization, transnationalize and/or link up with 'privatizing' elements in the state class. Dispossession of the state class is then a final stage and precondition of integration. However, as the case of Russia illustrates, this process may stagnate and even reverse. A return to a directive state may occur even though major slices of state property have been privatized, ending up in the hands of a class of 'tycoons' with billion-dollar size empires carved out of the disintegrating Soviet economy. Indeed it would seem that the tentative, transnational connections with the West are being suspended again.

Such connections are developed through an infrastructure of informal networks, from business boardrooms to the policy bodies such as Bilderberg. These bring together, in the private surroundings required to allow the expression of differences, key statesmen, media managers, and other 'organic intellectuals' and actual hereditary members of the transnational capitalist class (see Gill 1990; Graz 2003). I will speak of these people as 'class strategists', again on both the productive and foreign dimension—they develop strategies of capital to exploit society and nature, but also strategies for the liberal West to educate, neutralize, or lay siege on contenders. Their transnationality is their key asset: as Gramsci (1971, 182n) recognized, transnational class networks 'propose political solutions of diverse historical origin, and assist their victory in particular countries—functioning as international political parties which operate within each nation with the full concentration of the international forces'. They add a final component to the cohesion (always fluid and responsive to the changing configuration of forces) of the Western ruling classes and their auxiliary managerial, technical and political cadre.

The cadre forms in the process of socialization inherent in capitalist development, as a new pole in between the capitalist class properly speaking, and the large mass of the population with the working class at its centre. The transition from a sovereign equality mode to a global governance mode of foreign relations, is also accompanied by the growth of a cadre of international civil servants associated with the Western-dominated infrastructure—IMF and World Bank, OECD, EU. Leslie Sklair's (2001) work on the transnational capitalist class appears to focus, more than anything else, on this transnationalizing cadre. The hegemonic influence of the Western way of life and the economic and political forms this hegemony entails embraces both capitalist cadre and the mass of the populations under a concept of control—the overarching political formula in which this hegemony is expressed. Today we can observe how the neoliberal concept of control, built around market fundamentalism, and radiating across the heartland/contender divide as much as it percolates through each society 'vertically', is coming apart.

Networks of interlocking directorates serve as a ground floor of the formation of a transnational class interest (Fennema 1982). Now, as William Carroll and Colin Carson (2003a) have demonstrated, the policy groups in addition connect class strategists who otherwise would remain peripheral to the network of interlocking directorates. Adding membership and/or attendance at meetings of the International Chamber of Commerce, Bilderberg, the Trilateral Commission, the World Economic Forum and the World Business Council for Sustainable Development to the network of interlocking directorates among the Fortune Global 500 of 1997, they conclude that the policy groups considerably intensify the concentration of the core of the network. When these memberships are taken into account as communication links,

[c]ompanies sited in the three Anglo-American countries—heavy participants on the policy boards—become fully integrated with the continental European block [whilst] … for corporate Japan the policy groups play an important bridging role into global management.

(Carroll and Carson 2003a, 95–96; and see 96, Figure 7)

My own research with Otto Holman and Or Raviv (Holman and van der Pijl, 2003; van der Pijl and Raviv 2007) does indeed show that Japanese firms remain peripheral to the network of interlocking directorates through 2000 and 2005. And yet it would be hard to imagine a global ruling class that would not include a Japanese pole. The overwhelming presence of the Anglophone heartland in these networks and the marginal position of Japan are, however, also a reminder that we cannot simply assume that the capitalist class in its entirety has become transnationalized as argued by William I Robinson and Jerry Harris (2000). The contradiction between the national and the global here plays out as a complicating structure that inflects and moulds the fraction structure. It is a contemporary modality of the basic contradiction between community and humanity that constitutes and drives forward foreign relations.

To interpret how the West, in combination with transnational capital, exerts a determining influence in the global political economy through the hegemony of the Western way of life, I will disassemble the participants of the 2007 Istanbul Bilderberg Conference under three headings, each referring to one 'sublime object'—the West ('W'), transnational capital ('C'), and the hegemonic structure as such ('H'). In combination, these project an imperialistic global governance on the planet at large. In the process, they encounter obstacles and opposition (from current and past contender states in international relations, to social forces fleeing or resisting capitalist discipline and its consequences). Let me confine myself here to the role of the Bilderberg group.

Since its inception in the early 1950s (building on discussions among exiles in wartime London), Bilderberg has been the key channel of communication for the Atlantic ruling class (see van der Pijl 1984; 1998; and 2006). If we go over the list of participants of the Bilderberg group meeting of 31 May–3 June 2007 in Istanbul, it is obvious that for every possible problem, there is so to speak one or more 'interested' representative who embodies the experience of prior responses to comparable problems, and thus can contribute meaningfully to developing a strategic consensus to related challenges today.

In Table 3.1, I have reordered the official list of participants of (as provided by the Bilderberg Secretariat) into three categories, 'w 1–3' as a subset of 'W', the liberal West as a political formation; 'c 1–3' of 'C', transnational capital, and 'h 1–4' of 'H', the instances of the hegemonic order on which the two converge.

From this list, it transpires to what extent the West has remained the 'West' in spite of NATO and EU enlargement. Although both the EU Enlargement commissioner (Rehn, h.1) and the key strategist involved in NATO enlargement (Donilon, w.3) attended, not a single representative of the newly integrated, former Warsaw Pact/CMEA countries was present—Austria and Finland are obviously the furthest east the Atlantic ruling class reaches (Turkey has been an established member much longer). Of course, the level of government members of the lesser countries tends to be higher than those of the main Western states. All the big globalizing investment banks, key industrial sectors such as energy and informatics, are present. Those missing will be kept informed through key links with adjacent networks such as the World Economic Forum, the Council on Foreign Relations and others, represented by

Table 3.1 Participants of Istanbul Bilderberg meeting 31 May to 3 June 2007 by category (w: politics, h: hegemonic order, c: business)

w.0. Royalty

NL	Netherlands, H.M. the Queen of The	
B	Philippe, H.R.H. Prince	
E	Spain, H.Ms. the King and Queen of	

w.1. Members of Government

GR	Alogoskoufis, George	Minister of Economy & Finance
TR	Babacan, Ali	Minister of Econ. Affairs
A	Bartenstein, Martin	Minister of Economics and Labour
S	Bildt, Carl	Minister of Foreign Affairs
S	Borg, Anders	Minister of Finance
A	Gusenbauer, Alfred	Chancellor
NL	Heemskerk, Frank	Minister of Foreign Trade
FIN	Katainen, Jyrki	Minister of Finance
E	Léon Gross, Bernardino	State Sec for Foreign Affairs
USA	Luti, William J.	Special Asst to the President & Dir of Defense Policy, NSC
IRL	McDowell, Michael	Minister of Justice c.a.
USA	Silverberg, Kirsten	Ass Sec of State, Bureau of Int'l Organization Affairs
FIN	Tiilikainen, Teija	Sec of State, Ministry for Foreign Affairs
USA	Wood, Joseph R.	Dep'y Advisor to the Vice Pres, Nat'l Sec Affairs

w.2. Other politicians and government personnel

GB	Clarke, Kenneth	MP
GR	Diamantopoulou, Anna	MP
TR	Duna, Cem	Fmr ambass to EU
DK	Federspiel, Ulrik	Perm Sec of State for Foreign Affairs
USA	Feldstein, Martin	Pres/CEO Nat'l Bureau of Econ Research
USA	Geithner, Timothy F.	Pres/CEO Fed Reserve Bank of NY
CND	Kenney, Jason	MP
D	Klaeden, Eckart von	Foreign policy spokesman CDU/CSU
DK	Lykketoft, Mogens	MP
GB	Osborne, George	Shadow Chancellor of the Exchequer
GB	Patten, Christopher	Member, House of Lords [fmr UK Governor of Hong Kong until hand-over to China in 1997]**
USA	Perry, Rick	Governor of Texas
USA	Sebelius, Kathleen	Governor of Kansas
USA	Summers, Lawrence H.	University Professor, Harvard [fmr Sec of Treasury at the time of the Asian crisis]**

(continued)

Table 3.1 (continued)

D	Westerwelle, Guido	Chair, FDP
USA	Wilson, Ross	Ambass to Turkey

w.3. Military-Strategic and Intelligence Related Functionaries & Consultants

USA	Boyd, Charles G.	Pres CEO BENS [Business Executives for Nat'l Security]**
USA	Bremmer, Ian	Pres, Eurasia Group
TR	Çetin, Hikmet	Fmr Min of For Affs, fmr NATO rep for Afghanistan
B	Daele, Frans van	Perm Rep at NATO
GB	Dearlove, Richard	Master Pembroke College Cambridge [Fmr Head, MI 6]**
USA	Donilon, Thomas E.	Partner, O'Melveny & Myers LLC [involved in NATO expansion under Clinton]**
USA	Grossman, Marc	ViceChair The Cohen Group
USA	Kissinger, Henry A.	Chair, Kissinger Associates
USA	Perle, Richard N.	Fellow, American Enterprise Institute
USA	Weber, Vin (J.V.)	Partner, Clark and Weinstock [Chair, Nat'l Endowment for Democracy]**
USA	Zelikow, Philip D.	Prof of History, University of Virginia [Terrorism adviser State Dept]**

h.1. International Financial and Economic Organizations

INT	Derviş, Kemal	Administrator UNDP
INT	Kroes, Neelie	Commissioner, European Commission [Competition]**
INT	Monti, Mario	Pres, Luigì Bocconi University [predecessor Kroes EU Commission until 2004]**
INT	Rato y Figaredo, Rodrigo de	Managing Dir IMF
INT	Rehn, Olli	Commissioner, European Commission [Enlargement]**
USA	Sheeran, Josette	Exec Dir UN World Food Programme
INT	Trichet, Jean-Claude	Pres, Central European Bank
INT	Wolfowitz, Paul	Pres, The World Bank [fmr Under Sec of Defence]**

h.2. Other Foundations and Policy Councils

P	Belcza, Leonor	Pres., Champalimaud Fnd
USA	Haass, Richard N.	Pres., Council on Foreign Relations

(continued)

Table 3.1 (continued)

USA	Kravis, Marie-Josée	Snr fellow, Hudson Institute
USA	Matthews, Jessica T.	Pres, Carnegie Endowment for International Peace
D	Perthes, Volker	Dir., *Stiftung Wissenschaft und Politik*
CH	Schwab, Klaus	Exec Chair, World Economic Forum

b.3. Media and Public Opinion

USA	Barone, Michael	*US News & World Report*
TR	Birand, Mehmet	Columnist
A	Bronner, Oscar	Publisher/Editor *Der Standard*
TR	Çandar, Cengiz	Journalist
E	Cebrián, Juan Luis	CEO PRISA *El Pais*
D	Döpfner, Mathias	Chair CEO Axel Springer AG
USA	Gigot, Paul A.	*Wall Street Journal*
USA	Hart, Peter D.	Chair, Peter D. Hart Research Association
FIN	Jääskelänen, Atte	Director of News etc, *YLE*
GB	Micklethwait, R. John	Editor, *The Economist*
D	Nass, Matthias	Dep Editor, *Die Zeit*
F	Ockrent, Christine	Editor in Chief, *France Télévision*
D	Bredow, Vendeline A.H. von*	Business correspondent, *The Economist*
GB	Wooldrige, Adrian D.*	For correspondent, *The Economist*

b.4. Academics

USA	Allison, Graham	Prof of Government, Harvard
USA	Bierbaum, Rosina	Prof Nat Resources/Environment U of Michigan
TR	Gönensay, Emre	Prof of Economics, Işik Univ, fmr Min of For Affairs
NL	Halberstadt, Victor	Prof of Economics, Leiden University
F	Roy, Olivier	Snr Researcher, CNRS
TR	Soysal, Ayşe	Rector, Bosporus University
GB	Taggart, Paul A.	Prof of Politics, University of Sussex

c.1. Private Business: Financial

I	Bernabè, Franco	ViceChair, Rothschild Europe
USA	Blankfein, Lloyd	Pres CEO Goldman Sachs
F	Castries, Henri de	Chair CEO AXA
USA	Collins, Timothy C.	Snr Manag Dir CEO, Ripplewood Hdgs LLC
ISR	Gilady, Eival	CEO Portland Trust Israel [private investment into Palestinian territories]**
IRL	Gleeson, Dermot	Chair Allied Irish Bank Group
USA	Holbrooke, Richard C.	Vice Chair Perseus LLC
USA	Jacobs, Kenneth	Dep Chair, Head, Lazard US, Lazard Frères & Co LLC
USA	Johnson, James A.	Vice Chair Perseus LLC
USA	Jordan, Vernon E., Jr	Snr Man Dir, Lazard Frères & CO LLC

(continued)

Table 3.1 (continued)

TR	Koç, Mustafa V.	Chair, Koç Hldg
USA	Kovner, Bruce	Chair, Caxton Associates, LLC
USA	Kravis, Henry R.	Founding Partner, Kravis Kohlberg Roberts & Co
N	Kreutzer, Idar	CEO Storebrand ASA
A	Nowotny, Ewald	CEO BAWAG psw
E	Rodriguez Inciarte, Matías	Exec Vice Chair, Grupo Santander, Ciudad Grupo
A	Scholten, Rudolf	Member of Board Exec Dirs, Oesterreichische Kontrollbank
USA	Scully, Robert W.	Co-Pres, Morgan Stanley
I	Siniscalco, Domenico	Man Dir and Vice-Chair, Morgan Stanley
USA	Thiel, Peter A.	Pres, Clarium Capital Manag't LLC
NL	Tilmant, Michel	Chair, ING NV
N	Ulltveit-Moe, Jens	CEO UMOE AS
S	Wallenberg, Jacob	Chair, Investor AB
USA	Zoellick, Robert B.	Man Dir, Goldman Sachs fmr US trade repres; pres-elect, World Bank**

c.2. Private Business:
Energy

B	Davignon, Etienne	Vice-Chairman, Suez-Tractebel
DK	Eldrup, Anders	Pres DONG A/S
GB	Kerr, John	Member House of Lords; Dep Chair Royal Dutch Shell plc
N	Myklebust, Egil	Chair Board of Directors, SAS, Norsk Hydro ASA
FIN	Ollila, Jorma	Chair, Royal Dutch Shell plc
I	Scaroni, Paolo	CEO, ENI SpA
IRL	Sutherland, Peter D.	Chair, BP PLC and Chair, Goldman Sachs Int'l
NL	Veer, Jeroen van der	CEO, Royal Dutch Shell PLC

c.3. Private Business:
Other

P	Balsemão, F. Pinto	Chair/CEO Impresa, fm PM
F	Barnier, Michel	VPres Mérieux Alliance, fm M of For Aff
F	Baverez, Nicolas	Partner, Gibson, Dunn & Crutcher LLP
TR	Boyner, Ümit N.	Exec Council, Boyner Hdg
D	Burda, Hubert	Pres CEO Burda Media Hdg
GR	David, George A.	Chair Coca Cola HBC SA
USA	Dyson, Esther	Chair EDventure Hdgs Inc
I	Elkann John	ViceChair FIAT SpA
F	Hermelin, Paul	CEO Cap Gemini
NL	Hommen, Jan H.M.	Chairman, Reed Elsevier
USA	Kent, Muhtar	President and COO, Coca Cola Company
USA	Mundie, Craig J.	Chief Research & Strategy Officer, Microsoft Corp
F	Parisot, Laurence	President MEDEF [employers' fed]
CDN	Reisman, Heather	Chair & CEO, Indigo Books & Music

(continued)

Table 3.1 (continued)

USA	Schmidt, Eric	Chair of Exec Committee and CEO, Google
D	Schrempp, Jürgen	Fmr Chair Manag't Board, Daimler-Chrysler
S	Svanberg, Carl-Henric	Pres CEO LM Ericsson
USA	Taurel, Sidney	Chair CEO, Eli Lilly & co
GB	Taylor, J. Martin	Chair, Syngenta International AG
CH	Vasella, Daniel L.	Chair CEO, Novartis AG
TR	Yücaoglu, Erkut	Chair Board, MAP, fmr pres, TUSIAD [employers' fed]

- - * Rapporteurs
**Added to information provided by the official list.

their respective heads; Henry Kissinger (w.3) and Peter Sutherland (c.2) have key roles in the overlapping Trilateral Commission.

Now, because of its secretiveness, every Bilderberg meeting is followed, as surely as a comet is followed by its tail of ice and debris, by heated accounts on covert world government, dark conspiracies to subject the globe to capital, etc. Whereas the other policy boards have fairly sophisticated public relations operations attached to them, glimpses of Bilderberg discussions therefore come into the public domain through the investigative work of conspiracy buffs talking to loose-lipped or concerned participants, interpreters, waiters, or whoever else may have bits of information. Only later, the occasional set of typed documents may be passed on by somebody cleaning a participant's desk (I had that luck with the records of the 1989 meeting, van der Pijl 2006, 243–44). But what was discussed at Istanbul must for now be gleaned from the comet's tail. The idea is always that what is at stake is to demarcate the lines of legitimate debate and ideally, to achieve some sort of strategic consensus.

If I try to systematize from two such sources (*Bilderberg.org* 2007 and Estulin 2007), it would seem that the following items were prominent in the discussions. First, the ongoing and possible new wars waged by the Anglophone West and Israel—Palestine, Iraq, Afghanistan, and Iran. One source for *Bilderberg.org* gave '[h]ow to divide Iraq into 3–4 new nations' and '[n]ot if, but when to invade Iran and which nations will participate in the invasion' as the first two items in this tentative consensus agenda. But from other glimpses reported by the same source, it would seem that there was continuing disagreement on Iraq, pressure by Americans (Kissinger among others) to admit Turkey into the EU, as well as the need to confront Iran, for its oil as much as against its nuclear ambitions. It was argued however that strategic air bombardment should do the trick and that unlike Iraq, there should be no 'boots on the ground'.

On Afghanistan, it was 'commonly agreed' that 'the situation in that country is getting worse', a result, according to one British attendee, of 'unreal expectations' (quoted in Estulin 2007, 22). Prompted by interventions from Kissinger and 'one European royal' that the limits of Western power were coming to light in Afghanistan, a NATO representative 'categorically stated that the West has neither the political intelligence nor the understanding to fight a protracted, decade-long counter-insurgency campaign in Afghanistan' (Estulin 2007, 23). The control of oil and natural gas reserves around the world, item 3 of *Bilderberg.org*'s agenda source, was obviously imbricated in this discussion as well as those in the third block listed here, Russia and China. Second, there was the need to solidify the structures of global governance and confront anti-globalization populism.

Bilderberg.org's agenda source in this context mentioned the Free Trade zone project for the Americas and achieving the substance of the EU Constitution, as well as the need to create a Pacific Rim Union, as goals. Sutherland (*c.2*) was quoted by *Bilderberg.org* as saying that it had been a mistake to have referenda on the EU constitution: 'You knew there was a rise in nationalism; you should have let your parliaments ratify the treaty, and it should be done with'. Kissinger said words to the same effect concerning unification of the Americas, stressing the need to mobilize the enlightened media behind its propagation. To deal with the Third World, Robert Zoellick (*c.1*, named the new president of the World Bank to replace Paul Wolfowitz, *h.1*, later that month) also attended the Istanbul conference although he was not officially listed. As one Scandinavian attendee claimed, replacing one Bush appointee with another would not solve the World Bank's current governance problems (Estulin 2007, 20). One unidentified European according to the same source asked Zoellick whether 'he was planning to patch up his relationships with Third and Fourth World nations', which he compelled as US trade representative to adhere to US-imposed intellectual property laws on medicines—the implication being that this approach no longer works. This limit is even more apparent in the relations with Russia and China.

On this, the third group of issues, the conference conclusions state that 'the US can no longer ride roughshod over, nor bully, nor simply ignore resurgent Russia, rising China or the globe's regimes that supply the vital oil that fuels the US economy' (quoted in Estulin 2007, 22). As to Russia, one US participant observed (clear in intent if not in words) that 'Russia is acting against unipolarity's accommodating ideologies and politics, against its recently resurgent manifestations and machinations, and against the instruments of its perpetuation, such as [NATO]' (quoted in Estulin 2007, 21). Related to energy matters, the controversy over the TNK-British Petroleum licence in Russia apparently caused real anger at the meeting.

Russia's current strategy of 'actively dismantling what remains of "the acquiescence to America's will"', as another attendee put it, which had arisen in the Yeltsin period, was seen as a key issue to achieve a consensus on. As Estulin (2007, 21) concludes, 'to the Bilderbergers, energy imperatives are the end game', and 'Russia was the beginning of the end game'. The conference conclusions continue by saying that '*(s)omething must be done, and urgently, in order to cut deeply into Russia's mounting global energy leverage*. The US-Russia strategically deteriorating relations are one victim of this geopolitical struggle for energy supremacy' (Estulin 2007, 22 emphasis added). Perle (*w.3*) was quoted as saying that Russia had undertaken 'asymmetric steps to undermine the ability of the US to project its military power effectively into their neighbourhoods and into those of their partners and allies'.

As to China, *Bilderberg.org*'s agenda source summed up the China issue as follows: 'When [will it] be appropriate to start talking about China as the World's next Evil

Empire and next enemy. They must always have an enemy in order to justify the massive military spending'. However, as a European delegate pointed out, this was already happening, and it was noted that China's response to the US intentions to weaponize space, had been the simple and relatively inexpensive demonstration of how it could destroy a satellite in orbit (Estulin 2007, 22).

What transpires from these glimpses of the Bilderberg discussions is a less than confident mood. Such a sentiment would reflect what appears to be the inescapable conclusion that the West and capital are approaching the limits of their historic reach. Capital has brought the world to the threshold of a globally integrated economy; the hegemony of the liberal West has done the same as far as global governance goes. Neither can cross that threshold without a qualitative change in the nature of both the economy and the rules under which world politics are conducted.

Notes

1 This chapter builds on my contribution to the debate in the *Cambridge Review of International Affairs* (2007).
2 Quoted in *Financial Times*, 25 July 2000, emphasis added.
3 This argument is developed at greater length in van der Pijl (2007).
4 On the concept of 'passive revolution' also see Morton in this volume.

4 Beyond the theory of imperialism

Global capitalism and the transnational state

William I Robinson[1]

I live the worldsourced life. As CEO of Lenovo, I am an American CEO based in Singapore. Our chairman, who is Chinese, works from North Carolina. Other top executives are based around the globe. A meeting of my company's senior managers looks like the United Nations General Assembly. My company is like some of the world's most popular consumer products. It may say 'Made in China' on the outside, but the key components are designed and manufactured by innovative people and companies spread across six continents. The products of companies that practice worldsourcing may be labeled 'Made in Switzerland' or 'Made in the USA' or 'Made in China', but in the new world in which we all now live, they should be more truthfully be labeled 'Made Globally'. In today's world, assessing companies by their nation of origin misses the point.

- William J. Amelio (2008), President and CEO of Lenovo,
a leading global PC firm

We now have global financial markets, global corporations, global financial flows. But what we do not have is anything other than national and regional regulation and supervision. We need a global way of supervising our financial system ... we need very large and very radical [political, institutional] changes.

- British Prime Minister Gordon Brown in 2008 (Brecher *et al.*)

Introduction

Theories of a 'new imperialism' that proliferated in the years following the events of September 2001 assume that the United States has set about extending global empire to offset the decline in its hegemony amidst heightened inter-imperialist rivalry. These theories rest on a crustaceous bed of assumptions that need to be peeled back if we are to get at the root of twenty-first century global social and political dynamics. Grounded in the classical statements of V.I. Lenin and Rudolf Hilferding, they presume a world of rival national capitals and economies, conflict among core capitalist powers, the exploitation by these powers of peripheral regions, and a nation-state centered framework for analyzing global dynamics. Hilferding, Lenin, and others analyzing the world of the early twentieth century established this Marxist analytical framework of rival national capitals that was carried by subsequent political economists into the latter twentieth century via theories of dependency and the world system, radical IR theory, studies of US intervention, and so on. This outdated framework of competing national capitals continues to inform observers of world dynamics in the early twenty-first century. The following assertion by Michael Klare is typical:

> By geopolitics or geopolitical competition, I mean the contention between great powers and aspiring great powers for control over territory, resources, and important geographical positions, such as ports and harbors, canals, river systems, oases, and other sources of wealth and influence. Today we are seeing a resurgence of unabashed geopolitical ideology among the leadership cadres of the major powers ... the best way to see what's happening today in Iraq and elsewhere is through a geopolitical prism.
>
> (Klare 2003, 51–52)

Such thinking provides the scaffolding for a torrent of 'new imperialism' literature that appeared after 2001 (see, *inter alia*, Foster 2003; 2006; Wood 2003; Harvey 2003; Pozo-Martin 2006; Kiely 2006; Henwood 2003; Brenner 2002; Arrighi 2005; Gowan 1999; Klare 2003; Bello 2005; *Monthly Review* 2003).

But capitalism has changed fundamentally since the days of Lenin and Hilferding. We have entered a qualitatively new transnational stage in the ongoing evolution of world capitalism marked by a number of fundamental shifts in the capitalist system, among them:

- the rise of truly transnational capital and the integration of every country into a new global production and financial system;
- the appearance of a new transnational capitalist class (TCC), a class group grounded in new global markets and circuits of accumulation, rather than national markets and circuits;
- the rise of transnational state (TNS) apparatuses, and;
- the appearance of novel relations of power and inequality in global society involving a changing relation between space and power.

The dynamics of this emerging stage in world capitalism cannot be understood through the lens of nation-state centric thinking. This is not to say that the nation-state is no longer important, but that the system of nation-states as discrete interacting units—the interstate system—is no longer the organizing principle of capitalist development, or the primary institutional framework that shapes social and class forces and political dynamics (for elaborations on these propositions, see, *inter alia*, Robinson 2008; 2007; 2006a; 2005a; 2005b; 2004; 2003; 2002; 1996).

The myth of national economies and the reality of transnational capital

The hallmark of 'new imperialism' theories is the assumption that world capitalism in the twenty-first century is made up of 'domestic capitals' and distinct national economies that interact with one another, and a concomitant 'realist' analysis of world politics as driven by the pursuit by governments of their 'national interest'. In one leading treatise on the 'new imperialism', *Empire of Capital*, Ellen Meiksins Wood (2003, 23) asserts that 'the national organization of capitalist economies has remained stubbornly persistent'.

We are asked by Wood and others writing from the 'new imperialism' perspective to assume—although they provide not a shred of empirical evidence—that capital remains organized along national lines and that the development of capital has stopped frozen in its nation-state form. The interstate/nation-state framework obliges 'new imperialism' scholars to advance this unproblematized notion of 'national interests' to explain global political dynamics. What does 'national interests' mean? Marxists have historically rejected notions of 'national interests' as an ideological subterfuge for class and social group interests. What is a 'national economy'? Is it a country with a closed market? Protected territorially-based production circuits? The predominance of national capitals? An insulated national financial system? No capitalist country in the world fits this description.

There is a mounting body of empirical evidence that demonstrates the transnationalization of capital. This evidence strongly suggests that the giant conglomerates of the Fortune 500 ceased to be 'US' corporations in the latter part of the twentieth century and increasingly represented transnational capitalist groups (for summaries and assessments of this evidence, see inter-alia, Robinson 2004; Sklair 2001; 2002; Kentor 2005; Kentor and Jang 2003; UNCTAD, various years; Carroll and Carson 2003b; Carroll and Fennema 2002; Dicken 2003). This reality of transnationalization can no longer be disputed, nor can its significance for macro-social theories and for analysis of world political-economic dynamics. One need only glean daily headlines from the world media to discover endless reams of anecdotal evidence to complement the accumulation of systematic data on transnationalization (see, for example, the citation by Amelio that opens this chapter, and my discussion in the earlier version of the present chapter: Robinson, 2007)

A number of my critics misread my argument entirely in associating it with Karl Kautsky's earlier 'ultra-imperialism' or 'superimperialism' thesis (see, for example, Anievas, 2008). Yet, my global capitalism approach shares little or nothing with Kautsky's thesis. In his 1914 essay 'Ultra-Imperialism', Kautsy assumed capital would remain national in its essence and suggested that national capitals would collude internationally instead of compete, whereas my theory on the TCC emphasizes that competition and conflict among capitals is endemic to the system, but that such competition takes on new forms in the age of globalization not necessarily expressed as national rivalry. The TCC thesis does not suggest there are no longer national and regional capitals, or that the TCC is internally unified, free of conflict, and consistently acts as a coherent political actor. Nonetheless, the TCC has established itself as a class group without a national identity and in competition with nationally-based capitals. There is conflict between national and transnational fractions of capital. Moreover, rivalry and competition are fierce among transnational conglomerations that turn to numerous institutional channels, including multiple national states, to pursue their interests.

Reification and theoreticism in 'new imperialism' theories: the case of David Harvey

Most 'new imperialism' theorists acknowledge to varying degrees that changes have taken place, and particularly, that capital has become more global. Yet, capital in these accounts has not transnationalized; it has 'internationalized'. These accounts are concerned with explaining the *inter*national order, which by definition places the focus on interstate dynamics exclusive of the *trans*national. This need to accommodate the reality of transnationalizing capital within a nation-state centric framework for analyzing world political dynamics leads 'new imperialism' theories to a dualism of the economic and the political.

David Harvey, in perhaps the landmark treatise among this literature, *The New Imperialism*, argues that capital is economic and globalizes, but states are political and pursue a self-interested territorial logic. Harvey's theory starts with the notion that

> the fundamental point is to see the territorial and the capitalist logic of power as distinct from each other. ... The relation between these two logics should be seen, therefore, as problematic and often contradictory ... rather than as functional or one-sided. This dialectical relation sets the stage for an analysis of capitalist imperialism in terms of the intersection of these two distinctive but intertwined logics of power.
>
> (Harvey 2003, 29–30)

Harvey's is *not*, however, a dialectical but a mechanical approach. The different dimensions of social reality in the dialectical approach do not have an 'independent' status insofar as each aspect of reality is constituted by, and is constitutive of, a larger whole of which it is an internal element. Distinct dimensions of social reality may be *analytically distinct* yet are *internally interpenetrated* and *mutually constitutive* of each other as internal elements of a more encompassing process, so that, for example, the economic/capital and the political/state are *internal* to capitalist relations.

It is remarkable that Harvey proposes such a separation since the history of modern critical thought—from Polanyi to Poulantzas and Gramsci, among others, not to mention 50 years of historical materialist theorizing on the state—has demonstrated both the *formal* (apparent) separation of the economic and the political under the capitalist mode of production and the illusion that such a separation is organic or real (for discussion, see Robinson, 1996). This separation has its genealogy in the rise of the market and its apparently 'pure' economic compulsion. This separation appears in social thought with the breakup of political economy, the rise of classical economics and bourgeois social science, and disciplinary fragmentation (see Therborn 1985; 1999; Zeitlin 2000). Such a separation of the economic from the political was a hallmark of the structural functionalism that dominated much of mid-twentieth century social science. Structural functionalism separated distinct spheres of the social totality and conferred a functional autonomy to each sub-sphere which was seen as *externally* related to other sub-spheres in a way similar to Harvey's notion of separate state and capital logics that may or may not coincide.

Harvey offers no explicit conception of the state but he acknowledges that state behavior has 'depended on how the state has been constituted and by whom' (Harvey 2003, 91). Yet dual logics of state and capital ignore the real-world policymaking process in which the state extends backward, is grounded in the forces of civil society, and is fused in a myriad of ways with capital itself. It is incumbent to ask in what ways transnational social forces may influence a reconstitution of state institutions. To the extent that civil society—social forces—and capital are transnationalizing our analysis of the state cannot remain frozen at a nation-state level. The essential problematic that should concern us in attempting to explain phenomena associated with the 'new imperialism' is the political management—or rule—of global capitalism. The theoretical gauntlet is how to understand the exercise of political domination in relation to the institutions available to dominant groups and sets of changing historical relations among social forces—that is, how are the political and the economic articulated in the current era? This requires a conception of agency and institutions.

But instead of offering an ontology of agency and how it operates through historically constituted institutions, much of the 'new imperialism' literature reifies these institutions. Institutions are but institutionalized—that is, codified—patterns of interaction among social forces that structure different aspects of their material relations. When we explain global dynamics in terms of institutions that have an existence or agency independent of social forces we are reifying these institutions. Critical state theories and Gramscian IPE (see, for example, Cox 1987; Simon 1991) have taught us, despite their limitations, that the story starts—and ends—with historically situated social forces as collective agents. To critique a nation-state framework of analysis as I do is not, as my critics claim (see, *inter alia*, Pozo-Martin 2006; Kiely 2006), to dismiss the nation-state but to de-reify it. Reifying categories leads to realist analyses of state power and the interstate system. Realism presumes that the world economy is divided up into distinct national economies that interact with one another. Each national economy is a billiard ball banging back and forth on each other. This billiard image is then applied to explain global political dynamics in terms of nation-states as discrete interacting units (the interstate system).

The state, says Harvey (2003, 26), reverting to the realist approach, 'struggles to assert its interests and achieve its goals in the world at large'. But Harvey does not stop with this reification of the state. He introduces an additional territorial reification, so that territorial relations become immanent to social relations. 'The wealth and well-being of particular territories are augmented at the expense of others', writes Harvey (2003, 32). In this remarkably reified image—'territories' rather than social groups have 'wealth' (accumulated values) and enjoy 'well being'—Harvey gives space an independent existence as a social/political force in the form of territory in order to advance his thesis of the 'new imperialism'. It is not how social forces are organized both in space and through institutions that is the focus. Rather, for Harvey, territory acquires a social existence of its own, an agentic logic. We are told that 'territorial entities' engage in practices of production, commerce, and so on. Do 'territorial entities' really do these things? Or is it not that in the real world, individuals and social groups are the agents that engage in production, commerce, and so on? And they do so via institutions through which they organize, systematize, and demarcate their activities as agents. Social groups became aggregated and organized in the modern era through the particular institutional form of the territorial-based nation-state. But this particular institutional form does not acquire a life of its own and neither is it immutable. Nation-states continue to exist but their nature and meaning evolve as social relations and structures become transformed; in particular, as they transnationalize.

It is true that the social does not exist outside of the spatial and that space is relative and experienced subjectively (see, for example, Lefebvre 1991). Drawing on such insights from Henri Lefebvre, Marx, Luxemburg, and others, Harvey (1982) introduced the highly fertile notion of spatial (or spatial-temporal) fixes to understand how capital momentarily resolves contradictions (particularly, crises of over-accumulation) in one place by displacing them to other places through geographic expansion and spatial reorganization. Following Marx' famous observation that the expanded accumulation of capital involves the progressive 'annihilation of space through time', he also coined the term 'time-space compression' in reference to glo-balization as a process involving a new burst of time-space compression in the world capitalist system (Harvey 1990).

But 'places' have no existence or meaning in and of themselves. It is people living in particular spaces that do this dis-placing (literally), these spatio-temporal fixes. The 'asymmetric exchange relations' that are at the heart of Harvey's emphasis on the territorial basis of the 'new imperialism' must be for Harvey territorial exchange relations. But not only that: they must be nation-state territorial exchanges. But exchange relations are social relations, exchanges among particular social groups. There is nothing in the concept of asymmetric exchanges that by fiat gives them a territorial expression; no reason to assume that uneven exchanges are necessarily exchanges that take place between distinct territories, much less specifically between distinct nation-states. That they do or do not acquire such an expression is one of historical, empirical, and conjunctural analysis. Certainly spatial relations among social forces have historically been mediated in large part by territory; spatial relations have been territorially-defined relations. But this territorialization is in no way immanent to social relations and may well be fading in significance as globalization advances.

If most of the people in one place that we can call a territory or nation-state achieve 'wealth' and 'well being' by having displaced contradictions to most of the people in another place then we may be able to justify the view that social relations acquire a territorial expression—hence the territorial (nation-state) basis to classical theories of colonialism and imperialism and later world-system and related theories of geo-graphically-defined core and periphery. But we know that under globalization, masses of people in core regions such as Los Angeles or New York may suffer the displace-ment of contradictions off-loaded on them from people in the very same city. Whereas rising middle class and affluent sectors in India, Brazil, or South Africa may benefit as much from spatio-temporal fixes that off-load crisis to the global poor through neo-liberal mechanisms as their counterparts in First World global cities.

Any theory of globalization must address the matter of place and space, including changing spatial relations among social forces and how social relations are spatialized.

This has not been satisfactorily accomplished, despite a spate of theoretical propositions, ranging from Manuel Castells' (1996) 'space of flows' replacing the 'space of
place' and Anthony Giddens' (1990) 'time-space distanciation' as the 'lifting' of social
relations from territorial place and their stretching around the globe in ways that may
eliminate territorial friction. This notion of ongoing and novel reconfigurations of
time and social space is central to a number of globalization theories. It in turn points
to the larger theoretical issue of the relationship of social structure to space, the
notion of space as the material basis for social practices, and the changing relationship
under globalization between territoriality/geography, institutions, and social structures.

The crucial question here is the ways in which globalization may be transforming
the spatial dynamics of accumulation and the institutional arrangements through
which it takes place. The subject—literally, that is, the agents/makers of the social
world—is not global space but people in those spaces. What is central, therefore, is a
spatial reconfiguration of social relations beyond a nation-state/interstate framework,
if not indeed even beyond territory.

States are institutionalized social relations and territorial actors to the extent that
those social relations are territorialized. Nation-states are social relations that have
historically been territorialized, but those relations are not by definition territorial. To
the extent that the US and other national states promote deterritorializing social and
economic processes they are not territorial actors. The US state can hardly be considered as acting territorially when it promotes the global relocation of accumulation
processes that were previously concentrated in US territory. Harvey's approach is at
pains to explain such behaviour since by his definition the US state must promote its
own territorial aggrandisement. Harvey (2003, 106) observes that as local banking
was supplanted by national banking in the development of capitalism 'the free flow of
money capital across the national space altered regional dynamics'. In the same vein,
we can argue that the free flow of capital across global space alters these dynamics on
a worldwide scale.

Let us return to the question: why would Harvey propose separate logics for the
economic and the political—for capital and the state? By separating the political and
the economic he is able to claim that indeed globalization has transformed the spatial
dynamics of accumulation—hence capital globalizes—but that the institutional
arrangements of such global accumulation remain territorial as nation-states. The
state has its own independent logic that brings it into an external relation to globalizing capital. Here we arrive at the pitfall of theoreticism. If one starts with the
theoretical assumption that the world is made up of independent, territorial-based
nation-states and that this particular institutional-political form is something immanent to the modern world—Wood (2003) makes the assumption explicit, a law of
capitalism; for Harvey it seems implicit—then the changing world of the twenty-first
century must be explained by theoretical fiat in these terms. Reality must be made to
conform to the theoretical conception of an immutable nation-state based, interstate
political and institutional order. But since Harvey acknowledges the reality of globalizing capital he is therefore forced to separate the logic of that globalizing capital
from that of territorially-based states; he is forced either to abandon the theoretical

construct altogether or to build it upon a dualism of the economic and the political, of capital and the state.

Following closely Harvey's dualist logic, Alex Callinicos (2007) also argues that capital accumulation and the state system are to be understood as 'distinct determinations'. Two groups of actors—capitalists and state managers—respond to distinct rules of reproduction that are driven by respective processes of economic and geopolitical competition. There is a non-identity of interests, but pursuit of these distinctive interests, he argues, draws each into an alliance with the other. But state managers and political elites are dependent for their own reproduction on the reproduction of capital, as Callinicos (Chapter 1, 53) himself acknowledges.

Yet, once we acknowledge such dependency we are forced to examine the form of the structural power that capital exercises over the state. Stated in simplified terms, the transnationalization of capital transnationalizes the basis upon which state managers and political elites achieve their reproduction. To the extent that accumulation becomes transnational or to the extent that transnational capital becomes dominant among the capitals operating in their distinct political jurisdictions, state managers would come to reproduce themselves as a status group not through Harvey's and Callinicos's 'territorial aggrandizement', but through the reproduction of the dominant transnational accumulation processes on which they depend.

Theory needs to illuminate reality, not make reality conform to it. The pitfall of this theoreticism is to develop analyses and propositions to fit theoretical assumptions. Since received theories establish a frame of an interstate system made up of competing national states, economies and capitals, then twenty-first century reality must be interpreted so that it fits this frame one way or another. Such theoreticism forces theorists of the 'new imperialism' into a schizophrenic dualism of economic and political logics. In any event, Harvey has trapped himself in a blind alley that underscores the pitfall. Despite his acknowledgement of capital's transnationalization he concludes that the US state's political/territorial logic is driven now by an effort to open up space vis-à-vis competitor nation-states for unloading national capital surplus, hence the new US imperialism. This inconsistency in Harvey's argumentation reflects a general contradiction in the 'new imperialism' literature: the dualism of the economic and political, of capital and the state, is negated by the claim that the state functions to serve (US national) capital.

Global capitalism and the transnational state apparatus

'New imperialism' theories more generally analyze US foreign policy in relation to the realist assumption of competition among national capitals and consequent political and military rivalry among core nation-states. 'Intercapitalist rivalry remains the hub of the imperialist wheel,' claims John Bellamy Foster. 'In the present period of global hegemonic imperialism the United States is geared above all to expanding its imperial power to whatever extent possible and subordinating the rest of the capitalist world to its interests' (Foster 2003, 13). 'The European Union,' writes Wood (2003, 156), 'is potentially a stronger economic power than the US'. Yet, to interrogate Wood's affirmation, an empirical study of the global economy reveals that *trans*national corporations operate both inside and outside of the territorial bounds of the EU; that transnational investors from all countries hold and trade in trillions of Euros and dollars each day, and; that European investors are as deeply integrated into transnational circuits of accumulation that inextricably pass through the 'US' economy as are US investors into such circuits that pass through the 'EU' economy. These transnational capitalists operate across US-EU frontiers and have a material and political interest in stabilizing the 'US' and the 'EU' economy and 'their' financial institutions. Once we belie the realist notion of a world of national economies and national capitals then the logical sequence in 'new imperialism' argumentation collapses like a house of cards since the whole edifice is constructed on this notion. By coming to grips with the reality of transnational capital we can grasp US foreign policy in its organic, not merely functional, relation to the actual structure and composition of the dominant social forces in the global capitalist system.

My claim that a TNS apparatus is emerging does not imply that supranational institutions such as the IMF or the WTO *replace* or—in Wood's words—'make irrelevant' the national state. Rather, the national state, to the extent that it is captured by transnationally-oriented capitalists and elites, becomes transformed and increasingly absorbed functionally into a larger transnational institutional structure that involves complex new relations between national states and supra- or transnational institutions, on the one hand, and diverse class and social forces, on the other. Transnational bodies such as the IMF and the WTO have worked in tandem with national states to rearticulate labour relations, financial institutions and circuits of production into a system of global accumulation. As national states are captured by transnational capitalist forces they tend to serve the interests of global over local accumulation processes. The TNS, for instance, has played a key role in imposing the neoliberal model on the old Third World and therefore in reinforcing the class relations of global capitalism.

Few commentators suggest that the nation-state is disappearing, or that capital can now—or ever has been able to—exist without a state. The observation by Wood and others that global capital needs (local) states is neither original nor particularly controversial. I, among others, have argued for many years that a fundamental contradiction of global capitalism is that for historic reasons economic globalization has unfolded within the political/authority framework of a nation-state system, and moreover, that this system is functional to the reproduction of the class power of transnational capital. The real issue is not whether global capitalism can dispense with the state—it cannot. Rather, it is that the state may be in a process of transformation in consort with the restructuring and transformation of world capitalism. The question is, to what extent and in what ways may new state forms and institutional configurations be emerging, and how may we theorize these new configurations?

There are vital functions that the national state performs for transnational capital, among them, sets of local economic policies aimed at achieving macroeconomic equilibrium, the provision of property laws, juridical arbitrage, infrastructure, and of course, social control and ideological reproduction. However, national states are ill equipped to organize a supranational unification of macroeconomic policies, create a unified field for transnational capital to operate, impose transnational trade regimes, supranational 'transparency', and so forth. Emergent transnational state apparatuses may never be able to provide these conditions or perform such functions. Nonetheless, transnationally-oriented capitalists, state managers and other elites have in recent years attempted to transform existing international institutions, to create new transnational ones, and to operate through transnational institutional networks to construct a supranational legal and regulatory system for the global economy and to manage the contradictions of global capitalism—efforts that they accelerated in the wake of the late 2008 global financial meltdown, as suggested by the quote by British Prime Minister Gordon Brown at the start of this chapter. The policy prescriptions and actions of these transnational institutional networks have been synchronized with those of neoliberal national states that have been captured by local transnationally-oriented forces.

This transnational institutional structure has played an increasingly salient role in coordinating global capitalism and imposing capitalist domination beyond national borders. This transnational institutionality needs to be theorized. Clearly the IMF, by imposing a structural adjustment program that opens up a given country to the penetration of transnational capital, the subordination of local labour, and the extraction of wealth by transnational capitalists, is operating as a state institution to facilitate the exploitation of local labour by global capital. 'New imperialism' dogma reduces these IMF practices to instruments of 'US' imperialism (see, for example, Bello 2005; Gowan 1999; Wood 2003). Yet I know of no single IMF structural adjustment program that creates conditions in the intervened country that favours 'US' capital in any special way, rather than opening up the intervened country, its labour and resources, to capitalists from any corner of the world. This outcome is in sharp distinction to earlier imperialism, in which a particular core country sealed off the colonized country or sphere of influence as its own exclusive preserve for exploitation.

The continued existence of the national state is a central condition not for 'US hegemony' or a 'new US empire' but for the class power of transnational capital. The TCC has been able to use local core states to mould transnational structures and to impose these on distinct nations and regions. The real issue is not the continued existence of national states and of powerful national states in a globalized system—a fact that does not contradict the thesis of a TCC and a TNS—but their function. We must analyze US foreign policy in relation to this structural role of US state power in advancing global capitalism. US policies such as the imposition of neoliberal structural adjustment programs and the sponsorship of free trade agreements by and large served to further pry open regions and sectors around the world to global capitalism. And an analysis of TNS institutions suggests that they act not to enforce 'US' policies but to force nationally-oriented policies in general into transnational alignment.

The crisis of global capitalism and the US state

'US' imperialism refers to the use by transnational elites of the US state apparatus to continue to attempt to expand, defend and stabilize the global capitalist system. We face an *empire of global capital*, as I have argued elsewhere (Robinson 2004; 2005b), headquartered, for evident historical reasons, in Washington. The questions for global elites are: In what ways, under what particular conditions, arrangements, and strategies should US state power be wielded? How can particular sets of US state managers be responsive and held accountable to global elites who are fractious in their actions, dispersed around the world, and operating through numerous supranational institutional settings, each with distinct histories and particular trajectories?

We are witness to new forms of global capitalist domination, whereby intervention is intended to create conditions favourable to the penetration of transnational capital and the renewed integration of the intervened region into the global system. US intervention facilitates a shift in power from locally and regionally-oriented elites to new groups more favourable to the transnational project. The result of US military conquest is not the creation of exclusive zones for 'US' exploitation, as was the result of the Spanish conquest of Latin America, the British of South Africa and India, the Dutch of Indonesia, and so forth, in earlier moments of the world capitalist system. The enhanced class power of capital brought about by these changes is felt around the world. We see not a reenactment of this old imperialism but the colonization and re-colonization of the vanquished for the new global capitalism and its agents. The underlying class relation between the TCC and the US national state needs to be understood in these terms.

In sum, the US state has attempted to play a leadership role on behalf of transnational capitalist interests. That it is increasingly unable to do so points not to heightened national rivalry but to the impossibility of the task at hand given a spiraling crisis of global capitalism. This crisis involves a number of interrelated dimensions that by 2008 acquired systemic dimensions, among them, social polarization, overaccumulation, legitimacy, and sustainability (Robinson, 2004; 2008).

This multidimensional crisis of global capitalism generated intense discrepancies and disarray within the globalist ruling bloc that had begun to congeal in the 1990s. The political coherence of ruling groups always frays when faced with structural and/ or legitimacy crises as different groups push distinct strategies and tactics or turn to the more immediate pursuit of sectoral interests. Faced with the increasingly dim prospects of constructing a viable transnational hegemony—in the Gramscian sense of a stable system of consensual domination—the transnational bourgeoisie did not collapse back into the nation-state. Global elites, instead, mustered up fragmented and at times incoherent responses involving heightened military coercion, the search for a post-Washington consensus, and acrimonious internal disputes. The more politically astute among global elites began to clamour by the turn of the twenty-first century for a 'post-Washington consensus' project of reform—a so-called 'globalization with a human face'—in the interests of saving the system itself (see, for example, Stiglitz 2002). But there were others from within and outside of the bloc that called for more radical responses.

Neoliberalism 'peacefully' forced open new areas for global capital in the 1980s and the 1990s. This was often accomplished through economic coercion alone, made possible by the structural power of the global economy over individual countries. But this structural power became less effective in the face of the three-pronged crisis mentioned above. Opportunities for both intensive and extensive expansion dried up as privatizations ran their course, as the 'socialist' countries became integrated, as the consumption of high-income sectors worldwide reached ceilings, as spending through private credit expansion could not be sustained, and so on.

As the space for 'peaceful' expansion, both intensive and extensive, became ever more restricted, military aggression became an instrument for prying open new sectors and regions—for the forcible restructuring of space in order to further accumulation. The train of neoliberalism became latched on to military intervention and the threat of coercive sanctions as a locomotive for pulling the moribund Washington consensus forward. The war on terrorism provided a seemingly endless military outlet for surplus capital, generated a colossal deficit that justified deeper dismantling of the Keynesian welfare state and locked neoliberal austerity in place, and legitimated the creation of a police state to repress political dissent in the name of security.

The Bush White House militarized social and economic contradictions, launching a permanent war mobilization to try to stabilize the system through direct coercion. Was this evidence for a new US bid for empire? We need to move beyond a conjunctural focus on the Bush regime to grasp the early twenty-first century moment and the US role in it. In this sense, interventionism and militarized globalization was less a campaign for US hegemony than a contradictory political response to the crisis of global capitalism—to economic stagnation, legitimation problems, and the rise of counter-hegemonic forces.

Despite the rhetoric of neoliberalism, the US state undertook an almost unprecedented role in creating profit-making opportunities for transnational capital and pushing forward an accumulation process that left to its own devices (the 'free market') would likely ground to a halt. A Pentagon budget of nearly $500 billion in 2003, an invasion and occupation of Iraq estimated at upward to $3 trillion and a proposed multi-billion dollar space program that would rest on a marriage of NASA, the military, and an array of private corporate interests must be seen in this light, as a spectacular mobilization of global resources by the US state in function of militarized global accumulation. Some saw the trillions invested by the US state in the war on terrorism and the Iraq invasion and occupation as evidence that the US intervention benefits 'US capital' to the detriment of other national, for example 'EU', capitals.

However, Bechtel, the Carlyle Group, and Halliburton are themselves transnational capital conglomerates. It is true that military, oil, and engineering/construction companies, many of them headquartered in the US, managed to secure their particular sectoral interests through brazen instrumentalization of the US state under the Bush presidency. Yet, these companies were themselves transnational and their interests were those not of 'US capital' in rivalry with other countries but of particular transnational clusters in the global economy.

Transnational capitalists are themselves aware of the role of the US state in opening up new possibilities for unloading of surplus and created new investment opportunities. 'We're looking for places to invest around the world,' explained one former executive of a Dutch-based oil exploration and engineering company, and then 'you know, along comes Iraq' (as quoted in Monthly Review 2004, 64). The picture that emerges is one in which the US state mobilized the resources to feed a vast transnational network of profit making that passed through countless layers of outsourcing, subcontracting, alliances and collaborative relations—the open veins of the global economy—benefiting transnationally-oriented capitalists from many parts of the globe and sustaining, until 2008, global accumulation circuits in the face of severe overaccumulation and limits to financial speculation. The US state was the pivotal gear in a TNS machinery dedicated to reproducing global capitalism.

Concluding comments: imperialism and the extensive and intensive enlargement of capitalism

Let us recall that there are two inter-related components to classical and more recent theories of imperialism: 1) rivalry and conflict among core capitalist powers; 2) exploitation by these powers of peripheral regions. Much of my concern here has been with the premise of competing national capitals that informs the first. But what about this second component? If the world is not divided into rival national economies and national capitals, do we still need a theory of imperialism? Is there any contemporary relevance to the concept?

In the post-WWII period, and drawing on the tradition established by Rosa Luxembourg, Marxists and other critical political economists shifted the main focus in the study of imperialism to the mechanisms of core capitalist penetration of Third World countries and the appropriation of their surpluses. Imperialism in this sense referred to this exploitation and also to the use of state apparatuses by capitals emanating from the centres of the world system to facilitate this economic relation through military, political, and cultural mechanisms. If we mean by imperialism the relentless pressures for outward expansion of capitalism and the distinct political, military and cultural mechanisms that facilitate that expansion and the appropriation of surpluses it generates then it is a structural imperative built into capitalism; not a policy of particular core state managers—to see it as such was John A Hobson's fallacy—but a practice immanent to the system itself.

Alexander Anievas (2008), Adam David Morton (2007), and Callinicos (2007), among others, have argued that Trotsky's 'law of uneven and combined development' proves that capitalism inherently develops (accumulates) unevenly and that this uneven development belies my thesis on the transnationalization of the state. 'The central question then is whether there is anything inherent to capitalism which would perpetuate a territorial configuration of class interests and state power, and therefore, a multiplicity of states', states Anievas. 'The answer lies in what Trotsky termed the "law of uneven and combined development"' (Anievas 2008, 200). But why must the uneven accumulation of capitals be a territorially-uneven accumulation in which the spatial unit of this uneven accumulation is the nation-state? Lenin and Hilferding theorized an historical moment in world capitalism on the basis of an application of the laws of capitalist development, specifically, the manifestation of the outward expansion of competing capitals as imperialism. Trotsky, similarly, applied the laws of capitalist development—the uneven accumulation of capital as a consequence of the competition among capitals—to the world of the early twentieth century that he was analyzing. The historical forms that are thrown up by the laws of motion of a social order are just that: historical and therefore subject to transformation as the system evolves.

The centre-periphery division of labour created by modern colonialism reflected a particular spatial configuration of the law of uneven development that is becoming transformed by globalization. I suggested above that there is nothing in the concept of asymmetric exchanges that by fiat gives them a territorial, much less a nation-state, expression. And I have argued at length elsewhere (Robinson 2003; 2008), it is not that globalization does away with space or territory but that it reconstitutes the spaciality of world capitalism. I concur with Sassen (2007) on the historicity of scale and on the need to recode national and local processes as 'instantiations of the global' without assuming, as she observes, that if processes or conditions are located in national institutions or national territory they must be national. According to Alexander Anievas (2008, 201),

> another central factor perpetuating this uneven development, manifested in territorialized and geographical forms, is the construction of spatially-embedded physical infrastructures (e.g. transport and communication technologies) necessary for the expanded reproduction of capital. Investments in built environments come to define regional spaces for the circulation of capital.

As a result, he argues, 'capital demonstrates a clear tendency towards concentrating in specific regions at the expense of others, thereby producing a somewhat porous but nevertheless identifiable "territorial logic of power"—regionality—inherently arising out of the process of capital accumulation in space and time' (Anievas 2008, 201 quoting in part Harvey 2003).

Political economists have long observed what is known as agglomeration dynamics or the tendency for capital to concentrate in particular built environments. But there is nothing in this theory of agglomeration economies that would suggest these spaces must be nation-state spaces and in fact a great deal of empirical evidence indicates an ongoing erosion of the correspondence of national space with such economies and the accumulation circuits and levels of social development that adhere to them. The literature on global cities, for instance (see especially Sassen 2001; for a summary, Robinson forthcoming), and my own case studies on Latin America (Robinson 2003; 2008), show how capital accumulates unevenly in space and time and results in sharp social and spatial polarization within agglomeration economies nested in local, sub-national, cross-border and other spaces that do not correspond to nation-state spaces in an interstate logic.

These and other studies show that uneven accumulation tends to increasingly unfold in accordance with a social and not a national logic. Different levels of social development adhere from the very sites of social productive activity—that is, from social, not geographic, space. Moreover, privileged groups have an increasing ability to manipulate space so as to create enclaves and insulate themselves through novel mechanisms of social control and new technologies for the built environment. The persistence, and in fact growth, of the North-South divide remains important for its theoretical and practical political implications. What we must ask is whether the divide is something innate to world capitalism or a particular spatial configuration of uneven capitalist development during a particular historic phase of world capitalism, and whether tendencies towards the self-reproduction of this configuration are increasingly offset by countertendencies emanating from the nature and dynamic of global capital accumulation. To explain the movement of values between different 'nodes' in globalized production, clearly we need to move beyond nation-state centric approaches and apply a theory of value to transformations in world spatial and institutional structures (the nation-state being the central spatial and institutional structure in the hitherto history of world capitalism).

It is in the nature of global capitalism to create uneven spaces if only because of the mapping of functions onto space with the system. The law of uneven and combined accumulation postulates that the unevenness or inequality between regions together with their combination in a single international division of labour underlies capital accumulation. The spatial distribution of unequal development between North and South (or centre and periphery) as a particular territorial feature of the world system was determined in large part by the role of states as instruments of territorially bound classes and by the distinct socioeconomic and historical conditions that capitalism confronted in its genesis and worldwide spread.

The reality of capital as a totality of competing individual capitals, and their concrete existence as a relation within specific spatial confines determined geographically as nation-states, worked against a trans- or supranational unifying trend. Now globalization reconfigures the spatial relations of accumulation. Capitalists regardless of their national origin are able to use the uneven accumulation of capital and distinct spaces and political jurisdictions to their advantage in accumulation strategies. The Mexican multi-billionaire Carlos Slim and his Grupo Carso conglomerate, for instance, have operations that span all six continents (Robinson 2008). The conglomerate utilizes the Mexican and the US states as well as state agencies and managers in many other countries where it operates, taking advantage of uneven accumulation between Mexican and US territorial spaces for its own transnational accumulation strategies. The Grupo Carso has no intrinsic interest in 'developing' Mexico and no intrinsic aversion to uneven accumulation across national and other spatial boundaries; to the contrary, these often work to its advantage. Global capitalism, it is clear, has a global social base; it is a relation internal to virtually all countries and regions of the world. North-South contradictions are real yet complicated by capitalist globalization. The fundamental global social contradiction in global society is between subordinate and dominant classes in a transnational setting.

We need tools to conceptualize, analyze, and theorize how the expansionary pressure built into the capitalist system manifests itself in the age of globalization. We need these tools politically so as to help make effective our confrontation with the system. I would agree to this extent with Ray Kiely (2006, 219) that a theory of imperialism 'remains indispensable for understanding both the contemporary world order and the place of the South in that order'. Yet, capitalist imperialism is considerably more complex under globalization than the facile North-South/core-periphery framework through which it is typically viewed.

The class relations of global capitalism are now so deeply internalized within every nation-state that the classical image of imperialism as a relation of external domination is outdated. Failure to comprehend this leads to such superficial and misleading conclusions as, for instance, that the failure of popular projects to materialize under the rule of the Workers Party in Brazil or the African National Congress in South Africa is a result of a 'sell out' by the leaders of those parties or simply because 'imperialism' undercut their programs. Imperialism is not about nations but about groups exercising the social power—through institutions—to control value production, to appropriate surpluses, and to reproduce these arrangements. The challenge for such a theoretical enterprise is to ask: how and by whom in the world capitalist system are values produced (organized through what institutions), how are they appropriated (through what institutions), and how are these processes changing through capitalist globalization? During the 500 years since the genesis of the world capitalist system, colonialism and imperialism coercively incorporated zones and peoples into its fold. This historical process of 'primitive accumulation' is coming to a close.

The end of the extensive enlargement of capitalism is the end of the imperialist era of world capitalism. The system still conquers space, nature, and human beings. It is dehumanizing, genocidal, suicidal, and maniacal. But with the exception of a few remaining spaces—Iraq until recently, North Korea, etc.—the world has been brought into the system over the past half millennium. The implacable logic of accumulation is now largely internal to worldwide social relations and to the complex of fractious political institutions through which ruling groups attempt to manage those relations. We need a theory of capitalist expansion—of the political processes and the institutions through which such expansion takes place, the class relations and spatial dynamics it involves.

Notes

1 This is a revised version of an article first published in *Sociologists Without Borders* (issue 2, 2007).

5 Many capitals, many states

Contingency, logic or mediation?

Neil Davidson[1]

Introduction: three imaginary futures

Imagine that at some point in the future a single global polity has come into being and taken ownership and control of the entire world economy. Society under these conditions could be organized in one of two different ways. One way would be without classes, where the state has been replaced by a 'proto-governmental' or 'proto-political administration' (on these concepts see Draper 1978, 240). The other way would leave class divisions intact, but with state managers now directly occupying the position of the ruling class. The first would be world socialism. The second would be entirely new in human history, although comparable futures have been imagined in science fiction since HG Wells' *A Modern Utopia* (1905), and many attempts to classify the USSR as either 'totalitarian' or a new form of class society envisaged a dictatorial world state as the outcome of Russian victory in the Cold War.[2] From a Marxist perspective, such a monolithic economic entity would have one thing in common with socialism: it too would have ceased to be capitalist. For the nature of capitalism is determined by competition, and competition requires 'many capitals'. A 'universal' capital, as Marx put it, is a 'non-thing', an impossibility (Marx 1973, 414, 421fn2).[3] But how feasible is this hitherto unknown form of class society?

Marx (1976, 779) thought the 'entire social capital' of an individual society could be united under a single capitalist or company. Subsequent Marxist theorists of imperialism projected this theoretical possibility onto a global scale, with capital continuing to become ever-more concentrated and centralized until it formed one body, which they variously described as a 'general cartel', a 'universal capitalist trust' or a 'single world trust' (Hilferding 1981, 234, 311; Bukharin 1972, 133–43; Lenin 1972, 12–14). For the thinkers of the Second and Third Internationals, however, this new and universal Leviathan was highly unlikely ever to be realized. It is sometimes claimed that this was because they expected working class revolution to cut short developments in this direction (Lacher and Teschke 2007, 576). But there was another reason. Any consummation of trends towards centralization and concentration would also be prevented by political-military conflicts, both among the imperialist powers and between them and emerging capitalist states. The development of a global state is even less likely now, since the aspect of the period which made them most plausible—the interpenetration of state and capital towards an integral 'state capitalism'—is no longer the dominant tendency within contemporary economies.

Leave aside this object of literary fantasy, political paranoia and Marxist speculation, and envisage instead the completely opposite configuration: no state, but many capitals. Those who have come closest to advocating this outcome have been adherents of what might be called anarcho-capitalist thought, from Max Stirner and John Calhoun in the mid-19th century to Murray Rothbard and Ayn Rand in more recent times (Heider 1994, 92–150). Yet, the career path as a state manager followed by one of Rand's leading devotees, Alan Greenspan, suggests that their hostility is more to certain state functions—above all those concerned with welfare provision—than to the institution itself. As he enquires in his autobiography: 'if taxation was wrong, how could you reliably finance the essential functions of government, including the protection of individual's rights through police power?' (Greenspan 2008, 52). Marxists have not seriously entertained the possibility of capitalism dispensing with the state as a feasible option, but some have wondered why class rule takes this particularly 'public' form rather than private means of coercion (Pashukanis 1978, 139). The question has arisen in a different form more recently, in the context of debates over globalization. Fred Halliday, for example, has charged Marxists with failing to explain, 'why, if there is a world economy in which class interests operate transnationally, there is a need for states at all' (Halliday 1994, 91). Why indeed?

Capitalism always consists of many capitals and capitals always require a state. Does it follow that many capitals necessarily require many states? For if neither the bureaucratic collectivist nightmare nor the anarcho-capitalist dream is feasible, we are left with one alternative to the existing situation, which draws elements from them both: a single global polity under which economic life is still carried on by many competing capitals. The notion briefly surfaced in classical sociology, for example in Ferdinand Tönnies' Gemienschaft und Gesellschaft (1887), which speculated on whether it would be possible to 'abolish the multiplicity of states and substitute for it a single world republic, coextensive with the world market' (Tönnies 1957, 221). Most Marxist writers, however, believe that theoretically desirable as this outcome may be from the point of view of capital, it is unlikely to be achieved in practice (see, for example, Leys 2001, 26–27; and Brenner 2007, 84). Even those who are often grouped together as identifying the emergence of a 'single state' are usually arguing something quite different. Hardt and Negri (2000), for example, claim that nation-states and imperialism as traditionally understood are no longer central to the capitalist world order; they have been superseded by a new and metaphysical 'logic of rule' which they conceptualize as 'empire'. But while they argue that some states, notably the US, may be better adapted to these new conditions, they do not argue that states are ceasing to exist: 'empire' has superseded states without replacing them (Hardt and Negri 2000, xi–xvi). At the other end of the spectrum, Panitch and Gindin (2003) claim that the US is now a global imperial power without precedent or peer, and has successfully incorporated all potential economic competitors into a single imperial protectorate, within which geopolitical rivalries are no longer conceivable. But here again there is no suggestion that all other nation-states are to be literally absorbed into the US. Indeed, the consolidation of US hegemony implies the continued existence of other states over which hegemony can be exercised (Panitch and Gindin 2003, 13–33).

I do not find either of these arguments convincing, but the point is that neither suggest that a world state is imminent, or even possible. Among Marxists, William I Robinson is virtually alone in claiming that a global capitalist state is in the process of coming into being through existing transnational state apparatuses and the problems with his position have already been convincingly demonstrated (see Robinson 2007, 8, and his chapter in this collection; cf. Cammack 2007 and Morton 2007, 140–50). The debate is therefore less to do with whether a global state will emerge in the future, as with precisely why one will not, and what the implications of this are for relationships between capitalist states. A plausible argument for the continued existence of many states can, of course, be made from sheer practicality, or what Wood calls 'the insurmountable difficulty of sustaining on a large geographical scale the close regulation and predictability capital needs' (Wood 2006, 25; see also Wood 2003, 141 and Smith 1990, 142–43). But even size is not decisive. As Vivek Chibber (2005, 157) notes, 'one could certainly imagine a federated system, in which administrative and regulative authority is localized, but sovereignty is not'. Something more fundamental is involved here.

In the *Grundrisse*, Marx (1973, 85) comments that some determinations exist throughout history, while others only at certain times in that history. To which category do states belong? States have certainly existed in different forms since the origins of class society, but as Alasdair MacIntyre (2008, 55) once noted, 'the difference between one form of society as another is not just a difference in basis, and a corresponding difference in superstructure, but a difference also in the way basis is related to superstructure'. The issue is therefore whether we treat these different forms of state as also being different types of determination or not. Are there simply 'states' which relate in particular ways to different social formations, or are there 'feudal states' and 'capitalist states', the character of which is determined by the dominant mode of production? What is capitalist about a capitalist state?

Any state has to play two roles: one of representation, to 'promote and defend the ruling class and its mode of exploitation or supremacy'; the other, mediation of 'the exploitation or domination of the ruling class over other classes and strata' (Therborn 1978, 181). In neither case is every action necessarily in the direct collective interest of the ruling class. It is rather that 'all other interests are regularly subordinated to the interests of the ruling class' (Draper 1978, 262). There are particular functions which capitalist states must perform, of which three are particularly important. The first is the imposition of a dual social order: horizontally over competing capitals so that market relations do not collapse into 'the war of all against all'; and vertically over the conflict between capital and labour so that it continues to be resolved in the interest of the former. The second is the establishment of 'general conditions of production' which individual competing capitals would be unwilling or unable to provide, including some basic level of technical infrastructure and welfare provision (Barker 1978, 20–23). These are mainly 'internal' to the territory of the state; the third is the way in which each capitalist state has to represent the collective interests of the 'internal' capitalist class 'externally' in relation to other capitalist states and classes. But capitalist states also engage in other external activities—variously described as 'international relations' or 'geopolitics'—which sometimes appear to play no role in supporting national capitals and may even be detrimental to their interests. Does this mean that, in some respects at least, the states system is (absolutely or relatively) autonomous from capitalism? If so it would mean effectively treating the state as a 'capitalist state' only for the purposes of internal class relations, including inter-capitalist class relations, but as a 'state under capitalism' for external interstate relations.

States as moments in a 'mediated totality'

An alternative has to transcend the two most coherent Marxist explanations for the continued coexistence of many capitals and many states. Both deny that there is any intrinsic connection between capital accumulation on the one hand and the interstate system on the other. One is the argument from historical contingency associated with Robert Brenner, Hannes Lacher, Benno Teschke and Wood. The other is the argument from overlapping autonomous logics associated with Giovanni Arrighi, Alex Callinicos and David Harvey. Of these two explanations contingency suggests an accident of history, whereas logic implies a coincidence of interests, but neither allows any deeper underlying relationship; it is simply fortuitous, for reasons of either timing or motivation.

Both positions invoke the same reason for denying any necessary connection between them, although it is expressed in different terminology. Callinicos, for example, treats the states system as 'a set of determinations' with 'specific properties that are irreducible to those of previously introduced determinations' (Callinicos 2007, 542). While Lacher supports his argument for a purely contingent relationship between capitalism and territoriality by claiming that the alternative is to treat everything that exists under capitalism as an emanation from the capitalist relation and to thus treat capitalism as an 'expressive totality' (Lacher 2005, 35; 2006, 42, 60). This term was first used by Louis Althusser, who associated it with Hegel and contrasted it with his preferred alternative: the unity of a 'structure articulated in dominance' (Althusser 1969, 200–204). According to Nicos Poulantzas, Marxists—above all Györg Lukács—had also mistakenly embraced expressive totality (Poulantzas 1973, 14, 197–99).

The concept of totality was in fact one of the fundamental components of classical Marxism. And while there were certainly problems with Lukács' elevation of totality to the single most important aspect of Marx's analysis of capitalism, notably his neglect of internal contradiction, the concept itself is indispensable (Rees 1998, 247–49). In any case, Lukács did not himself refer to an 'expressive totality'—that expression has been 'ascribed' to him by the Althusserians and Political Marxists—but rather to a 'mediated totality'. To be part of a totality is to be part of 'a total social situation caught up in the process of social change' and to say that a totality is mediated is to overcome what Lukács calls 'the mere immediacy of the empirical world', in which moments are 'torn ... from the complex of their true determinants and placed in artificial isolation' (Lukács 1971, 162–63).

To what extent is Lukács following Marx here? Callinicos reminds us that Marx begins *Capital* with the commodity and, as the work proceeds, he introduces a series of ever more complex and non-reducible, free-standing determinations, each resolving problems which are posed earlier in the process of explanation, until a full picture of the capitalist mode of production as a whole emerges. The explanatory power of the successive determinations, of which the states system is one, is therefore derived precisely from their externality to the original starting point (Callinicos 2001a, 38–40; Callinicos 2007, 542–43). Callinicos has consistently contrasted this methodology with that used by Marx in the introduction to the *Grundrisse*, where these additional determinations are generated precisely by the original starting point, thus remaining in classical Hegelian style mere emanations of 'capital-in-general' (Callinicos 1982, 138–39; Callinicos 2005a, 57–58).

Now, it is unclear whether *Capital* is as radically anti-Hegelian as Callinicos claims. Marx himself noted in a letter to Engels during 1858 that his 'demolition' of the existing theory of profit was methodologically inspired by a rereading of Hegel's Logic (Marx and Engels 1983, 249). In any case, it is possible to establish a genetic connection between determinations while avoiding unreconstructed Hegelianism. Derek Sayer argues that determinations form 'a hierarchy of conditions of possibility'; so Marx analyzes the commodity before money, because the first is 'a condition of the second' (Sayer 1979, 101). But while a determination like money cannot be explained without recourse to the commodity, none of the chain of concepts of which they are both part is a 'condition of possibility' for the states system. The states system enters stage left, as a fully-formed determination whose origin is unexplained. What seems to be involved here are tendencies criticized long ago by Lukács for 'tak[ing] over ... determinations without either analysing them further or welding them into a concrete totality' or 'forg[ing] arbitrary unmediated connections between things that belong together in an organic union' (Lukács 1971, 9). Nor can the states system itself be explained by the separate application of this methodology, for what could be the starting point analogous to the commodity?

Part of the problem here seems to be the confusion of two types of methodology. In *Capital* Marx sets out a mode of conceptual presentation, not one of historical explanation or logical interconnection (Marx 1973, 107–8; Marx 1976, 102; see also Lukács 1972, 221). For this purpose it need not explain the origin of the determinations, which can be taken as pre-given. But this is different from Marx's actual method of historical and social analysis. As Bertell Ollman writes, Marx conceives of reality 'as a totality composed of internally related parts' and that each of these parts 'in its fullness can represent the totality'. This involves more than simply affirming that the different aspects of social life are related to each other—a position from which few people would dissent—but that for each aspect 'the conditions of its existence are taken to be part of what it is' (Ollman 1979, 105).

In his mature work Marx argued that there were three different forms of human practice, which together explain how societies emerge, develop and transform themselves. One form of human practice involves those activities which bring together natural and technological capacities and qualities into directly producing and reproducing human existence. These activities entail (or set the 'conditions of possibility' or 'conditions of existence' for) the social relationships of cooperation, exploitation and conflict within which they take place. These in turn entail those institutions—of which the states system is fundamental—and ideologies by which these relationships are justified, defended and challenged.[4]

As we shall see, this can explain not only 'the innermost secret, the hidden basis' of the state (Marx 1981, 927), but of the system of states. It is true, as Gonzalo Pozo-Martin reminds us, that the state system cannot be 'deduced from the concept of capital'; but to then argue that 'it exerts its own set of determinations, quite independently of capital', is effectively to abandon the notion of totality central to Marx's method (Pozo-Martin 2007, 556–57). The problem can be illustrated by looking at two central claims respectively associated with the arguments from contingency and from two autonomous logics: in the case of the first, that there is a separation of function between the economic and the political under capitalism; in the case of the second—which in some respects is a specific example of the first claim—that there is a divergence of interest between those who run the state and those who embody capital.

'The separation of the economic and the political under capitalism'

Under all pre-capitalist modes of production exploitation took place visibly through the extraction of a literal surplus from the direct producers by the threat or reality of violence: economics and politics were 'fused' in the power of the feudal lord or tributary state. Under the capitalist mode of production exploitation takes place invisibly in the process of production itself through the creation of surplus value over and above that required in reproducing the labour force. Wood (1981) identifies a resulting 'division of labour' between the moments of appropriation and coercion, with the former in private hands and the latter in those of the state. Furthermore, unlike previous exploiting classes, capitalists exercise economic power without 'the obligation to perform social, public functions' (Wood 1981, 81–82). This is one reason for what Hal Draper calls 'the political inaptitude of the capitalist class' compared to other ruling classes in history: feudal lords combine an economic and political role; capitalists perform only the former—although the necessity for capitalists to devote their time to the process of accumulation and their own multiple internal divisions also militate against their functioning directly as a governing class (Draper 1978, 321–24).

Claims for the separation of the political and the economic do therefore have scientific validity and highlight a central distinction between the process of exploitation under capitalism and other modes of production. According to Teschke, there is a 'complete separation' between the political and the economic under capitalism, where 'the capital circuits of the world market can in principle function without infringing on political sovereignty. As a rule, capitalism can leave political territories intact' (Teschke 2003, 267). The qualifiers introduced by Teschke here suggest a certain conceptual unease, as if these rules and principles might not actually apply in reality, which is indeed the case.

'Capital circuits' do operate outside the control of states in so far as they involve money capital; but money capital is ultimately dependent on the moment of production, which cannot escape territoriality and consequently a relationship with state power. Failure to distinguish between the logical development of categories in theory and their development in history leads to the danger of working with platonic or 'ideal' conceptions of the capitalist economy and capitalist states which do not correspond to the operation of any actual capitalist economies or capitalist states. As China Miéville (2005, 221) remarks, Political Marxists such as Teschke err in both of these respects, first by erecting an abstract model of capitalism and then by taking 'capitalism at its own word'. In fact, capitals can perform some of the functions of states and states can act as capital.

Throughout the history of the system capitalists have employed extra-economic means to recruit, retain, coerce and control labour. The self-expansion of the total social capital can never be completely based on unfree labour, of course, because it assumes and requires general labour mobility; but 'general' does not mean 'universal', and individual capitals can employ, have employed and continue to employ unfree labour (Banaji 2003, 79–80). As Chibber (2005, 155) has noted, even the extent to which these supposed deviations from the capital relation have been discarded has not been because system grows nearer to some abstract model, but because of successful resistance by the labour movement. In many cases the type of controls exercised by capitalists relate specifically to the use of violence, and only adherence to Weberian definitions of the state can explain failure to recognize this fact (Weber 1994, 310–11).

From the use of private armies by Rockefeller in America after the Civil War through to the current universal expansion of private security firms, violence has never been the monopoly of the capitalist state, for, as Timothy Mitchell (2007, 30) argues, violence is not 'contingent or external to the logic of history' but is 'constitutive of both markets and monopolies'. In terms of external relations, of course, states have always fought to retain the sole right to exercise violence, but even this is now challenged by the rise of war-making capacity in private hands; the rightly derided notion of the 'Global War on Terror' is an ideologically refracted recognition of this fact (Hobsbawm 2007, 25).

Capitalists, state managers and politicians

The argument from the twin logics of state and capital is more concrete and, at first sight, more plausible than unfounded assertions about the supposed separation of functions under capitalism, not least because it discusses actual social groups rather than reified abstractions like 'the economic' and 'the political'. Fred Block, who popularized the term 'state managers' in the first place, writes that, 'since the bourgeoisie or other propertied classes cannot survive without a state, those classes have little choice but to seek a *modus operandi* with the state managers' (Block 1980, 250). Callinicos follows Block on the grounds that his position 'has the great merit of starting from the non-identity of interests between capitalists and state managers' (Callinicos 2007, 543). Callinicos is rightly concerned not to succumb to economic reductionism, or to display what, following Chibber (2005, 157), he calls a 'soft functionalism', and sees this as a way of avoiding it (Callinicos 2007, 538). Nevertheless, claims for the 'non-identity' of state managerial and capitalist interests are, in effect, a specific example of the separation of the political and the economic under capitalism. If the latter is nowhere near as total as has been claimed, then there are also reasons for doubting the completeness of the former.

At the most fundamental level, the common interest between capitalists and state managers stems from their common class position. Both are part of the bourgeoisie: Departmental Permanent Secretaries in the British home civil service as much as say the Chief Executive Officers of major companies. If we visualize the bourgeoisie as a series of concentric circles, then the capitalist class as such occupy the centre and a series of other layers radiate outwards; with those closer to the periphery being progressively less directly connected to the core economic activities of production, exploitation and competition, and more directly involved with those of the ideological, administrative or technical aspects, which are nevertheless essential to the reproduction of capitalism (Davidson 2000, 33–34). The incomes which state managers are paid from state revenues ultimately derive from the total social surplus value produced by the working class, as are the profits, interest and rent received by different types of private capitalist (Harman 1991, 16–17). And this applies not simply to the source of their income, but also to its level, since the relatively high levels of remuneration, security and prestige enjoyed by these officials depend on the continued exploitation of wage labour. At that level, the interests of state managers and capitalist are the same.

But if we expand on the notion of 'interests' from material rewards to a broader sense of shared ideological commitment, it is not that their interests are 'non-identical' so much as they arise from distinct regions of the totality of capitalism, in its various national manifestations. A shared background in institutions like schools, universities, and clubs helps to consolidate a class consciousness which articulates these interests, but a more fundamental reason however is that the activities of states are subordinated to the accumulation of capital. And, regardless of their class origins, state managers and capitalists are drawn together into a series of mutually-supportive relationships: the former need the resources provided by individual national capitals, principally through taxation and loans, in order to attend to the needs of the national capital as a whole; the latter need specific policy initiatives to strengthen the competitive position of their sector of the national capital within the global economy.

Two apparently contradictory aspects of these relationships are particularly important. First, in order to maintain links to capital's multiple and mutually hostile incarnations, the state apparatuses must partly mirror capital's fragmentation (Hirsch 1978, 100). Second, if policies were however being framed for the benefit of sectional capitalist interests this would constitute a problem for the local capitalist class as a whole. In the US particularly, the penetration of the higher reaches of government by executives, notably those associated with the oil and automobile industries, has in some respects overtaken even the most deranged imaginings of vulgar Marxism (Henwood 2005, 73; Phillips 2006, 87; Davis 2007, 23, 26). But American foreign policy is not determined solely by the localized interests of oil and automobile executives.

In Britain, following hard on the heels of the US as always, there has been a more generalized influx of private-sector appointees into the civil service, which Peter

Oborne describes as being increasingly 'emasculated' as a result, to the point where it has been effectively subject to a 'corporate takeover' (Oborne 2007, 113–53). In other words, state managers may see their interests as being distinct from *specific* national capitals or even specific *sectors* of national capital, but not from the national capital as a whole. Indeed, the reason why the first capitalist state, the United Netherlands, was unable to sustain its pre-eminent position was not simply because it was territorially fragmented into an unwieldy compromise between a federal and confederate structure (Israel 1998, 276–84). It was also because the governments of the main provinces, especially Holland, were too closely aligned with particular capitalist interests for the central apparatus of the States General to make decisions which could advance their collective interest.[5] The English and subsequently British state did not suffer from this disadvantage.

It could however be argued that this ascribes too great a level of class consciousness to state managers; they may well share a class location with capitalists, but this does not mean that their actual motivations are inspired by the same economic considerations. The behavioural mechanisms driving the actions of state managers can certainly involve non-economic considerations, even the achievement of what might call 'reformist' objectives, in which support for national capitals is merely a means to an end. Oliver James, for example, recounts the response of one senior civil servant to the argument that economic growth does not necessarily increase human happiness. The official in question (after 'sighing as if I were a tiresome four-year-old who had asked what God is') replied that 'if economic growth was no longer the goal, unemployment would increase and there would be less funding for projects such as child poverty, and people would be *un*happier' (James 2007, 321–22). But does this matter?

Take one society in which there were no individual capitalists, and their role was collectively performed by state managers: the USSR between 1928 and 1991. In debates on the nature of the USSR, the late Ernest Mandel claimed that Stalinist bureaucracy was not compelled to accumulate, but sought to retain its collective managerial position for the purpose of satisfying its desire for consumption (Mandel 1973, 17). But for those like Callinicos and myself who believe that the USSR was a form of bureaucratic state capitalism, whatever motivations brought individual members of the bureaucracy to seek those roles (and the material benefits of a place among the ruling class would have exercised attractions, regardless of the risks), whatever *post hoc* justifications they may have used to rationalize their behaviour, once in post they were compelled to behave in such a way as to enable Russia to match American military spending or face being overwhelmed by their Western imperial rival (Cliff 2003, 90–92; Harman 1984, 71–74, 84–86). Even allowing for the exceptional fusion of state and capital under Stalinism, is the situation of Stalinist bureaucrats different *in principle* from that of state managers in situations where multinational capital is still dominant?

Nor are the motivations of state managers and capitalists as different as might be thought. Michael Kidron once noted that accumulation did not take place automatically, but through decisions taken by individuals and groups who had both criteria for success and incentives to pursue it. From the point of view of the system, however, the nature of these incentives and the motives of these actors are irrelevant except in so far as they contribute to the expansion of capital (Kidron 1974, 80–81). In other words, once capitalists enter the system as competitors, they are compelled to accumulate, but their reasons for entering the system are not, generally speaking, because they want to become the living embodiments of capital. Whatever the motivations, it is only by submitting to the imperatives of accumulation and successfully competing with other capitals that they stand any chance of fulfillment.

Like capitalists, state managers can be motivated to act in the interest of capital accumulation as a means to quite other ends, they simply do so from a position of greater distance in the process of capital accumulation, and less concern with the fate of individual capitals. After all—to take one of Callinicos' and Ashman's (2006) examples—why do state managers have an 'interest' in developing the military capacities of their state, if not in their capacity as representatives of capital? And they do so not only in preparation for war, but for economic reasons. 'A soft state that yields on vital national security issues cannot project an image of a tough negotiator on trade and commerce' (Greenfield 2001, 482). But arms need not be involved in any sense. As Edward Luttwak notes,

> ... investment capital for industry provided or guided by the state is the equivalent of firepower; product development subsidised by the state is the equivalent of weapon innovation; and market penetration supported by the state replaces military bases and garrisons on foreign soil as well as diplomatic influence.
>
> (Luttwak 1998, 128)

These are not simply analogies. War may be 'different from commerce, but evidently not different enough', as the response to a perceived threat, in the form of retaliatory trade restrictions, for example, is similar (Luttwak 1998, 129). There are, however, areas where there are genuine differences of interest between capitalists and state managers, but to understand them we need to introduce a further category; namely that of politicians, whose functions overlap in some respects with those of state managers, but in at least two others involve central differences.

First, their importance for capital occurs in different historical situations. The virtues of state managers for capital are those associated with a consolidated regime: stability, continuity and predictability. In such periods, these are also expected of political actors. In times of crisis, however, the significance of the latter is quite different and this has been the case from the bourgeois revolutions onwards. In these, political leadership was rarely provided by merchants, industrialists or bankers, but by journalists, lawyers or priests, groups whose boldness was in inverse proportion to their ownership or control of capital, and who consequently had less to lose (Davidson 2005, 42–44). At certain points, however, one view of the 'national interest' must prevail and one strategy to achieve it must be followed, if military defeat, economic relegation or successful working-class insurgency is to be avoided. In contemporary terms then, the importance of the elevation of political actors above the economic core of the bourgeoisie comes in periods of crisis where major restructuring of capital is required, when the intra-capitalist conflicts have to be resolved, at least until the immediate danger is passed. The establishment of neoliberal hegemony was one such reorientation. It was not originally articulated in any systematic way by the capitalists who ultimately benefited from it. It was rather the obsession of peripheral ideologists employed mainly as academics and journalists, then by politicians who accepted these ideas as a means of restoring profitability, and only then by the majority of capitalist owners and managers, even in the US, which had the most developed tradition of business activism. The Thatcher government directly represented capital in so far as it was opposed to the working class movement ('vertically'), but could not represent every component of capital ('horizontally'), because there was no general agreement on strategy during the late 1970s, not least because individual capitals would and did suffer from the one eventually adopted from 1979 onwards (Gamble 1988, 194–97, 224–27). In this sense the state under the minority Thatcherite wing of the Tory Party acted as the *avant garde* of the British capitalist class.

The second major difference between state managers and politicians is that the latter have to some extent to reflect the interests of their electoral supporters, which is easier when those interests are coincident or at least compatible with those of capital. Politicians in all the main parties are increasingly converging on openly capitalist notions of the national interest, but in some cases, the beliefs of their supporters may inadvertently cause difficulty for the accumulation process, as in the case of US Republican reliance on communities of fundamentalist Christian believers (Phillips 2006, 393–94). But politicians themselves can act in ways which are either irrelevant or detrimental to the interests of capital. The Nazi regime presents us with several examples of policies which were irrational, not only from the capitalist perspective, but from that of the state as a war-making machine (Mason 1995, 74; Kershaw 2000, 563, 567–68, 713). But the unavoidable example, and one of the most difficult of historical problems, is the motivation behind the Holocaust.

In an outstanding discussion Callinicos rightly points out that, in general terms, 'the extermination of the Jews cannot be explained in economic terms'. And although he does not use the terminology of 'logics' in this context, he clearly sees the connection between the Holocaust and German capitalism as an example of the same type of interpenetration of interests, in this case between 'German big business' and 'a move-ment whose racist and pseudo—revolutionary ideology drove it towards the Holocaust'. Callinicos sums up his position: '"German capitalism didn't need the Holocaust. But it needed the Nazis, and *they* needed the Holocaust"' (Callinicos 2001b, 403, 406, 413fn95).[6] But where did the Nazi 'racist and pseudo-revolutionary ideology' come from in the first place?

Callinicos seems to regard claims for a connection between Nazism and capitalism as involving the immediate needs of the economy at a time of crisis, which would indeed be reductionist. But the ideological formation of the Nazi worldview took place over a much longer period, which saw the combination of a series of determinations arising from the contradictions of German and European capitalism, including extreme right-wing nationalism, racism in its anti-Semitic form, disappointed imperialism, a taste for violence acquired in the trenches and so on (see Evans 2003, 22–76; Kershaw 2007, 438–44). In other words, we might say that German capitalism didn't need the

Holocaust, but the long-term development of German capitalism produced, through a series of mediations, the ideology of Nazism which contained the possibility of a Holocaust. When German capitalists turned to the Nazis in the moment of crisis, the latter were given the opportunity to realize that possibility. The barbaric ideology of Nazism and the socio-economic crisis of Germany to which they provided one solution were already connected as different moments in the mediated totality of capitalism.

Competitive accumulation: the essence of capitalism

Is there an alternative explanation for the continuation of the states system than the two discussed above? Marx wrote that, 'the anatomy of … civil society … has to be found in political economy' (Marx 1975, 424). Civil society in its turn contains the anatomy of the state—the 'concentration of bourgeois society in the form of the state' (Marx 1973, 108). Each is a different, but inter-related moment in the totality of capitalism. As Henryk Grossman emphasized, Marx was attempting to understand social phenomena, not by focusing on their 'superficial attributes … at any given moment or period', but 'in their successive transformations, and thus to discover their essence' (Grossman 1943, 517). For Marx (1973, 414), the essence of capitalism, its 'inner nature', is competition. And 'competition on the world market' is the 'very basis … of the capitalist mode of production' (Marx 1981, 205). But competition has both a precondition and consequence: the precondition is the creation of a class of wage labourers; the consequence is the compulsion to accumulate (Marx 1976, 874, 739).

Capitalism is a system of competitive accumulation based on wage labour and these two defining aspects also point to the reasons for the persistence of the states system: on the one hand, the need for capitals to be territorially aggregated for competitive purposes; on the other, the need for that territory to have an ideological basis—nationalism—which can be used to bind the working class to the state and hence to capital. It is the first of these that I want to consider here.[7] Fernand Braudel once argued that capital has *always* existed beyond the limits of 'the state and its particular preoccupations' (Braudel 1985, 554). But despite these complications, the capitalist class in its constituent parts continue to retain territorial home bases presided over by states for their operations (Harman 1991, 32–38; Anderson 1992, 6; Harvey 2005, 35–36). Why?

Capitalism is based on competition, but capitalists want competition to take place on their terms; they do not want to suffer the consequences if they lose. In one sense then, they require from a state more than simply providing an infrastructure; they need it to ensure that effects of competition are experienced as far as possible by someone else. A global state could not do this. Indeed, in this respect it would be the same as having no state at all. For if everyone is protected then no-one is: unrestricted market relations would prevail, with all the risks that entails. The state therefore has to have limits; it has to be able to distinguish between those capitals who will receive its protection and support, and those who will not. But what sets the territorial limits of a state? Here Harvey's early writings are helpful.

The confines are set by the limits of what he calls 'a *structured coherence* to production and consumption within a given space', a space within which 'capital can circulate without the limits of profit within socially-necessary turnover time being exceeded by the cost and time of movement' and 'a relatively coherent labour market prevails (the space within which labour power can be substituted on a daily basis)'. It is this space of 'territorial coherence' which is 'formally represented by the state' (Harvey 2001a, 328–29). Two conclusions follow. First, capitalism would have produced a similar states system to the one that currently exists no matter what preceded it. Second, even if a global super-state were to come into being (and this hypothesis is extremely unlikely, given the catastrophic levels of interstate violence which would be required to bring it into being), capitals within it would tend to group together to create new states or recreate old ones: it would be unsustainable as long as there were many capitals.

If the preceding argument is correct, then we should expect to find, not only the persistence of many states, but that these many states will persist in competing with each other—that is, capitalist competition will find *expression* in geopolitical competition. Pozo-Martin (2007, 560) claims that any attempt to show that the latter is 'directly determined' by the former will 'crash against reality time after time'. Quite a lot hinges here on the words 'directly determined', since it is precisely in order to show the indirect routes by which economic competition is manifested politically that I have insisted on the need for the concept of mediated totality. In order to demonstrate this point it is not necessary to show that, say, France is likely to go to war with Germany in the near future—a scenario which I agree is unlikely—but that capitalist states are engaged in forms of competition which have the potential to end in war, whether or not that potential is ever realized.

Capitalist competition versus perpetual peace

Some Marxists reject even the possibility of conflict. Brenner for example, argues that, while states generally act in support of capital, the system of multiple states which capitalism inherited from feudalism means that even the biggest cannot predict or control the outcomes of their actions, since every other state is also acting in a similar way, potentially leading to counter-productive outcomes (Brenner 2006a, 84–85). At an extreme, these outcomes can involve catastrophes like the First World War, which is presumably why Brenner believes that a 'global-state solution' would be in the best interests of capital. Now, if Brenner was simply pointing to the incommensurability of outcomes it would be difficult to disagree. His position goes further than this, however, to suggest that, not only are the consequences of certain actions unpredictable, but that from the point of view of capitalism, they are incomprehensible.

The theoretical difficulty behind these arguments is a conception of capitalism as essentially involving market competition on the basis of price, behind which lies the compulsion to achieve cost savings through technical innovation. Brenner famously distinguishes 'horizontal' *competition* between capitals from 'vertical' *conflict* between labour and capital, which is helpful up to a point, but inter-capitalist competition does not take place only through the market (Brenner 2006a, 25). In 1920 Nikolai

Bukharin described 'the struggle for spheres of capital investment ... for the very opportunity to expand the production process' as an example of capitalist competition by other means (Bukharin 1979, 62). Chris Harman has argued that other non-market forms of competition involve 'spending surplus value on ways of manipulating the market, advertising goods, creating a "product image", bribing buyers in firms and state agencies' (Harman 1984, 43–44). Capitalist competition can be external to markets, but so too can the agents of competition be separate from capitals: they can be states, and competition between states tends to lead to *conflict*.

As Arrighi notes, there are two kinds of competition between capitals. The first amounts to a form of regulated cooperation in which all benefit from the expansion of trade. The second, however, involves 'substantive' competition in which the profits of one capital are achieved at the expense of another; the situation ceases to be 'positive-sum' and becomes 'zero-sum'. This type of competition is not restricted to firms, however, but involves states, beginning with the behaviour of the Italian city-states during the Hundred Years War (Arrighi 1996, 227). Arrighi thus concludes that 'inter-capitalist competition has indeed been the predominant influence' in causing contractions in profitability, as this is only tenable 'provided that we include inter-capitalist wars among the most important forms of that competition'. If we do not, then it can lead to 'the virtual eviction of world politics from the analysis of capitalist dynamics' (Arrighi 2007, 130, 132).

In this context, the situations which state managers and politicians face are similar to those which face individual capitalists. When a firm invests in new labour-saving technology which will reduce its costs, rival capitalists ultimately must make similar investments, even at the risk that the initial cost of purchase, installation and training will be so great as to threaten to force them out of business before the savings can be realized. Not investing means the virtual certainty of failure; investing means it is only a possibility. State managers and politicians behave similarly to capitalists in relation to national economies. But state managers and politicians also have to take decisions which, on balance, are likely to result in disaster because the alternative exposes them to even greater risk in the longer term. And this does not only apply only in situations which are directly economic in nature. The invasions and occupations of Afghanistan and Iraq have turned into disasters for the US (they were always so for the Afghans and Iraqis), but this outcome was not preordained. A failed strategy does not become irrational simply because it fails. Politicians make calculated gambles, the results of which appear inevitable if they pay off and irrational if they do not. There is therefore no need to regard Dick Cheney and the other neo-conservatives as insane or following a perverse political strategy in relation to American capitalist interests, which their actions have nevertheless undermined, with certain negative implications for the future of US geopolitical power (Arrighi 2007, 178–203; Jha 2006, 319–21; Wallerstein 2006b, 90–92).

Future conflicts are therefore unlikely to be restricted to the attempted imposition of US dominance over recalcitrant states of the global South: They will involve the states of the developed world themselves, above all for resources. Does this mean that war is imminent between the core states of the world system? In the short term, of course not; but this is scarcely the only form of geopolitical rivalry. Since the end of the Cold War one expression has been war 'by proxy', where the dominant states jostle for influence by supporting different sides in inter- or intra-state conflicts. The different sides supported by France, Germany and the US during the disintegration of Yugoslavia was perhaps the first example of this strategy in the post-Cold War world; the conflict between NATO and Russia over Georgia (and the divisions *within* the NATO member states over attitudes to Russia) is the most recent. But similar alignments are beginning to take shape in Central Africa where France is already in the dominant position among the Western powers. And proxy wars have, after all, preceded full scale imperialist wars before now. As Boris Kagarlitsky reminds us, the key opponents in the First World War had already been engaged in conflict-at-one-remove before 1914: 'The Anglo-Boer War was in many ways a conflict between Britain and Germany who backed, encouraged, trained and supplied the Boers. The Russo-Japanese war was a clash between Germany (backing Russia) and England (supporting Japan)' (Kagarlitsky 2004, 274fn3).

As the current crisis deepens, we can expect the first manifestations of renewed interstate conflict to take the form of direct pressure by larger states on smaller states at the same point in the developmental spectrum: Britain threatens Iceland with the seizure of assets (under anti-terrorist legislation) because the latter refuses to guarantee British deposits in Icelandic banks; Russia invades Georgia because the latter refuses to countenance the secession of areas with majority Russian populations. If the argument here is correct, then rather than being different kinds of event, they represent different points on a continuum, the end point of which is the escalation to violence. The moment of maximum danger for humanity will come when the capitalist great powers no longer express their different competitive interests by proxy in the Global South, or assert their interests over lesser states in the developed world itself, but when they directly confront each other on the geopolitical stage.

Conclusion

Capitalism did not inherit the feudal-absolutist states system. Instead it destroyed and rebuilt the internal structures of the constitutive states, and then reconfigured their external relationships on a different basis. Once the new system emerged, the dynamics of competition between the component states assumed a distinctive logic, but it was the geopolitical expression of the same logic that impels the most rudimentary moments of competitive accumulation involving commodities. There are not two logics. As Father Merrin says in *The Exorcist*: 'there is only one', although our demon is called Capital rather than Pazuzo (Blatty 1972, 282). What are the implications of this for the classical Marxist theory of imperialism?

Critics of the theory are fond of listing its supposed inadequacies, not only as a guide to the current situation, but even in relation to the period in which it was formulated (Panitch and Gindin 2003, 4–9; Lacher and Teschke 2007, 578). Inadequacies there certainly were: Lenin over-generalized from the German fusion of banking and industrial capital and was empirically wrong about the destination of overseas capital investment; Bukharin gave too one-sided a picture of the tendency towards state capitalism, and so on. But when all these criticisms have been registered, there remains the fact that the theory identified aspects of the system which have largely been lost by subsequent generations of Marxists.

The theory involved two sets of relationships: those of domination by the metropolitan powers over the colonial and semi-colonial world and those of rivalry between the metropolitan powers themselves. The former came popularly to define 'imperialism', not least because during the Cold War inter-capitalist economic rivalries were held in check—not abolished—by their enforced political and ideological solidarity against the Eastern Bloc. The Cold War further obscured this aspect of the system by appearing to make geopolitical rivalry an aspect of the supposedly 'inter-systemic conflict', rather than a function of the system itself. But it was the latter that most concerned the theorists of classical Marxism.

During the inter-war period several argued that the next world war would be between the Britain and US, the declining and rising world powers (for example, Maclean 1977, 182–90 and Trotsky 1971, 28–37). They were right in that these very different empires could not coexist, but wrong about the means by which the latter would achieve its ascendancy over the former. As Arrighi points out, the US 'had no need to challenge Britain militarily to consolidate its growing power'. During the Second World War the US used three tactics: 'one, let Britain and its challengers exhaust one another militarily and financially; two, enrich itself by supplying goods and credit to the wealthier contestant; and, three, intervene in the war at a late stage so as to be in a position to dictate terms of the peace that facilitated the exercise of its own economic power on the largest possible geographical scale (Arrighi 2007, 312). The final stage in the transfer of hegemonic status occurred however during Britain's imperial self-immolation at Suez, which the US hastened by pressurizing the pound and refusing to allow the IMF to offer support. It is less often remembered that Eisenhower also instructed the Sixth Fleet, then permanently based in the Mediterranean, to harass and obstruct the Anglo-French expedition between Malta and Port Said (Hennessy 2006, 426, 450). Nor should this surprise us. The official report to President Truman by the National Security Council (NSC-68) in 1950 is usually considered to be the foundation of the ideology of total mobilization against the USSR and its allies. It also speaks of the achieve 'order among nations'—code then as now for US supremacy—'even if there were no Soviet Union' (National Security Council 1975, 9).

I am not suggesting that the end of the Cold War has simply seen a reversion to the situation which existed between 1914 and 1945, and that the classical theory of imperialism can be reapplied as if there had been no developments in the intervening decades. On the contrary, I want to suggest that the aspect of the theory which deals with conflict between the capitalist states is relevant precisely because it transcends the issue of imperialism. If there is a general problem with the classical theory, it is not, as critics suggest, that it is irrelevant because imperialism has changed into new forms. *It is rather that the theory is not a theory of imperialism at all, except in so far as it dealt with relations between the metropolitan powers and the colonial and semi-colonial world; it is instead a theory of how capitalism itself would work in a world where all the major economies were dominated by the capitalist mode of production.* In other words, the 'inter-imperialist rivalry' aspects of classical imperialism should be seen as simply the first manifestation of the type of geopolitical conflict between capitalist states which is the *normal* condition of the system. Capitalist states have always competed with each other, in military as well as market terms, from Italian city-state and Anglo-Dutch rivalries onwards, but until the later decades of the 19th century there were simply too few states dominated by the capitalist mode of production for any generalizations about their conduct to be made—indeed, it was precisely why many early theorists of capitalism could assume that a world of capitalist states, happily trading with each other, would be one of peace. From some point in the last third of the 19th century, it became apparent that capitalism in fact meant war, but this was theorized as an aspect of a special stage in capitalist development, rather than as permanent aspect of the system once it reached full maturity.

There will be many capitalist states as long as there are many capitals; and as long as there are many capitalist states they will behave as capitals. The trajectory of geo-economic competition ultimately ends in geopolitical rivalry. This is why explaining the persistence of the state system is more than an academic issue: it is central to a realistic assessment of what we can expect from the capitalist system in terms of its destructive capabilities, which we should not complacently assume will only ever be directed towards the Global South. And that in turn should give added urgency to our considerations on how we might bring it to an end.

Notes

1 Thanks to Alex Anievas, Colin Barker, Pepijn Brandon, Gareth Dale and Chris Harman for helpful comments. This chapter was written with the support of Economic and Social Research Council Grant RES-063–27-0174.
2 See respectively Arendt (1986, 415–17) and Castoriadis (1988, 86).
3 See also Rosdolsky (1977, 41–53); Arthur (2002, 128–48) and, in relation to state capitals, Cliff (2003, 93–94).
4 I owe the notion of 'entailment' to Colin Barker.
5 I owe this point to Pepijn Brandon, who is developing the analysis for his PhD at the University of Amsterdam.
6 Quoting an intervention by Kreiger at Marxism '93.
7 The necessity of national consciousness and nationalism for capital, and consequently in maintaining the state system is discussed in Davidson (2009), from which parts of this section are drawn.

6 Post-Fordist capitalism and imperial power

Toward a neo-Gramscian view

Mark Rupert[1]

Introduction

In recent years imperialism has been something of a growth industry, both in the military-industrial complex and academy. In the latter, scholars of critical bent have asked to what extent reviving classical Marxist theories of imperialism can help us to understand contemporary global power or whether some more radical innovation might be necessary. Among the contested issues central to these discussions are whether geopolitics and globalizing capitalism ought to be understood in terms of 'one logic or two' (Hobson 2007), or indeed whether the problem of capitalist geopolitics can usefully be reduced to some abstract causal logic or logics. Breaking with classical theories of imperialism, Hannes Lacher and Benno Teschke (2007) argue that a formal or deductive approach which imputes imperialist tendencies to an essential logic of capital is misguided:

> While geopolitical competition characterizes the entire period of capitalist modernity, the specific dynamics of international competition (and cooperation) underwent conjunctural transformations that have to be set in the context of the variable resolution of specific social and international conflicts in the political and economic organization of capitalist modernity.
>
> (Lacher and Teschke 2007, 577)

The purpose of this chapter is not to intervene directly in these debates, dissecting the theoretical arguments of various contributors with an eye toward determining the best or most authentically Marxist explanatory framework; but rather to sketch out the broad contours of what I might describe as a neo-Gramscian view of contemporary geopolitics and multi-layered account of the evolution of US global power from the mid-twentieth century into the twenty-first. From this perspective, politics entails relations of coercion and consent which are historically situated and socially contested, and a satisfactory account would need to incorporate not just the historical structures of global capitalism—with their economic, political, and cultural aspects—but also the ideologies and actions of human agents variously situated in terms of these historical structures, reproducing or contesting those historical structures in ways which may not be determined a priori. The resulting account would interweave multiple threads of varying temporality, seeking to explain: (1) how the structures of capitalist modernity create the possibility of particular kinds of world politics; (2) how those possibilities were realized in the particular forms of the twentieth-century capitalist world order; (3) within those historical structures, the key relationship between capitalism, Fordism, and the geopolitics of petroleum, along with the ideologies of 'economic security' which have animated US policymakers from the Cold War to the Bush administration; (4) ideologies of popular legitimation for the exercise of imperial power and cultural formations in which these have been embedded (and contested), ranging from longstanding narratives of American exceptionalism to post-Vietnam representations of resurgent militarized American masculinity, and; (5) the ways in which these historical structural possibilities are activated in the politics of a particular conjuncture. The result will be not a logic of causality, but an historical-structural sketch of a complex and contradictory conjuncture.

Capitalism and geopolitics

The historical structures which make possible contemporary forms of geopolitics have been usefully explored by Justin Rosenberg (1994) and Ellen Meiksins Wood (1995; 2003). I would summarize as follows the lessons I draw from their seminal contributions. The possibility of imperialism is built into the historical social relations that constitute the core of capitalism. In its fully developed form, capitalism entails a structural separation between the economic and political aspects of social life—that is, the de-politicization and privatization of the economy which makes possible capitalist private property and compels those who are not members of the owning class to sell their labour-power in order to survive. This structural separation means that the state in a capitalist context is generally dependent upon the economic activities of capitalists—private investors and employers—in order to generate enough economic growth and employment within its territory to legitimate the government and the social order as a whole, and to produce resources which the state can tax so as to fund its operations. The state has, therefore, a compelling interest in the overall success of accumulation—that is, private profit reinvested in the growth of capitalist enterprise—by capitalists whose operations are based within its territory. But since capitalist economic activity routinely overflows the juridical boundaries of particular nation-states, the imperatives of capitalist market competition and geopolitical competition among states may converge to generate imperialism—the deployment of military power in the service of capital accumulation.

Capitalist imperialism, as distinct from pre-capitalist tribute-extracting or commerce-controlling empires, has involved the use of coercive power in order to create and maintain conditions necessary for capitalist production, exchange, investment and accumulation to occur on a transnational scale (Wood 2003). This has entailed forcibly integrating new areas into the world market, destroying non-capitalist ways of life and commodifying social relations (that is, creating widespread market dependence), generating an exploitable 'proletarianized' labour force (a class of people who own no means of production and therefore must sell their labour-power), and/or enforcing the dominance of private property and capitalist access to important resources. The global expansion of capitalist social relations over the last two centuries has prepared the way for the recession of explicitly political coercive force into the background of global capitalism, never entirely absent, but not as a rule directly present or visible in economic relations. When conditions of transnational accumulation have been more-or-less secured, capitalism can function without ongoing recourse to directly coercive exploitation. On this view, the contemporary capitalist world represents a 'mode of economic domination managed by a system of multiple states', for

> neither the imposition of economic imperatives nor the everyday social order demanded by capital accumulation and the operations of the market can be achieved without the help of administrative and coercive powers much more local and territorially limited than the economic reach of capital.
>
> (Wood 2003, 152, 154)

When local states and ruling classes are unable or unwilling to maintain the political conditions of transnational accumulation, coercive force may be brought to bear by an imperial power in order to re-impose those conditions.

Building on the work of Rosenberg, Wood and others, Hannes Lacher (2006) offers a powerful theoretical and historical argument against the thesis that the modern state and—by extension, the system of states—was born out of the very historical processes that gave rise to capitalism. Lacher argues instead that the emergence of a system of multiple, rivalrous territorial states—a process driven by the historically distinct politico-economic imperatives of absolutist rule in early-modern Europe—preceded the emergence of capitalist production relations and cannot adequately be understood as their product. However, following the emergence of capitalist production relations in 17th century England, the dynamics of absolutist geopolitics were transformed and the system of territorial states was *internalized* within, and became integral to, a distinctly capitalist system of transnational social relations. The nature of sovereignty itself was transformed as absolutist rule and 'politically constituted property' (characteristic of absolutism) gave way to capitalist social formations based on the formal separations of politics and the economy, domination and appropriation. 'By starting from the historical constitution of political-economic authority', Lacher shows

> that anarchy itself may best be understood not as perennial structure, but very concretely as the historical product of the consolidation of absolutist states through the disempowerment and demilitarization of the kings' rivals in the struggle for political authority, aristocrats foremost among them. This evacuation of social content (the feudal forms of suzerainty, subordination and obligation, and the overlapping forms of authority and politically constituted property that were previously expressed through them) from the relations between sovereign dynastic proprietors was constitutive of the new absence of rule between those actors that had successfully become sovereign and were recognized as such. With the transition to capitalism in the nineteenth century, this anarchical space was once again

(though partially, and in a way that was very different indeed from feudal lordship) penetrated by transnational power relations, as the now privatized power to appropriate surplus was deployed by individual actors beyond national boundaries, creating an 'empire of civil society'.

(Lacher 2006, 148; quoting in part Rosenberg 1994)

In this way, Lacher argues that capitalism's 'political space has been fractured by sovereign territoriality', and this historical-structural disjuncture has put states in a position of rivalry. He summarizes as follows the crucial implications of this historically particular relational constellation:

> Whereas the state domestically stands apart from the competition between individual capitals, and seeks to regulate the economy through universal forms of governance like the rule of law and money, in the international sphere it is or can itself be a competitor seeking to promote the interests of its capital with political and economic means.

(Lacher 2002, 160–61)

Lacher argues that capitalism's globalizing tendencies were shaped and channelled through inter-relations with rivalrous territorial states and their socio-political and geopolitical strategies. 'The international relations of capitalist modernity came to mediate the emergence and expansion, but also the crises and contradictions, of a historical form of society in which surplus is primarily appropriated privately by "economic" means'. Further, 'this "internalization" of the system of territorial states also entailed the "imbrication" of the interstate form of capitalist political space into the "base" of capitalism' (Lacher 2006, 149).

The geopolitics of the capitalist world therefore represents neither the intersection of two ontologically distinct spheres each with its own distinctive 'logic' of determination (Harvey 2003; and see Callinicos this volume), nor the subsumption of political life under the single 'logic' of capital accumulation (Brewer 1990). Rather, it is the dialectic of territorialization and globalization which Lacher (2006) identifies as the central dynamic through which contemporary geopolitics has been produced. In contrast to scholars who argue that the system of territorially exclusive states is likely to remain into the indefinite future as the problematic political infrastructure of economically universalizing capitalism (for example, Wood 2003), and those who posit the tendential subsumption of nation-states by global relations and processes of capitalism (for example, Robinson 2004), Lacher views the persistence of territorially based rule as very much an open—and quintessentially political—question in the era of capitalist globalization. From a neo-Gramscian perspective (see Rupert 2005), I find this approach congenial insofar as it contextualizes contemporary geopolitics in terms of the historical structures of transnational capitalism without imposing, *a priori*, a particular causal logic (or logics) upon the political struggles which are played out in that historical structural context. If these are the structural conditions of capitalist modernity, which generate the possibility of various forms of capitalist geopolitics, how then may we account for particular historical structures of US global power which have shaped our world from the mid-twentieth century?

US hegemony and Fordist geopolitics

The United States is no stranger to the imperial exercise of coercive force. From its colonial origin to its role in reshaping the twentieth century capitalist world order, the US has been intimately involved with imperial power. Expansion into a continental and then hemispheric power entailed the forceful expropriation and near extermination of Native Americans and the forceful absorption of substantial territories formerly belonging to Mexico. The US would establish domination in the hemisphere and enforce capitalist property rights on a transnational scale through enactment of the Monroe Doctrine and the Roosevelt corollary. By the late 19th century, pursuit of an 'Open Door' for US capital seeking to expand its sphere of operations led to annexation of Hawaii and conquest of Cuba, Puerto Rico, the Philippines, and other territories used as strategic bases. In the twentieth century the US became central to global order struggles leading to the destruction of fascism—with its political economy of militarized autarky—and the subsequent reconstruction of the infrastructure of the capitalist world economy.

The geopolitics of sustaining this US-centred capitalist world order involved the 'containment' of a putative global communist threat which was invoked to justify numerous bloody interventions both overt and covert to secure the 'free world'—understood as a hospitable environment for US political and economic interests—during the second half of the twentieth century (see Stedman Jones 1970; Kolko 1988; La Feber 1989; Blum 1995; Kinzer 2006; Saull 2007). Such exercises of imperial power were not always consistent with professed values of human rights and democracy. But neither has US global power relied exclusively upon overt coercion, directly applied. Since the mid-twentieth century it has been embodied in structures of world order, forms of state-society complexes, and the relations among various social forces—to adapt some of Robert Cox's (1986) justly famous conceptual vocabulary—in which global power has had both coercive and consensual aspects, interrelated in varying combinations across space and time.

Fordism may be understood as a particular historical form of capitalist social organization—a constellation of political, economic and cultural relations enabling the mass production and consumption of commodities. In the first half of the twentieth century, Fordism emerged from social struggles in the US linking the social organization of production,the US state-society complex, and the emerging US-centred system of global power (Rupert 1995). Through these historical structures, US power and Fordist accumulation became inextricably bound up with the geopolitics of the Middle East, especially the oil-rich Persian Gulf. While scholars such as Michael Klare (2004) and Andrew Bacevich (2005; 2008) have pointed toward the special geopolitical significance of this region and its unparalleled oil resources for US foreign policy, I would contend that this significance cannot be fully appreciated unless it is explicitly linked to historical forms of Fordist production, the US state-society complex which emerged in that context, and the kinds of geopolitical project which these made possible.

While petroleum may be said to have been a strategic commodity since Winston Churchill committed the Royal Navy to a new generation of oil-fuelled warships prior to World War I, its decisive strategic significance was clearly established when Fordism went to war during World War II. With the development of mechanized warfare, mass-produced armadas of oil-powered military machines—on land and in the air as well as at sea—proved indispensable to victory. Direct access to American oil, supplies of which were at that time relatively plentiful, and the denial of similarly abundant supplies to Germany and Japan, was a crucial factor underlying the Allied victory in that global struggle (Yergin 1991, 306–88). Effective global power clearly required reliable access to enormous supplies of oil in order to fuel the projection of massive military force over sea, air and land; and the ability to deny such access to rivals had been shown to be a decisive strategic instrument.

In addition to oil's military significance, Fordist capitalism depended upon oil as fuel for internal combustion engines in automobiles, trucks and tractors, airplanes and ships, as well as diesel-powered railroad locomotives; as a lubricant for machines of all sorts; and as a necessary raw material for the burgeoning petro-chemical industry. All of this was essential not just for Fordist industry but also for ever more capital- and chemical-intensive agriculture. The very landscape and quality of the lived environment was transformed as part of this Fordist reconstruction of America. Cheap and plentiful oil made possible the construction of 'increasingly industrialized and urbanized society which involved the suburbanization of cities, the switch from public to private transport, the mechanization of housework and better standards of heating' (Bromley 1991,105). In short, oil was becoming indispensable to the energy-intensive forms of Fordist capitalism which the US sought to reconstruct as the core of the postwar world economy, and the emerging culture of mass consumerism which helped to submerge class-based tensions deeply embedded in the Fordist organization of capitalist production (Rupert 1995).

American global strategy after World War II was aimed not just at 'containing' the power of the Soviet Union, but also at creating a world which would be hospitable to the growth of American-centred capitalism, understood in terms of a systemic vision of 'economic security' (Pollard 1984). Widely regarded as a foundational document of US post-war geopolitical strategy, National Security Council document 68 (NSC-68, 1950) called upon the US to assume a role of 'world leadership' in order 'to create conditions under which our free and democratic system can live and prosper' (NSC-68 in May 1993, 26, 29). The 'free and democratic system' which US leaders wanted to promote and protect worldwide was axiomatically identified with capitalism. US strategists explicitly envisioned a symbiotic relationship between the vitality and robustness of the capitalist 'free world'—in their words, 'an international economy based on multilateral trade, declining trade barriers, and convertible currencies'—and globally projected US military power capable of defending 'any of several vital pressure points' where the free world might be vulnerable to incursion or subversion (NSC-68 in May 1993 48; see also 29, 41–43, 46, 53–54, 73). In a polarized, zero-sum world where 'a defeat of free institutions anywhere is a defeat everywhere', US national security and the survival of 'civilization itself' was thus seen to depend upon a liberalized and reinvigorated world capitalism and the possession of 'clearly superior overall power' by the US and its free world allies (NSC-68 in May 1993, 26, 43).

Viewed through the lenses of this strategic vision, protecting the free world was closely identified with promoting a vigorous US-centred capitalist world economy, and it was this worldview which appeared to justify US interventions in order to counter political forces—even if not directly related to the USSR—which might inhibit the growth of American-dominated global capitalism. Though the relative balance between coercive and consensual aspects of US global domination may have shifted from one historical conjuncture to another, and had different doctrinal expressions, variants of this basic strategy governed US world order policy throughout the Cold War period (Gaddis 1982; Saull 2007).

The US strategic goal of establishing a post-war hegemonic world order in which the US might attain its systemic goal of 'economic security' required rebuilding 'Western' (or non-Soviet) Europe and Japan along Fordist lines as industrial bulwarks of the capitalist free world. And since US oil supplies were finite while global demand was not, this had crucial implications for global petro-politics. As Simon Bromley (1991, 105–6) argues:

> ... Although US oil provided nearly six-sevenths of allied oil during the war, it was clear that future supplies to Western Europe ... and Japan would have to come primarily from the Middle East. Indeed, [post-war] US hegemony depended on rapid and stable growth in these areas, and in turn this depended on plentiful supplies of cheap oil. US control over the international oil industry was therefore seen by wartime planners as a key element to their designs for the post-war order ... Specifically, control over Middle East oil reserves and the displacement of the erstwhile imperial power, the United Kingdom, was required in order that US possession of low-cost Middle East oil could underpin European (and Japanese) recovery.

The major waypoints along the historical path to the contemporary imperial episode—the 'Global War on Terror' and the invasion of Iraq—may then be understood against the backdrop of this constellation of political economy and geopolitics.

The US geopolitical project in the Gulf was centred on Saudi Arabia and Iran. Franklin Roosevelt's 1945 inauguration of a long-term commitment to the Saudi kingdom and its royal family coincided with the post-war formation of a consortium of major US oil companies named the Arabian-American Oil Company (ARAMCO) whose goal was to exploit the incomparable wealth of Saudi Arabia's oil fields (Yergin 1991; Klare 2004). These longstanding geopolitical commitments may be seen to have culminated in Operations Desert Shield and Desert Storm to insert massive US forces into the Saudi kingdom and remove Iraqi troops from Kuwait in 1990–91. During the ensuing decade of regional containment directed at Saddam Hussein's Iraqi Ba'ath regime, the ongoing presence of smaller numbers of US troops in the Saudi kingdom (in whose territory are situated Islam's holiest sites) proved a major irritant for Islamist militants such as Osama bin Laden and his al-Qaeda network who declared that America was waging war upon Islam in Arabia and Iraq, and that violent retaliation was religiously warranted (bin Laden 1998).

A second important thread of this geopolitical tale involves the US and Iran. US influence in Iran was secured for a quarter century by the 1953 CIA-sponsored coup in which the democratically elected Prime Minister, Mohammad Mossadegh, was overthrown by forces who re-established the autocratic power of the Iranian monarch, the Shah. Mossadegh was an ardent Iranian nationalist whose political movement directly challenged British control of Iran's rich oil resources by nationalizing facilities of the British-owned Anglo-Iranian Oil Company. Insofar as a successful Iranian nationalization might appear to peoples around the region—or indeed the world—as an example of how they could themselves reclaim control over the natural resources being exploited by dominant foreign firms, this was a strategic threat to Anglo-American control over the increasingly important oil reserves of the Persian Gulf region, and perhaps even Western access to Third World resources more generally. Mossadegh was painted in the West as a communist sympathizer and menace to the capitalist free world, and Cold War strategic rivalry was invoked as the rationale for his removal. After a false start, American and British intelligence agencies ultimately engineered a successful coup, and Mossadegh's elected government was replaced by the militaristic and repressive—if also reliably pro-American—regime of Mohammad Reza Shah (Kinzer 2003).

In the wake of the coup Iran's oil concessions were renegotiated, with British and American firms now equally sharing control. Meanwhile, the Shah's SAVAK secret police organization—trained and equipped by US military and intelligence—terrorized Iran's population, brutally repressed dissent and enabled the Shah to impose a program of state-led, Western-oriented, secular modernization. Along with the US-Saudi relationship, the Shah's Iran became a cornerstone of US strategic dominance in the oil-rich Persian Gulf region. America's subversion of Iranian parliamentary democracy in 1953 and subsequent support for the autocratic but pro-Western Shah of Iran culminated in the Iranian Revolution of 1979 and the rise of a militantly anti-American Shiite clerical regime and an American strategy of 'dual containment' aimed at perceived challenges to the US position in the Gulf from both Iran and Iraq.

Following the Iranian revolution and the Soviet military incursion into Afghanistan, the Carter Doctrine was announced in 1980 declaring that the US had vital national interests at stake in the Gulf region—explicitly identified with the continuing free flow of Gulf oil to the West—and intended to defend those interests with military force. Pursuant to the Carter doctrine, the US substantially strengthened its capabilities for projecting military power into the region (eventually creating the Pentagon's Central Command to institutionalize that capability) and orchestrated US-Saudi-Pakistani support for mujahedeen waging guerrilla war against Soviet forces in Afghanistan. Of course, the most militantly Islamist elements of these forces subsequently evolved into the core of al Qaeda (Coll 2004), reacting violently against the continuing presence of US power in the region and US support for putatively un-Islamic autocracies in the region (bin Laden 1998). These Islamist forces thereby became the *bête noir* of America's 'Global War on Terror' and central to the official justification for the invasions of Afghanistan and Iraq.

The Bush administration's notorious National Security Strategy of 2002 not only announced the doctrine of preventive warfare to head off the emergence of perceived threats from possible state sponsors of terrorism, it also reaffirmed the fundamental geopolitical vision of 'economic security'. 'A strong world economy enhances our national security by advancing prosperity and freedom in the rest of the world' (White House 2002). And it contextualized the geopolitical commitments which would become the Global War on Terror in terms of that vision:

> Today, the United States enjoys a position of unparalleled military strength and great economic and political influence. In keeping with our heritage and princi-ples, we do not use our strength to press for unilateral advantage. We seek instead to create a balance of power that favors human freedom: conditions in which all nations and all societies can choose for themselves the rewards and challenges of political and economic liberty. ... the United States will use this moment of opportunity to extend the benefits of freedom across the globe. We will actively work to bring the hope of democracy, development, free markets, and free trade to every corner of the world. The events of September 11, 2001, taught us that weak states, like Afghanistan, can pose as great a danger to our national interests as strong states. Poverty does not make poor people into terrorists and murderers. Yet poverty, weak institutions, and corruption can make weak states vulnerable to terrorist networks and drug cartels within their borders.
>
> The United States will stand beside any nation determined to build a better future by seeking the rewards of liberty for its people. Free trade and free mar-kets have proven their ability to lift whole societies out of poverty—so the United States will work with individual nations, entire regions, and the entire global trading community to build a world that trades in freedom and therefore grows in prosperity.
>
> (White House 2002)

There was, then, a fundamental continuity between the Bush doctrine and the guiding concepts of post-war US geopolitics, reflected in an abiding commitment to create a global environment of economic security (for other arguments suggesting continuity, see Callinicos 2003; Harvey 2003; Bacevich 2008). So strongly did the Bush White House believe in this connection that they placed in the heart of their national security doctrine a neoliberal policy blueprint which would allegedly create conditions conducive to market freedom, enhanced productivity, prosperity and security worldwide—right down to specifying explicitly that a world of economic security entailed lower marginal tax rates to create incentives for the wealthy to become wealthier.

Taken together, these webs of geopolitical commitments—power and resistance, terror and counter-terror—form the background against which America's latest imperial episode has played itself out. My point here is not to deny the political agency of the region's people or to reduce these complex chains of events entirely to consequences of US geopolitical projects. Rather, my aim is to suggest that the US geopolitical project in the Middle East, and the historical structures which supported that project, were conditions of possibility for these processes of power and resistance to unfold as they did. Acknowledging that, it seems to me, requires contextualizing this tangled narrative in the historical structures of Fordist capitalism, for it was the economic, political and cultural aspects of those structures—including the culture of Fordist mass consumption—which generated American interest in the Middle East and animated the geopolitical project which has led us to where we are today.

Domination in the name of liberty: the paradox of imperial consent

Especially from a Gramscian perspective, with its emphasis on the complex interplay of coercion and consent, the Bush administration's ability to mobilize broad segments of the American public behind its thinly justified war and broader imperial policy constitutes a significant political puzzle. America's founding mythology is one of anti-imperial struggle and the defence of liberty, so how is it possible for an imperial project of global military domination to secure the consent of an American public whose 'common sense' is deeply imbued with this original myth? (for another expression of this puzzle, see Stedman Jones 1970) In the remainder of this chapter, I sketch out some working hypotheses which, taken together, may help to explain this apparent paradox, and to construct a fuller and more satisfactory account of contemporary imperial power.

Rationalizing double standards: ideologies of American exceptionalism

Somewhere near the core of popular common sense in America is a family of belief systems which suggest that the United States is an extraordinary nation with a unique role to play in the world. Such beliefs are commonly referred to as 'American exceptionalism' and typically revolve around a peculiarly American political origin story. The American origin story paints the emergence of republican government in the New World as born out of revolutionary upheaval against the feudal legacies of European monarchy and tyranny. This New World republic was to be based on the collective sovereignty of the people, guaranteeing their rights and liberties (crucially including private property rights) as part of the constitutional framework, and limiting in manifold ways the powers which government may rightly exercise. Insofar as the national power of the United States was axiomatically identified with the progress of the republican cause and therefore of human liberty, it became possible to justify American expansionism in terms of the spread of liberty. Those non-Americans who failed to perceive this were either malevolent enemies of freedom or people too benighted and backward to be self-governing. These latter were often characterized in terms of explicitly racialized hierarchies in which they were assigned positions of biological and civilizational inferiority in relation to 'white' Americans (Hunt 1988). In either case, Americans were able to justify (to their own satisfaction) the deployment of coercive force against others represented as outside the frontiers of, or alien to, liberty's empire.

This kind of dualistic world view has been influential among American leaders and in public political rhetoric since before the revolution, when Tom Paine's *Common Sense* depicted the New World as 'the asylum for the persecuted lovers of civil and religious liberty' in contrast to the monarchical and aristocratic abuses of liberty characteristic of the Old World. From World Wars I and II through the Cold War, such dualistic representations—anointing Americans as defenders of liberty against tyrannical aggressors—have been crucial in mobilizing US public support for the most significant global struggles of the last hundred years. Helping Americans to make sense of their most profound world-historical experiences, these narratives of American exceptionalism have become deeply anchored within popular common sense (see Rupert 2000, Chapter 2). Accordingly, Andrew Moravcsik reports, '[f]ully 71 per cent of Americans see the United States as a source of good in the world ... 70 per cent have faith in their domestic institutions and nearly 80 per cent believe "American ideas and customs" should spread globally' (Moravcsik 2005).

It should not be surprising, then, that the Bush administration called upon such longstanding and deeply resonant aspects of US political culture in order to justify what might otherwise appear to be an imperial project of global military dominance. This is clearly evident in the National Security Strategy's axiomatic equation of US supremacy with 'a balance of power that favors freedom'. Ensconced within this self-justifying world view, President Bush was unable to imagine how global others might harbour even remotely legitimate grievances against the United States: 'I'm amazed that people would hate us. Like most Americans, I just can't believe it. Because I know how good we are' (quoted in Ford 2002). If legitimate grievances against the United States are unthinkable, then those who oppose America must do so out of sheer malevolence: 'You've probably learned by now, I don't believe there's many shades of gray in this war. You're either with us or against us. You're either evil, or you're good' (Bush quoted in McManus 2002).

In the context of this Manichean mythology of global politics, military intervention in the Middle East was rationalized by representing its targets as 'evil-doers': dangerous enemies of America/freedom who are collectively implicated in 9–11 and in terrorism more generally. Al-Qaeda was portrayed as part of a larger threat posed by radical Islamists allegedly motivated not by resentment of US power and the policies it pursued in regions inhabited by Muslims (al-Qaeda's repeated declarations of precisely such grievances notwithstanding, see for example bin Laden 1998), but rather driven entirely by deep-seated antipathy to modernity and its quintessence in putatively American principles of liberty and democracy. In his 2002 State of the Union address, President Bush (in)famously claimed that such terrorist networks were enabled by sinister rogue states: 'States like these, and their terrorist allies, constitute an axis of evil, arming to threaten the peace of the world' (quoted in Sifry and Cerf 2003, 250).

In order to avoid moral ambiguity, the Bush administration downplayed past US support for Saddam's regime during periods of massive human rights abuse in Iraq, aggression against Iran, and repeated use of chemical weapons against both military and civilian targets. Instead, it portrayed Saddam Hussein as intrinsically evil, a dictator of unsurpassed brutality and ruthlessness, a serial aggressor, and an implacable enemy of the United States who if given the chance would not hesitate to do the most grievous harm to Americans. Hours before the bombing of Baghdad began, the President laid out his case for war:

Peaceful efforts to disarm the Iraqi regime have failed again and again because we are not dealing with peaceful men. Intelligence gathered by this and other governments leaves little doubt that the Iraqi regime continues to possess and conceal some of the most lethal weapons ever devised. This regime has already used weapons of mass destruction against Iraq's neighbors and against Iraq's people. The regime has a history of reckless aggression in the Middle East. It has a deep hatred of America and our friends. And it has aided, trained and harbored terrorists, including operatives of al Qaeda. … The United States and other nations did nothing to deserve or invite this threat, but we will do everything to defeat it.

Many Iraqis can hear me tonight … And I have a message for them. If we must begin a military campaign, it will be directed against the lawless men who rule your country and not against you. … We will tear down the apparatus of terror. And we will help you build a new Iraq that is prosperous and free. In a free Iraq there will be no more wars of aggression against your neighbors, no more poison factories, no more execution of dissidents, no more torture chambers and rape rooms. The tyrant will soon be gone. The day of your liberation is near.

(Bush quoted in Sifry and Cerf 2003, 503)

Reframed in terms of the discourse of American exceptionalism, and bolstered with dubious claims about Iraqi weapons and links to Al Qaeda, the invasion of Iraq became an extension of the War on Terror, and the massive exercise of imperial power became a defence of liberty and democracy. Anatol Lieven has summarized in the following terms the effect of this reframing:

Most Americans genuinely believe all this to be a matter of self-defense—of their economy, their 'way of life', their freedoms or the nation itself. The US under George W. Bush is indeed driving towards empire, but the domestic political fuel being fed into the imperial engine is that of a wounded and vengeful nationalism. After 9–11, this sentiment is entirely sincere as far as most Americans are concerned and all the more dangerous for that; there is probably no more dangerous element in the nationalist mix than a righteous sense of victimhood.

(Lieven 2004)

Thus, a policy which might not otherwise have been acceptable to the American public was recast in terms which resonated with themes deeply embedded in popular common sense and so were able for a time to secure their support.

Enlisting the working class: post-Fordist capitalism and blue-collar patriotism

Embedded within this enduring cultural context of American exceptionalism are the class and gender politics of globalizing capitalism. The globalization of post-Fordist or neoliberal capitalism has entailed relentless pressure on the economic position and cultural status of working class American men; pressures which have destabilized their historical identification with the Democratic Party of the New Deal and the industrial union movement. This, in turn, has created opportunities for these working class men to be re-recruited into an imperial coalition via a hyper-masculinized ideology of American martial virtue. The role of an all-volunteer military in offering a secure livelihood to increasingly insecure working class Americans has enhanced the effect of a militarized culture of working class masculinity.

At the core of Fordism, with its institutionalized correspondence between mass production and mass consumption, had been the implicit social norm of the 'family wage'—the notion that working class men should receive wages sufficient to support their families at some basic (socially determined) standard of living. Under this institutional framework, Keynesian macroeconomic policies oriented toward relatively high levels of employment (and therefore wages) were combined with industrial unionism and pattern bargaining in core sectors of the economy in order to secure three decades of steadily growing real wages for working class Americans, especially men. The characteristically Fordist pattern of real wages and productivity growing more-or-less in tandem came under attack in the late 1970s as profit rates stagnated and a lean-and-mean neoliberal market fundamentalism gained ascendency. That productivity growth has consistently outpaced the growth of real wages in the US during the post-Fordist, neoliberal era reflects the enhancement of the class-based powers of employers and investors, and goes a long way toward accounting for the historically sharp increases in inequality of both income and wealth (Harvey 2005, Chapter 1). Attempting to sustain family incomes and consumption norms in this environment, more women have joined the workforce and women's wages (historically lower than the male 'breadwinner' wage) have not fallen as drastically as those of formerly privileged male workers As a result, the ability of working class American men to maintain the social identity and cultural status of breadwinners is increasingly problematic (Rupert 2000, Chapter 2).

It is in this context that sociologist Arlie Hochschild (2004) situates the symbolic politics of the Bush administration's appeal to blue collar men. According to Hochschild, the administration's symbolism represents a strategy to redirect chronic insecurity and anger away from the policies of the administration and the aggrandisement of the wealthy few, and instead to target the Taliban, Osama, Saddam, or some other evil-doer *du jour* as the source of America's insecurity—a redirection which implicitly promises that the underlying anxiety might be eased through a reassertion of American masculinity through global military mastery. All of this represents, she writes,

> an aggressive right-wing attempt to mobilize blue collar fear, resentment and a sense of being lost—and attach it to the fear of American vulnerability, American loss. By doing so, Bush aims to win the blue collar man's identification with big business, empire, and himself. ... Whether strutting across a flight deck or mocking the enemy, Bush with his seemingly fearless bravado— ironically born of class entitlement—offers an aura of confidence. And this confidence dampens, even if temporarily, the feelings of insecurity and fear

exacerbated by virtually every major domestic and foreign policy initiative of the Bush administration.

(Hochschild 2004)

Further contributing to a working class culture of allegiance to American militarism has been the economic and social significance of military service in an economy undergoing restructuring and globalization. According to the *New York Times*, 'today's professional, blue-collar military' offers working class Americans an open source of secure employment and, for many, the gateway to an otherwise difficult to afford college education.

> With minorities overrepresented and the wealthy and the underclass essentially absent, with political conservatism ascendant in the officer corps and North-easterners fading from the ranks, America's 1.4 million strong military seems to resemble the makeup of a two-year commuter or trade school outside Birmingham or Biloxi far more than that of a ghetto or barrio or four-year university in Boston. ... Compared to their contemporaries in civilian life, the armed forces have a greater percentage of minorities, a higher proportion of high school graduates and better reading levels. As a group, about 60 percent of enlisted men and women are white; they tend to be married and upwardly mobile, but to come from families without the resources to send them to college.

(Halbfinger and Holmes 2003)

Military officers acknowledged that the relative availability of alternative civilian employment was crucial to their wartime recruitment efforts (Schmitt 2003). Also crucial to fielding an ongoing occupation force in Iraq have been the part-time 'citizen soldiers' of the reserves and the National Guard (as state militias are known in the US). At one point, about half of the 150 000 US troops serving in Iraq were from Guard and reserve units. According to the *Los Angeles Times*, '[t]hey tend to be older, and are more likely married with children. They're also much more entrenched in their civilian communities than the regular military' (Tempest 2005). Such close connections between working class life and military service may then help to explain the proliferation of yellow ribbons, bumper stickers, and banners commanding readers to 'support the troops'. In an environment where working class connections to military service are strong, criticism of America's imperial policies is popularly interpreted as an attack on the morale of 'our troops' as they go into harm's way—providing aid and comfort to the enemy.

Recreating a culture of masculinized militarism within the US state-society complex has entailed re-writing the history of failed imperial episodes such as the Vietnam War. The popular disillusionment of the Vietnam era suggested to imperial state managers and allied social forces that domestic support for a global geopolitics, and especially its military interventions, cannot be taken for granted and must be constructed and fostered through extensive cultural interventions of various kinds. Through popular appeals and outreach campaigns such as 'America Supports You', the Pentagon under the Bush administration deliberately played upon and promoted pro-troop sensibilities in order to sustain support for the wars in Iraq and Afghanistan and prevent another Vietnam-like collapse of popular support and troop morale (Rupert 2009).

More broadly, among the cultural constructions which have effectively redefined the Vietnam experience and made possible a resurgence of popular militarism are the factually baseless but broadly and deeply resonant mythologies of valiant and manly American soldiers 'denied permission to win' in Vietnam (as Ronald Reagan put it), the heinous betrayal and abandonment of POWs left behind in Vietnam after the war's official conclusion, and returning soldiers allegedly spit upon and vilified by antiwar protesters and hippies. Echoing the notorious Nazi fable of the 'stab-in-the-back', which purported to explain German surrender despite the absence of crushing battlefield defeat at the end of World War I, all of these omnipresent popular mythologies speak of a virile, virtuous, and noble US military which could have 'won' in Vietnam had it not been betrayed by liberals, leftists, feminists, gays, peace and anti-nuclear groups, and sundry other wimps, traitors, commies, enemies of freedom, and elitists scornful of popular culture and the manly virtues of militarized American patriotism (Jeffords 1989; Franklin 1992; Gibson 1994; Lembke 1998; Bacevich 2005; Baker 2006). In terms of these popular cultural narratives, then, restoring American greatness requires silencing these disloyal social forces, re-masculinizing America, and re-establishing the preeminence of a culture of militarism, which is to say that these mythologies embody a comprehensive conservative agenda for America and the world.

Accordingly, representations of America's military engagement in Iraq and Afghanistan have had strongly gendered themes. From the fabulous epic of Jessica Lynch in which army commandos enacted a gendered script of redeeming American masculinity by rescuing one of 'our' women from the sinister clutches of 'their' men, to the lionization of professional football player Pat Tillman as an icon of masculinized patriotism whose enlistment as an Army ranger was celebrated while his inglorious death by friendly fire was covered up by the military, to the feminization and sexualized humiliation of Iraqi prisoners in Abu Ghraib, to President Bush's triumphal swagger across an aircraft carrier flight deck to announce 'Mission Accomplished', the War on Terror has been saturated with gendered narratives, images and associations. Neatly encapsulating masculinist-militarist fantasies of feminizing and sexually humiliating the Arab world, *New York Times* triple-Pulitzer winner Thomas Friedman notoriously explained to television interviewer Charlie Rose that the Iraq war was 'unquestionably worth doing' because it was necessary to defend 'our open society' and respond to terrorism with moral clarity by picking a place in the Arab world and sending the US military, 'going house to house, from Basra to Baghdad', kicking in the door and declaring 'Suck On This' (Rose 2003).

I believe these representations are neither entirely top-down nor bottom-up in origin, but reflect longer-term dynamics of American state-society relations and popular culture; cultural resources which state managers and their allies have attempted to marshal and mobilize behind their war, and the underlying project of global military supremacy. The managers of the imperial state and their allies have tried to use these cultural resources to sustain the allegiance of their core supporters, to marginalize dissidents as effeminate, weak, and incapable of defending the American way of life, and to deter defection among those whose support for imperial militarism might be wavering as the Iraq war drags on. Although the election of a less overtly masculinist and militarist Obama administration might suggest the failure of these efforts to find an audience, I would point out that despite the manifest and manifold failures of the Bush administration, John McCain's overtly militaristic (and neoconservative advised) Republican candidacy managed to secure some 57 million votes, disproportionately among white men, and voters with relatively less education. I believe that these sorts of masculinist and militarist representations continue to resonate powerfully with a large segment of the US population, and constitute an active component of US political culture from which we have not heard the last, especially since the geopolitical tensions of post-Fordist capitalism continue to boil and bubble.

Conclusion

Accounts of contemporary global power and imperial force need not be torn between the false dichotomies of reductionism or reification. I hope to have plausibly suggested here that it is possible to draw on the conceptual resources of historical materialism and to situate imperial power within the historical structures of capitalist and Fordist geopolitics without producing a formal, mechanistic, or deterministic account from which politics in all its various forms has been effectively evacuated. Rather, these historical structures and their dynamics may be understood as the sites, and the products, of a rich variety of political struggles not all of which are immediately reducible to class or to the 'logic' of capital accumulation. Instead of taking such a formal, deductive, or broadly causal approach to the question of geopolitics, I wish to suggest a contextualized historical-structural account of a particular instance of global power. In my view, this system of global power has structural conditions of possibility rather than a cause, and those conditions may be actualized in particular ways under specific historical circumstances by the struggles of situated social agents. This is what I understand as a dialectical explanation of post-Fordist capitalism and imperial power.

Notes

1 I am grateful to Alex Anievas for astute editorial criticisms. Despite the certainty that I have not allayed his concerns, I am equally certain that this chapter is stronger for his efforts.

7 To be or not to be a non-reductionist Marxist: Is that the question?

John M Hobson[1]

Introduction

There is no doubt, as this volume bears ample testimony, that Marxist International Relations Theory (MIRT) has undergone an important and exciting renaissance in the last decade or so. This particular volume is an extension of a forum that was published in *Cambridge Review of International Affairs* in 2007. The key issues raised in that forum, and in particular by Alex Callinicos's piece republished in this volume, were several-fold. These concerned the need to theorize the states system and the interrelated issue of 'empire versus anarchy', as well as the need to break with economic reductionism/ economism when formulating an adequate theory of world politics.[2] In this chapter I want to focus exclusively on recent Marxist attempts at solving the problem of economism. This makes sense in large part because the problem of economic reductionism has provided a key issue or pivot around which many contemporary Marxists are seeking to develop their own particular theories of world politics more generally.

With regards to the issue of economism it seemed to me, at least on *first sight*, that contemporary MIRT is going back to the future of the 'one logic or two' debate which emerged in the late-1970s/early-1980s. The phrase 'one logic or two' emerged in the well-known piece by Christopher Chase-Dunn (1981) within an *International Studies Quarterly* special forum. Interestingly, the issue back then was whether we could understand world politics through reference to a single economic logic—as was allegedly proposed by Immanuel Wallerstein (1974)—or through the two logics of a geopolitical states system *and* a capitalist world economy. In this respect the parallels between these two fora are striking. But on closer inspection, various crucial differences become apparent. First and foremost, the 1981 debate was conducted within the specific context of World Systems theory. However, by the late-1980s and early-1990s World Systems theory had receded into the background. On the one hand, the original approach has been largely superseded by this theory, which argues that there has been *one* world system that stems back anywhere between one and five thousand years (see especially Abu-Lughod 1989; Frank and Gills 1996; Denemark *et al.* 2000). And, on the other hand, World Systems theory has been outflanked by alternative Marxist approaches.

Leading the way in the growing renaissance of MIRT has been the development of Gramscianism (Cox 1986; Augelli and Murphy 1988; Gill 1993; Arrighi 1994; Van der Pijl 1997). This emerged slowly in the 1980s but accelerated and proliferated in the late-1990s and through the 2000s at the hands of a new generation of Gramscian scholars (for example, Rupert 2000; Ryner 2002; Payne 2005; Sinclair 2005; Pasha 2006; Bieler and Morton 2006; Morton 2007; Moore 2007; Bruff 2008; Shields 2009). This was followed by political Marxism, which includes the works of Justin Rosenberg (1994), Benno Teschke (1998; 2003), and Hannes Lacher (2005; 2006). One of the most innovative and interesting departures is the emergence of what might be called a 'Trotsky-lite' approach, found in the writings of Rosenberg (2005, 2006), as well as Alex Callinicos (2007), Kamran Matin (2007), Neil Davidson (2009), Jamie C Allinson and Alexander Anievas (2009), and Sam Ashman (2009).[3] In addition, a highly innovative non-Eurocentric literature has emerged within MIRT—some of which has inspired my own writings (see Frank and Gills 1996; Slater 2004; Shilliam 2006a; Pasha 2006; Gruffydd-Jones 2006; Matin 2007). This list is far from exhaustive, and it would be wrong to assume that all of these aforementioned scholars always fit neatly within one category as many of them combine insights from more than one approach (for example, Rosenberg 2005; Ashman 2009; Robinson 2004; Bieler and Morton 2008; Pasha 2006). In aggregate, these approaches have led to a much richer and more vibrant departure for MIRT than was the case 25 years ago, yielding genuinely innovative empirical and theoretical unsights that surely restore Marxism to the status of a major and important approach within IR.

Before outlining my framework, I want to emphasize the point that what follows is *not* a critique of MIRT per se. I have a good deal of sympathy for much of what some of the Marxist variants have to say about developments within world politics. Rather, my aim is to produce a typology within which the different proposed solutions to economism can be situated and to consider how successful these have been. Within this typology I identify three major proposals: the 'relative autonomy' approach, 'two logics pluralism' and 'collapsed base-superstructuralism'. Each approach is dealt with in separate sections. Although I argue that none of these has yet succeeded in their objectives, nevertheless I specify a set of criteria that need to be met before success can be declared. And my aim here is to either prompt Marxists into taking the final great leap forward by addressing these non-economistic criteria, or equally to prompt them to re-evaluate the strenghts of marxist economism.

The final section raises some of the deeper and most urgent issues that necessarily underpin the quest for non-reductionism; issues that are rarely considered within Marxist circles. In particular, because each anti-economistic strategy entails different ontologies, it is not possible to mix and match them (as sometimes happens). So clarity here is urgently needed. Also significant is the point that many Marxists assume axiomatically that the base/superstructure model is the source of economic reductionism. But we need to consider whether the source of the problem lies at a deeper level—namely with Marx's dialectical method. And Marxists also need to confront the possibility that a non-reductionist Marxism might not be the 'saviour' that so many of them axiomatically assume it to be, given that there are also negative side-effects of the proposed anti-reductionist drug. These, I suggest, should no longer remain in the closet but need to be openly discussed and confronted.

The 'relative autonomy approach': Or, the cul-de-sac of 'modified base/superstructuralism'?

The most well-known proposed solution to economism within Marxism is the 'relative autonomy' approach. It is often assumed that the original formula was laid out in Friedrich Engels's 'class-equilibrium' theory that was propagated in his *The Origins of the Family, Private Property and the State*. Here he argued that, '[b]y way of exception ... periods occur in which the warring classes balance each other so nearly that the state power, as ostensible mediator, acquires, for the moment, a certain degree of independence of both' (Engels 1970, 328). However, these moments were by definition exceptional given that the transition from one mode of production to another is a very rare event. Equally, Marx's (1969) argument in *The Eighteenth Brumaire of Louis Bonaparte* is also touted as one of the key original sources. But arguably the clearest original example is found in a rarely cited passage in *Capital* Volume 1, where Marx discusses the passage of the Ten Hours bill in the British parliament (Marx 1954, 226–81). He concludes that while the capitalist class was up in arms against the proposed shortening of the working day, the bill was passed as a means of pacifying the workers given that they were in open revolt against capital's rebellion against the bill. In short, the passing of the Ten Hours Act was deemed vital if capitalism was to be preserved—a claim which boils down to the general proposition that the state was prepared to go against the immediate short-term profit-making interests of capital so as to avoid social revolution, thereby ensuring the continued or long-term reproduction of the capitalist mode of production. Arguably, it was this formula that was taken up subsequently by the likes of Louis Althusser and Nicos Poulantzas, before it became a key part of the lexicon of neo-Marxist state theory more generally (see Hobson 2000, Chapter 4).

The classic statement is contained in Poulantzas' *Political Power and Social Classes* (1973, 255–321). The essential formula runs as follows. Because the members of the capitalist class are pre-occupied with everyday competitive struggles between themselves, so the class-as-a-whole inevitably becomes disunited. As such, this renders it incapable of maintaining unity in the face of proletarian challenges. Accordingly, the role of the state is to act as a 'general capitalist'—or an 'ideal collective capitalist' (Offe 1984)—so as to ensure that the capitalist class as a whole can survive in the long run. Being removed from the daily process of surplus-value extraction, and armed with a 'relative autonomy' from the dominant class, the state can and must ignore or go against the short-term needs of the bourgeoisie in order to secure the long-term reproduction of capitalism. In this way, the economic becomes determinant 'in the last instance', with the state being charged with the need to conform to the long-term survival requirements of the mode of production. One of the most common examples of the way in which the state goes against the short-term interests of the bourgeoisie is through welfare policy. So, while capitalists might vehemently resist the increases in personal income taxation that are necessary to finance welfare expenditures for the working class, nevertheless by undertaking such reforms the state is able to pacify the proletariat and thereby prevent it from attaining revolutionary consciousness. The result is, much to the pleasant surprise of the bourgeoisie, the securing of the long-term reproduction of capitalism in general.

However, the immediate problem with this formulation is that it does little to overcome the inherent problems with the base/superstructure model. All that has really happened is that the state is seen to act not in the short-term, but in the long-run, interests of the capitalist class. The key shift is from a short-term class instrumentalist model—as was famously presented in *The Communist Manifesto* (Marx and Engels 1977, 82)—to a long-term class structural-functionalist model. Thus, a soft-functionalist class-reductionist model ensues insofar as the state functions merely to maintain long-term bourgeois rule. This was enshrined in Poulantzas's (1973, 287) famous definition that the state functions as a 'factor of social cohesion—atomizing the working class and unifying the dominant class'. This is not unlike the current juncture in which British state interventionism in the financial markets is undertaken to shore up the long-term interests of free market capitalism in general and the long-term interests of the bourgeoisie in particular. Lest I be misunderstood: I am not arguing entirely against the validity of this argument, for it seems clear that states do their utmost to maintain capitalism in the long-run. But as a 'solution' to economism, the model is little more than a modified base/superstructuralism and, to my mind, as such constitutes the weakest of the three generic approaches since it clearly reverses Marxism full speed into the cul-de-sac of economism. Accordingly, I want to spend more time considering the two more recent and innovative approaches.

'Two-logics pluralism': or, the 'illusion of the realist moment?'

The second prominent proposed solution to economic reductionism—what I am taking the liberty of calling 'two logics pluralism'—is that advocated by Alex Callinicos (2007, and see Chapter 1 this volume) as well as by others (see Harvey 2003; Arrighi 1994). Here, I solely focus on Callinicos's formulation. The substantive context within which Callinicos constructs his proposal concerns his refutation of what might be called neo-Marxist 'capitalist imperial peace theory' found in the works of William I Robinson (2004) and Michael Hardt and Antonio Negri (2000). Callinicos thus seeks to reinvoke the Leninist critique of Karl Kautsky's theory of 'ultra-imperialism' by arguing that cooperation between the great powers is fictitious given that geopolitical (and geoeconomic) competition between them remains a fundamental aspect of contemporary IR. But, in implicit contrast to Lenin's economic reductionism (see Hobson 2000, 117–21; 2007, 583–84), Callinicos seeks to develop his argument by constructing a non-reductionist Marxism that accords ontological weighting to both class-economics and geopolitics. He insists that capitalist and territorial logics must be theorized as having a certain autonomy, even if they are at the same time reinforcing and entwined. Yet, while Callinicos goes a long way to achieving his objective, in the last instance he nevertheless takes a wrong move and ends up back in the land of economic/class reductionism. How so?

Callinicos begins by correctly claiming that many Marxist accounts embody a 'soft functionalism'—a term that he borrows from Vivek Chibber (2005)—wherein the states system owes its existence to the needs of capital (Callinicos 2007, 538). Rather than being criticized as economically reductionist, Callinicos prefers Gonzalo Pozo-Martin's (2006; 2007) important criticism that he veers towards a realist explanatory model. In this vein, Callinicos insists that territoriality or geopolitical competition has a logic of its own that is different to that of economic competition:

> Of course the state system has distinctive properties: if it did not, it could not play an explanatory role. One implication of this point is that there is, necessarily, a realist moment in any Marxist analysis of international relations and conjunctures: in other words, any such analysis must take into account the strategies, calculations and interactions of rival political elites in the state system.
>
> (Callinicos 2007, 542)

Moreover, Callinicos seeks to show that capitalist imperialism occurs through the interaction of economic and geopolitical competition. And because these logics differ in structure, their interrelations will necessarily vary over time. This insight is deployed to reveal how patterns of interstate competition differed between the first and second halves of the twentieth century. But this begs the question as to whether Callinicos has succeeded in producing a genuinely non-reductionist approach or whether he has in fact produced a lop-sided economic approach that 'adds geopolitics and stirs'? I suggest that at the crucial moment his argument enters extremely rocky terrain. This takes the form of his strategy of avoiding ending up in the 'bourgeois' cul-de-sac of Weberian multi-causality by according greater weighting to the economic logic, thereby issuing a causal hierarchy in contradistinction to multi-causal pluralism. In order to understand this move, it is necessary to contextualize it more generally within Marxist theory.

It is clear that Callinicos is completely aware of the pitfalls of an ontologically pluralist Weberian model. Though he does not mention it, it was, of course, Karl Marx who argued that the tendency to accord ontological autonomy to the state or, by inference, geopolitics (or any 'superstructural' process for that matter), is to fall into the trap of 'bourgeois fetishism'. And this claim was not a minor point that Marx issued simply in respect of liberal political economy's propensity for 'commodity fetishism'; rather, it provided the essence of his whole 'dialectical (scientific) method'. That is, he insisted that the everyday appearance of (all) things must be penetrated for their underlying essential base; a base that comprises contradictory social relations of production. Failure to uncover the underlying base of contradictory social relations is to fall into the trap of fetishism that is the *leitmotif* of 'bourgeois' theory (see Marx 1973, 267, 297, 308, 528–29, 585, 684, 700–702, 745, 758–59, 822; Marx 1972, 454–523; Marx 1954, 366, 483, 567–70; Marx 1959, 45–48, 168, 392–99, 827, 829–31).

In the famous case of the commodity, fetishism occurs when the observer assumes that it appears to have a value (or power) independent of the social relations that produced it. Such an analysis is extended not just to all economic phenomena but also to all non-economic ones. Hence, Marx issued his general claim that underpins his 'dialectical method': 'All [dialectical] science would be superfluous if the outward appearance and the essence of things did not coincide' (Marx 1959, 817). It is at least possible, then, that it was the dialectical method that informed his 'base-superstructure' metaphor that was in turn famously outlined in his 'Preface' to *A Contribution to the Critique of Political Economy* (Marx 1976)—a point I shall return to in the next section. Assuming this connection exists means that tampering with, or exorcizing, the base/superstructure model might be merely treating the symptom rather than the cause.

In light of this, Callinicos is fully aware that having got this far he now finds himself on the precipice between the realms of Marxist and 'bourgeois' theory. And the dilemma that he faces is one that every other neo-Marxist has confronted (or will confront) when trying to reconstruct a non-reductionist Marxism: Plough on too far and end up in a so-called bourgeois dead-end, or retreat from the abyss and reverse right back into the cul-de-sac of Marxist economic reductionism. The former strategy naturally protects him from the reductionist charge though it comes at a high political price, namely the sacrificing of a revolutionary Marxist politics, while the latter strategy enables him to maintain Marxist theoretical and political integrity at the cost of a reductionist ontology. It is in this sense that Callinicos finds himself between a Marxist rock and a bourgeois hard place. Which road does Callinicos take? The clue is found in his claim, in summarizing his critics' arguments, that 'by positing two distinct logics ... economic and geopolitical—we have surreptitiously embraced the explanatory [bourgeois] pluralism of Weber and of historical sociologists such as Mann and Skocpol' (Callinicos 2007, 585).

At this critical juncture he steers a course that, like the theorists of the 'relative autonomy of the state' before him, seeks to *elevate the economic* to create an ontologically hierarchical model in order to avoid the pitfalls of a fully Weberian pluralism. This 'elevation of the economic over the geopolitical' entails revealing that which is inherent within capitalism that keeps states plural. Though sharing in their non-reductionist aspirations, here he critiques Hannes Lacher (2002) and Benno Teschke (2003) who assert that there is a highly *contingent* relationship between capitalism and the state system and, most importantly, that capitalism could do away with the multi-state system and replace it with a different form of state—specifically a transnational state (Callinicos 2004, 429; 2007, 538). Paradoxically, this schema is emerging as an important one in the construction of a non-reductionist Marxism in IR, one that I consider in the next section.

But for the moment I note that Callinicos charts a course which sets out to reveal how capitalism secures the reproduction of a multi-state system so as to avoid falling into the trap of bourgeois pluralism and thereby retaining Marxist integrity. Specifically, he argues that it is the tendency to uneven and combined development inherent within capitalism that ensures the multi-state system's reproduction. Thus, the logic of competition between capitals ensures the unequal development of capitalism. And while he rightly notes that 'it would contradict what I have already argued simply to assume that it carries over to the political', he then goes on to say immediately that

> [a]ll the same, there would seem to be good reason to believe that it *does* carry over: the tendency not simply to uneven development, but to destabilizing shifts in its pattern, would constantly subvert attempts to construct a transnational state. ... The centrifugal pulls generated by the inherently geographically

uneven distribution of resources under capitalism are likely to keep the state system plural.

(Callinicos 2007, 544–45, emphasis original)

But in so doing, Callinicos leans ultimately towards an economistic explanation of the geopolitical system. Of course, there is nothing problematic in arguing that the multi-state system is (at least in part) reproduced by capitalism when constructing a non-reductionist approach: failure to do so can lead to a neo-realist geopolitical reductionism and all the attendant problems that this throws up. But to secure non-reductionism he must also show how the multi-state system constitutes not just the reproduction of capitalism, but shapes the directions that capitalism takes beyond an economic/class-functionalist framework.

Indeed, he would need to show how geopolitics (defined partly in non-class ways) enters into the constitution of global economics—and how geopolitics partially constitutes and creates the uneven development of capitalism. In addition, he would need to reveal how class relations are shaped not only by the mode of production but also by a non-class definition of geopolitics (beyond a soft functionalist conception). Unfortunately, it is these imperatives—which would square the circle, so to speak—that are missing in his analysis. Instead, Callinicos sketches a picture that reveals how geopolitical competition between the great powers remains important especially in the modern era. Though interesting, this approach effectively side-steps the issue and 'adds geopolitics and stirs' it into an economistic mixture.

Of course, this retreat from bourgeois multi-causal doomsday has the advantage of retaining Marxist integrity even if it comes at the cost of the theoretical target that he set himself at the beginning of his journey—that of achieving a genuinely non-reductionist Marxist model of IR. None of this, however, is to deny the point that much of what he has to say is insightful and original. Indeed, his capitalist explanation of the multi-state system certainly adds something to MIRT. Nor is this to belittle his efforts in transcending economism, for I believe that he has gone further than most, whether they be Marxist or otherwise. Indeed, here I want to emphasize the vital point that the majority of IR theories are ontologically reductionist. Accordingly, if my conclusion is correct, Callinicos and other Marxists are far from alone in this regard.

Interestingly, my interpretation inevitably clashes with the readings of Callinicos made by various neo-Marxists. Their claim, as alluded to earlier, is that a two-logics pluralism inevitably leads to a realist moment; a moment that they find unacceptable. Moreover, it is unlikely that Callinicos himself would agree with my reading. More likely he would continue to call for a 'realist moment'. Because the problems with this have been discussed much more fully by others (Pozo-Martin 2006; 2007; Callinicos and Rosenberg 2008), I shall merely add a few points to conclude my discussion here.

The main problem with trying to aim for a realist moment concerns the point that modern neo-realism (which is really what I think he has in mind) invokes a pure reductionist ontology. That is, the logic of anarchy trumps all other logics. This means that trying to graft a realist/geopolitical moment into Marxism is logically fraught at best and impossible at worst. Neo-realism's ontology is simply too inflexible to allow for the sort of two-logics pluralism that Callinicos has in mind. Of course, the flip-side of this coin lies in the question as to whether Marxist ontology itself is sufficiently flexible to import geopolitics without denying its effectivity by stirring it into a class-based mixture. And it is precisely here where another group of Marxists enter into our discussion through their deployment of a third proposed solution to the challenge of economic reductionism, to a consideration of which I now want to turn. But to conclude, it seems that the realist moment which Callinicos searches for turns out to be an elusive quest.

'Collapsed base-superstructuralism': or, the 'illusion of the non-reductionist promised land?'

The third generic formula that has been recently developed within MIRT is that which I am once more taking some liberty in calling 'collapsed base/super-structuralism'. Though a clumsy term, I feel that it conveys the essence of this approach. Although this approach is undoubtedly an innovation within MIRT it is in fact a revival of the formula first laid out by Political Marxists, most notably Ellen Meiksins Wood and Robert Brenner (though there were some cues for it in the works of Perry Anderson (1974b) and Terrell Carver (1982)). The starting point for Political Marxists (within and without IR) is a forthright rejection of the base-superstructure model as famously outlined in Marx's 1859 'Preface' (Marx 1976). The extreme frustration with the economistic straitjacket that the base-superstructure model inevitably imposes is aptly conveyed in the words of Ellen Wood (1995, 49): 'The base/superstructure model has always been more trouble than it is worth. Although Marx himself used it very rarely ... it has been made to bear a theoretical weight far beyond its limited capacities'. The recent words of one prominent Political Marxist within IR, Hannes Lacher (2005, 29), echo this in content and spirit:

> To be sure, those utterly misguided passages from the Preface ... that suggest that 'the economic structure of society' determines the legal, political, ideological 'super-structures' have found their followers in Marxist IR/IPE, especially in world-systems theory. Significantly, like their liberal critics, these economic determinists conceptualise capitalism as the 'economic factor', though they accord it much more historical and explanatory power than the former. An alternative historical materialist perspective may start from the proposition that capitalism is not an economic category at all. ... The capitalist economy, far from being some primordial sphere that imposes itself on the state and society, is itself the product of the societal disposition of extractive and coercive powers. ... [None of this can] be conceptualised in terms of a base/superstructure relationship.

This particular strategy to counter economic reductionism explicitly involves collapsing the 'superstructure' into the 'base' (the mode of production). Perry Anderson originally captured this key point succinctly:

previous [pre-capitalist] modes of exploitation operate through extra-economic sanction—kin, customary, religious, legal or political. It is therefore, in principle, always impossible to read them off from economic relations as such. The superstructure of kinship, religion, law or the state necessarily enters in to the constitutive structure of the mode of production in pre-capitalist social formations.

(Anderson 1974b, 403; see also Carver 1982, 27)

Thus, echoing Anderson and explicitly evoking Wood, Lacher goes on to assert:

not only is the 'ultimate secret' of capitalism 'political' ... more specifically, the 'relations of production' themselves take the form of particular juridical and political relations—modes of domination and coercion, forms of property and social organisation—which are not mere secondary reflexes, nor even just external supports, but constituents of these production relations.'

(Lacher 2005, 29 quoting in part Wood 1995, 27)

More generally, the initial formula for political Marxism—as it was for Althusser's (1969) and Poulantzas's (1973, 13–18) critique of economism—lies in the claim that in any particular mode of production, the economic level 'assigns' the other levels certain powers or roles.

Drawing on Marx's discussion in *Capital* Volume 3 (1959, 790–93), Political Marxists argue that in feudalism, the economic level assigns 'dominance' to the political level, in the sense that the political is the dominant force that is responsible for the extraction of a surplus from the producer class. Violence and militarism are both tied up with the extraction of surplus-value. Thus, coercion is deployed in order to extract a surplus in the first place, while part of this product is then allocated to funding warfare (given that the nobles were the mainstay of the feudal army). Accordingly, they argue that the mode of domination/violence can attain a certain *constitutive* power vis-à-vis the economic—with the resulting formation being labelled the 'mode of exploitation' (Teschke 2003; Lacher 2006). This in turn leads them to claim that non-economic forces cannot be separated from the social relations of production, but nor can they be reduced analytically to the mode of production.

The base-superstructure framework is problematic, then, because while it does not fully separate out non-class from economic forces (as *allegedly* occurs in 'two-logics pluralism'), the former are nevertheless seen as a direct product of the latter and that the superstructure simply functions to reproduce the class base. This functional role that is played by the superstructure, which Marx originally proposed in 1859, is viewed by political Marxism (as well as by most Marxist variants) as *the* source of economic reductionism; an assumption I question below.

In considering this approach in MIRT, I focus here on two of the most prominent and creative Political Marxists in IR—Hannes Lacher and Benno Teschke. Significantly, both have applied Political Marxist insights into theorizing IR in the context of the emergence of the interstate system (Lacher 2005; 2006; Teschke 1998; 2003; Lacher and Teschke 2007). However, it is important to recognize that what follows is *not* a critique of their arguments about world politics. My aim, rather, is to consider in critical detail their proposed solution to economism, using their discussion as an example of 'collapsed base/superstructuralism'. Moreover, the discussion also applies to other Marxists who utilize this anti-reductionist formula, not all of whom are Political Marxists (for instance, Anderson 1974b; Rosenberg 1994; Bieler and Morton 2008; Ashman 2009).

The starting point, which is aimed fundamentally at overcoming economic reductionism, lies in the claim that the states-system cannot be derived or read-off from capitalism given that the former emerged *before* the latter. Both Lacher and Teschke argue that the interstate system emerged during the absolutist era and was pre-capitalist. Capitalism-proper, they argue, emerged only in the 19th century via industrialization and was, therefore, born into a pre-existent interstate system; an argument similar to those made by Theda Skocpol (1979) and Michael Mann (1986). This claim appears to break with the familiar soft functionalist Marxist position, which conceives of the states-state system as a requirement of the reproductive needs of capitalism (insofar as its presence enables capital to play off different states in order to maximize its global profits); an approach that was developed initially by World Systems theory (Wallerstein 1974). And it certainly enables them a degree of flexibility when thinking about the relationship between capitalism and geopolitics. Thus, they argue, in direct contradistinction to Callinicos, that under a global capitalist system a multiple sovereign states system could be done away with in favour of an imperium (Lacher 2002; Teschke 2003; Lacher and Teschke 2007). This enables them considerable wiggle-room vis-à-vis the soft functionalist position.

Both Lacher and Teschke emphasize the process of *internalization* by which they mean that economic, political and geopolitical forces mutually constitute each other. Thus, rather than separating economic from non-economic forces as allegedly occurs in two-logics pluralism, they collapse these forces into each other. But for this to be successful the same challenge that we considered earlier applies equally here. For, if the various non-economic forces attain no ontological weighting in their own right then we end up back in the economistic *cul-de-sac*. Put differently, if there is nothing specific to non-economic forces that *cannot* be reduced to economic/class factors however partial this residual might be, then by definition they do not exist other than as an instantiation of the economic, again returning to economism.

The problem here is that I can find no instances in this approach wherein non-economic forces are not essentially defined by class forces of one sort or another. Teschke, for example, in his discussion of the European 'international system' of the Middle Ages, asserts:

> Induced by collective peasant resistance and the needs of external conquest and defense, lords self-organize in a 'state of associated persons'. The 'state' guarantees noble property and lordly survival. Lordly reproduction follows the logic of political accumulation, being both an economic (lord-peasant) and a geopolitical (lord-lord) process.
>
> (Teschke 1998, 352)

Hence, Teschke offers up a class-based definition of geopolitics in which the base of the states system rests on inter-dominant class struggles. But if the geopolitical turns out to be merely a condensation of dominant class struggles, then there is by definition nothing specific to it other than class factors. In this vein, Lacher and Teschke (2007, 569–70) assert that:

> a territorially defined geopolitical pluriverse preceded the rise of capitalism and modern sovereignty. It was not the contingent legacy of an untheorizable past or the independent by-product of autonomous military or political sources of power, as neo-Weberians would want us to believe, but the determinate long-term consequence of centuries of social conflicts over rights of domination and appropriation over land and people amongst pre-capitalist classes.

They go on to assert that a two-logics pluralism, which grants a realist ontology to state managers and a capitalist logic pursued by firms, is problematic and that *the* challenge is to 'show historically what constellation of socio-political forces struggled at any point in time over the control of the state, to establish which social interests prevailed' (Lacher and Teschke 2007, 570). Once again, though, the problem remains that at no point do they identify anything that is specific to non-economic forces (states and geopolitics) beyond a pure class definition. States are the product of struggles between classes and are the condensation of a particular constellation of class-based property rights at any point in time; as much as the absolutist state serves to shore up the nobility.

On a *prima facie* reading, this Marxist conceptualization of the 'collapsed base-superstructuralist' method, wherein the mutual constitution of different forces— economic and non-economic—can be understood through an *internalization* causal process, appears to exhibit just the kind of Weberian approach which they seek to distance themselves from. Indeed it appears on first sight to be virtually the exact same formula produced by Mann (1986), where the various *partially autonomous* sources of power mutually shape or *constitute* each other and retrack one another in promiscuous and complex ways. Of course, their task is not to effect a Marxist convergence with Weberianism: far from it. And, on closer inspection, their avoidance of a Weberian ontology is achieved successfully given that for their internalization method to live up to the promise of mutual constitution/internalization/non-reductionism, they must be able to specify something that is specific to these non-economic variables (even if the ontology of such forces is one of partial rather than absolute autonomy).

But the irony is that by distancing themselves from this Weberian formula, they are in danger of throwing the reductionist baby out with the 'bourgeois bathwater'. And precisely because, as I explained above, at no point are non-economic forces granted a specificity outside of a class definition, then it becomes very difficult to identify a successful break with economism on their part. As noted, there is nothing problematic in arguing that the multi-state system is, at least in part, reproduced by capitalism (or dynastic semi-feudalism) when constructing a non-reductionist approach: failure to do so can lead to a neorealist geopolitical reductionism, which would be a step backwards. But if the geopolitical turns out to be a pure instantiation of the economic, then logically we have not taken the crucial step forward beyond economism.

It is worth reiterating the two key criteria that need to be met to satisfy the anti-reductionist goal. First, it needs to be specified how states engage with each other in ways that are based neither on a pure externalizing of internal class relations or the playing out of inter-dominant class struggles (conducted across countries). In short, there can be no one-to-one correspondence between class forces and geopolitics. Second, it is important to show how the states system constitutes 'external' economic relations and internal class relations in ways that are not connected to a pure class logic of any sort. To be clear, this is *not* to say that the multi-state system should be deemed to be wholly autonomous of class relations. Rather, it should be understood as attaining a *partial* autonomy; having a certain specificity that is non-reducible to class forces, on the one hand, but also being partially shaped by class factors, on the other. Failure to do this ends up in a pure realist moment. And so to reiterate the point made earlier: here I agree entirely with Lacher and Teschke (2007) and others that a Marxist ontology is incompatible with a (neo)realist one, precisely because the latter embodies a wholly reductionist ontology which cannot allow an inclusion of class forces as causal or constitutive. But, in the end, the very same problem that haunts two-logics pluralism also bedevils 'collapsed base-superstructuralism': namely that the failure to pinpoint that which is specific to the states system beyond class forces leads us back into the cul-de-sac of economism. Until these two criteria are satisfied, and despite their many ingenious efforts, those Marxists that adhere to a version of 'collapsed base-superstructuralism' are yet to break successfully with economism. Once again, therefore, it seems that the search for the non-reductionist solution appears to be, if not an impossible, then at least an elusive, quest.

Resuscitating and confronting the obscured subliminal underpinnings of Marxist anti-economism

None of the three proposed strategies have yet succeeded in delivering Marxism to the promised land of non-reductionism. Nevertheless, I was struck by how both 'collapsed base/superstructuralism' and two-logics pluralism got so far but then, at the very last turn so-to-speak, forked left onto the highway that returned them home. Thus throughout these journeys, my deep sense of anticipation turned out to be dashed at the very last turn: the climax of my voyage turning instead to be a mirage that vaporized into thin air, leading me to recall the famous adage that 'all that is solid melts into air' (Marx and Engels 2002, 223). But had my aforementioned criteria been met, then success would surely have crystallized.

An important implication of my typology is that there are quite different ontologies that underpin the three strategies. Accordingly, it is worth heeding an intellectual health warning: that it is not possible to mix and match them. Robert Cox's seminal work, for example, falls into this trap. He frequently uses the relative autonomy approach (or 'modified base/superstructuralism'), but the statement for which he is most well-known approximates with a 'collapsed base/superstructuralism'.

Thus, for example, he argues that in non-hegemonic orders the state gains consider-able levels of 'relative autonomy' (Cox 1987, 236–44; see also, 124–28, 137–38, 148–49, 189–210; Cox 1986, 216). But his 'collapsed base/superstructuralism' becomes apparent when he asserts that '[t]hree categories of forces (expressed as potentials) interact in a structure: material capabilities, ideas and institutions. ... No one way determinism need be assumed among these three; the relationships can be assumed to be reciprocal' (Cox 1986, 218). Or again, speaking of the anti-economistic conception of the historic bloc he asserts that 'the juxtaposition and reciprocal rela-tionships of the political, ethical and ideological spheres of activity with the economic sphere avoid reductionism. ... ideas and material conditions are always bound toge-ther, mutually influencing one another, and not reducible one to the other' (Cox 1996, 131). But joining together the 'modified base/superstructuralism' of the relative autonomy approach with the 'collapsed base/superstructure' approach is ontologically highly problematic. So, if nothing else, I hope that my typology can enable greater levels of clarity to emerge within MIRT when trying to develop anti-economistic strategies.

There is, I believe, a need to resuscitate some of the deeper, subliminal issues that underpin the anti-economistic project but that hitherto have remained obscured. These need to be confronted by MIRT, if not by Marxists more generally. First, the general assumption—taken to its logical extreme in political Marxism—is that reconstructing the base/superstructure model can deliver Marxism to the non-reductionist terminus. But what has not been confronted thus far is whether the base/superstructure model is a symptom or product of a deeper source, namely Marx's dialectical method. As was explained earlier, this method assumes that to attribute autonomy to any non-class force is to fall into the trap of bourgeois fetishism. The assumption that is so often made within Marxist circles is that the base/superstructure model is some kind of incon-venient, abstract add-on and that, as such, it is dispensable within a Marxist frame-work. But *if* Marx's dialectical method turns out to be the source of the base/superstucture model, then this suggests that reforming or tampering with the latter is to treat the symptom rather than the cause.

This, then, throws up a number of central issues and questions that require further consideration. First and foremost, if it is the dialectical method rather than the base/superstructure model wherein the source of economism lies, then is it game-over for a non-reductionist Marxist approach? But if this negative conclusion is rejected, then second, we need to know what the cues are within Marx's dialectical method for a non-economistic approach. Third, if there is wiggle-room within the dialectical method then we need to know exactly where the cut-off point between Marxist integrity and bourgeois theory lies. Or, is it the case that diluting even to a small degree Marx's pure dialectical method undermines Marxist integrity and leads inevitably into the realm of bourgeois theory? Or again, does allowing non-class forces some kind of autonomy alongside class analysis lead into a critical theory rather than Marxism *per se*? If not, then we need to specify exactly the nature of the interstitial space that exists between Marxist, critical, and bourgeois theory, as well as locate precisely where the boundary lines are situated. Fourth, what are the pay-offs from ditching economism and are these necessarily superior to the benefits of retaining it?

Picking up on the fourth question above, a second deep issue that needs to be brought out into the open for consideration is whether non-reductionism constitutes the theoretical nirvana that most neo-Marxists axiomatically assume it to be. One way into considering the potential pitfalls of a non-reductionist Marxism is to invoke the old adage: 'be careful what you wish for'. For the possible perils that a break with class reductionism entail *might* outweigh the many advantages that non-reductionism necessarily yields, thereby making economic reductionism a somewhat attractive proposition. Ditching economism imperils a Marxist-revolutionary politics, as Lenin was consistently at pains to point out; which is precisely why he embraced economic reductionism so fervently (Hobson 2000, Chapter 2; 2007, 583–84). Or, as the prominent Marxist scholar, Gerry Cohen asked rhetorically: 'if the economic structure is constituted of property ... relations, how can it be distinct from the legal super-structure which it is supposed to explain?' (Cohen 1978, 217–18). The failure to distinguish class relations within the mode of production from non-economic forces ultimately risks denying Marxist theoretical integrity thereby propelling such analysis into the realm of bourgeois theory (Cohen 1978, 216–48). It is in this sense that we might ask: 'To be or not to be a non-reductionist Marxist—is that the question?' For in contemporary MIRT it is taken as axiomatic that non-reductionism is the only way to proceed. But Marxists rarely interrogate this question by considering what the negatives might be in breaking with economism. In this sense, then, one at least needs to ask whether (rather than assert that) the non-reductionist promised land is possibly a spectre or dangerous illusion that Marxists should seek to exorcize. And in turn, this necessarily leads us back to the questions posed in the previous paragraph.

It is interesting to consider why Marxists are so committed to critiquing econo-mism. Rarely, if ever, do we hear neorealists or neoliberals or constructivists/post-structuralists agonizing over the problem of geopolitical reductionism, market reductionism or ideational reductionism, respectively. Why, then, do Marxists feel the need to beat themselves up over the issue of reductionism? We know that Marxists are in part reacting to the clearly unacceptable politics of Stalinist/Third International economism. Added to this is the point that for many Marxists econo-mism produces too crude a theoretical tool for analyzing world historical develop-ment; one that is, *inter alia*, insensitive to the subtleties of historicist notions of change through time. And for many, countering the reductionist charge is seen as crucial for defending Marxism *per se* from its critics (which is why many reading this piece would, wrongly as it turns out, assume that it constitutes a critique of Marx-ism). But it seems to me that Marxism's most fundamental claim, that world politics is an emanation of class struggles, is a very powerful one in its own right. One might well ask, therefore, why so many Marxists feel the need to shy away from this pro-foundly important Marxist claim? But if the anti-reductionist avenue is the preferred route, then Marxists need properly consider the deeper set of questions and issues raised here that necessarily underpin the challenge of anti-economism. Bringing them out of the closet and confronting them is, I believe, a necessary first task.

My task here is not to suggest that a non-reductionist Marxism is unattainable, or that a non-reductionist Marxism is a non-sequitur. Rather, my questions are posed in an open and constructive fashion rather than being pre-determined to intentionally sink the Marxist ark. I want to close by saying that in the course of writing this chapter I have enjoyed reading through many Marxist books and articles, as much as I have sincerely enjoyed talking to quite a few of those mentioned here.

Notes

1 Without implicating them, I wish to thank Alex Anievas and John C Smith for their extensive and extremely useful comments on the original journal article from which this chapter is derived, as well as Justin Rosenberg, Adam Morton, Stuart Shields, Ian Bruff (and Alex once again) both for their invaluable advice concerning this present chapter, as well as for putting up with what was for me a most enjoyable dialogue but for them must have seemed like a never-ending stream of emails and phone calls.
2 Note that I am using the term 'economism' only as a short-hand for economic reductionism.
3 The term 'Trotsky-lite' is used to denote crucial differences in this body of literature; one in which these scholars display a certain 'relative autonomy' from pure Trotskyism.

8 Industrial development and international political conflict in contemporary capitalism

Peter Gowan

Introduction

In the field of the International Political Economy of development, in the recent past there have been two broad schools of thought in conflict. One is the familiar Anglo-Saxon neoclassical school and the vulgarized varieties of it peddled by the Atlantic states within the International Financial Institutions (IFIs) and the GATT/WTO over the last few decades. The other is often labelled the 'industrial mercantilist' school. The first of these schools finds no necessary link whatever between the strategy and practice of industrial development on the one hand and interstate political harmony on the other. It claims, on the contrary, that so long as market organization is constructed in line with liberal norms all states should accept this free market organization from the angle of their own long-term, self-regarding interests.[1] The second of these schools sees industrial development within any one state as being, if successful, inevitably linked to international political tensions and conflicts. It also views industrial development as being strikingly different as a process and as entailing much greater political, administrative and budgetary intervention by states than the market-based neoclassical tradition.

While these debates (and political battles) are overwhelmingly focused upon the international political economy of North-South Relations, most of the fundamental issues at stake are of a much more general character and concern the entire relationship between international industrial competition amongst capitalisms and political tensions between them. On this broader field, the recent line-up has been somewhat similar though more complicated. There has been a clearer split between neoclassicals and their vulgarizers. The latter are best called the neoliberal globalizers. And there are simultaneously industrial mercantilists, whose public voice has been somewhat muffled in the recent past but who remain influential at elite levels and amongst IR theorists inclined towards realism,[2] lately of the George W Bush administration.

But Erik S Reinert and his co-thinkers (2004, Chapter 1) have recently argued rather persuasively that all the debates which I have mentioned above, along with a number of others, have recurred over a number of centuries between two broad schools of thought: a market-exchange tradition, centred in Britain historically, and an industrial economics tradition stretching back to the renaissance in continental Europe. Reinert calls this second tradition 'the Other Canon'. Reinert and his school situate Karl Marx in the tradition of the 'Other Canon'. In one sense this is obviously true in that Marx was deeply concerned with problems of economic development and of the dynamics of industrial change. Yet, at the same time, Reinert's elaboration of the substance of this tradition says next to nothing about Marx's contribution to it or place in it. Marx's fundamental concern with economic development is evident in what he saw as the central goal of communism—the achievement of human freedom, understood first and foremost as human liberation from 'the realm of necessity'. Also fundamental for Marx's ontology was the centrality of human creativity in its labouring activity and hence the great possibilities of learning economies, of innovations and of historical change. Further, Marx gave great importance to the possibilities of increasing returns to scale, the application of science to industry, etc.

The purpose of this chapter is to explore what the relationship between Marxism and these issues of industrial development and international political tensions within contemporary capitalism actually may be. In particular, I am interested in exploring what Marx's relationship with the industrial-mercantilist school may be. I should say that this chapter consists overwhelmingly of hypotheses along with some very limited empirical and analytical research. Addressing these issues in adequate depth would require a much more rigorous and much for far-reaching programme of empirical research.

Part I explores issues concerned with industrial competition in contemporary capitalism. Part II looks at elements which may not only exacerbate the political tensions between capitalist states resulting from this competition but may also mitigate such tensions. It then concludes with some reflections on the critical edge of Marx's treatment of these problems.

Industrial competition and necessary political tensions arising from it

Increasing returns to scale

Marx was far from being alone in his recognition that in most branches of industry, increasing returns to scale operate. Adam Smith had noted the same reality and so did Alfred Marshall, not to speak of such other Marx contemporaries as John Ramsey McCulloch and Nassau Senior. This reality also played a central part in the thought of Joseph Schumpeter. All these economists grasped that in most industrial branches, the more units of a product you could produce, the cheaper would be the marginal unit produced. They also grasped that the logic of increasing returns to scale was to generate 'imperfect' competition and monopoly.[3] The founder of modern Marginalism, Alfred Marshall, explained this as follows in his *Principles of Economics:*

> We say broadly that while the art which nature plays in production shows a tendency to diminishing return, the art which man plays shows a tendency to increasing return. The *law of increasing return* may be worded thus: An increase of

labour and capital leads generally to improved organization, which increases the efficiency of the work of labour and capital. Therefore in those industries which are not engaged in raising raw produce an increase of labour and capital generally gives a return increased more than proportion; and further this improved organization tends to diminish or even override any increased resistance which nature may offer to raising increased amounts of raw produce. ... In most of the more delicate branches of manufacturing, where the cost of raw material counts for little, and in most of the modern transport industries the law of increasing return acts almost unopposed.

(Marshall 1925, 318–19)

And, as Schumpeter points out, Marshall was thus led to stress the centrality of the trend towards monopoly and imperfect competition 'whose patron saint Marshall may indeed be said to have been' (Schumpeter 1972, 975).

This issue of increasing returns to scale is not a theoretical one, but an empirical one—yet of great theoretical significance. If a given sector exhibits strong increasing returns to scale (or, which is the same thing, 'economies of scale') then the more production within that sector is concentrated within a single productive organization, the cheaper the unit costs should be and thus the greater the productive efficiency should be. Thus the efficiency logic of increasing returns to scale is, other things being equal, to construct monopolistic productive organizations—single producers concentrating all production in their hands and thus reducing unit costs to the minimum.

Now, it was evident to Marx and many other 19th century economists that one of the distinctive consequences of the rise of capitalist relations of production was that these tended to enhance the *scale of production* in the industrial field. This was for Marx (1962) an absolutely central *historical* achievement of capitalism. But the phenomenon itself of increasing returns to scale belongs not to the field of social relations of production but rather to the nature of the productive forces and it can and does operate not only in and through *capitalist* social relations but also in precapitalist, in Soviet-type and in any future socialist socio-economic system—a point of great importance for Marx.[4]

It is worth situating Marx's ideas on economies of scale (and learning economies, a topic treated below) within his overall analysis of capitalist dynamics. Marx saw the accumulation of capital as being accompanied by the mechanization of production and by a rising productivity of labour. This means that the proportion of capitalists' spending on materials and machines in their overall spending goes up—in Marx's terminology, the 'organic composition of capital' rises. But this will in turn mean that the rate of profit will go down, *assuming that the capitalists' rate of surplus value remains unchanged.* Here we have the starting point of Marx's famous theory of crisis generated by the tendency of the rate of profit to fall. But we should note that this tendency predominates, for Marx, only insofar as it is not cancelled out by a rise in the rate of surplus value. And it is precisely just such a rise in the rate of surplus value that may occur through the development of increasing returns to scale, learning economies, etc.[5]

While twentieth century Marxist economists have tended to focus on the crisis tendencies outlined in Marx's theories, the countervailing tendencies linked to sharp increases in the rate of surplus value—precisely the issues which concern us here—have been given less attention in Marxist empirical research. Marx (1965, 626) writes:

> The battle of competition is fought by cheapening of commodities. The cheapening of commodities depends, *ceteris paribus*, on the productiveness of labour, and this again on the scale of production. Therefore the larger capitals beat the smaller.

He underlined that the drive for economies of scale expresses itself under capitalism as the tendencies towards the concentration and centralization of capitals. Concentration refers to enlargement of the scale of production. It thus operates mainly at the level of the plant, rather than at the level of the firm. Small plants get knocked out by big plants because the latter enjoy economies of scale denied to the smaller plants.

Centralization, on the other hand, operates at the level of the firm, rather than the plant. It means one firm gobbles up other firms, combining capitals that are already in existence. As Marx (1965, 626) puts it,

> it only presupposes a change in the distribution of capital already to hand and functioning. ... capital grows in one place to a huge mass in a single hand because it has in another place been lost by many. This is centralization proper, as distinct from accumulation and concentration.[6]

For the moment, we leave these issues to one side in order to remind ourselves of a rather bizarre feature of orthodox neoclassical economic theory today: the fact that it is absolutely centrally premised on the claim that increasing returns to scale *do NOT operate* in modern industry. Instead, it requires that we assume that modern industry is marked by constant or diminishing returns to scale. Walras's (1954) attempts to use the calculus to produce a general equilibrium theory on assumptions of perfect competition involved him in assuming constant or declining returns. As Schumpeter (1973) points out, many neoclassical economists then tried to find ways of claiming that constant returns were *necessary* features of market economies, denying the obvious fact that whether returns increase or diminish is a purely empirical question!

We are, of course, used to the idea that neoclassical economics makes unrealistic assumptions, for simplifying purposes, about perfect information and the like. And we are familiar with the idea of subsequently modifying such assumptions as we introduce greater complexity into our analysis. But here we have an assumption which is a little different: it is more like a very precise empirical claim to the effect that human beings have four feet rather than two. And worse, the claim is not only factually directly contrary to the truth, but is at the same time is a very foundation of the entire neoclassical model. And indeed, Sir John Hicks, the great neoclassical synthesizer in the 1930s, acknowledged that abandonment of the idea of constant returns destroys the assumption of perfect competition and threatens the 'wreck-age. ... of the greater part of [orthodox] economic theory' (Hicks 1939, 84 as cited by Schumpeter 1973, 972).[7]

It is the assumption of constant or decreasing returns to scale on which the whole neoclassical idea that firms are price-takers rather than price-makers depends. And this in turn provides the basis for the claim that market price signals drive economic efficiency. From this derives the policy claim that states should welcome fully free markets in which their industries are subjected to unrestrained market pressures (through price signals) which make all more efficient. Yet industry after industry turns out to be marked by increasing returns to scale. And where this applies the most efficient firm structure in a given industry is not actually competition between a multitude of firms but the dominance in the industry of the most efficient firm: the one that can exploit to the maximum the logic of increasing returns to scale. Indeed, one industry, one firm would be the best outcome from an efficiency point of view.

For neoclassical economists, blinded to this reality, the trend towards monopoly is explicable basically as the subversion of the free market by rent-seekers using politics. Such 'rent seeking' activity does, of course, go on but it is far from being the root cause of monopolistic tendencies in modern industry. Neither does this root cause lie in the *social relations of capitalism*, but rather in characteristics of the productive forces. Marx also grasped this. After explaining how the logic of increasing returns generates concentration and centralization of capital, Marx (1965, 688) writes that for society as a whole, the ultimate goal would not be reached 'until the entire social capital would be united either in the hands of one single capitalist, or in those of one single cor-poration'. Here is the drive's ultimate monopolistic logic.[8] Engels makes a similar point when he notes how the technical logic towards a single firm dominating one industry occurred in the English alkali industry in 1890. He goes on: 'freedom of competition changes into its very opposite—into monopoly; and the production without any definite plan of capitalistic society capitulates to the production upon a definite plan of the invading socialist society. ... ' (Engels 1962, 147).

Economies of scale are, like all productivity increases, time-economies. They can be fostered by a whole host of measures, many of which are not generated/facilitated simply within the firm but are of much broader origin. Indeed, since Marx we have seen ever-increasing involvement of states in efforts to generate or help generate increasing returns: constructing secure market bases for their companies, training workforces, supplying transport and communication infrastructures—and, of course, the exercise of geopolitical influence to open and protect overseas markets. Much of the huge expansion of state resources in the twentieth century has, indeed, been devoted precisely to activities in this area.

Learning economies and the role of the public sector

Economies of scale are, of course, closely associated with learning economies—effi-ciency gains through technological learning and upgrading on the part of work-forces. This aspect of economics also fascinated Marx and he foresaw the possibility of a fusion of science and production that would begin under capitalism but flower under socialism. Such learning activity connected to the production process is centred on public education systems for the working class and technical intelligentsia, on university research and on outlays for Research and Development (R&D). Thus the bigger the state budget for these activities the more effective the drive for learning economies will be. Crucial also will be learning feedback from the workforce within the production process itself—what came to be called Toyotism in the 1980s because of Toyota's extremely effective way of generating such feedback from its workforce.

The impact of both economies of scale and learning economies within some high-tech sectors can be illustrated with the examples of semi-conductors and computers. In semi-conductors, since the invention of integrated circuits, memory chip prices have dropped at a rate of about 35 per cent a year. And in mainframe computers the quality adjusted annual price decline has been roughly 20 per cent (Flamm 1996, 7). These dramatic rises in what Marx would have called the rate of surplus value have come above all from so-called learning economies. Cumulative production experience has taught workforces how to dramatically reduce unit costs. But to exploit economies of scale and learning economies to the full, the role of the public sector is very pervasive.

By the mid-1990s, the cost of establishing a plant for leading edge semi-conductor production was over $1bn. In other words, very large sources of cheap credit are needed for heavy investment in such new fixed capital, and the state is deeply implicated in creating the conditions for the supply of such credit. Physical infrastructures of all kinds must be supplied for such industries and those who work in them and these also require very large state outlays. Transport and communications systems are also central. As Rodrik and others have pointed out, markets create very powerful barriers against radical innovation by private entrepreneurs (Hausmann and Rodrik 2006). Such radical innovation presupposes the existence of markets which will necessarily be absent: there will be no markets for the new sector's labour and raw materials inputs, none for its fixed capital, none for its marketing and sales networks. Thus, the private entrepreneur is required to create all such market systems for themselves and still make profits—usually an impossible task. Such radical innovation must be fostered and protected and pump-primed by states and those states with the resources to do this place their business organizations at an immense competitive advantage in new growth sectors (see Hausmann and Rodrik 2006).

Implications for analysis of contemporary capitalism

These sides of the economic thought of both Marx and other economists outside the neoclassical dead-end have very obvious and large implications for our understanding of contemporary international capitalism. First, they enable us to grasp the imperialist character of the organization of trade rules in the contemporary world economy. And, secondly, they enable us to grasp certain basic social power relations between core capitalist economies and sources of tension between them. We will look very briefly at each of these in turn.

The prevalence of economies of scale brings us face to face with the imperialism of free trade in industrial goods. The organizing principles of the WTO, premised upon neoclassical assumptions, are simply instruments for perpetuating the subordination and industrial underdevelopment of the countries of the South. Breaking from such an imperial approach would involve going over to the trade principles in the industrial field pursued by the United States in the 19th and first half of the 20th centuries: Hamiltonian principles of industrial protection (given a pale reflection in List's work).[9] Secondly, a grasp of the centrality of learning economies makes us aware of two fundamental features of the contemporary world: first the blatantly imperialist character of the intellectual property monopoly regimes in the WTO—a vulgar and crude example of monopoly rent seeking. But far more important is another feature of contemporary international reality: the centrality of the size of state budgets in the competition for dominance in various economic sectors, and the huge advantages gained by private economic organizations based in states with relatively large state budgets to supply them with a whole range of environments crucial for generating or enhancing economies of scale and learning economies. The size of such state budgets is, of course, completely unregulated within the framework of the WTO, etc. despite the fact that it massively shapes the competitive conditions facing companies.

The most obvious consequence of pervasive economies of scale is the importance of both the size of national market bases and the size of state resources for providing the infrastructures to enhance economies of scale. A core capitalism with a secured market base of 300 million people can provide a framework for achieving great scale economies not open to those capitalisms with much smaller market bases. Thus, the fact that the US product market is far bigger than any other national capitalist product market is enormously important.[10]

Of course, industrial capitalisms with relatively small national industrial markets have sought to overcome this problem by constructing what German theorists of the 1930s and 1940s called 'economic *grossraums*': German hegemony in war-time Europe, Japan's 'East Asian Co-Prosperity Area', etc. The contemporary EU Single Market can be viewed as possessing key characteristics of an economic *grossraum*, though with the distinctive characteristic that US capitals have full access to it.[11] In this context, the relatively small size of the Japanese domestic market, and Japan's post-war prohibition from rebuilding strong ties with China, ensured that Japan became critically dependent on access to the US market for acquiring the scale to compete effectively.[12] But the second conclusion which we should draw from what we have said about increasing returns to scale and about the battle for learning economies is that we should expect to find strong tendencies towards socio-economic tensions between core capitalisms and towards mercantilist strategic interaction between them (see Section II).

The notion that such strong conflict tendencies exist between core capitalisms has not been fashionable over the last 20 years, at least in the Anglo-Saxon world. Here the discourse of a global capitalism or global capitalist class has predominated (see, for example, Robinson this volume). We will therefore proceed in the following steps: (1) evidence of such tensions and such mercantilism; (2) a suggested hypothesis for explaining both such tensions and the limits of such tensions. We first turn to evidence of such tensions within the core over the recent past.

Intra-core tensions and mitigating possibilities

Evidence of tensions and mercantilism within the core

The official discourse of the Atlantic world over the last 20 years has been that of a progressive advance since 1945 towards completely open markets and free trade, culminating in the Uruguay Round and the founding of the WTO. This is empirically false: the Atlantic states have used trade negotiations to open markets for *new growth sectors* that they want to drive into international markets. But they have simultaneously been taking new measures to protect or *close* their markets. The GATT trade rounds tended over the decades to open more and more of less and less: by the start of the 1990s, GATT covered only about 5 per cent of world trade. We take just four examples of the new mercantilism in the triad, focusing particularly on the US and the EU: (1) anti-dumping policy; (2) anti-trust policy; (3) Free Trade Agreements, and then; (4) two examples of core mercantilism in high-tech sectors, the examples of semiconductors and commercial aircraft.

1. Anti-dumping policy

Dumping used to be defined as selling goods abroad more cheaply than in your home market. But since the 1970s, US trade law has redefined dumping as selling products below 'fair value'. Since 1980 about 60 per cent of all US anti-dumping cases have been based on this fair value concept (Nivola 1990; Horlick 1989). 'Fair value' is calculated by the US Commerce Department by working out what should be the long-run *average costs of production* in a given industry, and then adding on a fixed 8 per cent mark-up to reflect 'normal' profits:[13] sales below that can be treated as dumping by the US and can simply be driven out of the US market. But in industries marked by increasing returns to scale and by large learning economies—a feature of most industrial sectors and especially of high-tech sectors—pricing a product on the basis of long run average costs makes no economic sense. Even pricing products at current marginal cost is often inefficient.

Companies typically engage in 'forward pricing'—pricing below current marginal cost—particularly in industries which exhibit strong learning economies. This has long been understood in the US, where it was first spelt out in the early 1980s (Spence 1981). Forward pricing in this context is not dumping but is simply rooted in the knowledge that current marginal costs are bound to fall in the future (Flamm 1996, 307). Yet, as Flamm (1996, 358) points out 'pricing below a constructed long-run average cost has become the principal grounds for applying the US dumping laws to US imports of some foreign products'. Thus, US anti-dumping policy is a very powerful instrument of economic protectionism or even economic warfare. It has been used on countless occasions and across any sector of production, not least those which are formally tariff-free. And to avoid being hammered in this way, states are typically required to introduce 'voluntary export restraints' (VERs), 'voluntary price floors' etc.

The EU also engages in a whole range of bogus anti-dumping measures for exactly the same mercantilist purposes as the US. During the 1980s and the first half of the

1990s, the US adopted a trade policy which Jagdish Bhagwati (1990) has called 'aggressive unilateralism' under Section 301, Super 301 and Special 301 of US trade law.[14] This policy gave the US authorities the unilateral right to decide who was adopting hostile trade policy towards the US and what action the US should adopt towards such centres. And although it was attenuated after the formation of the WTO, the Bush administration has shown that this tendency is far from dead.

2. Anti-trust

Anti-trust regulation in the US and the EU would seem, on the face of it, to be a pillar of liberal international political-economic norms, protecting companies and consumers from monopolistic practices. Anti-trust is thus often presented as a bastion of liberal internationalist free market principles. And so it was in the early post-war decades when American ascendancy in so many industrial sectors seemed assured: anti-trust meant a domestic anti-monopoly drive. As Edward Graham (2000, 61) of the *Institute of International Economics* explains:

> Until the late 1970s, this was done pretty much without regard to whether these distortions might be offset by factors that would enhance efficiency ... This unwillingness to consider efficiency defences, however, changed during the 1980s, when these enforcement agencies—the Federal Trade Commission and the Antitrust Division of the Department of Justice—upgraded their analytical techniques to recognize that mergers could create offsetting efficiencies.

The phrase about 'upgrading' analytical techniques is a pleasant little joke. What Graham means is that the relevant agencies grasped that in industries characterized by increasing returns to scale, monopoly could be good (for American capitalism) if it was judged to enhance increasing returns and global market dominance.

The same pattern is visible at the West European level: the European Commission established a merger regulation in 1989. This was supposedly to implement article 82 of the Treaty of Rome against 'the abuse of a dominant firm position'. But the regulation specifically allows European Commission Competition Directorate (DGIV)—the Commission authority on mergers and acquisitions—to take account of efficiency considerations in its judgement on mergers. Since in industries characterized by increasing returns to scale efficiency can be enhanced by maximum concentration of capital to the point of complete market dominance for one firm, the regulation supposedly against market dominance can assure market dominance in the name of efficiency. And the regulation has the great virtue, from the angle of European big business, of giving no explanation of how the efficiency criterion will relate to other factors. In other words, DGIV has more or less complete discretion as to what policy to adopt on monopolization.

Graham goes on to explain that efficiencies should be understood 'dynamically' and not in a static way. So the authorities can be 'tolerant of mergers that create dynamic efficiencies even if these create some static welfare losses due to increased market power' (Graham 2000, 62). This interesting remark then softens us up for the next. For Graham explains:

in recent years in the United States and implicitly in the EU, merger and acquisition review has operated largely under the premise that market concentration is in most circumstances a self-correcting distortion. In other words, it is largely held that, if monopoly rents are created by merger or acquisition, in the absence of greater efficiency of the merged enterprise, these rents will in most instances draw new entry into the market. This entry, in turn, will correct the inefficiencies created by market power held at the outset by the merged firm.

(Graham 2000, 64)

This is a piece of cant. A Japanese company, say, entering the US or European market in a given sector for the first time, will not do so because of the existence of monopoly rents on the part of domestic producers. It will do so if it judges it can cover its costs of entry. And amongst such huge overhead costs are those of having to establish a new distribution system and those of having to face a host of other privileges of the domestic competitor, not least their easy access to domestic political influence. Graham in fact illustrates this when he says that while the creation of dynamic efficiency is the key criterion of anti-trust bodies, a second best criterion is to ignore inefficiencies on the grounds that the foreign competition is bound to enter the market! Thus, in a concluding remark, Graham is honest enough to admit, in splendid understatement: 'in both jurisdictions [i.e. US and EU] the thresholds for challenging a merger or acquisition on grounds that the merger creates a monopoly ... have been quite high'.

It is also striking that the EU and the US define the relevant market for anti-trust cases in variable ways: if the market is judged to be global, then just about any degree of monopolization within the jurisdiction can be justified. Yet the market definition can be reduced, often quite drastically, in the case of a foreign firm seeking an acquisition domestically which faces strong domestic opposition. And because of their huge market access power, both the US and the EU antitrust authorities are able to exert powerful extraterritorial jurisdiction, with the capacity to judge, say, mergers of two foreign firms with some presence in their market but with the bulk of their activities outside it monopolistic.

To put matters more bluntly we are in a normless and politicized zone. Some experts in transatlantic anti-trust openly acknowledge this. Simon Evenett *et al.* (2000, 14–15), for example, explain that

> anti-trust is a political phenomenon and is therefore subject to all the normal interest group pressures that affect policy across the spectrum. ... the larger firms that will be the actual targets of anti-trust intervention are far more likely to be foreign than domestic, as the former will have considerably less domestic lobbying power.

Thus, since the late 1980s in both the US and the EU anti-trust policy has become a 'political phenomenon' in the sense that it targets foreign companies entering the market much more than domestic firms.

3. Free trade agreements (FTAs)

Another striking example of how liberal language is turned inside out is the pro-liferation of FTAs. These are, in reality, key instruments for the mercantilist expansion of accumulation from the main triadic centres. The key feature of them is the fact that they allow free trade only in the specified products of 'national origin' amongst the contracting states. Thus an FTA between say the EU and State X will allow the specified products from State X into the EU if the products are produced either by EU companies in State X or by State X's own territory-based productive activities above various specified thresholds. These thresholds are designed to ensure that no US or Japanese multinational enterprise (MNE) could enter State X to assemble products for sale in the EU. They also give state X extremely powerful incentives to privilege FDI from the EU in its territory since only EU companies will be sure not to face barriers to entry into EU markets.

At the present time, bilateral FTAs centred on each of the triadic centres are proliferating, undercutting the multilateral principles of the WTO. They are an evident sign of attempts by each centre to draw national economies lower down the international division of labour into dependence on one triadic centre as against the others.

4. High tech economic warfare

Despite all the neoliberal ideology about the efficiency of free markets, about the triumph of free markets over states and about the efficiency-necessity for removing the state from any role other than policing competition, triadic state policy in strategic industrial sectors has been marked by ruthless mercantilism—not least on the part of the US. By strategic sectors we do not mean those with military significance. We mean those which generate chain-reaction effects across many industrial sectors. We take two examples in order to illustrate this theme: semi-conductors and civilian aircraft. Semi-conductors stand at the top of the industrial food chain of the computer and electronics industries. Civilian aircraft production is the motor of a whole range of high-tech components sectors which can have economies of scope leading into other industrial sectors.

In the mid-1980s, Japan achieved global dominance in advanced semi-conductor production. It had achieved this dominance through strongly mercantilist state industrial support. But the fact remained that it was producing the highest quality semi-conductors at the cheapest price. The Reagan administration complained about Japanese mercantilism in this field. However, it is worth examining US industrial policy in semi-conductors as well.

The US Federal Government between 1958 and early 1970s directly or indirectly funded between 40 and 45 per cent of all industrial semi-conductor R&D (Flamm 1996, 36–39). By the late 1980s, Federal funding of semi-conductor-related research was running at about half a billion dollars a year. At the same time, over one quarter of all semi-conductors produced in the US during the late 1980s had a captive state market in US defence agencies alone. Along with such assistance would come a whole range of tax breaks and tax credits and other kinds of subsidies to boost the profitability and lower the costs of production in semi-conductors and other sectors. Thus in 1981 the US Congress passed a 25 per cent incremental tax credit for R&D in semi-conductors (Flamm 1996, 147). Thus we find that the entire development of the US semi-conductor industry has been the result of massive state support.

By the mid-1980s, the Japanese semi-conductor industry had achieved global leadership in semi-conductor production with about 70 per cent of the global market. In the face of this Japanese ascendancy, the US government adopted a policy that can best be described as economic warfare on the Japanese in this sector and some others. In 1986, the US imposed upon Japan the Semi-Conductor Trade Arrangement (STA). In 1991 the STA was renewed in a somewhat different—and more explicit—form for another five years to 1996. In 1992, the approach which the US used on the STA was extended to car parts. And the Clinton Administration in 1993 indicated that it would use the approach contained in the STA more widely in its economic diplomacy towards Japan (David 1993). This turn involved the following measures.

From late 1986, the US Commerce Department worked out the prices which each Japanese chip maker had to charge for each of its products in the field of DRAMs and EPROMs (advanced semi-conductors). From March 1987, the Commerce Department was fixing price floors for these sales not only in the US but also in 19 other markets (including 6 European markets).The Japanese government had to accept that by 1992 foreign companies would have a 20 per cent share of the Japanese domestic market in DRAMs. The Japanese foreign trade ministry (MITI) was required to reduce both output and investment on the part of specific Japanese semi-conductor producers. Thus a MITI memorandum in April 1987 circulated to Washington stated:

> In February, MITI exercised administrative guidance to the companies to reduce production during the first quarter of 1987 by 23% below fourth quarter 1986 levels. Last month, MITI again exercised administrative guidance to the companies to reduce production still further in the second quarter to 32% below fourth quarter 1986 levels.
>
> (as quoted in Flamm 1996, 185)

And US trade negotiators gave MITI detailed demands for limiting investments by Japanese firms in new capacity well into 1988 (Flamm 1996, 195).

These impositions of managed economics on the Japanese were justified at the time in large part by claims of a 'national security threat' to the US in military terms. Yet, US military demand for semi-conductors had been, since the late 1970s, no longer a demand for the most advanced chips. The Japanese lead was rather in the civilian, commercial sector (Flamm 1996, 36). At the start of the 1980s, the US government started funding R&D to counter the Japanese commercial threat in what was a major policy shift.[15]

Civilian aircraft production is another strategic, high-tech industrial sector marked by huge economies of scale and with very large spin-offs across related sectors. In the post-war years, the British failed to exploit their opportunities in this field and American producers, above all Boeing, achieved ascendancy. In the early

1970s, the French led other Western European states into the Airbus consortium to mount a challenge to US dominance in this field. For the next 20 years, Boeing—which had emerged as the dominant US player—and Airbus were supported by their respective state sponsors to continue in business. According to the US government, Western European governments have given Airbus preferential government loans of more than $15bn over the last five years (Garten 2005). According to the EU, Boeing has received around $23bn (€17.1) in governmental development aid since 1992, mostly in the form of military and NASA contracts, R&D expenditure and tax subsidies.

The total US Government indirect support of the US civil aircraft industry in 2003 alone was about $2.74bn. This represents around 11.9 per cent of the 2003 commercial turnover of the US industry. In addition, since 1990 Boeing has avoided paying more than $1.2 billion in federal taxes through the use of off-shore Foreign Sales Corporations (FSC) (a tactic ruled illegal by the WTO). And Boeing also receives large subsidies from American state governments. Planned subsidies for Boeing's new 7E7 aircraft production amount to $3.2bn from Washington State, $0.5bn from Kansas, and $0.35bn from Oklahoma (European Commission 2004). The EU also claims that Boeing's Japanese subcontractors, who will produce about 60 per cent of the new 7E7, receive more than $1bn in subsidies from Japanese state sources. On the other side, the US government claims Airbus is moving the same way, having recently cut a deal with state-owned China Aviation Industry Corp (Garten 2005).

In the early part of the new millennium, Airbus overtook Boeing in share of the world market. In 1993, Boeing had controlled about 73 per cent of the market. But 10 years later, its share of the world market dropped to 48 per cent. Airbus sold 305 aircrafts in 2003, compared with Boeing's 281. And in 2004, Airbus delivered 320 planes compared to 285 from Boeing (Bloomberg 2005). Against this background, the US government threatened to take Airbus to the WTO for illegal state subsidies and the EU has responded by threatening to take Boeing to the WTO on the same grounds. But the key point is that the reality of inter-triadic rivalries in high-tech sectors. And the picture in semi-conductors and aircraft is far from unique. Indeed, at the launch of Airbus's new A380 superjumbo in January 2005, President Jacques Chirac of France held up the Airbus joint government-company industrial model as the way forward in other sectors, mentioning specifically energy, transport and medicine (Garten 2005).

What of economic globalization?

Despite all this evidence of substantial mercantilist activity and conflict, it would appear from the vast outpouring of academic and journalistic writing concerning 'economic globalization'—not to speak of the rhetoric of Atlantic political leaders—that market forces have overcome such statist mercantilism and have been able to implement the neoclassical dream of full factor mobility (though excluding, of course, labour) on a global scale. On the basis of such claims, the evidence of mercantilism at the very centre of the system has been bracketed out. Yet one problem with these claims is that they have lacked a firm basis in empirical research, most particularly on the actual reach of supposedly global capitalist industrial firms.

Amongst the few studies which have attempted to give us solid quantitative evidence on the scope of multinational enterprise (MNE) activity, the work of Alan Rugman and Alain Verbeke has demonstrated that we are more accurately in a world economy precisely of regional *grossraums* rather than of global companies at the present time. They divide the world into three regions: North America, Europe and East Asia. They define a MNE as having a base in any one region by the criterion of having at least 20 per cent of its sales in that region. Thus a global MNE would have at least 20 per cent of its sales in each of the three triadic regions, a bi-regional MNE would have at least 20 per cent of its sales in each of two regions, etc. At the same time, they define a home-region MNE as one having over 50 per cent of its sales in a single region. Their definition of the Asian region includes Japan, China, South Korea and the Association of Southeast Asian Nations (ASEAN) (Rugman and Verbeke 2004).

These are rather dramatic figures. First, of the 380 MNEs for which sales data is available, a miserable 2.6 per cent are global companies, while 84.2 per cent are home region oriented. Only 6.6 per cent are bi-regional. There are obvious limitations to this data and possible challenges to Rugman and Verbeke's methodology— both of which they fully acknowledge. But at the very least, this data strongly contests the sweeping claims of the economic globalization discourse and fits very well with the image of inter-regional mercantilist tensions offered by our earlier material.

Explaining international political tensions and their limits

We have so far sought to demonstrate that the prevalence and importance of economies of scale and learning economies in the competition between capitals tends to generate political tensions between states. This claim has become controversial amongst supporters of globalization theory, including Marxists. Yet, as shown above, there is plenty of empirical evidence to support this claim from the recent past. Moreover, once the centrality of scale economies and learning economies is grasped, we may also understand the deep and many-sided implication of capitalist states in directly supplying inputs into their corporate sectors that are central to their competitive success. The notion that private sector profitability and capital accumulation is the result of purely private sector activity within modern capitalism is hopelessly wide of the mark: state financial and coercive resources and rule-making play a vastly important daily role in establishing the qualitative and quantitative conditions for private sector profitability.

Yet it is equally the case, surely, that the political tensions arising from these economic sources have remained manageable within the capitalist interstate system over the last half century, at least as far as intra-core relations have been concerned. We have not experienced a return to the kind of interstate political rivalry that led to the destruction of European dominance over the international political economy in the first half of the twentieth century. The question thus arises: why not? What are the limits or counter-acting tendencies within the contemporary interstate system?

A systematic answer to these questions would, of course, demand a complete account of the political and economic dynamics of contemporary international relations. We will, however, limit ourselves to one, often overlooked aspect of these issues—namely the extent to which the nature of the contemporary productive forces can, in a capitalist context, exacerbate interstate political tensions and the extent to which the nature of capitalist relations of production can actually *mitigate* such tensions. To explore these issues we must first look rather more closely at the consequences of economies of scale and learning economies within the international political economy.

The international division of labour as a power hierarchy/process

When we examine the international economy from a sectoral point of view, exploring the international division of labour, we find evident distinctions between Branch 1 products (means of production) and Branch 2 (consumer goods produced by branch one plant) and along with this distinction we find differences between high-tech, medium-tech and low-tech sectors. We thus also notice relations of dependency between national economies resulting from this international division of labour.

These dependencies are most obvious in the production chains pushed upon countries of the South by the Atlantic world since the 1980s (and indeed before), where production-for-sales activity in the South depends upon inputs from core

Table 8.1 Distribution of world's largest 500 MNEs

	1981	1991	1996	2000
No. in Triad		410	443	430
No. in US	242	157	162	185
No. in EU	141	-	155	141
No. in Japan	62	119	126	104

Table 8.2 Classification of top 500 MNEs in 2001

Type of MNE	No. of MNEs	% of 500	% of 380	Weighted av. % of intra-regional Trade
Global	10	2%	2.6%	38.2%
Bi-regional	25	5%	6.6%	42%
Host-region Oriented	11	2.2%	2.9%	30.9%
Home Region Oriented	320	64%	84.2%	80.3%
Insufficient data	14	2.8%	3.7%	40.9%
No data	120	24%		Na

Note: Weighted averages were calculated by assuming the lowest point in intra-regional sales (i.e. 10=90 > 90=90)
Source: Rugman and Verbeke (2004)

capitalist countries and upon sales outlets there. But it also extends to relations between core capitalist countries. As Robert Cooper (2003, 38) points out, US preservation of Japanese security is probably a vital interest of the United States 'because Japanese industry is an integrated component of the global market, vital for many Western manufacturers and retailers ... '. In blunter terms, inputs from Japanese plants are vital for the very functioning of a number of important sectors of both the US and West European economies. And this dependence on Japanese products also gives Japan leverage over the US in the event of sharp political conflicts with Washington.[16]

At the same time, high-tech sectors, though small in their overall weight in GDP, bring multiple economic benefits. On average, they have more rapid sales growth and more than double the profits growth of medium-tech industries and they provide wide positive externalities for other firms supplying components or working lower down the industrial food chain. And very commonly, key high-tech sectors are also the sources of important economies of scope: technological breakthroughs generating new growth in one sector opening up possibilities of new growth sectors being spun off from that initial sector.[17] The battle to advance up this hierarchized international division of labour is what economic development is centrally about. But equally, those core capitalist states at the top of the technological division of labour create multiple dependencies across the world economy and shape and reshape the actual structure of the international division of labour itself. It was precisely this aspect of economic dynamics to which Schumpeter gave such weight in his theoretical work. But none of these ideas are in the slightest alien to Marxist theory. On the contrary, Marx was acutely aware of the core processes and of their social power significance in the international political economy. Yet Marx located these issues within his theory in a distinctive way and it is by grasping this aspect of his work that we can find a very interesting, distinctive and important research agenda for analyzing contemporary dynamics.

Forces of production and capitalist relations of production

Marx makes a very important categorical distinction in his theory between the concepts of forces of production and relations of production, running parallel to his central distinction between use-value and exchange-value. Both these sets of antagonistic realities/concepts are, in Marx, inextricably linked together. Nevertheless, for Marx, the telos of capital is not the production of use-values or the development of the productive forces: it is the production of more capital. In other words, private value-generation and value-extraction is the governing goal. Thus, the development of the productive forces, including the enhancement of productive scale and the generation of cumulative learning economies must be seen as by-products of, or means towards, the capitalist drive for value expansion and extraction. At any given time and place they may not at all be the only or even the main means to such value-expansion/extraction. Capitalism by no means has to go for high-tech and the generation of ever-greater 'relative surplus value' via technological upgrading. It can very happily go, so to speak, 'down-market': the ferocious drive for the cheapest possible labour working the longest possible hours in the worst possible conditions should be all too familiar to us in the contemporary world, not only in the global South but in the North as well. And if we look at league tables of industries credited with generating the highest (before tax) value-added today we will typically find that at the top of the list comes not semi-conductors but cigarette production!

Marx also stressed that actual capitalist drives are mediated not only by the telos of value-maximization but also by the internal politics of the given capitalist state and capitalist class. Class conflict counts in economics. To take an obvious example: The leaders of British capitalism debated in the late 1970s whether they should use the coming North Sea Oil bonanza to rebuild and modernize Britain's industrial base or to revive Britain as a financial power. The course they chose was an anti-industrial one and that choice was decisively influenced by their subjectivity concerning Britain's industrial working class.

That example illustrates how the drive for maximizing productive efficiencies through exploiting scale economies and learning economies can be very far from being predominant in the accumulation strategies of particular capitalist classes. Sandra Halperin (2004) has argued rather persuasively that the 19th century British bourgeoisie quite deliberately eschewed such strategies because of their unpleasant consequences for class (political) structures. Thus the inevitable tensions and conflicts that would result if such productive efficiency drives were predominant may be modified or muffled if conditions are created in which the capitalist classes of the main core economies are focused upon value-extraction strategies which decentre such efficiency drives. One such strategy would focus upon exploiting cheap labour in the South in the new value-chains which have been the fruits of 'structural adjustment' and WTOism over the last quarter of a century. Another such strategy has been the 'globalization' of financial and business services: Giving the financial operators of the Atlantic states great new fields for the operation of money-capital, not least in the form of speculative arbitrage.[18]

The example which we looked at of economic warfare on the part of the US towards Japan in the 1980s and 1990s suggested that the subjectivity of the leaders of the American capitalist class makes it hyper-sensitive to the threat that some other centre could acquire industrial dominance in a decisive new growth sector such as the Information and Communication Technologies (ICT) was perceived to be in the 1980s and 1990s. Once it became clear that the US had largely won the battle for dominance in ICT in the late 1990s, Washington offered Japan a new framework for cooperation.

At the same time, the Japanese case itself was specific: Here was a ruling class which surrendered its geopolitical orientation entirely to the US after its defeat yet at the same time systematically worked to exploit scale and learning economies to achieve ascendancy at the top of the international industrial division of labour (Johnson 1982 and 1995; Werner 2003). The Japanese state's way of organizing its capitalism for this purpose proved extraordinarily effective, panicked US elites for a decade from the early 1980s and produced a no-holds-barred American drive to systematically reorganize the internal regimes of Japanese capitalism to end this competitive struggle—a drive which has by no means been fully successful.

Tensions in the industrial field generated by the nature of modern productive forces with their huge potential for economies of scale (and scope) and for learning economies are not easily containable in the contemporary period. American hopes that an international financial system offering extraordinary financial gains to the bourgeoisies of the world and thus integrating them culturally under US hegemony have blown up in the Wall Street Crash of 2007–9. At the same time, the possibility of containing such industrial tensions through the ascendancy of the American state over other capitalist centres in the geopolitical field (as their 'protector' or discipliner) has declined as the collapse of the Soviet Bloc and integration of both China and Russia into the world market has weakened the disciplines of an US-centric capitalist world. The efforts of the Bush administration to repair this have evidently backfired. In this context then of the inability of the US to provide a secure world order for the main political-economic centres, all the main centres will tend towards self-strengthening through industrial development with resultant political tensions.

The tensions have been principally active in two zones: firstly, in the main centres of industrial competition in the capitalist core (in other words, the US and Japan and Germany), and; secondly, along the North-South battle line on those fronts where the dominant social groups within states have been driving above all for scale and learning economies. Here, of course, the enormous challenge for the twenty-first century will be that of China's economic and political development. Insofar as China retains a state organized for development it possesses unique potentials to exploit extraordinary scale economies and learning economies and to acquire great state resources for upgrading its production to rise up the international division of labour.

Marx's critical edge

Marx and Engels did not themselves bring out strongly the link between the drive of capitalisms for increasing returns to scale and for learning economies and international political tensions. But they do provide us with the conceptual apparatus for grasping this and most especially for grasping its public-private dimensions. On one side, the gains from scale and learning economies pass into the hands of private owners. On the other hand, public state authorities play a central role in generating and maintaining these economic gains. And they play this role not only through their domestic infrastructure activities but also through their international political action to open markets and to consolidate the market power of their economic operators. Given these economic-political logics for individual states, the result at an interstate level is what we might call an 'armed peace' in the international political economy of the core: each main centre using 'anti-trust' and trade instruments to protect themselves against the possibility of a decisive defeat in the international division of labour as one centre gains a more or less unassailable lead in a key new growth sector.

The result of such an 'armed peace' is a global industrial landscape marked by enormous industrial redundancy (surplus capacity) in sector after sector as each protects its own. At the same time, we find extraordinarily aggressive drives by the core centres of the Atlantic world to open and grab markets in the global South. The liberal solution to these problems is not merely specious—free trade as the road to market domination—it is also quite utopian outside of a world in which one centre overwhelmingly dominates the rest of the world *and* seeks to impose a liberal imperialism of free trade on the rest. The recent Atlantic project for a liberal globalization is simply a joint US-European drive to open the markets of the rest of the world in those sectors—notably high-tech industrial products and business services—where the Atlantic states dominate. And this project is not in evident deep crisis in the WTO and elsewhere.

There is simply no solution to these problems within the field of power politics, never mind trade policy principles. The key to a solution does, however, come into sight if we focus on the taboo topic of the private profits of international industries. If these were socialized under public control at an international level, the terms of the problem begin to be transformed. All countries of the world need semi-conductors of the highest quality and lowest possible cost. Why should not the world semi-conductor industry be organized to achieve these goals in an optimally sustainable way? If the profits of the resulting industry were then distributed among states according to some internationally agreed principle of justice, this could provide the *beginnings* of a transcendence of the international political tensions resulting from industrial development: *All* would gain benefits from optimal global organization of the semi-conductor industry. Such an industrial organization need not be on a monopolistic basis. There could be elements of competition between a semi-conductor Fannie Mae and Freddie Mac.[19] And the resolution of how the profits of such international public organizations should be distributed might be subject to power political distortions, along the road to the emergence of a genuinely global, accountable political authority. But a post-capitalist social logic would have been set in motion, with potentially enormous global efficiency gains.

These were, of course, precisely the kinds of arguments in Marx and Engels' critique of capitalism which pointed towards the necessity of a socialist alternative organization of economic life. Since the collapse of the Soviet Bloc, arguments to the effect that there are more efficient possible forms of social organization of economic life than capitalism have been more or less silenced, at least in the Anglo-American world. The old materialist arguments of the classical political economists to the effect that capitalism was a natural, market mechanism for most efficiently exploiting nature have been faithfully preserved in the discourse of economic globalization: A natural progress of the market and market actors onto a globalized level of economic efficiency in finance and other sectors.

Yet capitalism is not a market mechanism for optimum development of the productive forces. It is a social class system for value-extraction by ruling classes (via market exchange media) and this has no necessary link whatever to economic efficiency: It can fit very well with decades of stagnation or even regression across entire continents, not to speak of a host of worse horrors. Marx's point was not to replace capitalism with a system of manic productivism for its own sake. On the contrary, his goal was human freedom, understood as the expansion of our free time and the reduction of that proportion of our lives chained to the 'realm of necessity'—the struggle to meet our survival needs. But such a leap towards a dramatic reduction of the working day required the fullest possible exploitation of the possibilities of productive efficiency in the economic system, the 'realm of necessity'.

This was, of course, the central *economic* claim which Marx and Engels made for socialism: Its productive superiority over capitalism. By bringing economics under public control, the full possibilities for exploiting economies of scale and learning economies, while eliminating the huge waste of productive forces under capitalism, could be realized. But by and large Marx and Engels wrote on such matters within what might be called a 'national framework' (see, for example, Engels 1962). It was only later with Lenin and Trotsky and other Marxists of the inter-war period that the economic arguments for overcoming the international fragmentation of the capitalist world through socialism became more central. This was, of course, particularly true of Trotsky from the 1920s onwards (see Trotsky 1962).

Conclusion

If the arguments here are valid, then Marx does have strong affinities with what Reinert has called his 'Alternative Canon'. However, he cannot be contained within that tradition because he also includes within his theory all the material usually grouped under the heading of 'market relations' within the mainstream Anglo-Saxon tradition. For Marx, this material is in reality that of the social relations of production within capitalism, understood as a social class system. And that dimension of real modern economic life cannot be other than central to economic dynamics.

The arguments here also contain implications for the debates about imperialism and globalization. For liberalism, imperialism, understood as the domination by one entity over another in the international field, is a power political violation of liberal norms. But the critique of the liberal international economics of free trade made here suggests that such imperial domination may be achieved precisely *through* the implementation of current liberal economic norms. The above arguments also have implications for recent debates about economic globalization and for liberal cosmopolitan theories. They suggest, first, that liberal theories of the role of the state in modern economics are hopelessly thin since they imply that the state's role is largely confined to market regulation. If that was the case, 'economic globalization' transcending the nation-state may be easily achieved via some sort of regulatory 'governance' of markets at a cosmopolitan level. But we have argued that state budgetary resources and diplomatic resources are crucial in fostering and expanding economies of scale and learning economies which are in turn decisive for companies' abilities to dominate markets. If so, cosmopolitan governance that ignores these aspects of state activity which loom so large in national economic life (roughly 40 per cent of National Income in the UK passed through the state sector) is simply another case of liberal pseudo-norms legitimating imperial power politics. Simultaneously, liberal theory gives far too much weight to the supposedly endogenous capacity of firms to gain market dominance: Firms in reality depend upon a wide range of supports from their socio-economic and political environment, not least a wide range of state agencies, in order to mount any challenge in international markets.

This reality also vitiates neo-Weberian theories of economic globalization with their pluralistic stress on the mutual autonomy of states and business organizations, each with its own distinctive 'logic'. On this reading, MNEs expand to the global level, autonomously rationalizing economic life for endlessly improved efficiency, escaping, as far as possible, the constraints of power-maximizing states. In place of such visions of pluralistic logics of different types of organizations, a stress on social systems marked by class dominance and class conflict offers a perspective which shows how states and firms are deeply interlinked in common efforts towards capital accumulation, although how these links are articulated at any given time is a matter for empirical research.

This last point is not a small one for Marxists. Only systematic empirical research can establish which of the various contradictory trends within capitalisms predominate in a given place and time. Marx's entire approach to theorizing the real dynamics of capitalism requires that we can establish the actual, contemporary dynamics only in and through such empirical research. The empirical material in this chapter is far from adequate. But it hopefully suggests some possible leads.

Notes

1 Deriving originally from David Ricardo's theory of natural comparative advantage, its neoclassical variant gained its main current form in the so-called Heckscher-Ohlin Model of international trade. This centres not only on goods produced, but on free mobility for all factors of production (with some qualifications). For a sophisticated mainstream discussion see Feenstra *et al.* (1996)

2 Significant American examples being Samuel Huntington (1992), Robert Gilpin (1987) and Stephen Krasner (1982 and 1999).

3 On increasing returns see in particular see Brett (1983). This book is seminal not only for its treatment of economies of scale but also for its extremely valuable analysis of international monetary relations.

4 Indeed, Schumpeter (1973, 258–59) points out that the first theorist to note and stress economies of scale in manufacturing industry was Antonio Serra in his *Breve Trattato* of 1613. And Serra also figures as a crucial founding father of Erik Reinert's 'alternative cannon'.

5 This is a condensed and simplified account, glossing over such distinctions as those between absolute and relative surplus value. For an excellent summary, see Sweezy, (1968, Chapters 4 and 6).

6 And centralization of capital may be driven not only by the consequences of scale economies but by many other factors of quite different sorts.

7 The neoclassicals try to hide this secret by analytical immediatism and by excluding the range of forces generating increasing returns, such as technological change and learning, the role of the credit system and the roles of the state.

8 Again, I don't think that Marx himself was necessarily hostile to a monopolistic form of organization of modern industry. What he opposed was monopoly under *private capitalist control*. Indeed, part of the argument for a socialist organization of production's greater efficiency surely lies here.

9 It should also be said that even if free trade *were* on the side of development, the benefit that could be claimed for it would be small: a single one-off gain in supposed allocative efficiency. For the sake of argument, let us assume that this gave a one-off gain in productivity of as much as 30 per cent according to neoclassical calculation. That would be a trifling gain in the battle for catch-up through industrial development; a battle that entails

not merely a doubling of productivity but a tenfold increase in productivity. Neoclassical economics simply has had no answer to that development task, except the vague idea of knowledge diffusion from rich to poor countries. On these issues see the excellent discussion in Skarstein (2005).

10 An interesting exploration of this dimension of inter-war rivalries, particularly in relation to US industrial advantages in this area is Chase (2004).

11 They do so through the 1955 West German-American Economic Agreement preparing the way for the end of the US occupation of Germany in the economic field. Under this agreement US capitals had complete freedom to establish economic undertakings in Germany with full 'national rights'—that is, the rights of West German companies. The subsequent Treaty of Rome then gave such US companies free access to the product markets of West Germany's neighbours.

12 For insight into the centrality of the drive for economies of scale in Japanese policy elite thinking, see Murakami (1996).

13 There are also key administrative and accounting rules in the Commerce Department's fair value calculations and these are widely seen as systematically biasing the system towards findings of dumping and toward higher dumping margins (see Boltuck and Litan 1991).

14 For a detailed, but sympathetic account of the use of these measures by the US in the 1980s and early 1990s see Bayard and Elliott (1994).

15 This shift was signalled with the Very High Speed Integrated Circuit Programme (see Alic *et al.* 1992, 269).

16 The resultant US imperative to supply Japanese security should be, in this context, understood as the ability of the US to impose a 'protection racket' on Japan, ensuring Japanese dependence on the US in the military-political field, when in reality Japan has more than adequate state resources for assuring its own security in this field.

17 For a classic historical account of economies of scale and scope in the Atlantic world see Chandler (1990).

18 This strategy, so central to the Anglo-American project for re-organizing core capitalism, has been placed under threat by the financial blow-out of 2007–9.

19 The two state-owned American housing finance corporations.

Part II
Marxism and 'the international'

9 Uneven and combined development

The social-relational substratum of 'the international'? An exchange of letters

Alex Callinicos and Justin Rosenberg[1]

Introduction

What is 'the international' from the point of view of social theory? Can its significance be apprehended from within existing social theories, suitably applied? Or does it necessitate a revision of the most basic shared assumptions of those theories—the 'general abstractions' by which they frame their conception of the social world itself? What, moreover, and in the light of these considerations, is the intellectual and political standing of Realism as an approach to international theory? In the following exchange of letters these questions are debated by two authors who, sharing the language and principles of historical materialism, enter the issue from different directions—and, thus far, with differing results.

Alex Callinicos has, over the years, developed a distinctive argument about the nature of the sociological abstractions deployed by Marx in *Capital* and about the method of applying them to historical events and processes (Callinicos 2001a; 2005d). In this method of 'non-deductive concretization', the international, particularly in the form of the state system, is one among a number of dimensions of the social world which, though not deducible from Marx's concept of 'capital', must (and can) be critically incorporated in the course of his concretization. One of the benefits of such a strategy, Callinicos believes, is that it would permit the integration of a version of the classical Marxist theory of imperialism into a broader theory of the capitalist mode of production.

From a different starting point—from the difficulties encountered by historical sociology in the field of International Relations (IR)—Justin Rosenberg has begun reconstructing and interrogating Leon Trotsky's idea of 'uneven and combined development' (U&CD) (Rosenberg 1996; 2006; 2007). This has led him to claim that the challenges faced by Marxism in IR are in fact generic to the legacy of classical social theory as a whole: they arise from the latter's failure to incorporate the multilinear and interactive dimension of sociohistorical development into its basic conceptions of 'society'. Thus, according to Rosenberg, it is not so much in the application of sociological concepts as in the assumptions already built into them as abstractions of the real world that the nub of the issue lays. The peculiar challenge posed by 'the international' for social theory has been long and widely recognized; distinctive to Rosenberg is his belief that the idea of U&CD may provide a solution.

In 2005, Callinicos participated in a forum on a previous article by Rosenberg (Callinicos 2005d, Rosenberg 2005). When Rosenberg (2007) later sent Callinicos a response to that forum Callinicos' reply included the draft of a third article ('Does Capitalism Need the State System?'). What follows is an edited version of the correspondence that ensued.

Brighton, 6 June 2006

Dear Alex,

I've just read your piece 'Does Capitalism Need the State System?' (Callinicos 2007), and I find it fascinating, not least because of the way that you progressively refine and deepen the issue being addressed. Your title question is of course one that Marxists have often asked themselves. But it's a slippery one nonetheless, because anyone who wants to avoid asserting a merely contingent relation between these two seems driven, by the very form of the question, towards an unhelpfully functionalist kind of answer. So I think you're wise to begin by reformulating the issue as, in effect, 'why has the end of the Cold War not brought about the end of geopolitical competition between states?' And from this alternative starting point, you then proceed to deepen the question, pressing it, on my reading, through two further permutations. First it becomes, roughly: 'how can we integrate the significance of multiple states into Marxist theory without falling into either a reductionism (which misses the causal reality of "the international") or a reification (which, like Realism, treats the existence of multiple states as an independent source of causality)?' And finally, the conundrum reappears in its most elemental form: 'why *are* there many states (Callinicos 2007, 544).

Now, as it stands, your explanation for why geopolitics has not disappeared with the Cold War seems to me a perfectly good one. Capitalism, you argue, necessarily reproduces the political fragmentation of the state system as a by-product of its tendency to 'U&CD'. The shifting historical geography of competition for surplus value gives rise to conflicts of interest among state organizations which are differentially located in the global accumulation process. And that in turn means that accommodations among capitalist states represent adjustments to a given, temporary configuration of power, will likely not outlast that temporary configuration, and at any rate do not signal an approaching supercession of geopolitics through either a world state or a durable ultra-imperialism.

All this strikes me as a creative extension of the classical Marxist theory of imperialism. And yet I sense that something beyond this is also going on in your paper. With your further permutations of the core question—and this is what I find so intriguing— you effectively lead the argument beyond the familiar terrain of Marxist theories of imperialism and onto the adjacent but much less explored territory of Marxism and the question of 'the international' itself. The difference between these two is that while theories of imperialism take the existence of multiple societies as given, and then analyze the forms of domination operating among them,[2] international theory also contains a half-buried question about the causal significance of inter-societal multiplicity *per se*.

In one form or another, *that* question is one to which both hostile and sympathetic critiques of Marxism in IR have returned again and again (Waltz 1959; 1979; Berki 1971; Kubalkova and Cruikshank 1980; 1989; Holsti 1985; Linklater 1990). The 'horizontal' fact of political fragmentation, they have variously argued, generates causal pressures and behavioural patterns which cannot themselves be derived from a theory of the 'vertical' divisions of society into classes, as postulated, for example, by Marx's concept of the 'mode of production'. Attempts to deploy the latter in international theory, therefore, will tend towards one (or both) of two outcomes. Either they will superimpose their *intra*-societal categories of social structure onto *inter*-societal phenomena, thus obscuring whatever determinations might arise from the fact of geopolitical multiplicity itself (the 'fallacy of the domestic analogy' (Bull 1966)). Or they will dilute the claims made for those categories by allowing that an additional 'geopolitical' logic, whose source lies somehow elsewhere, modifies or over-determines the more strictly 'sociological' causes which they nonetheless still prioritize (a problem which might be termed 'proto-realism' (Rosenberg 2006, 337)). Either way, the facticity of 'the international', whether allowed or not, eludes *theorization* by Marxism—as it must, according to these critics, for any 'second image', 'unit-level' form of analysis. And indeed for this latter reason the challenge exists not just for Marxism, but also for all historical sociological approaches to the subject.[3]

How have Marxists in IR responded to this charge? Have we ever tackled it head on? I wonder—and I think you do too.[4] My own impression is that we have more usually sought to turn the tables on the Realist orthodoxy. By this I mean that we have concentrated instead on demonstrating how the social character of this multiplicity (and of its causal mechanisms) has in fact varied crucially according to historical changes in the dominant mode of production.

Certainly, a thumbnail review of the major Marxisant contributions to IR theory seems to confirm this picture. Over time, the classical theory of imperialism has been joined first by Dependency and World Systems Theory, then by 'neo-Gramscian' and other 'Critical' approaches, then by a kind of historical materialism of geopolitics (whether returning directly to Marx (Rosenberg 1994) or via Brenner's restatement of Marxism as a 'theory of social property relations' (Teschke 2003)) and finally, if fleetingly, by Michael Hardt and Antonio Negri's (2000) 'postmodern' reflections on 'Empire', together with other 'globalization'-inspired approaches (Robinson 2001). By now, all this amounts to a very rich tradition of ideas, leaving far behind that 'paucity of Marxist scholarship in IR' which Hazel Smith (1994, 145) felt obliged to report as late as 1994.[5] And yet, insofar as it has addressed the central question of IR—the generic significance of inter-societal multiplicity—the direction of the argumentation has remained almost entirely one-way:[6] from the unique historical form of capitalist society to the no less distinctive character of its international relations. And this, as you yourself imply at one point, still 'begs the question' (Callinicos 2007, 15) of plurality itself. In this sense, what Marxism (and other non-Realist approaches) have yet to provide is a *sociological* answer to the question of why the 'international' dimension of social reality exists in the first place.[7] Lacking this, we seem to be driven either to discount its generic effects or, since we can't derive them from our existing categories, to concede an irreducible reality to them, opening the door once again to Realism.

Now, as you know, I've recently come to the conclusion in my own work (Rosenberg 2006) that Trotsky's term U&CD, which you apply to the social logic of capital, simultaneously captures, at a more general level, a sociological characteristic of all historical development; furthermore, that it is this sociological characteristic— entailing, as it does, an inner differentiation and interactivity to the historical process—that accounts for the transhistorical fact of geopolitical multiplicity; and finally, that this claim—present, but not worked through, in Trotsky's own writings[8]— might hold a solution to the intellectual problems which Marxism has faced in IR.

But here's the rub: if we say that in some wider sense *all* development is 'uneven and combined', then I think two important qualifications might have to follow concerning your own argument.

First, the issues of why capitalism does not end political multiplicity and why multiplicity exists in the first place overlap but are no longer fully co-extensive. Hence—referring to page 544 of your article—I'd be driven to say that the question 'Why are there many states?' is not (as your 'or' seems to imply) fully reducible to the question 'is there anything inherent in capitalism that tends to keep states plural?'

And second, it might also follow that the 'place' where Marxism (or any other historical sociology) really needs to broach the issue of 'the international' is not, in the first instance, at the level of its theory of capitalism (or 'modernity'),[9] but rather at the more fundamental level of historical materialism itself (or whatever other general abstractions of the historical process are being used). Only then, I think, can one avoid a situation in which the transhistorical circumstance of multiplicity evades theorization at the start, only to return later in the reified form of proto-Realist premises.

Now, I must say that your own intellectual method—progressive but non-deductive concretization—is an ingenious way of controlling for the effects of this problem: It allows for the determinacy of the geopolitical while denying it substantive autonomy. But my question then would be: what exactly is the standing of the determinations that are admitted to the argument in what you describe as the necessary 'realist moment' of a Marxist analysis of IR? To put it another way: where comes the positive non-Realist *theorization* of the geopolitical determinations, which Realism rightly emphasizes but wrongly conceptualizes? After all, just because liberal approaches to IR have infinitely more to say than Realism about the significance of the international economy, we don't correspondingly conclude that there must be a necessary 'liberal moment' to a Marxist analysis of IR. Why should Realist theory be 'cleaner' in this respect, less needful of fundamental reformulation? Or am I being unfair here?

Personally, I think we ought to be able to crack the shell of this reification ('geopolitics') and resolve its contents back into generative sociological categories. But because its historical referent extends back beyond capitalism, that can't be done exhaustively by working from a theory of capitalist development alone. Elaborating U&CD as, in the first instance, a *general* abstraction of the historical process is the only means I've yet found for getting behind this problem in order to crack the reification in its generality (rather than just controlling its effects in the particular cases of Absolutism or capitalism). I try to illustrate this in the 'Interim Synopsis' of the idea contained in my rejoinder to the 'Globalization Theory' forum (Rosenberg 2007).

So I guess this is the difference between our positions: your position implies, I think, that at any rate there's a great deal more to be said about how capitalism in particular generates U&CD—and I'm sure that's right. My position—mostly a hunch since I haven't done enough of the work yet—is that even when that 'more' is said, the fact of multiplicity itself and what arises from it will not have been addressed in a way that finally deals with the problem of Realism (and with it, the problem of 'the international' for social theory). Hence my enormous, continuing detour through the idea of U&CD as a 'general abstraction'. Perhaps we'll meet in the middle at some future point—what do you think?

All the best,

Justin

Brighton, 9 June 2006

Dear Justin,

Thanks for your letter, which I found very stimulating. My interim report on the puzzling ideas you have provoked follows:

1. In a general sense, the answer to your concluding question must be yes: we will 'meet in the middle at some future point'. In principle, there are multiple strategies for 'crack[ing] the shell of this [and other] reification[s]'. Proceeding by 'general abstraction' and a more 'mode of production' focused analysis are on the face of it mutually compatible strategies.

2. I do, however, have a preference for my strategy, just as you have for yours. In my case this reflects the following thought: 'general abstractions' are a necessary part of any conceptual construction in social theory and it is important to acknowledge this rather than kid oneself that one can historicize everything, as with the traditional Marxist hostility to the idea of human nature. So I think it is fine and, as you have amply shown, fruitful to explore U&CD as a constitutive dimension of the social. But general abstractions do at the same time carry a risk, recognition of which is the justification for the hostility just referred to—namely that they may give rise to essentialisms that deduce transhistorical elements of the social from supposed properties of human nature. I understand that you are precisely seeking to avoid this in your own, strongly historical treatment of U&CD, but this doesn't alter the fact that the danger exists.

My preferred strategy for (to borrow one of your formulations) controlling for essentialism is not to deny the existence of general abstractions, but to seek to contextualize their referents' operation relative to the structures of some mode of production. This is why I like Brenner's concept of political accumulation:[10] it provides a materialist way of accounting for part of the extension of your concept of 'multiplicity'—premodern state-building—by invoking the rules of reproduction of actors in precapitalist production relations (my way of putting it, not his) that avoids any appeal to human nature or the 'will to power' or whatever. I think it is likely that when you move from identifying the wider patterns of U&CD you have discussed to explaining them you are likely to push in the direction of mode of production analysis of this kind (or perhaps a more complex form of such analysis involving more than one mode of production in the case, for example the interactions between empires and nomads or of the expansion of European feudalism into its Irish and East European peripheries). Or, if you don't move this way, you would have to give some account of the kind of alternative explanations on which you relied and of how these avoid the problem of essentialism. But my hunch is that once you seriously explore the inter-societal across some large span of space and time you will be pushed toward cashing general abstractions into more historically specific mode of production-based analyses (all this is of course a gross oversimplification: any mode of production analysis would have to be combined with all sorts of other things to produce a plausible historical interpretation).

3. Your challenge about the 'realist moment' is a really good one: I have greatly enjoying thinking about how to reply to your question why 'we don't correspondingly conclude that there must be a necessary "liberal moment" to a Marxist analysis of IR'. I have a strong and weak answer.

The weak answer is that we should so conclude because there *is* a liberal moment, if not in the 'Marxist analysis of IR', then in the larger theory of the capitalist mode of production. We can situate it in the stage of Marx's argument in *Capital* Volume I, Part 1, where he analyzes the structure of generalized commodity production without positing that labour-power is a commodity. This is famously 'the exclusive realm of Freedom, Equality, Property and Bentham', which is subverted once Marx (to put it in Hegelese) posits the presupposition and introduces labour-power as a commodity, so leading to exploitation and the rest.[11] One might also see the liberal moment in those famous passages in the *Communist Manifesto* and the *Grundrisse* where Marx highlights the revolutionary and progressive character of capitalism (Marx 2002; 1973).

My strong answer is that while of course liberalism and Realism are both theoretical ideologies, liberalism is in quite a different class from Realism. It is a much richer and more complex ideology with far more normative resources and the conceptual range denoted by such names as Locke, Smith, Kant, Hegel, Tocqueville, Mill, Keynes, Hayek and Rawls. By comparison, Realism is a much thinner ideology, which may be why it is so easy for contemporary exponents such as Waltz (1979) and Mearsheimer (2001) to axiomatize it. It can be worked up into something more dramatic when conjoined with Nietzsche's ontology or Weber's sociology, but, on its own, its theoretical content it is not 'cleaner' than liberalism, but much more limited.

I'm inclined to think of Realism as a theoretical articulation of the spontaneous ideology of state managers (which is pretty obvious in the case of its contemporary influence on American policy intellectuals). To that extent it's like neoclassical economics, whose ancestor vulgar political economy Marx criticizes for systematizing the forms in which capital appears 'on the surface of society, ... in competition, and in the ordinary consciousness of the agents of production themselves' (Marx 1959, 25; this may help to explain why both are so hospitable to rational choice theory). So Realism is a bit like the kind of conceptualizations of capitalism derived from the perspective of actors on the financial market. If you take these conceptualizations at face value, you get—as Marx points out when discussing the credit system in *Capital*, Volume III—the most fetishized form of capital. He doesn't deny the kind of self-understanding that actors on the financial markets have *any* reality (the credit system does function, financial assets do allow their holders to appropriate a portion of total surplus-value and so on), but seeks to expose its limitations by setting them in the context of capitalist production relations as a totality.

So why can't one think of Realism in the same way: as a cluster of theories that articulate the self-understanding of a specific set of actors (the managers of the state system) and that are therefore not completely false, but that first require contextualization within the larger theory of the capitalist mode of production and of its historical development (including the intersection of economic and interstate competition)? This doesn't mean simply sticking realist concepts and axioms undigested into a Marxist discourse on capitalism and imperialism, but one way to reformulate concepts is to set them alongside other, unfamiliar concepts.

I'm really grateful to you for forcing me to think through the implications of my position, and would be interested in any further thoughts you had about all this, though I will, of course, quite understand if (particularly because of the piles of scripts that the suspension of the exam boycott has dislodged)[12] you would prefer to call it a day.

All the best,

Alex

Brighton, 17 July 2006

Dear Alex,

Many thanks for your latest comments. Their clarity and pertinence have been really helpful in pushing me to try and pinpoint exactly why I find the idea of U&CD so significant. Reading through my responses set out below, I see that they return again and again to different versions of the same point—a fact which I hope illustrates the many implications of this point, rather than just wearying you with excessive repetition. I'm also struck by the following thought: because you yourself fruitfully invoke Trotsky's idea in your recent article in these pages, it may be that our difference will eventually reduce to one of degree. At any rate, I shall try below to convince you that the implications of this idea are wider, deeper and, in a way, more indispensable to the success of your own arguments than your usage of it so far implies.

As I see it, you've raised three basic issues for us to discuss: the liabilities of working with general abstractions; the ways in which a more mode of production-based approach might deal with 'the international' as an issue; and finally, the question of how to construe the relationship between Marxism and Realism in international theory. Perhaps inevitably, it was while trying to respond to the last of these that matters really came to a head for me. But since some necessary clarifications were also forced by your other reflections, I shall work through the three issues in their existing order.

The danger of general abstractions

I must begin by noting a large area of agreement. General abstractions, as you say, are both necessary and risky—permanently prone, in fact, to essentialism, reification and Robinsonades.[13] This means that their relationship to other, more 'concrete' categories—and to empirical reality itself—requires extremely careful positioning. The idea of U&CD has given me no end of grief on this score, not least because, like any general abstraction, it can appear to say everything and nothing at the same time. But, for what it's worth, my current assessment of this 'everything' and 'nothing' is as follows.

At the most basic level, U&CD formulates a much-needed alternative conception of the historical process. It invokes that dynamic, interactive (Trotsky would say 'dialectical') texture of social reality from which, arguably, both the unsociological Realist conception of 'the geopolitical' and sociology's monadic, unilinear conception of 'society' are one-sided and intrinsically misshapen abstractions.

If this latter diagnosis is correct, it would help explain why the specifically methodological challenge of extending an historical sociological method into the field of IR has proven so intractable: this challenge must initially take the form of trying to reintegrate two dimensions of social reality by using the very same conceptions (of 'geopolitics' and 'society') through which, at a deeper theoretical level, these dimensions have been externalized from each other. The record suggests that this approach does not work. Either it leads back to the fallacy of the 'domestic analogy' where liberal and Marxist sociologies of international relations have traditionally been accused of ending up (Bull 1966), or, as I suggested in my previous letter, the interpolation of 'the international' takes the form of a proto-Realist *deus ex machina* which leaves 'the international' itself untheorized in sociological terms—arguably the point reached by such 'neo-Weberian' writers as Charles Tilly, Theda Skocpol and Michael Mann.

In such a situation, with the classical inheritance spent to so little avail, we seem entitled to consider more drastic solutions. Perhaps what we actually need is not a combination or rebalancing of existing concepts—not even the 'dialectical' one you cite Harvey as proposing (Callinicos 2007, 539–40)—but a more radical reconceptualizing of the nature of the historical process itself in order to remove the intellectual source of the antimony. And this, I believe, is what Trotsky's idea provides. By positing 'development' ontologically as the subject matter of the analysis, it identifies the evolution of social structures in historical time as the basis of its explanatory method. It comprises in that sense an emphatically historical sociological conception. However, by simultaneously asserting the 'uneven and combined character' of that development overall, it recovers for social theory those properties of multilinearity and interactivity which would otherwise unavoidably give rise to a sociologically impregnable and rival discourse of geopolitical explanation. I know of no other idea that can do this. And I think it should follow that by concretizing *this* general abstraction—rather than those of 'anarchy' or 'society' which have underpinned the disciplines of IR and sociology—we can finally formulate *sociologically* exactly that dimension of human social existence with which Realism has always been able to trump attempts at sociological explanation in IR.

Yet here, hard on the heels of the 'everything', comes the 'nothing'. By itself, axiomatic assertion of the multilinear and interactive character of human social development cannot tell us much at all at the level of concrete historical explanation, and it cannot provide the basis of a substantive social theory. By itself, after all, it lacks any tools for specifying the causal properties of those processes of social life to whose multiplicity and interaction it draws attention. Whatever the importance of this idea, therefore, it cannot operate as a replacement for the classical social theories whose limitations we are trying to overcome. In fact, without being attached to one of these—historical materialism for example—it cannot reach down to the level of concrete historical explanation at all. The intellectual results of any attempt to turn the general *abstraction* into a general *theory* of U&CD would thus be very slight indeed.[14] In a similar way, and for similar reasons, Kenneth Waltz could squeeze no more than a highly general 'permissive' causality from his early reflection on the international system as a level of determination in its own right (Waltz 1959). Yet there is a difference too.

Waltz took the conceptual determinacy of 'the international' as a warrant for theorizing it in abstraction from 'the social'. For me, by contrast, the significance of U&CD lies in its utility for exactly the opposite exercise: namely, for reintegrating 'the international' within the remit of 'the social'. And although this does, as Trotsky's own analyses showed, have considerable intellectual consequences for social theory, radically transforming any logic of historical process derived from it, the overall balance of the equation does, as you suggest, need firm reiteration. More than just an *ad hoc* caveat for the variety of historical circumstances, but less than a replacement for existing social theory, Trotsky's idea provides the anterior assumptions about the texture of the historical process in which existing theories need to be regrounded if they are to avoid the 'domestic analogy' problem and find their way through to concrete historical explanations of international relations.

The conclusion I draw from this is as follows. While general abstractions are both necessary and risky, we also can and must distinguish among the variety on offer to us in terms of how intellectually 'fit for purpose' they are. A general abstraction of 'society' as singular is not fit for general use.[15] Harmless though it might be for some forms of analysis, its limitations are starkly exposed whenever it comes anywhere near the field of IR. Nothing requires that the conception of 'society' presupposed in Marx's concept of the capitalist mode of production should be a singular one. Equally, however, nothing in Marx's thought prevents it from being assumed to be such. And most Marxist approaches in international theory have in fact left this assumption itself untouched. Trotsky's idea corrects this problem at the level where it needs to be corrected—at the level of the general abstraction itself. By positing unevenness as general, it sublates the resultant fact of inter-societal coexistence into a reformulated general abstraction of society as multiple and interactive. Here, I think, we might possibly agree.

Limits of a mode of production approach

Still, one upshot of all this is that, as you rightly say, my own line of argument cannot, in principle, generate historical explanations until it is brought into relation with a 'more mode of production-focused analysis'. Why then do I remain inclined to start with the general abstraction, rather than following your own 'preferred strategy' of beginning with the historically specific forms of social development?

The reason relates to your comment on 'Brenner's concept of political accumulation'—the concept by which he links the geopolitical struggle for territorial acquisition in medieval Europe to the 'extra-economic' form of surplus extraction characterizing the feudal mode of production. This provides, you say, 'a materialist way of accounting for part of the extension of your concept of "multiplicity"'. Agreed, but that's a very judicious formulation! Exactly which part does it account for—and which not? I would say it accounts somewhat for the sociohistorical *form* of multiplicity (and thus of geopolitical interaction), but not for the *fact* of it. Does this really matter?

I didn't use to think so. I used to think that in the face of Realism's ahistorical claims about geopolitics, historical materialist demonstrations of the changing social forms and dynamics of geopolitical behaviour were all that was required. Now I'm not so sure. As I wrote in my last letter, if the fact of geopolitical multiplicity extends historically beyond any individual form of society then any determinations arising from that fact itself will in principle elude derivation from the particularities of any given mode of production, or even—if such an exercise were possible—of each and all of them considered individually and serially. For the fact itself is not particular, but general (and perhaps therefore something general remains uncaptured—even about contemporary capitalist geopolitics—by your argument about the historical 'subsumption' of interstate competition 'under that between capitals' (Callinicos 2007, 541)).

Yet, what determinations *do* arise from that fact? Here of course I must beware the essentialism that you rightly warn against. So the limit on what I can say is: that all societies coexist with and interact with others, and that this super-adds a lateral field of causality over and above the 'domestic' determinations arising from each and every one of the participant societies. I cannot from this specify in principle how wide the margin of difference opened up by that 'over and above' will be. In Trotsky's analysis of capitalist development, it turned out to be enormous. But the real issue here is not the scale of difference in any given case, so much as its existence in every case: there *are* no societies whose development has not been fundamentally inflected by relations with others. And there *is* no case of a wider social formation whose developmental trajectory does not include a significant dimension composed of the course of interactions among its parts. We all know this empirically; on what grounds has it been excluded from our theoretical abstractions of 'society' and 'historical process'?

Pressed to choose between Brenner's 'concept of political accumulation' and a Realist explanation of medieval geopolitics, I would do everything I could to avoid making a choice. I would rather turn to Perry Anderson's (1974a) *Passages from Antiquity to Feudalism*. There, the dimension I'm referring to is incorporated via a nomenclature of differentiated, interactive temporalities of development within a wider social formation. And the result, *inter alia*, is that historical unevenness plays a quite crucial theoretical role (not least in the climactic explanation of the 'second serfdom'[16]), and in ways that could not be approached by invoking 'political accumulation' (or, in Anderson's case, 'parcellised sovereignty') alone.

Thus my second conclusion is that if we're going to 'meet in the middle', we both have (if I may borrow your term) a 'non-deductive' leap to make. I must, and do, accept that the general abstraction of U&CD cannot furnish the particularities of any given mode of production, which, I also agree, are necessary for the general abstraction to be 'cashed in'. But I suspect that you will also reach a point where the acknowledgment of the inter-societal is not something fully derivable from any conventional mode of production approach. And I think U&CD can solve both problems—mine, because the subject of the predicates 'uneven' and 'combined' remains 'development' and that means that this general abstraction can *only* be concretized by specifying particular historical structures—and yours because, conversely, the operation of those same predicates on 'mode of production' means that the inter-societal, and all that goes with it, need not be encountered as a theoretical externality.

To put it another way, there turns out to be not one but two sources of essentialized conceptions of geopolitics of which we must beware. One, as you indicate, comes from misapplication of a general abstraction. The other, however, has a quite different origin: It operates by default whenever the inter-societal dimension is not explicitly included in the definition of 'the social' itself. For then geopolitical effects, which are generated beyond the reach of the given 'social' theory, seem to take on either a contingent (hence ungeneralizable) or a strictly supra-sociological appearance.

This, incidentally, is why I'm uneasy with attempts to solve the problem by invoking what you call 'the intersection of economic and interstate competition'. Exactly where, after all (since you yourself allow it an existence extending back beyond its 'subsumption' under capitalism), does the 'interstate competition' *come* from? Perhaps I'm mistaken, but I don't think this question can be answered entirely by working 'upwards' from a conventional mode of production-type approach. And at least part of my preference for starting at the other end (with the general abstraction) derives from a professional predicament: working in IR, one inevitably confronts this question very early in any enquiry. Indeed, little else can be 'cashed in' until it is answered.

This brings me to your two ingenious arguments for a 'Realist moment' of Marxist analysis. It may be that I have mis- or over-interpreted these arguments. But at any rate, I have hugely benefited from them; they have forced me to work out in some detail what I now think about Realism. My reasoning may well have gone awry. If you can show me how, I'll be yet further indebted to you. If not, however, I think we may both have quite a lot more thinking to do about the relationship between Marxism and IR.

The status of realism

I'd like to bracket out for a while your 'strong answer' (about liberal riches and Realist poverty), and concentrate first on the methodological parallel you draw concerning Marx's critique of liberalism.

Yes, Marx described the categories of bourgeois economics as 'socially adequate' (Marx 1976, 169), faithfully reflecting the phenomenal or 'surface' form in which the essential relations of capitalist society appear to their agents. Hence, in any intellectual journey from 'the surface' to 'the depths', there will indeed be a 'liberal moment' as we pass through a layer of appearances that are both real and mystifying. Why, you ask, can't we view Realism—'the spontaneous ideology of state managers'—in the same terms? Allowing it a 'moment' would enable us both to take due account of the 'interstate competition' on which it focuses *and* then to 'expose its limitations by setting them in the context of capitalist production relations as a totality'.

As you'd expect, I have instinctive sympathy for this proposal. But I also have a problem with it, which I'll try to draw out in three steps.

First, as you point out, the 'liberal moment' in *Capital* is rapidly subverted as Marx digs deeper into its presuppositions. Although it retains an authentic *connection* to reality—as a 'form of appearance'—its *explanatory* standing dwindles in the face of an alternative discourse (the 'critique of political economy') which asserts it to be the mystified expression of something else which its own categories cannot comprehend. If the 'Realist moment' you propose for the 'Marxist analysis of IR' is a parallel to this, then would we not also have to include a long, long 'after-moment' of deconstruction? Isn't Realism too 'an enchanted, perverted, topsy-turvy world' of appearances in which, to paraphrase Marx, *Monsieur le Souverein* and *Madame la Balance de Pouvoir* 'do their ghost-walking as social characters and at the same time directly as mere things' (Marx 1959, 830)?[17] You do say of your proposal that '[t]his doesn't of course mean simply sticking realist concepts and axioms undigested into a Marxist discourse on capitalism and imperialism. ... ' But I'm still not yet clear exactly where in the process of critical co-optation of Realism this 'digestion' occurs, and into what elements Realist categories are broken down.

Second, this may be just terminological but I can't help feeling that in order to facilitate the analogy (between the critiques of liberalism and Realism) you may have loosened the definition of Marx's method beyond what you yourself might wish. Yes, one way of describing Marx's critique of liberal ideas is to say that it sets 'them in the context of capitalist production relations as a totality'. But that, I think you'd agree, is a broad description of the result, rather than a tight definition of the method. The latter is approached more nearly when you say that the realm of liberal ideology is 'subverted once Marx ... posits the presupposition'.

Now, I wonder whether these two spatial metaphors (the horizontal one of widening contextualization, and the vertical one of surface and depth) don't actually reflect two different intellectual procedures: the latter being Marx's method for the *construction* of a dialectical abstraction and the former being your own method (and possibly his too) for the *re-concretization* of an abstraction. One could argue that in *Capital* both of these are happening at the same time, but I want, if only for purposes of self-clarification, to separate them out for a moment.

One can, as many of us have tried to show, take the 'vertical' approach and 'posit' capitalist social relations as the 'presupposition' of the abstracted 'sovereign' form of the modern state (and, by extension, state system).[18] But my sense is that although you'd agree with that, it's not quite what you're proposing here. When you rightly say that 'one way in which concepts are reformulated is when they are set alongside other, unfamiliar concepts', I *think* you have in mind the procedure of non-deductive concretization outlined in your 2001 paper (Callinicos 2001a). There the emphasis is upon showing how capitalist determinations reach into zones of social reproduction whose generic properties are not deducible from the concept of capital itself—and whose incorporation correspondingly introduces additional, irreducible logics of their own into an increasingly concrete concept of capital (indeed, you cite this irreducibility as both legitimate and advantageous, and I can see why).

Now, each of these two procedures might conclude that Realism is a 'spontaneous ideology'—either of the abstracted, capitalist form of state or of some more generic, limited 'worldview' of 'state managers'. But, as I must try now to elaborate in my third step, I no longer think that, either singly or in combination, this says quite enough. To explain what I mean by this, and to answer my own earlier question about what a 'digestion' of Realism might involve, I too would like to draw an analogy with Marx's method.

Once again, I begin with some points on which I think we agree. Central to Marx's method, as you say, is the positing of an undiscovered social-relational substratum to apparently self-evident phenomena and categories, a positing which then generates a radically alternative explanatory idiom. Significantly, however, the first such exercise in *Capital* comes long before any mention of wage labour, or any explicit critique of liberalism. And although it turns out to have enormous consequences for the latter, its scope, as the exuberant claim to have bettered Aristotle himself implies (Marx 1976, 151–52), is far wider. I'm referring of course to Marx's opening engagement with the question: what is the substance of value?[19]

It's logical that this question must precede the more apparently consequential one of 'what is *surplus* value?', which comes later. Less immediately obvious, though subject to incessant demonstrations, is Marx's assertion that previous attempts to answer this question—let alone our everyday assumptions about its answer—involve either naturalistic or metaphysical premises which, as soon as they are made explicit, are manifestly untenable. The challenge, then, is to identify a human relational content to the exchange of things that could explain what 'their' value is as a 'social substance'.

And the first part of Marx's answer is where I want to build my analogy. This part is worked out, not by reference to 'the totality of capitalist production relations', but through interrogation of what Marx calls the 'the simple, isolated or accidental form of value' (Marx 1976, 139–54). Here, he says, the hardest part of the question is already posed. In an oft-misunderstood claim, Marx observes that in any act of exchange, the relation of equivalence posited between the things exchanged in fact simultaneously relates as equivalent whatever human activities have brought the objects of exchange to this point. Of course, and despite his use of the term, this is not yet 'value'. The relational substance of value—'socially necessary abstract labour time'—comes into systematic being only with modern capitalist society. And in fact, there's a world of difference between saying that human productive activities are passively equated to each other as an *effect* of exchange and saying that this relation between them actively conditions the process of exchange itself (hence, I think, the misunderstandings). But why then analyze 'simple value' at all? Answer: because a crucial element of the phenomenon that Marx is anatomizing—though it becomes truly significant only in the developed (capitalist) case—is already present, *in nuce,* in every instance of exchange.

There is, Marx argues, something peculiar about the form taken by any human relation—even if momentary, inadvertent and inconsequential—when it is mediated by the exchange of things. On the one hand, it is inverted: an actual social relation between persons (for things cannot exchange themselves) appears as a quantitative relation between things, governed by the imputed properties—material or spiritual— of the things themselves. And on the other hand, this perceptual reification expresses a real 'objectification' of human agency: it is, after all, intrinsic to exchange as a human act that it is inverted and refracted through 'the instrumentality of things' in this way. Still, it is a riddle with a solution, not an illusion without substance. And according to Marx, it is a riddle that must be solved if the real but mystified surface appearance of capitalist relations is to be penetrated sociologically.

For it is this peculiar potential of inversion and reification, latent in all exchange relations, which is uniquely activated into a generalized phenomenology by the capitalist form of society; this is due to the central role of exchange in production relations themselves. Thus his opening analysis of the inverted relational architecture of exchange *per se* becomes a crucial sociological key to the 'hieroglyphic' of capitalist sociality.[20] Without it, we would have no cognitive procedure for revealing the inverted, reified (capitalist) *relations* encased in the otherwise irreducible materiality of things and their movement. And without *that,* the theory of *surplus* value would be, well, vulgar: all mathematics and no ontology (indeed, Marx does later—climactically in his discussion of the Trinity Formula—suggest that 'wage labour' itself is a mystified category).

Now, the analogy I wish to draw here with geopolitics is imperfect in many ways (interpersonal and inter-societal relations are, after all, quite different orders of phenomenon). Yet I do think the requirement we face—and even something of the solution—is the same. In both cases, what looks like an elemental datum of social reality—exchange of things on the one hand, geopolitical interaction on the other—in fact secrets a further layer of relational constitution which must be excavated *sociologically* if the datum in question is not to licence a reifying discourse of 'vulgar economy' or Realist geopolitics. Moreover, in both cases, what Marx elsewhere calls the perceptual mechanism of *'camera obscura'* (Marx and Engels 1976, 36), which makes the appearance seem irreducible, derives not from any given historical form of the datum, but from properties inherent in that particular kind or fragment of human sociation in general. Whenever things are exchanged, in whatever kind of society, the inverted, reified form of social relation which capitalist society uniquely develops into the 'social substance' of value is momentarily, even if inertly, posited. It is a latent sociological property of exchange relations *per se*.[21] Something parallel, I shall suggest below, can be said—and must be excavated—concerning inter-societal relations.

Well, you and I would agree that Marx solved his riddle—but can we now solve ours? '[I]t is', say Thucydides' Athenians to their Melian victims,

> A general and necessary law of nature to rule wherever one can. This is not a law that we made ourselves, nor were we the first to act upon it when it was made.

We found it already in existence, and we shall leave it to exist for ever among those who come after us. We are merely acting in accordance with it, and we know that you or anybody else with the same power as ours would be acting in precisely the same way.

(Thucydides 1972, 404–5)

How can we prevent this statement from legitimating—as Realist thought *does* legitimate—a notion of geopolitics as both *sui generis* and extra- or even supra-sociological? Invoking an intersecting 'interstate logic' seems to me only to restate the problem, which, if we strip away the historically (and anthropologically) limited form of relations between states, now reduces to the following question: what *is* geopolitics, *sociologically*?

And here there is a real parting of the ways. One path leads indeed to a pragmatic accommodation: There is a 'Realist moment' to any developed sociological analysis because the geopolitical 'level' or 'dimension' exists and must be included, not least because its effects handily extend the grounds for a critique of liberalism. Viewed from any starting point outside the discipline of IR, this must appear as (and indeed often is) a genuine augmentation of a sociological analysis. Viewed from *inside* IR, however, talk of a 'Realist moment' appears, however unintentionally, to give the game away. For as you know, within IR, treating geopolitics, however pragmatically, as an elemental datum of reality is precisely what we're up against. The imputation of autonomous behavioural properties to political entities—whether derived from their nature or from the structure of their coexistence—lends an irreducible, thing-like quality to geopolitics. From this, Realism distils a power-political essence that is simultaneously as sociologically impossible (states do not subsist autonomously) and yet as empirically inexpungeable (states do behave power-politically) as the idea that things have values. I find this echo telling: surely some 'objectification' is at work here. But objectification of what? And how?

This question leads us onto the other path, which points to some kind of parallel to the exercise performed by Marx on the sociology of exchange. But how? How can we break down, or subsume, the *fact* of geopolitics sociologically without dissolving its determinacy and social reality? This is the question which sociological approaches to IR have been unable to answer. It drives them, if they reject the pragmatic accommodation mentioned above, into one version or another of 'domestic analogy'. Thus, if we don't want to end up with either an essentialized or a reductionist notion of geopolitics, we need to posit a presupposition here—one which, like Marx's presupposition of an inverted human relational content to the exchange of things, can provide a sociological key to the hieroglyphic of Thucydidean Realism. *Hic Rhodus, hic salta!*[22] Needless to say, I would not dare propose such a challenge if I didn't think we already had the answer to it, but such an answer is exactly what U&CD, worked through as a *general* abstraction, enables.

In my view, the point about 'unevenness' is not in the first instance that it posits inequalities and differences *among* coexisting societies; it is rather that, posited of social development, it makes sense of the existence of a *plurality* of societies in the first place—and with that, of the extension of a lateral field of interaction which is both intrinsic to, and behaviourally distinct within, the expanded conception of social development now posited.

I wish I could say that positing unevenness is a big theoretical discovery, but I can't. For on the one hand, it is a matter of mere historical record that the unevenness of human development has always found expression in a multiplicity not just of the forms, levels, shapes and sizes of society but also, somehow crucially, of its numerical instances; that a number of these instances therefore always coexist concretely in historical time; that all societies thus confront the fact that the human world extends beyond themselves; and that the resultant imperative to manage the 'outside' world, if only minimally for reasons of survival, compels them into interaction with each other, which in turn is part-constitutive of what they are as societies. In sum, a strategic interactive dimension is intrinsic to development itself. And on the other hand, the enormous theoretical difference made by conceding these empirical points is almost entirely achieved by simply *avoiding* the negative results that their neglect has produced in existing social theories.

Still, the theoretical moral must be drawn, before it escapes and is lost again in the empirical obviousness of all this. The very existence of 'geopolitics', its imputed transhistorical 'logics', and its varying forms and causal weight, can all be explained via a generative sociological presupposition—the first two by reasoning from the *general* abstraction of U&CD and the third by developing *concrete* abstractions of the latter's particular historical configurations. For what has been objectified in Realism is the strategic dimension of development—a dimension whose existence in fact expresses the 'uneven and combined character' of development itself.

As with Marx's argument about 'value', the real trick of this point is to see that the question is even there—that there must be a sociological substratum to the fact of geopolitics, rather than just to its changing forms—and that not to pose this question leaves one with unwittingly essentialized assumptions. Indeed it seems to follow that without the idea of U&CD (or some equivalent), the Marxist theory of imperialism—or indeed *any* theory of geopolitics—is rather like the theory of surplus value without the theory of value itself. It is 'vulgar' in the strict Marxian sense that it operates with reifying categories for which it has not yet found the critical presupposition that needs to be posited. But then here, as I shall hint again several times below, one would be hard pressed to argue that Marx himself provided the actual presupposition which is needed (hence my suggestion, in the opening paragraph of this letter, that the importance of Trotsky's idea for the problems you and I are both trying to tackle may be far greater than any restriction of it to capitalist geopolitics allows).

Where then does the objectification come from? Clearly, the perceptual and real objectifications of geopolitics are not the *same* as those intrinsic to exchange. But, to complete the analogy, they have this much in common: In both cases, there is a sociologically intelligible reason, rendered visible by the presupposition, which explains why the basic ontology of the phenomenon is initially obscured from its own agents. In the case of geopolitics, the reason is that U&CD actually does constitute its agents as political subjects of a simultaneously fragmented but interactive historical process. Within the resultant fragments homogenizing and centripetal processes obtain (not a few sustained by the existence of a differentiated outside), which appear, *post festum*,[23] to constitute the nature of society itself. Outside, among the fragments, but nonetheless arising from the selfsame fragmentation, different circumstances, and hence forms of behaviour, apply, generating the appearance of a supra-sociological realm. Because reflection begins from within, it is always the inter-societal which appears as different—a dimension which must either be reduced (analytically or practically) to the likeness of the domestic, or else asserted as autonomous and *sui generic*. But actually, the multiplicity of the inter-societal is no less intrinsic to this process than is the inward singularity of any individual fragment. Neither is any more or less definitive of 'the social' than the other.

Well, I've tied a bit of a knot for myself here, one that I must now undo if I'm to draw a line under the argument so far. Have I not myself, in the foregoing pages, added a large argument of my own *in favour* of a 'Realist moment'? I find this tricky to answer, but I think the long and the short of it may be as follows. We can, after all, speak coherently of a 'Realist moment' to social analysis in a manner somewhat analogous to the 'liberal moment' you identify in the downward journey of Marx's argument in *Capital*. But, like the liberal moment, the Realist one is a symptom of a problem, not a formula for a cure. Moreover—*cave! Hic draconis!*[24]— the presupposition which needs to be posited in order to 'get to the bottom' of the phenomena which Realism describes is not the same as the one used by Marx to break through to the relational substance of value—and it cannot be found in *Capital*. This spells possible danger, I think, for your (otherwise very compelling) method of non-deductive concretization. It raises the possibility that the mystified 'moment' will be incorporated, undigested, for lack of the analytical means to break it down. And this leads me back to my earlier suspicion that the issue of the geo-political cannot be fully grasped from within a theory of capital. For by then, in a way, it's too late: the problem itself, and its solution, belong at a higher level—that of the general abstractions of historical materialism itself. To put it another way— and in some tension perhaps with your claim elsewhere about the legitimate irreducibility of a geopolitical logic—geopolitical categories *can* be translated back into a generative sociological discourse, but only if the latter has already been reformulated by incorporating the general abstraction of U&CD. And in the field of sociological approaches to IR, including Marxist ones, this reformulation has yet to occur.

Yet all this, you might say, addresses only the weaker of the two answers you give to the question of how and why a 'Realist moment' can be safely incorporated into a Marxist analysis. You also provide a 'strong answer'—that Realism is a much 'thinner' ideology than liberalism. Whereas the latter expresses the forms of self-consciousness organic to capitalist society as a totality, the roots of Realism extend no further down than the limited worldview of a specialized professional group: it is 'the theoretical articulation of the spontaneous ideology of state managers'. One might make it look deep by attaching it to 'Nietzsche's ontology or Weber's sociology'. But the connec-tion—unlike that between liberal ideology and the underlying wealth of liberal philo-sophy—would be a kind of rearguard defence of an ideology which 'on its own' has a 'much more limited ... theoretical content'. Liberalism is 'rich'; Realism is 'thin'. Hence the liabilities of allowing a 'Realist moment' are far less.

These days, I'm uneasy with this line of thought. When I first encountered Realism, I formed exactly the impression you describe. And, like you, I still find the substantive political analyses of neo-Realist writers (as opposed to their sometimes splendid demolitions of liberal ideology) to be dissemblingly thin. Still, as that mysterious Realist power to puncture liberalism already suggests, the relationship is somehow more complex—and more paradoxical—than any simple contrast of 'rich' and 'thin' implies. In fact, in international theory, I think it would be truer to say that it is liberalism which is intrinsically shallow, and Realism which, for all its problems, is connected to a circumstance of profound significance. How so?

There is a real sense in which liberalism (and actually most Marxist thought) is not, and does not possess, an international theory. What liberalism and Marxism have to say about international relations is reasoned not from the circumstance of inter-societal coexistence, but rather from the impact upon that circumstance of social development occurring 'elsewhere' (thus Waltz's (1979) charge of illicit reductionism has undeniable substance, though I denied its importance for a long time). Realism, meanwhile, (and neo-Realism especially) is *only* an international theory: it reasons exclusively from the bare circumstance itself, and its results are indeed correspondingly 'thin'.

Yet, to repeat the question: if so thin, why so powerful? Well, I have a suggestion: because Realism is the reified abstraction of a real dimension of the historical process—a dimension, meanwhile, which has been unconsciously repressed by all the theories which Realism criticizes. If this is what Realism is—the return in distorted form of the repressed multilinear and interactive dimension of social existence—then the conundrum of how it can be simultaneously so empty and so strong is explained. Hypostasize this dimension of reality (on its own) and the result will indeed be not just thin but false. Repress it, however, and the resultant social theory will forever be mysteriously vulnerable to the 'return' in question. And since, in my view, it is the repression which generates the hypostasizing, admission of a 'Realist moment' has this paradoxical outcome: while at one level it controls for the effects of the problem, at another level it places the problem itself yet further beyond solution. For then, either the inter-societal is allowed as an irreducible 'geopolitical logic', or it is falsely reduced to the expression of a particular historical form of society.

Correspondingly, I no longer believe (as I once certainly did) that Realism lacks deep normative resources. From the same circumstance of political fragmentation, after all, Realism derives, when so minded, an ontological critique of easy, self-serving universalisms; a highly developed moral and practical sense of the tension between ends and means; and a genuinely tragic appreciation of the anarchically inscribed conflict of particularist (national) and common (international) interests.[25]

The lines of connection here run back, as you suggest, to Max Weber and in particular to his preoccupation with 'the ethical irrationality' of the world. But I think that the connection is actually an organic one. And I want to suggest that there's an objective sociological reason why this preoccupation should loom so large in international theory.

Ethical irrationality—the fact that desirable outcomes do not necessarily follow from morally well-intentioned actions—is no peculiarity of international relations. Yet it does perhaps assume a peculiar salience there. And the reason does appear somehow to be bound up with the geopolitical fragmentation of human existence. It is that wider circumstance, after all, in which 'domestically' universal identities, interests and purposes are necessarily encountered (by their foreign equivalents) as partial (in both senses of the word) particularisms. Here too, internal concentrations of 'legitimate' violence reappear as non-concentrated, dispersed military potentials, reopening existential issues of security normally suspended within individual societies. And finally, into this particularized, combustible mix, geopolitical fragmentation also adds the special causal unpredictability that characterizes the mutual management of political actors who, whatever differentials of power and leverage exist among them, do not formally control each other.

Identity, mortal violence and anarchy are not unique to the inter-societal dimension, and they are far from the only sources of determination operating there (an international theory that saw only these would be as inadequate as a social theory which could not see them at all). But they do come together in international relations in ways that both intensify the experience of existence as 'ethically irrational' and entail wider problems of moral meaning and identity which will tend to pile up, unresolved, at this level.

They will pile up there because in a secular world there is no higher register in which to pose a general idiom for their (intellectual and practical) resolution; and yet they will remain unresolved because at this level of social reality, far from being dissolved in an experience of common humanity, they are only further compounded by the additional existential implications that geopolitical fragmentation necessarily generates. In fact, it is precisely the attempt to find an empirically universal vantage point of moral and political judgment that opens a canvas wide enough to reveal the ways in which the fact of inter-societal plurality generated by unevenness problematizes such a vantage point.

I have no solution to the intractable form in which they present themselves in normative international theory, where they sustain a dichotomy of 'cosmopolitan' and 'communitarian' approaches—neither of which is sociologically any more plausible than the other. Nonetheless, it seems important to say that what they express is a fatality bound up with the specifically 'uneven and combined' character of human social development.

This fatality, I think, is the deeper issue to which Realism is connected. And, as the twisted histories of modern nationalism and internationalism attest, it is by no means a problem for state managers alone. Marx's own journalistic writings and revolutionary political analyses continually encountered it, as one international relationship after another—Franco-German, Russo-Polish, Anglo-Irish, even Euro-Chinese—were perceived as holding (or withholding) the key to metropolitan revolution. Indeed, is it not a specifically inter-societal 'ethical irrationality of the world' with which Marx was indirectly struggling in the following exasperated judgment, a year before his death?

The little bit of republican internationalism between 1830 and 1848, was grouped around France, which was destined to free Europe. *Hence it increased French chauvinism* in such a way as to cause the world-liberating mission of France and with it France's native right to be in the lead to get in our way every day even now.

(Marx quoted in Kandal 1989, 38, emphasis in original)

Surely there is something important here which merits theorization. But Marx himself does not tell us, theoretically, where it comes from.[26] And nor, if the analogy I pursued earlier has any cogency, can Realism. It is driven, as you say, to impute it rather to human nature, or to 'power politics', or—so near and yet so far—to the 'structure' of 'the international'. This is why I persist in my, perhaps quixotic, view of the intellectual status of Realism: thus far, it is the only international theory we have, but it is nevertheless the wrong one. And once again therefore, it seems that the answer cannot lie with a 'Realist moment', but must rather involve a deeper recapture of these phenomena by a non-Realist social theory.

In conclusion, let me have one last stab at clarifying the theoretical provenance of my overall argument. This time, I'd like to recall one of those 'back of the envelope' formulations of Marx's overall intellectual project that crop up from time to time in his writings. 'The order', he writes at one point in the *Grundrisse,* 'obviously has to be:

1   The general, abstract determinants which obtain in more or less all forms of society ...
2   The categories which make up the inner structure of bourgeois society ...
3   Concentration of bourgeois society in the form of the state ...
4   The international relation of production ...
5   The world market and crises. (Marx 1973, 108)

Interestingly, Marx's translator (Nicolaus) says of this schema that Marx subsequently dropped the first step (Marx 1973, 53–54). I think that's only half true. For sure, what we call the '1857 General Introduction' did not make it into the first volume of *Capital*. And yet, as I've suggested above, Marx does quite crucially weave the interrogation of a general abstraction (the simple form of value) into the opening movement of chapter one. This part of 'the order' therefore stands. But, to come to the point: where in this five-step order should 'the international' come in? My answer would be as follows. There is no period of history in which one cannot find a plurality of societies or social formations coexisting in time. And yet, for reasons I'm not entirely clear about myself, I would hesitate before placing 'intersocietal coexistence' itself into step one—'the general, abstract determinants which obtain in more or less all forms of society'. What I do think needs to be in step one, however, is the general abstraction of that property of social reality which operates to produce a strategic dimension to all social development, irrespective of whether the latter takes the form of juridically differentiated, visibly separate 'societies'. For if 'all forms of society' are not explicitly conceived as 'uneven and combined' in their development, then when the consequences of this fact are later addressed—say in step four—they will either be falsely derived from the historical particularisms of steps 2–3, or else they will be encountered as contingencies which have no theoretical 'depth'. In short, neglect the significance of U&CD in step one, and either reductionism or proto-Realism will unfailingly result further down the line.

Whatever else the achievements of Marxism in international theory, I don't think it (or any other approach, for that matter) has ever cracked this problem. I have yet to think through exactly what would be the cascading implications of a solution for those other steps of the schema. The problem itself, however, is there. And so, I believe, somewhere in this idea of U&CD, which I'm still fumbling to unpack, is the solution.

And yet I must wonder, in closing, whether I've said anything in this letter with which you'd actually disagree. After all, part of the distance separating our positions was always down to our different points of entry into the same issue. And even where we might have seemed to be at odds—the question of the 'Realist moment'—my response has been to take up part of your own account of Marx's method, and to apply it to 'the international'. On the other hand, I must acknowledge that the more I work with the idea of U&CD, the more I find myself carried not only beyond my own earlier thinking, but also potentially in directions for which Trotsky's texts themselves provide at best little direct warrant. But then, as the man himself was wont to say: 'Marxism is above all a method of analysis—not analysis of texts, but analysis of social relations ... ' (Trotsky 1962, 196). And surely few phenomena stand in more urgent need of a genuinely 'social relational' analysis than this thing which we call 'the international'. What do you think?

As ever,

Justin

London, 29 July 2006

Dear Justin,

Thanks very much for another challenging, wide-ranging and penetrating set of thoughts. I hope you'll forgive me if I concentrate on a relatively limited set of issues in this response, three to be more specific: the uses of the transhistorical, the limits of the value analogy and the virtues of Realism.

The uses of the transhistorical

This seems to be the substantive question at issue in our discussion: Of what use are transhistorical 'general abstractions'—above all, U&CD—in understanding 'the international'? The line I took in my last letter was to acknowledge the legitimacy of resort to such concepts but to insist that, as far as possible, the main burden of explaining inter-societal relationships and trends should be borne by concepts speci-fying the structures and tendencies of definite modes of production. Your reply is that accounts that rely on the latter kind of concepts (what as shorthand I call 'mode of production analysis') will always leave behind an unexplained surplus that reflects the fact 'that all societies coexist with and interact with others, and that this super-adds a lateral field of causality over and above the "domestic" determinations arising from each and every one of the participant societies'. Failure to thematize explicitly this fact and its implications creates an ideological space that can be filled by Realism and its reifications.

All this is fine and I'm very happy to endorse it (I particularly like the formulation that the inter-societal is 'a lateral field of causality' super-added to domestic determinations). I also take your point that Trotsky's inherently historical conception of U&CD is designed, as it were, to control for the danger of essentialism. So, at this level of generality, we're in agreement. If I stick slightly stubbornly to a preference for pushing mode of production analysis as far as it will go, this is because I think this analysis is needed in order to grasp the specific modalities of the inter-societal. I was a bit surprised at your dismissal of Brenner's concept of 'political accumulation', as if it were incapable of registering 'differentiated, interactive temporalities of development within a wider social formation'. In fact, one of his main uses of the concept is to analyse the divergent patterns of state-building in mediaeval England and France—monarchy as, respectively, the class organization of the lords, reinforcing the capacity of each to extract surplus-labour from his own peasants, and as an expanding super-lord whose growing military and fiscal capabilities compensated for the declining extractive powers of individual lords—understood explicitly as a case of U&CD:

> English feudal class self-government appears to have been 'ahead' of the French in the twelfth and thirteenth centuries, not only because its starting point was different, but because it built on advances in this sphere already achieved on the Continent, especially in Normandy. In turn, when French centralization accelerated somewhat later, it was influenced by English development, and was indeed, in part, a response to direct English politico-military pressure. But French feudal centralization did not follow the English pattern and, over time, radically diverged from it. Thus the development of the mechanisms of 'feudal accumulation' tended to be not only 'uneven' but 'combined', in the sense that later developers could build on previous advances made elsewhere in feudal class organization.
>
> (Brenner 1982, 52)

This is a case where a theory of the feudal mode of production helps us to understand the specific form taken by inter-societal interactions where, broadly speaking, feudal relations obtain. But mode of production analysis is also needed if we are properly to historicize what are too easily described as centre-periphery relations. Robert Bartlett (1993) has brilliantly captured the colonizing, expansionist dynamic that thrust the feudal lords of western Christendom into Ireland, Moorish Spain, Outremer and the Slavic lands beyond the Elbe. Is this the same dynamic at work in the later incorporation of the entire globe in the capitalist word system? I don't think so, for reasons given once again by Brenner: where capitalist production relations obtain economic actors' 'rules of reproduction', reflecting their dependence on the market for access to the means of subsistence, give them an incentive to develop the forces of production intensively that was absent in precapitalist economic systems (Brenner 1986). If this line of reasoning is correct, then the nature of the production relations prevailing in different regions is likely to have a decisive effect on the form taken by inter-societal relations.

Let me emphasize that these examples aren't intended to wash away the inter-social as a 'lateral field of causality' amid a tide of historical specificities. I freely concede its irreducibility and indeed have always done so in our discussions of these matters. But, as I pointed out to you in our earlier correspondence on your 'International Historical Sociology' piece (Rosenberg 2006), you aren't the only contemporary social theorist to thematize the significance of the inter-societal. Michael Mann in effect affirms the analytical priority of the inter-societal when he puts forward the idea of the social as power networks in opposition to the concept of society as a closed totality effectively bounded by a nation-state (Mann 1986, Chapter 1).

Granted by using the concept of U&CD to frame the inter-societal, you give the latter a historically dynamic character. But, in a way, so does Mann, albeit in an explicitly essentialist mode, by invoking the ingrained human capacity to outflank established power-configurations. For example: 'Human beings are restless, purposive, and rational, striving to increase their enjoyment of the good things of life and capable of choosing appropriate means for doing so' (Mann 1986, 4). Mode of production analysis is needed to block this kind of relapse into humanism; more positively, it seems to me that it is also required once you go beyond generic affirmation of the historical and dynamic character of U&CD to explore its actual modalities in specific regions and periods. But I can see that I am in grave danger of simply repeating what I have already said, so I shall say no more on this point.

The limits of the value analogy

So far I'm clear enough, whether or not my argument is correct. But I must say that I found your treatment of my suggestion that there should be a Realist moment in the theory of the capitalist mode of production—just as (I also contended) there is a liberal one in *Capital*, Volume I, Part 1—quite hard to follow. On the one hand, you warn that this amounts to a 'pragmatic accommodation' with Realism that leaves its reifications intact. On the other hand, you endorse a much more generous assessment of Realism as a political ideology than I can bring myself to accept. What compounds my confusion is that you seek to bring out the problematic nature of my own strategy by developing an analogy between the kind of move from U&CD to the inter-societal that you recommend and Marx's progression from value to surplus-value in *Capital*. In this section I want to try and puzzle out how this analogy is meant to work before returning to Realism in the next one. Forgive me if I proceed slowly and clumsily, but I am puzzled.

You develop the analogy through a discussion of Marx's treatment of value at the beginning of *Capital* (excuse me for quoting at length but I can best deal with your argument by working through it fairly pedantically):

> Central to Marx's method ... is the positing of an undiscovered social-relational substratum to apparently self-evident phenomena and categories, a positing which then generates a radically alternative explanatory idiom. Significantly,

however, the first such exercise in *Capital* comes long before any mention of wage labour, or any explicit critique of liberalism. And although it turns out to have enormous consequences for the latter, its scope, as the exuberant claim to have bettered Aristotle himself implies, is far wider. I'm referring of course to Marx's opening engagement with the question 'what is the substance of value?'

> This ... is worked out, not by reference to 'the totality of capitalist production relations', but through interrogation of what Marx calls the 'the simple, isolated or accidental form of value'. Here, he says, the hardest part of the question is already posed. In an oft-misunderstood claim, Marx observes that in any act of exchange, the relation of equivalence posited between the things exchanged in fact simultaneously relates as equivalent whatever human activities have brought the objects of exchange to this point. Of course, and despite his use of the term, this is not yet 'value'. The relational substance of value—'socially necessary abstract labour time'—comes into systematic being only with modern capitalist society ... But why then analyse 'simple value' at all? Answer: Because a crucial element of the phenomenon that Marx is anatomizing, though it becomes truly significant only in the developed (capitalist) case, is already present, *in nuce*, in every instance of exchange.
>
> (Rosenberg, this chapter, 167–68)

I have several problems with all this. First of all, I don't think it's true that Marx answers the question of what value is by interrogating the 'simple, isolated, or accidental form of value'. His discussion of the latter is simply the first step in his analysis of the value-form in Section 3 of *Capital*, Volume I, Chapter 1, whose aim is to 'trace the development of the expression of value contained in the value-relation of commodities from its simplest, almost imperceptible outline to the dazzling money-form' (Marx 1976, 139). Moreover, though Marx does praise Aristotle when discussing the simple form of value as 'the great investigator who was the first to analyse the value-form', the solution to the problem that the latter was unable to resolve— what makes qualitatively different use-values commensurable?—has already been settled in the first two sections of Chapter 1 (Marx 1976, 151). It is in Section 1 that Marx explains that the substance of value is socially necessary labour-time and in Section 2 that he introduces the critical distinction between abstract and concrete labour.

You are quite right that Marx develops his theory of value before formulating his account of capitalist exploitation and that he does so even though the law of value only becomes operative in capitalism. This strategy is justified, you say, 'because a crucial element of the phenomenon which Marx is anatomizing, though it becomes truly significant only in the developed (capitalist) case, is already present, *in nuce*, in every instance of exchange'. And you go on to explain how reification is generated by every exchange-relation. I'm not at all sure that this is the right way to justify the analytical priority of value over surplus value. Marx explains that Aristotle couldn't grasp the nature of the value-relation because it only becomes possible to recognize 'the equality and equivalence of all kinds of labour' in a system of generalized commodity production where 'the commodity-form is the universal form of the product of labour' (Marx 1976, 152). It is in such a system, he goes on to argue in Section 4 of *Capital*, Volume I, Chapter 1, that commodity fetishism emerges. The trouble with your *in nuce* formulation is that it can't capture the *systemic* and *coercive* character of the value-relation, the subordination of economic actors to the compulsion to increase productivity and reduce costs that derives from their own competitive interactions. By its nature an isolated act of exchange can't convey this. Hence, Marx moves from the simple form of value, where only two use-values are exchanged; to forms where indefinite varieties of use-values are rendered commensurable; and culminating in their universal exchangeability via the money commodity.

Marx constructs the theory of value in Part 1 of *Capital*, Volume I, without consideration of surplus-value and exploitation because he is developing here a model of generalized commodity production—of an economy of autonomous but interdependent and competing commodity producers. He needs to have this model before he deals with exploitation because it gives him a theory of the commodity and, of course, because his claim that labour-power is a commodity is central to his account of capitalist exploitation. He posits the presupposition in Volume I, Part 2, when he draws our attention to the fact that a system of generalized commodity production is one where labour-power itself is a commodity, thereby introducing a new level of determination. We must henceforth distinguish between the actual commodity producers, the sellers of labour-power and those who purchase labour-power thanks to their control of the means of production. This is a good example of what Gérard Duménil (1978, 89) admirably calls Marx's method of 'dosed abstraction ... a concretization constructed element by element'—the progressive introduction of more complex determinations. These different levels of determination coexist synchronically rather than representing a diachronic process. So you are mistaken when you say that, *stricto sensu*,[27] Marx shouldn't have talked of value when analyzing the simple form of value because '[t]he relational substance of value—"socially necessary abstract labour time"—comes into systematic being only with modern capitalist society'. His entire discussion of the value-form identifies distinctive properties of generalized commodity production that—though analytically they need to be introduced prior to the theory of surplus-value—can only be actualized where the capital-relation obtains.

You go on to claim that without 'the prior analysis of the inverted relational architecture of exchange', 'the theory of *surplus* value would be, well, vulgar: all mathematics and no ontology' (Rosenberg, this chapter, 168). It's certainly true that understanding the 'relational architecture' of generalized commodity production is a prerequisite to grasping the extraction of surplus-value. But Marx's detailed account of the valorization process in Parts 3, 4 and 5 of *Capital*, Volume I, is thoroughly relational and, indeed, intellectually and politically revolutionary in the way it treats production as a conflictual social process and not simply the realization of a set of technical conditions. His later suggestion that, as you put it, '"wage labour" itself is a mystified category' has to do with the fact that, as Marx (1976, 675, 677) says at the start of Part 6, '[o]n the surface of bourgeois society the worker's wage appears as the price of labour', the monetary expression of the value of labour, an ideological language that is functional to the operation of the labour market but in which 'the concept of value is not only completely extinguished, but inverted, so that it becomes its contrary'. But the distinction between labour and labour-power and the concept of the value of labour-power constitutive of the theory of surplus-value aren't implicated in this fetishistic inversion. On the contrary, by allowing us to conceptualize the real relations of exploitation, they define the norm relative to which we can say that the idea of the value of labour is 'an expression as imaginary as the value of the earth' (Marx 1976, 677).

As you can probably guess after all this rigmarole, I am sceptical about the analogy that you posit between exchange and geopolitics. You write:

> In both cases, what looks like an elemental datum of social reality—exchange of things on the one hand, geopolitical interaction on the other—in fact secrets a further layer of relational constitution which must be excavated *sociologically* if the datum in question is not to licence a reifying discourse—of 'vulgar' economy or Realist geopolitics. Moreover, in both cases, what Marx calls the perceptual mechanism of *'camera obscura'*, which makes the appearance seem irreducible, derives not from any given historical form of the datum, but from properties inherent in that particular kind or fragment of human sociation in general: whenever things are exchanged, in whatever kind of society, the inverted, reified form of social relation which capitalist society uniquely develops into the 'social substance' of value is momentarily—even if inertly—posited. It is a latent sociological property of exchange relations *per se*. Something parallel, I shall suggest below, can be said—and must be excavated—concerning inter-societal relations ...
>
> Thus, if we don't want to end up with either an essentialized or a reductionist notion of geopolitics, we need to posit a presupposition here—one which, like Marx's presupposition of an inverted human relational content to the exchange of things, can provide a sociological key to the hieroglyphic of Thucydidean Realism. *Hic Rhodus. Hic salta!* Needless to say, I would not dare propose such a challenge if I didn't think we already had the answer to it: but such an answer is exactly what U&CD, worked through as a *general* abstraction, enables.
>
> (Rosenberg, this chapter, 168–69)

I don't dispute the conclusion. But there is an important difference between the 'relational constitution[s]' secreted in exchange and geopolitics. U&CD is genuinely transhistorical—that indeed is your most general claim, which I have accepted. But generalized commodity production isn't. The thrust of Marx's argument in *Capital* is to show that this form of economy requires the prevalence of capitalist production relations in all their complexity. Inasmuch as you acknowledge that '[t]he relational substance of value ... comes into systematic being only with modern capitalist society' you seem at least partially to accept this. But the effect is to limit the scope of your analogy because in one case the 'relational constitution' obtains right across human space and time while in the another it proves to belong to the inner architecture of a historically specific mode of production.

Marx, you say, thought that 'the riddle of (exchange) value is present in all societies and yet solvable ... only within capitalist society', but this solution depends on a
detailed analysis of properties that solely obtain in the capitalist mode—as he makes
clear especially in his discussion of commodity fetishism. Thus he is not developing
what you call a 'generalized phenomenology' if by that you mean a theory of transhistorical scope: the simple form of value may, as you suggest, be a 'general abstraction' in inasmuch as use-values are exchanged in a wide range of societies, but Marx
treats it only as a step in constructing a theory of generalized commodity production
and hence of the capitalist mode of production. The paradox is thus that you stress
the insufficiencies of mode of production analysis in theorizing the inter-societal but
seek to validate your own approach by building up a detailed analogy with an argument that leads us into the mother of all mode of production analyses.

It may seem a bit cheeky of me to be emphasizing so much here the limits of value
theory in understanding the geopolitical after making so much of Marx's method in
Capital in the paper that started off this correspondence. But there I wasn't primarily
drawing an analogy with value theory—I was *using* it. To put it more precisely, I was
arguing that the Marxist theory of the capitalist mode of production can and should be
extended to incorporate a theory of the state system and of the geopolitical—*in capitalism*. I add the last clause to make clear that this argument does not commit me, as
you seem to imply, to denying that 'the issue of the geopolitical cannot be fully
grasped from within a theory of capital'. Of course it can't, for two reasons: first, in the
case of pre-capitalist inter-societal relations we will need, as I have tried to bring out
in section (1) above, theories of modes of production other than capitalism; and
second, we also need, as you argue, 'general abstractions' that can capture the transhistorical surplus of U&CD that escapes mode of production analysis.

The virtues of realism

You yourself point to the limits of the value analogy at a somewhat lower level of
abstraction: 'The presupposition which needs to be posited in order to "get to the
bottom" of the phenomena which Realism describes is not the same as the one Marx
used to break through to the relational substance of value—and it cannot be found in
Capital.' And you go on to warn that failure to recognize this gives rise to the danger
that 'the mystified [Realist] "moment" will be incorporated, undigested, for lack of
the analytical means to break it down'. Others have made much the same point—for
example, Pozo-Martin (2006) in the article on which I comment in my states system
paper (Callinicos 2007). I accept there is a danger of this nature, but I'm not sure
that there is a general formula for dealing with it. But a relevant methodological
point is worth stating to avoid misunderstanding: just because a Marxist theory of the
state system would analyse a phenomenon that Realism has made its privileged object
would not require it to employ the same concepts as Realism. A good Marxist treatment of the capitalist geopolitical need no more resemble, say, Mearsheimer's (2001)
The Tragedy of Great Power Politics than Marx's analysis of the credit system in *Capital*,
Volume III, Part 5, a neoclassical text on financial markets (I know, I've slipped into
analogizing despite what I said in the preceding paragraph). But, for all the chaotic

state of the manuscripts poor Engels had to splice together in order to publish that analysis, it reflects very substantial empirical and analytical work on Marx's part. The work required to develop a Marxist theory of the geopolitical lies before us.

One difference between us is that I think you tend to stress more the conceptual side of this effort. Thus you write:

> Geopolitical categories *can* be translated back into a generative sociological discourse, but only if the latter has already been reformulated by incorporating the general abstraction of U&CD. And in the field of sociological approaches to IR, including Marxist ones, this reformulation has yet to occur. (Rosenberg, this chapter, 171)

I take it that you have set yourself the task of helping to achieve this reformulation. I certainly await the results of these efforts with interest, but I think more historically and empirically oriented analysis is an essential complement to such conceptual under-labouring and, on the whole, it is what I am personally more interested in. All of which is slightly odd, since I am meant to be the philosopher and you the social scientist, though I suppose this only goes to show how useless disciplinary distinctions are.

I do have some mainly philosophical comments to make on your concluding discussion of Realism. This was another point at which I felt a bit dizzy since, having warned me against swallowing Realism undigested, you overleapt me with your favourable treatment of the normative dimension of Realism. Thus you challenge my unfavourable comparison of Realism with liberalism as political ideologies:

> I no longer believe, (as I once certainly did), that Realism lacks deep normative resources. From the same circumstance of political fragmentation, after all, Realism derives, when so minded: an ontological critique of easy, self-serving universalisms; a highly developed moral and practical sense of the tension between ends and means; and a genuinely tragic appreciation of the anarchically inscribed conflict of particularist (national) and common (international) interests.
>
> (Rosenberg, this chapter, 172)

Once again I have a strong and weak answer to this. The strong answer is this: I know that there is a current trend in international theory to explore Realism as a normative theory, but come on! What you evoke here can very easily turn into what one might call the Statesmen's Lament: decisions are complex and require a choice of evils, we are constantly defeated by the consequences of our actions, life is tough and cruel but fortunately some of us are man enough to take it on and don the imperial purple (or more usually the counsellor's more modest garb). There are bathetic cases of this kind of discourse—Schlesinger's and Sorenson's mythologization of John F Kennedy and his 'grace under pressure'—or, worse still, Kissinger's apologias in his memoirs and *Diplomacy* (1994).[28]

EH Carr is a much more substantial figure, but *The Twenty Years' Crisis* (1939) reeks of the spirit of Munich. You also cite Hans Morgenthau's *Scientific Man versus*

Power Politics. You aren't the first person to have commended this text to me as evidence of Realism's moral depth. I'm afraid I just can't see this at all. Morgenthau's argument here as elsewhere is rooted in rampant essentialism—the postulation of 'the *animus dominandi*, the desire for power', as a universal and irreducible source of human motivation (Morgenthau 1946, 192).[29] It is moreover incoherent since Morgenthau combines a pertinent critique of liberalism's conception of 'the international' with the affirmation of one of the main premises of utilitarianism (which he rightly treats as one of the principal forms of liberal ideology) and offshoots such as neoclassical economics; namely, that the goals of action are, as Talcott Parsons puts it, random, so that reason plays a purely instrumental role, selecting the most effective means of achieving these goals. 'Reason, far from following its own inherent impulses, is driven towards its goals by the irrational forces the ends of which it serves' (Morgenthau 1946, 152).

As for the 'tragic appreciation' of 'the international', is this the kind of stuff you mean? '[I]t is only the awareness of the tragic presence of evil in all political action which at least enables man to choose the lesser evil and be as good as he can be in an evil world' (Morgenthau 1946, 202–3). Or again:

> To act successfully, that is, according to the rules of the political art, is political wisdom. To know with despair that the political act is inevitably evil, and to act nevertheless, is moral courage. To choose among several expedient actions the least evil one is moral judgement. In the combination of political wisdom, moral courage, and moral judgement, man reconciles his political nature with his moral destiny.
>
> (Morgenthau 1946, 203)

Please tell me you don't take this guff seriously—it's pure Statesman's Lament. Liberalism may indeed lack 'an international theory' (I'll come back to that), and its aspirations are inherently liable to Realist debunking, but how are the horizons of these aspirations set? Merely by *liberté, égalité, fraternité*—that is, by the ideological heritage of the great bourgeois revolutions, by the ideals the Marxist critique does not reject but constantly reproaches capitalist society for systematically failing to realize. These conceptions seem to me more than 'easy, self-serving universalisms'. Liberty, equality and solidarity are ideals too powerful to abandon to the likes of Bush and Blair (Callinicos 2000). From a normative point of view, there just is no contest between Realism and liberalism. It's true that there is another form of political bathos that exploits liberal ideals. We are all too familiar with what one might call the Liberal Imperialist's War Song, currently much in use on both sides of the Atlantic to justify Israel's battering of Lebanon and Gaza. But isn't one main reason why people so detest Tony Blair's pharisaism is that it debases the very ideals to which it appeals? And to resort to Realism in order to overcome the manifest defects of contemporary liberalism is to get trapped in exactly the rat run of mainstream IR theory from which we both want Marxism to offer a way of escaping.

My weak answer is not that different from the strong one. One can find serious expressions of the moral outlook that you evoke. The most important is probably

Weber's 'Politics as a Vocation'[30] and the famous contrast it draws between the 'ethic of conviction' and the 'ethic of responsibility'.[31] But there are reasons for exercising care in approaching this text. In the first place, as Perry Anderson has brought out very well, the lecture's rhetoric is informed in part by what he calls Weber's 'vulcanism', his self-image as the embodiment of 'a combination of intense passion and iron discipline', in part by the animus of a German nationalist fiercely unreconciled with the Reich's double disaster of November 1918—military defeat and sociopolitical revolution (Anderson 1992a, 191). But, secondly, as Anderson also notes, 'Weber was an early twentieth-century liberal, of a distinctively German kind' (Anderson 1992a, 193). John Gray recognizes him as a case of what he calls *'agonistic liberalism'*, 'a stoical and tragic liberalism of unavoidable conflict and irreparable loss among inherently rivalrous values' (Gray 1995, 1). Weber relativizes liberalism, not only drawing attention to the mutual incompatibility of its constitutive values but also by stressing its historical fragility, its dependence on 'a unique, never to be repeated set of circumstances' (Weber 1995, 108). But he remains a particularly important and impressive representative of the liberal tradition.

The point of the foregoing is to suggest that serious statements of normative Realism are likely not to articulate a free-standing ideology but to express the values distinctive to Realism in combination with others derived usually from liberalism, as is demonstrable in Weber's case.[32] It seems to me that the excessive claims that you make for Realism are motivated by your (entirely legitimate) preoccupations with international theory. Thus, in support of your claim that, 'in International Theory, ... it is liberalism [and not Realism] which is intrinsically shallow', you write: 'There is a real sense in which liberalism (and actually most Marxist thought) is not, and does not possess, an international theory'. I think this latter statement is true enough, but it only warrants the conclusion of liberalism's narrowness within the domain of international theory, as your initial qualifying clause indeed makes clear. But this tells us nothing about the relative normative resources of the two theories. In *that* respect, my judgement remains that Realism is much the weaker of the two, and that it tends to be parasitic on other, richer philosophical traditions (most usually liberalism, but Nietzsche's ontology of the will to power offers another, albeit in its own way highly problematic, resource).

I certainly agree that Realism 'is the only international theory we have—but it is nevertheless the wrong one'. This seems to be one of the main reference points in our discussion, that we both intellectually respect Realism but want to develop a Marxist theory of 'the international' that can transcend it. Indeed *Hic Rhodus! Hic salta!* One aspect of Realism's strength that you don't discuss is the way in which, particularly in the work of structural realists such as Waltz and Mearsheimer, it thematizes the systemness of 'the international'. You inadvertently touch on this when you cite Polybius in one of your footnotes: 'In previous times, events in the world occurred without impinging on one another ... [then] history became a whole, as if a single body; events in Italy and Libya came to be enmeshed with those in Asia and Greece, and everything gets directed towards one single goal' (Rosenberg, this chapter, 187fn21).

There is of course one way of interpreting this statement, namely that the late Hellenistic Mediterranean world formed what Mann calls 'a multi-power-actor civilization' composed of interacting rival city-states and kingdoms. Here there are definitely dragons in the shape of the kind of comparative international theory practised by Barry Buzan and his associates, which seeks to identify the properties of international systems widely separated in space and time (Buzan and Little 2000). We would probably both agree that this represents an extreme form of reification because it abstracts political forms and geopolitical patterns from the historical processes and social relations in which they were embedded. Yet we both seem also to agree that there is something to this sort of reifying theory—that it captures something about the world that both liberalism and much mainstream social theory fails to address. As you nicely put it, 'Realism is the reified abstraction of a real dimension of the historical process'. You also state what's needed very well—'a deeper recapture of these phenomena by a non-Realist social theory'. Plainly we have different strategies for accomplishing this shared objective. This does not mean the critical comparison of these strategies can't offer illumination. I certainly have gained much from our exchanges.

All the best,

Alex

Notes

1 The authors would like to thank Alex Anievas and an anonymous reviewer for valuable suggestions in preparing this exchange for publication.
2 Here Brewer's updated study (1990) remains, I think, the authoritative survey.
3 While Marxism in IR has generally attracted the charge of 'domestic analogy' or reductionism, the neo-Weberian strand of historical sociology which has found its way into this discipline, associated with such writers as Charles Tilly, Theda Skocpol and Michael Mann, has more frequently been accused of being caught on the other horn of the problem, namely 'proto-realism'. See, for example, Jarvis (1989), Hobden (1998), Buzan and Little (2001), Halliday (2002b), Smith (2002).
4 You yourself nicely finger this question of multiplicity towards the end of your 2004 article on 'Marxism and the International' (Callinicos 2004).
5 It says something about the limited development of Marxism in international theory that her survey was included in a sub-section entitled 'Partial Theories in International Relations'. For more recent surveys, see Hobden and Wyn Jones (2005), Teschke (2008) and Dufour (2008). Despite its title, Andrew Linklater's *Beyond Realism and Marxism* (1990) is perhaps still the most comprehensive attempt to mobilize the wealth of Marxist thought outside IR, in order to focus it on the question of 'the international'.
6 I say 'almost' because Benno Teschke's (2003, 2005) recent work involves a rising claim about the theoretical significance of 'the international' which in many respects parallels my own developing preoccupation. *The Myth of 1648* initially proposes a 'core argument ... that the constitution, operation, and transformation of geopolitical orders are predicated on the changing identities of their constitutive units' (Teschke 2003, 7). Yet the work as a whole ultimately exceeds the 'second image' limits which such a formula usually entails. Indeed its concluding chapter, which invokes the idea of 'combined and uneven development' already contains many pointers to his later call for 'a general and systematic attempt to elevate the international from the start to a constitutive component of any theory of history. ... ' (Teschke 2005, 10). Whether and how such an exercise would reach into a reformulation of historical materialism itself remains to be specified. But clearly we have arrived, albeit from different directions, on very substantial common ground.

7 I use the term 'the international' as shorthand for 'that dimension of social reality which arises specifically from the coexistence within it of more than one society' (Rosenberg 2006, 308). Since this dimension has always existed, while 'nations' have not, the usage must appear anachronistic. Yet the obvious alternative term—'inter-societal'—brings not dissimilar problems of its own. And since this same dimension remains for social theory the unrecovered core of *modern* international relations too, I hope that this usage may be allowed, with all the qualifications it requires. For when the qualifications are made, be they ever so weighty, the dimension itself is still there. And the significance of its existence is not exhausted by analyses of its changing historical forms.

8 Overwhelmingly, Trotsky uses the term 'combined development' to refer to a specifically capitalist phenomenon. Yet he also describes 'unevenness' as 'the most general law of the historic process' (Trotsky 1980, 5), and adds that '[f]rom the universal law of unevenness ... derives another law which ... we may call the *law of combined development* ... ' (Trotsky 1980, 5–6). By implication, therefore, this second 'law' must also be universal. Yet though his account of the precapitalist development of Czarism operationalizes this wider, transhistorical meaning of U&CD in all but name, nowhere does Trotsky develop its theoretical implications.

9 Not even where this theory is historicized to locate the emergence of capitalism within an antecedent Absolutist state system, as Teschke (2003) and Lacher (2002) have both importantly done.

10 Because in feudal societies, wealth was extracted via political ownership of land and persons, feudal lords engaged in 'political accumulation' of territories, persons and the means of violence: 'A drive to political accumulation, or state building, was the feudal analogue to the capitalist drive to accumulate capital' (Brenner 1987, 174).

11 In *Capital* Volume I Marx argues that the exchange between capitalist and worker in the labour market apparently belongs 'the exclusive realm of Freedom, Equality, Property, and Bentham' (Marx 1976, 280), since the buyer and seller confront each other as legally free and equal property owners each pursuing their own interest. The real inequality between the two, consequent on the worker's lack of access to the means of production, becomes clear when they enter 'the hidden abode of production', where the capitalist's control of the production process allows him to exploit the worker (Marx 1976, 279).

12 In the summer of 2006, the University and College Union were engaged in an assessment boycott as part of a national campaign over university funding in the United Kingdom.

13 Marx uses the term 'Robinsonade' (Marx 1973, 83) to criticize the theories of liberal political economy. In his view, these theories unwittingly generalized the particular historical characteristics of capitalist sociality into transhistorical features of human behaviour—as if Robinson Crusoe's actions when isolated on his island revealed an unmediated 'human nature' rather than transferring into his new environment the norms of his native English capitalist society.

14 I am grateful to Simon Bromley for impressing this point upon me at an earlier stage of my explorations.

15 Tenbruck (1994) makes this point very powerfully.

16 On this term, consider the following: 'Europe knew two separate waves of serfdom, first one in the West (9th to 14th centuries) and then one in the East (15th to 18th centuries) ... ' The latter however, which Engels called the 'second serfdom', was no simple repetition elsewhere of the first: 'From the 12th century onwards ... no purely endogenous evolution was ever again possible. The destiny of the East was altered by the intrusion of the West. ... [I]t was henceforward irrevocably other than it would have been if it had developed in relative isolation' (Anderson 1974a, 263–64).

17 In a celebrated chapter of Volume III of *Capital*, chapter 47, 'The Trinity Formula' (Marx 1959, 814–31), Marx argues that the mystification of capitalist social relations reaches an intellectual climax in the categories of 'vulgar economy' which attribute creative powers to inert things—as if 'rent' grew out of the earth itself, or as if capital, as a thing to be invested, was itself pregnant with the 'interest' which it appears to generate. 'It is', writes Marx of such reifying categories, 'an enchanted, perverted, topsy-turvy world, in which

Monsieur le Capital and Madame la Terre do their ghost-walking as social characters and at the same time directly as mere things' (Marx 1959, 830).

18 This is what I attempted in chapter 5 of *The Empire of Civil Society* (Rosenberg 1994), building on the work of Derek Sayer and Ellen Wood.

19 In the opening chapter of *Capital*, Marx repeatedly abstracts from the question of what determines the quantitative magnitude of value in any given case in order to pose first and foremost the qualitative (ontological) question of what value *is* as a social phenomenon.

20 Marx (1976, 167) describes value as a 'social hieroglyphic'—meaning that (like the ancient Egyptian writing system for those who rediscovered it) the existence of value was unquestionably a human social artefact, but one whose coded form long defeated attempts to decipher it.

21 Arguably, this also explains how Marx could simultaneously argue that the riddle of (exchange-) value is present in all societies and yet solvable (that is, susceptible to a theory of value) only within capitalist society. And I wonder, parenthetically, whether there might be a parallel here too—whether somehow the question of the geopolitical, while general to all societies, becomes analytically soluble only with the rise of capitalism. If so, it perhaps has to do with the latter's universalizing tendency, the way that capitalism constitutes human development as both an empirical and an organic totality, such that the historically general but varying significance of the inter-societal is now systematically activated within a wider social process which renders it susceptible to an actual theory. Herodotus, one might say, echoing Marx's explanation for Aristotle's difficulties with exchange-value, had nothing like this to go on: his totalizing conception, while securing his place as 'the father of universal history', could only be a speculative one. Such an argument, however, would have to cope also with the following claim by Polybius in the 2nd century BCE: In previous times, events in the world occurred without impinging on one another ... [then] history became a whole, as if a single body; events in Italy and Libya came to be enmeshed with those in Asia and Greece, and everything gets directed towards one single goal. (quoted in Tenbruck 1994, 88) I haven't yet thought this through.

22 'Here is Rhodes: jump here!' Marx uses this saying, (derived from Æsop via Hegel), to dramatize his approaching solution to an apparently insoluble problem—which he is about to address via the procedure of 'positing a presupposition' (Marx 1976, 209).

23 'After the feast'. Marx uses this term to describe the practical starting point of any social-theoretical reflection: namely that it confronts an already completed social reality, in which emergent properties may have developed in such a way that their enduring social foundations are now concealed by their results (Marx 1976, 168). This necessitates a conscious procedure of working backwards from the 'finished form' in order to uncover the generative social phenomena—and without this the problem of reification cannot be overcome.

24 'Beware! Here be dragons!'

25 I'm thinking here in particular of Morgenthau's *Scientific Man versus Power Politics* (1946)—especially the last chapter, 'The Tragedy of Scientific Man'; Herbert Butterfield, 'The tragic element in modern international conflict', in *History and Human Relations* (1951); and Carr's *The Twenty Years' Crisis* (1946). There are even traces of this in the sometimes doggedly optimistic writings of Kenneth Waltz. His 1993 article on the emerging post-Cold War world ended as follows:

[o]ne may hope that America's internal preoccupations will produce not an isolationist policy, which has become impossible, but a forbearance that will give other countries at long last the chance to deal with their own problems and to make their own mistakes. But I would not bet on it. (Waltz 1993, 79)

26 For a fascinating analysis of the subterranean sway of 'international' determinations in the formation of Marx's own revolutionary political categories, see Shilliam (2006b).

27 Strictly speaking.

28 Soon after John F Kennedy's assassination, two of his aides wrote best-selling biographies that sought to provide detailed evidence for the portrayal of his administration as 'Camelot': Schlesinger (1965) and Sorenson (1965). Those still susceptible to such mythmaking should consult the great investigative journalist Seymour Hersh, previously a nemesis of Kissinger, and now Bush's and Cheney's. See Hersh (1997).

29 Morgenthau's attempt in *Power among Nations* to substantiate this assumption is particularly vulgar:

> The tendency to dominate, in particular, is an element of all human associations, from the family through fraternal and professional associations and local political organizations, to the state. On the family level, the typical conflict between the mother-in-law and her child's spouse is in its essence a struggle for power, the defence of an established power position against an attempt to establish a new one. As such it foreshadows the conflict on the international scene between the policies of the status quo and the policies of imperialism. (Morgenthau 1955, 31)

No wonder Waltz developed structural realism to escape such banalities. But then you know all this much better than me, since you write in *The Empire of Civil Society* that 'Morgenthau ... had some rather unflattering and unsophisticated views on human nature, and an embarrassing habit of parading them as the philosophical basis of realism' (Rosenberg 1994, 23). May I commend this excellent book to you as a corrective to your current tendency towards an overindulgent treatment of Realism?

30 'Politics as a Vocation' [*Politik als Beruf*] was a lecture given by Max Weber to the students of Munich University in January 1919 and published in October of the same year.

31 Thus, in his powerful conservative critique of the United States' grand strategy since the 1940s, Christopher Layne (2006, 203–5) invokes Weber's ethic of responsibility in support of an affirmation of Realism's 'moral sensibilities'.

32 For the sake of my own philosophical conscience, let me just emphasize that I use the expression 'normative realism' here not to refer to the meta-ethical doctrine moral realism, which holds that evaluative sentences are true or false in the same way that other assertoric sentences are, but to whatever normative theory might be worked up out of Realism as a positive theory of 'the international'. The terminological confusion is likely be increased by the profusion of strategic doctrines—'Wilsonian realism', 'ethical realism' and so on—being offered by the United States in the wake of the neoconservative debacle in Iraq.

10 Capitalism, uneven and combined development, and the transhistoric

Sam Ashman[1]

Introduction

That understanding 'globalization' and socio-economic development through the broad rubric of uneven and combined development (U&CD) has provoked debate is to be welcomed greatly. Within the discipline of IR, this is in large measure thanks to Justin Rosenberg's (1996; 2006; 2007) efforts to develop the concept as the basis of a theory of the international. This chapter explores some of the themes raised by Rosenberg, in particular in his exchange with Alex Callinicos (Rosenberg and Callinicos 2008). More specifically, it examines whether or not U&CD is usefully seen as a transhistoric general abstraction or whether it needs to be situated within particular modes of production, if not the capitalist mode of production in particular. According to Rosenberg (80–88), U&CD captures 'a sociological characteristic of all historical development' since 'all societies coexist with and interact with others' thus 'super-add[ing] a lateral field of causality over and above "domestic" determinations'. 'The real issue', suggests,

> is not the scale of difference in any given case, so much as its existence in every case: there *are* no societies whose development has not been fundamentally inflected by relations with others. And there *is* no wider social formation whose developmental trajectory does not include a significant dimension composed of the course of interactions among its parts.

U&CD entails 'differentiation', 'interactivity' and accounts for 'the transhistoric fact of geopolitical multiplicity' (Rosenberg and Callinicos 2008, 88, 80). Therefore, it is an essential tool for understanding the international sphere and the horizontal fact of political fragmentation between states—a major question confronting Marxists in IR. By contrast, Callinicos prefers to emphasize that mode of production analysis is critical to understanding the 'specific modalities of the inter-societal'. The nature of production relations prevailing in a particular region 'is likely to have a decisive effect on the form taken by inter-societal relations' and U&CD's 'actual modalities in specific regions and periods' (Callinicos and Rosenberg 2008, 101–2).

This chapter attempts to further develop Callinicos' argument about analysis based on a particular mode of production—indeed perhaps more so than he would himself, given his essential agreement with Rosenberg that U&CD is usefully seen as a transhistoric phenomenon. Rosenberg recognizes that U&CD as a general abstraction cannot 'furnish the particularities of any given mode of production, which ... are necessary for the general abstraction to be "cashed in"' (Callinicos and Rosenberg 2008, 88). Yet he persists in maintaining that U&CD's great transhistoric utility is that unevenness by definition posits difference and therefore multiplicity from the outset—that is, development between constituent parts can only be uneven because it involves more than one constituent part. We thus integrate the inter-societal into the social: it is no longer an 'add on' extra and we thus move beyond the limitations of Realism's 'anarchy' and sociology's 'society' (Callinicos and Rosenberg 2008, 88–94).

Whilst agreeing with this (surely it is difficult not to), it is rather thin gruel. How else could human beings develop relationships, languages, cultures, traditions, institutions and states other than in particular places at particular times? To imagine otherwise really would be a 'big bang' theory of history. To state that societies exist in the plural is mere description that neither helps explain the dynamic (or 'actual modalities') of combination between these societies (should it exist and Rosenberg does not demonstrate why it must exist) nor offers any explanation of unevenness or of the differences between societies. This is precisely because general (transhistoric) abstractions do not have explanatory power (Marx 1973). To the extent that something akin to U&CD can be discerned in pre-capitalist modes of production, we can *only* illuminate such a phenomenon with a theory of the particular mode of production in question, its relations and dynamics—that is, through the development of determinate abstractions. The laws of motion and tendencies of development of particular modes of production are of different historical types, they are not the same laws simply different historically (Fine 2004).

The first section of this chapter develops these points, arguing that U&CD is most usefully employed in the context of a theory of the capitalist mode of production, as capitalist social relations—and political forms—are historically unique in their systematic generation of both combination and unevenness. A danger with Rosenberg's analysis of U&CD as a transhistoric phenomena is that it loses sight of the 'great transformation' brought about by capitalist relations and political forms, despite the emphasis placed on this in earlier work (Rosenberg 1994). This is illustrated by looking at the specifically capitalist determinacy of combination and unevenness with particular emphasis on the spatially and technologically dynamic nature of the production process and inter-capitalist competition in the pursuit of surplus value.

In the second section, this chapter explores the variations in capitalist relations and political forms and points to some of the limitations in Trotsky's analysis. The distinctive dynamic of capitalist relations and political forms—particularly once the real subsumption of labour to capital is achieved in those societies which make the first transitions—forges a world economy and international division of labour which draws ever greater parts of the world into their orbit, incorporating some on a subordinate colonial basis as primary commodity producers in societies where the separation of the direct producers from the land is less complete (Marx 1976). This combined development leaves a critical legacy for uneven development and helps develop a relational conception of poverty and underdevelopment (Bernstein 1992).

Following this, we return to the discussion of the very limited value of transhistoric abstractions for Marxist theory. This emphasizes how 'science' lies not in the development of descriptive transhistoric general abstractions; but rather in the development of determinate abstractions (both abstract and concrete) *and* in the interaction of the tendencies and counter-tendencies (arising from the relations and processes these determinate abstractions seek to grasp) in historically particular circumstances. It is argued that U&CD operates at two levels: first, as a mediating level of analysis in the journey from an abstract conception of the capitalist mode of production to the more concrete concept of a specific social formation and; second, as a tool to analyze particular social formations or societies. This is not to 'falsely derive' unevenness from international production or world market as Rosenberg argues but to develop further our understanding of the variegated and unstable terrain capital is both produced by and in turn transforms, and of which the state system is a part (Callinicos and Rosenberg 2008, 99). This chapter concludes with some reflections on the status of U&CD in relation to a theory of the international.

The specificities of capitalist social relations and political forms

Marxism has a highly distinctive and powerful contribution to make to IR, to understanding the state and to understanding the state system. This concerns the primacy it gives to historically-specific social relations of production and the connection it makes between these relations and particular political forms. Marx and contemporary Marxist approaches refuse both to naturalize and universalize these relations and to analyze production in a manner which is divorced from social determinations. Production, by contrast, is as much of a black box for (Realist) IR as it is for mainstream economics. It is on the basis of this connection between historically-specific relations of production and political forms that Marxist approaches necessarily reject the reification of states and geopolitics so characteristic of mainstream IR (Rosenberg 1994).

This approach to the state, and to the state system, has been present in Marxism for some time. Indeed both contemporary and classical debates about imperialism explore this problematic (Halliday 2002; Sutcliffe 2002). Robert Brenner's (1977; 1986) account of the specificities of capitalist 'social property' relations (which, he argues, underpin modern economic growth) and Ellen Wood's (1981; 1995) account of the connection between these relations and the specificities of capitalist political forms are a useful departure point. This is not least because their approach is influential upon a growing body of Marxist scholarship in IR, including Rosenberg's earlier *Empire of Civil Society* (1994) which provided a powerful Marxist critique of Realism.

In Brenner's (1986, 31) rendition, for pre-capitalist modes of production both exploiters and exploited are 'free' of the market and the necessity of exchange. The direct producers have non-market access to their means of subsistence; they have effective control over the land and tools necessary to support themselves. Ownership of land does not in itself allow pre-capitalist exploiters access to part of the product. Surplus extraction usually takes the form of the transfer of surplus labour to the lord or to the state by means of labour services, rent and tax. Such bonds and duties are regarded as traditional but supported by a variety of forms of political, legal and military coercion. Under pre-capitalist modes, then, surplus extraction takes place by means of extra-economic coercion and is thus external to the production process itself. In this way, economic exploitation is 'achieved by political means' and coercive power is wielded by the appropriator (Wood 1981, 75). Where capitalist relations prevail, by contrast, surplus extraction is not done through political direction or duty or custom and obligation. Instead, surplus extraction takes place within the immediate process of production. The contractual relation between 'free' wage labour and private appro-priators ensures that the 'forfeit of surplus labour is an immediate condition of pro-duction itself' (Wood 1981, 80).

As surplus-labour is extracted through extra-economic coercion, feudal lords tend to direct resources to strengthening the means of coercion at their disposal in order to extract a greater amount of surplus from the direct producers, or dispossess others of their land and labour. For Brenner (1986, 32), the long-term developmental trend is 'toward stagnation, if not crisis'. But once the transition is made to capitalist relations 'where all the direct producers are separated from their means of subsistence, *above all the land*, and where no exploiters are able to maintain themselves through surplus-extraction by extra-economic coercion' (Brenner 1986, 33), the market-dependence of both capital and labour introduces rules of reproduction necessary to support modern economic growth. Units of capital have to compete to reproduce themselves and hence have an interest in reducing their costs of production (and therefore the price of their products) through productivity-enhancing investments (which also increase wages).

Capitalist relations thus introduce competition as a systematic dynamic under-pinning growth, expansion and crises. Wage-labour—'free' of all property and com-pelled to sell its labour-power—is organized cooperatively and on a growing scale. The extraction of surplus value in the process of production rests on the separation of labour from its conditions of production and the creation of a class of 'free' wage labourers in relation to capital. This separation is also the basis of a class of private owners of land, and the creation of capitalist (or modern) landed property. Indeed, it is this very ownership that acts as the means by which direct producers are dis-possessed of land (Neocosmos 1986). Capitalist landed property is a contradictory social relation, not a technical or natural factor of production where rent is a corollary of price theory (Fine 1994). Indeed, capitalist social relations can be usefully seen as based on a series of illusory separations, which are real but simultaneously deceptive. These include:

- the separation of the direct producers from the land and the means of production, making them dependent upon the sale of labour-power;
- competing units of capital separated from each other but dependent on each other for raw materials or means of production or consumption goods to repro-duce its workforce from other units of capital;
- the separation of landed property from both capital and wage-labour;
- the differentiation of the state from civil society;
- the separation of finance and commerce from other forms of capital.

What are the implications for the capitalist state form? Wood (1981) builds from Marx a distinctive account of the connection between the particularities of these relations and the emergence of a unique state form. As noted, under pre-capitalist modes, surplus extraction takes place by means of extra-economic coercion and is thus outside or external to the production process itself. Where capitalist relations obtain, surplus extraction is not done through political direction or duty or custom and obligation. Instead surplus extraction is internal, or it takes place within the immediate process of production. The contractual relation between 'free' wage labour and private appropriators ensures that the 'forfeit of surplus labour is an immediate condition of production itself' (Wood 1981, 80). The extraction of surplus value does not, therefore, require a coercive authority on a day-to-day basis once market dependence is established, and this coercive authority is not directly in the hands of private surplus appropriators. Instead there is a division of labour between the 'private' moment of appropriation by a class and the 'public' moment of coercion by the state, a division of labour which grants capital extraordinary control of (private) production and divests it of (public) social responsibility (Wood 1981, 81–82).

This is not to suggest that 'politics' is extraneous to capitalist relations or that a state and coercive authority is rendered redundant: force is necessary to dispossess; to protect private property and class rule in general; to enforce contracts between the buyer and the seller of labour-power; to enforce the norms of commodity exchange; to raise taxes; set interest and exchange rates. Whilst the power of surplus extraction is 'not directly grounded in the coercive apparatus of the state', it remains dependent upon such a coercive power that both serves surplus appropriation and is autonomous from it (Wood 1981, 84).[2] But the capitalist state form has a 'special character' as a consequence of the development of a division of labour rendered possible by the fact that 'the "moment" of coercion is separate from the "moment" of appropriation'. The 'two moments—appropriation and coercion—are allocated separately to a "private" appropriating class and a specialized "public" coercive institution, the state" (Wood 1981, 81–82). In this, we have the peculiar separation of the economic and the political under capitalism, and we have the particular form of the political under capitalism.

The specific form of the capitalist state and the specific form of private appropriation of capital develop together in a dialectical process over time, as does the 'privatization' of economic power. It is not necessary for private appropriation to develop prior to the capitalist state form. Indeed, the state is vital to the dispossession of the direct producers from the land and other means of production and to the concentration of capital upon which the development of capitalism depends and which is achieved also by non-market means. The state is not only critical to the act of dispossession, or the original primitive accumulation, it also aids the transformation of the dispossessed, over time, into a collective workforce (Marglin 1982). The original transitions to capitalism entailed interconnected processes, including the emergence of a capitalist class and the development of a home market. All these processes are dependent upon the intervening and mediating role of the state and, in addition, entail the rise of cities and the extension of the spatial division of labour (Walker and Buck 2007).

Wood and Brenner's development of the notion of the separation between economics and politics was a means to deal with specificities of *capitalist* politics, not evidence of 'real' autonomy or that the state—though modified in the post-war period by its welfare functions—is still a guarantor of capitalism's persistence. It was not therefore to surrender to a Weberian (or Giddens) inspired conception of modernity marked by the differentiation of politics and society. One limitation in these earlier debates was that the state was too often theorized in the singular (Barker 1978a; von Braunmühl 1978). There was also a neglect of tendencies that, in changing form, push towards the fusion of economics and politics. These are discussed in the next section. But for now there is one implication of the above analysis that is relevant to a discussion of whether U&CD can usefully be seen as a transhistoric general abstraction.

The extraction of surplus labour within the process of production gives capital the power to exploit workers beyond its immediate territory in a way not possible for feudal lords and so gives capital historically unprecedented geographical mobility. John Holloway (1995, 123) makes the point explicit when he suggests that 'the destruction of personal bondage was also the destruction of geographical constraint'.[3] Under the impetus of the competition between capitals and technological change, capitalist relations generate both unevenness and an unprecedented scale of interconnection; production and exchange relations on a world scale; and the extension of the sphere and the interconnections of generalized commodity production.[4] The competitive pursuit of surplus value creates a drive to reproduce the conditions necessary for capital accumulation elsewhere with its growing and changing demand for inputs, outlets and labour-power. But this extension of the terrain of accumulation is as dependent upon state power to achieve the conditions necessary for accumulation as the first transitions. At the same time, advanced capitalism can also create conditions conducive for its more 'primitive' forms, for example as capital intensive production releases workers for super-exploitation elsewhere.

Callinicos points to the process that Brenner has dubbed 'political accumulation' as an example of pre-capitalist U&CD (Callinicos and Rosenberg 2008). Surely the most important point is that the dynamics of feudal and capitalist expansion are different. Driven by the limits to productive development set by feudal relations, lords build up their military power for territorial expansion and state-building. This feudal political accumulation thus produces centralized monarchies, state bureaucracies, armies and war. As capitalist relations develop in Holland and England in the 16th and 17th century, they ensure wealth gathered in the mercantile period is channelled into productive investment. As the feudal monarchies of Spain and Portugal were to discover, the wealth plundered during the mercantile period did not fuel an industrial revolution on the Iberian Peninsula precisely because social relations were not transformed.

The transformation in social relations is the critical basis from which to explain the 'great divergence' that opened up between Europe and North America on the one hand and the rest of the world on the other.[5] On the foundation of this transformation, we can see the indivisibility of the creation of the 'core' and the 'periphery' of the world economy (Wolf 1997). In addition, on the basis of the industrial revolution and real subsumption of labour to capital, the world economy is transformed further. Capitalist relations are both rooted in international processes and transform these processes, including geopolitics.

The above may seem glaringly obvious, but suggesting U&CD is a transhistoric process loses sight of the importance of this moment. The 'great transformation' in England and Holland facilitated further external expansion, which further aided the development of capitalism at home. The new *capitalist* states thus expanded externally and developed domestically, but did so only on the basis of transformed social relations which then exerted pressure on other regions of the world at the level of both state and societal relations. In short, they established a symbiotic relationship between state building, colonial expansion and capitalist development at home. This exerted strong pressure on others to follow suit and continues to have a lasting impact on the social relations of the societies colonized. Thus, once capitalism is established in one part of the world it affects and changes the form of transition to capitalist development elsewhere.

The relatively advanced exert pressure on the relatively backward through both the international division of labour and the international system of states. These pressures compel (some of) the relatively backward to catch up, but they do so in a way which cannot simply replicate earlier transitions (Trotsky 1962; 1970; 1977). The geographical expansion of capitalism according to a single logic of accumulation thus produces diverse forms and social and political differentiation, not homogeneity. Peculiar combinations arise, the 'amalgam of archaic with more contemporary forms' (Trotsky 1977, 27). Moreover, capital seizes hold of existing forms and appropriates them for itself. Capital uses them for its own purposes, even at times intensifying non-capitalist modes of exploitation, expanding its sphere of influence through what on the surface appear to be archaic but are actually the most modern of forms (Trotsky 1977; Neocosmos 1986).

Understanding the capitalist state system: multiplicity and diversity

Through explicating the nature of capitalist social relations we can see combination created on a specifically capitalist basis that heightens differences between those who make the transition and those who do not. This means subsequent transitions cannot take precisely the same form again. Whilst there is only one type of capitalism, it is variegated in form. The problem of the international is not only that states are multiple in number, but that there are many different kinds of states. To address this, we need to examine the concrete variations in the process through which capitalist social relations and state forms are established in different places and times. To do so, we need to move on from the beginnings of a theory of capitalism which emphasizes the separation of economics and politics to the addition of further levels of determination that produce tendencies in the opposite direction—to the fusion of economics and politics.

As mentioned above, capital inserted itself into various territories in various waves: first in the form of merchant capital and later in the form of industrial capital. The nature and impact of colonial domination varies between periods in the development of capitalism (Bernstein 2000). Changes in capital—its restructuring and transformation in the 'core' of the world economy—are transmitted to the colonial world where social relations are restructured in varying and complex ways, transforming some class relations and preserving others. Particularly once the real subsumption of labour to capital is achieved in those states that make the initial transition to capitalism, production relations elsewhere are greatly affected as the world market is transformed (Marx 1976; Fine 1978; Fine and Harris 1979). As Marx (1981, 451) put it, 'it is not trade that revolutionizes industry, but rather industry that constantly revolutionizes trade'. Increasing productivity greatly strengthens competitive pressure.

Those on the 'periphery' of the system become tied or forced into an international division of labour where they specialize in the production of primary products and where the separation of the direct producers from the land is far less complete than in the societies that underwent the original transition. Large pools of surplus labour are not absorbed by industrial production and poor 'peasants' remain in possession of land (Bernstein 1988). This bequeaths a critical legacy for U&CD at a global level. Furthermore, it facilitates the development of a relational conception of poverty and 'underdevelopment'. The term is from Henry Bernstein (1992, 24) who argues relational approaches emphasize mechanisms generating wealth and poverty simultaneously. This is contrasted with residual conceptions of poverty which suggest that poverty is a result of being 'left out' of 'development' and can be addressed through extending the sphere of market relations (Kaplinsky 2005).[6] Whether and how these processes actually apply is of course highly contingent and requires the historical analysis of specific instances.

This discussion also highlights how the relationship between land, labour and the state varies in different historical contexts. As Trotsky argues, the pattern of the original transition can never be repeated with exactitude. It is, henceforth, shaped by the outcome of earlier transitions, and is marked by the period when the transition is made. For those parts of the world that are forced into capital's orbit via colonialism, the colonial state needs to be seen as a variant of the capitalist state—indeed as a remarkable example of the fusion of economics and politics (Lonsdale and Berman 1979). A very large set of questions pertain to the differences in processes of commodification in the transition to capitalism and within existing capitalism, and how differences in these processes generate different types or kinds of capitalism (Bernstein 2007). Thus, capital can be seen to introduce a single logic, but one which results in diverse forms.

Trotsky is brilliant in giving a sweeping vision of how capital binds together in a historically unprecedented manner, which results in an extraordinary complexity of relations and forms. But whilst Trotsky clearly assumes Marx's analysis of competitive accumulation as the driving force behind the creation of world economy—and therefore the basis for U&CD as a phenomenon—it is not something he ever articulates fully. Nor does he provide any clear specification of the impact of colonial and imperial expansion on the precise form of social relations in the colonized world or of the specificities of these forms. Yet Trotsky remains profound in his analysis of successful late industrialization, not only in his prescience in recognizing the importance of finance for late development. He would influence later work by Alexander Gerschenkron (1966), who analyzed how 'late developers' sought to emulate the global 'leader', Britain. Despite its tiny percentage of the world's population, Britain dominated global industrial output due to its advanced production techniques.[7] Gerschenkron described the 'advantages of backwardness' in very similar terms to Trotsky's 'privilege of backwardness'. He explored uneven development in the sense of the aggravation of pre-existing (sub-national) regional differences under the impact of industrialization (north and south in Italy) and in terms of the reversal of 'national order' by virtue of institutional innovation and intervention (Russia, France, Austria, Bulgaria and others). There are connections too with Gramsci's argument that Germany, Japan and Russia experienced 'passive revolutions' or 'bourgeois revolutions from above' under the pressure of the world market and state system (see Morton 2007c and this volume). For these late developers, the state facilitated rapid accumulation through a number of measures: overseas borrowing; the establishment of state-owned savings banks to concentrate savings; state investment in infrastructure; and the expansion of technical educational provision. For 'developmental states' in the post-war period too, the state, particularly in relation to the allocation of capital to industry, would again prove to be crucial.

Here the limitations of emphasis on the separation between economics and politics discussed above are important. Emphasis on this separation was seen as a way of overcoming the limitations of earlier theories of the state and/or base and superstructure models of economics and politics. But in emphasizing the separation of economics and politics, we may be left with the state as a territorially-based unit of coercion, a provider of legal norms, perhaps even as an ideological unifying force via nationalism. There is a danger, then, of neglecting those determinants that produce tendencies to push economics and politics together. It is not simply that the state is deeply connected with struggles over land, dispossession and commodification before capitalist relations and market imperatives are customary. The state is continuously involved in the appropriation and dispersal of surplus value through taxation and expenditure, the regulation of accumulation, the restructuring of capital, the regulation of exchange rates, and influencing relations of distribution through tax and income policy.

The German State Debate has the merit of discussing such factors as the inability of capitalism through the logic of competitive accumulation to provide the necessary preconditions for its own reproduction, and capital's tendencies to breakdown and failure (Hirsch 1978). This state involvement is not merely to 'sustain' the market but is often aimed at 'distorting' it in the interests of particular capitals or sections of capital as the state seeks to restructure to resume accumulation. In the advanced industrialized economies, this was not simply as a result of workers' political pressure but the necessities born of competition and reproduction as capitalism develops (Fine and Murfin 1984; Gough 1979). This is in evidence not only in the advanced industrialized economies in the post-war period, but in the countries of the former Soviet bloc and in the 'developmental states' of the post-colonial world. But in the post-war era, latecomers or 'developmental states' did not have the option of boosting domestic primitive accumulation with colonial primitive accumulation as the early capitalist powers did (Byres 2005).

Marx's method and the theoretical status of uneven and combined development

So far the argument has attempted to demonstrate the specifically capitalist determinacy of U&CD. What, then, of the discussion of the transhistoric with which we began? As we saw in the introduction, Rosenberg contends that the transhistoric value of U&CD lies in how it posits multiplicity and diversity from the outset and is thus a better basis from which to develop more concrete analysis than either anarchy (Realism) or society (sociology). Callinicos agrees that U&CD can be seen as a general abstraction, though is more wary of the dangers and pitfalls in the use of general abstractions, preferring mode of production-based analysis (Callinicos and Rosenberg 2008, 86). However neither really follows this through.

It is not simply that Marx makes use of general abstractions—he clearly does, most famously in the '1857 General Introduction' (Marx 1973)—but he develops the distinction between the two precisely in order to demonstrate the explanatory poverty of general abstractions, which are of very limited use for understanding reality or the actual (Murray 1988).[8] They do not, and cannot, move beyond the most general description to the provision of explanation. As Marx puts it (1973, 88): 'Common to all stages of production, there are determinations which are fixed by thought as general, but the so-called *general conditions* of all production are nothing other than these abstract moments with which no actual historical stage of production is grasped'. The inadequacy of general abstractions lies precisely in their transhistoric nature and inability to grasp difference.

> The labour process as we have presented it in its simple and abstract moments, is purposive activity toward the production of use-values; appropriation of the natural for human needs; universal condition of the material exchange between man and nature; eternal natural condition of human life and therefore independent of every form of this life, or better yet, equally common to all its forms of society.
>
> (Marx 1976, 290)

Marx thus contrasts labour with abstract labour; for example the labour process with the valorization process, and use-value with exchange-value (Marx 1976). Explanation requires the development of these latter determinate abstractions (and others) that make up the 'inner articulation' of capitalist society (Marx 1973, 108). Determinate abstractions in turn vary in their level of abstraction or complexity. It is precisely through making the second distinction between more and less concrete determinate categories that Marx is able to differentiate between surplus value and profit, and between the rate of surplus value and the rate of profit.

The capitalist mode may be 'a rich totality of determinations and relations' which exist simultaneously (Marx 1973, 100), but for purposes of analysis, determinations are introduced step-by-step. Furthermore, Marx's method demands that we identify which are the determinate abstractions appropriate for the particular object of study and how we order them properly among themselves, moving from the abstract to the concrete, understanding the interplay of tendencies and counter-tendencies in a historically given moment (Murray 1988). The position of concepts, the particular point at which a determination is introduced, is critical but this is not to say that determinations introduced relatively late are of lesser importance. The subject matter of *Capital* Volume III for example—the formation and equalization of the rate of profit, its tendency to fall and the counter-tendencies to this, the business cycle, commercial and money capital, rent and landed property—are crucial features of capitalism.

Rosenberg might well agree with this but he seems determined to have his cake and to eat it. He wants to recognize the value of the transhistoric nature of the inter-societal whilst also recognizing that U&CD 'cannot provide the basis of a substantive social theory'; cannot specify causal properties; and needs to be 'attached' to another major social theory such as historical materialism to be able to 'reach down to the level of concrete historical explanation' (Callinicos and Rosenberg 2008, 86). He points to the limits of mode of production analysis, rejects Brenner's theory of political accumulation—preferring to refer to 'differentiated, interactive temporalities of development within a wider social formation'—but then balks at placing U&CD at the level of 'the general abstract determinants which obtain in more or less all forms of society', as Marx put it. Yet Rosenberg thinks that at the level of 'general abstract determinants' we should put the 'strategic dimension to all social development' irrespective of whether it is the form of 'juridically differentiated, visibly separate societies'. This needs to be incorporated otherwise we will 'falsely derive' unevenness from international production or the world market and crises (Callinicos and Rosenberg 2008, 88–99).

It is argued here that it is perfectly possible to situate U&CD within analysis of the capitalist mode of production without such false derivation. If we do so, it aids the complex journey from the very abstract notion of the capitalist mode of production to more concrete kinds or types of societies or formations and particular forms of state. As Nicos Poulantzas put it, a mode of production is an abstraction that delineates the social characteristics of laws of motion arising from a specific relational form of human society, but it is an abstraction that does not exist in reality:

> The only thing which really exists is a historically determined *social formation*, ie a social whole, in the widest sense, at a given moment in its historical existence ... a social formation ... presents a particular combination, a specific overlapping of several 'pure' modes of production. (Poulantzas 1973, 15)

But in making the journey from the capitalist mode of production to a specific social formation, we must avoid Poulantzas' mistake of making the step in one leap, as though taking a flight of stairs 'with a single step on the way' (Fine, Lapavitsas and Milonakis 2000, 133).[9] This chapter suggests that mediating steps in this 'flight of stairs' are the state system and the U&CD of world economy and that both need to be understood in the context of the development of capitalism's different historical periods.

Callinicos (2007) thus seems correct to argue that the capitalist state system should be seen as a distinct level of determination within the capitalist mode of production. That the state system predates capitalism is no obstacle to such an analysis once we recognize how the state, the state system and geopolitical competition are transformed by the new capitalist powers in Holland and England. The state system develops prior to the dominance of capitalism but is incorporated into and adapted to the capitalist mode, producing specifically capitalist geopolitics. Late-comers striving to overcome 'backwardness' then consciously seek to develop particular state forms and are drawn into capitalist forms of geopolitical competition.

The state system must be treated as a dimension of the capitalist mode of production and geopolitical competition treated as capitalist geopolitical competition—not identical to the competition between capitals but certainly not a phenomenon that is external to capital. Gonzalo Pozo-Martin (2007, 556) thus seems correct to argue that we must 'theorize a *capitalist* geopolitical logic' shaped by class, accumulation, competitive struggles and crises; while Callinicos (2007, 542) seems mistaken to characterize this as a 'realist moment' of analysis. Capitalist states ensure the reproduction of economic and social relations as a whole and therefore simultaneously operate at economic, political and ideological levels. In doing so, the state is formed by and looks to domestic and international relations and the world economy—the latter itself a competitive, evolving, uneven and combined totality.

Conclusion

The above argument has emphasized the importance of situating U&CD within Marx's theory of the capitalist mode of production, as well as the significance of the capitalist determinacy of U&CD. The distinctive dynamic of capitalist relations and political forms create a world economy and international division of labour that incorporates some on a subordinate colonial basis and places historically unprecedented pressure on others to 'catch-up'. The relatively advanced exert pressure on the relatively backward through both the international division of labour and the international system of states. Capital has a historically unique drive to expand and in so doing create unevenness of its own making. It does not simply destroy all before it, but reshapes that which it finds to a much greater degree than any other mode of production. In the case of Russia's late development, Trotsky (1977) attempted to theorize how modern capitalist industry in the towns (financed from abroad) combined with state backed serfdom in the countryside, the latter strengthened by the former. His aim was to develop an understanding of the development of capitalism but also to determine how best to construct class and revolutionary alliances in such circumstances.

Trotsky's theory is specifically about capitalism: amalgams of the 'archaic and the contemporary' that are not transhistoric but very modern in form. It is not a theory of the initial or first transition to capitalism, but of 'late' capitalist development— that is, of development which occurs in the context, and perhaps also as a consequence, of capitalism's pre-existence elsewhere. Once capital exists in one small corner of north-western Europe, development for all others is immediately transformed. Trotsky clearly assumes Marx's analysis of competitive accumulation as the driving force behind the creation of the world economy and, therefore, the basis for U&CD as a phenomenon. However, it is not something he ever articulates fully. Nor does he provide any clear specification of the impact of colonial and imperial expansion on the precise form of social relations in the colonized world or of the specificities of these forms. Both Callinicos and Rosenberg are to be thanked for the debate they have stimulated on important matters for IR theory; clearly it would be foolish not to seek to develop Trotsky's notion.

But what are we to conclude about Rosenberg's persistent emphasis on U&CD's transhistoric possibilities for social theory? Despite a characteristically elegant discussion, all Rosenberg seems to assert in this respect is that we need to recognize multiplicity and unevenness at the historical outset. This assertion, it has been argued, only goes to demonstrate the poverty of general abstractions for understanding reality. As such, the argument remains sceptical about the results to be yielded by the insistence on the value of U&CD as a transhistoric category.

An alternative approach is suggested, which sees U&CD as operating at two levels: first, as a mediating level of analysis in the journey from the abstract concept of the capitalist mode of production to a concrete social formation or society—a concept which presupposes the existence of the state system, world economy and division of labour as distinct levels of determination, and; second, as a tool for looking at particular societies at particular points in time and how the 'amalgam of the archaic and the contemporary' shape them. This does not give us a fine-grained analysis of the relations and state forms that comprise those societies nor does it give full explication of the mechanism through which those societies might change. Nevertheless, the importance of the development of these intermediary concepts is that they aid the understanding of particular social formations without losing sight of the abstract tendencies of the capitalist mode of production or of capitalism as a dynamic and changing totality. This is not to suggest that U&CD alone helps us make that transition, but that it is a necessary stage on the journey that can help illuminate, at the level of both world economy and a specific society.

U&CD is thus useful for the 'problematic of the international' if situated firmly within a theory of the capitalist mode of production. Capitalist relations and the state system tie the world together on a particular basis generating both combination/connection and unevenness/divergence. Capital and the state system, via colonialism and imperialism, integrate large parts of world into the competitive dynamic of accumulation, which reproduces unevenness. U&CD does not replace analysis of the changing dynamics of capital accumulation, nor does it replace state theory (or the necessity to analyze geopolitics *as* geopolitics). It is however, one of the conceptual tools we need to develop an understanding of the international as an unjust, unequal and class-divided space.

Notes

1 I am grateful to Alex Anievas, Ben Fine and anonymous peer reviewers for their very helpful comments.
2 This is not to argue that extra-economic coercion does not exist under capitalism but that the system *as a whole* is based on free wage labour. See Banaji (1977; 2003) and Barker (1997).
3 This is not to argue that capital is 'a-spatial' once determinations at a lower level of abstraction are introduced. Capitalist development is spatially highly contradictory, producing tendencies to both geographical expansion and dispersal but also to unevenness and concentration (Weeks 2001).
4 Lacher and Teschke (2007, 579) thus seem mistaken to suggest that the *unevenness* of capitalist development does not arise as a consequence of its own nature but arises from the combination of the capitalist and the non-capitalist whilst *combination* arises at the geopolitical level. The *combination* of uneven and combined development is much deeper than just combination at the geopolitical level, as we come on to argue, whilst competition between capitals systematically generates its own unevenness.

5 The term is borrowed loosely from Kenneth Pomeranz (2000) but for an important Marxist critique of Pomeranz, see Brenner and Isett (2002).

6 For an example of the latter approach see Collier (2007), and for a critique see Grove (2008).

7 Needless to say, Gerschenkron's analysis is stripped of all the radical content to be found in Trotsky. Van Der Linden (2007) points to how Gerschenkron was an Austro-Marxist and critical supporter of the Soviet Union in the 1920s and 1930s. So it is highly likely he was familiar with Trotsky's work, especially as *The History of the Russian Revolution* was published in German in the early 1930s—though Gerschenkron did not refer to his left wing past during his later life as an émigré in the US.

8 Murray (1988) argues that the distinction is clearly present in Marx's 1844 'Paris Manuscripts' and *The German Ideology* in addition to the *Grundrisse* and *Capital*.

9 The metaphor is not employed in relation to Poulantzas, but is apt for present purposes.

11 Approaching 'the international'

Beyond Political Marxism

Jamie C Allinson and Alexander Anievas[1]

Introduction

In rebuke to those mainstream IR scholars who identified Marxist thought with Soviet diplomatic practice, the years since the collapse of the USSR have seen a flourishing of Marxist writing in the field. This trend has been stimulated, in the best traditions of praxis, by the need to account for actually existing international politics: in the debate on 'globalization' in the 1990s and the subsequent 'return to empire' in the early years of this century. For many Marxists, the issues of empire and imperialism had never really died away. These 'revived' debates have, however, revealed the persistence of a series of dilemmas in Marxist thought on international relations. In what follows, we focus on one dimension of these many issues—specifically what has been termed the 'problematic of the international' (Rosenberg 2000, 65). Most generally stated, this can be defined as the myriad theoretical, political, normative, and philosophical problems flowing from the division and interaction of humanity into a multiplicity of political communities. Here, we enquire into the theoretical issues emerging from Marxism's engagement with this international problematique, noting some of its political implications.

In our original contribution to the *Cambridge Review of International Affairs* section, we attempted to address some of these issues through an exploration of Leon Trotsky's concept of uneven and combined development (U&CD) and Justin Rosenberg's more recent reformulation of this idea into a transhistorical theory of 'the international'. We sought to demonstrate that although characteristics associated with U&CD can be found throughout history, it is only under the generalized commodity production of the capitalist epoch that U&CD's distinctive effects, articulated and expressed through inter-societal competition, are *fully* activated. From this perspective, we criticized the ambiguities in Rosenberg's use of U&CD as both a 'general abstraction' to be incorporated into our theoretic assumptions and a theory unto itself, whilst further illustrating the qualitative differences between 'simple' and fully-formed modes of U&CD in the pre-capitalist and capitalist eras, respectively.

We remain committed to this general line of argument. Nevertheless, it became apparent to us that our argument suffered from some haziness which, given our own criticisms of Rosenberg, needed to be addressed. In particular, the precise differences between pre-capitalist and capitalist forms of U&CD required further clarification.

We thus address some common issues raised in recent Marxist debates on the international whilst seeking to elaborate themes first brought out in our original contribution by further specifying some of the problems in applying U&CD to precapitalist world politics. In doing so, we work through a critical interrogation of the 'Political Marxism'[2] approach associated with Robert Brenner and Ellen Meiksins Wood and, in particular, the works of Hannes Lacher and Benno Teschke in IR. Given the latter's sustained and rigorous attention to the international problematic, as well their engagement with Trotsky's U&CD concept, this seemed an appropriate starting point for our investigation. We begin by examining the key theoretical claims of Political Marxism in relation to their 'solution' to the dilemmas derivative of Marx's basis/superstructure (*Basis/Überbau*) metaphor through which we then explore the larger problematic of the international in Lacher and Teschke's work.

Political Marxism and the international

Social property relations and the basis/superstructure problem[3]

A central claim of historical materialism is that the 'direct relationship of the owners of the conditions of production' (the production 'basis') determines 'the specific form of the state in each case' (the political 'superstructure') (Marx 1981, 927). As critics argue, however, the correspondence between any given relations and forces of production to particular states or politics is anything but direct. The Political Marxist concept of 'social property relations' is a parsimonious attempt at solving this basis/superstructure problem within historical materialism. In understanding the importance of the property relations concept, and its implications for the traditional historical materialist basis/superstructure conceptualization, it is helpful to briefly examine the theoretical origins of Political Marxism.

The works of Robert Brenner, Ellen Meiksins Wood and their students emerged as a loose-knit theoretical project intended to re-instate the crucial role of class agency to Marxism. They sought in turn to reconnect the severed link between abstract theory and concrete historical analysis viewed as symptomatic of the more structuralist forms of historical materialism influential at the time of their original interventions in the late 1970s and early 1980s. The dissociation of theory and history charge was particularly directed against the works of the Althusserian Marxists, World Systems Theory, and GA Cohen's (1978) seminal *A Defence of Karl Marx's Theory of History*. According to Brenner and Wood, these held a mechanistically reductionist conception of Marx's basis/superstructure metaphor, resulting in an overly techno-determinist analysis of the origins and development of capitalism and a 'de-socializing' of the materialist basis. In a critique leveled at Marxism in general, but which appeared primarily directed at the structuralists, Wood (1981, 68) charges historical materialists with adopting

> modes of analysis which, explicitly or implicitly, treat the economic 'base' and the legal, political, and ideological 'superstructures' which 'reflect' or 'correspond' to it as qualitatively different, more or less enclosed and 'regionally'

separated spheres. This is most obviously true of orthodox base-superstructure theories. It is also true of their variants which speak of economic, political, and ideological 'factors', 'levels' or 'instances', no matter how insistent they may be about the *interaction* of factors or instances, or about the remoteness of the 'last instance' in which the economic sphere finally determines the rest.

Following from this, Brenner and Wood stressed the ahistoricism of Marxist structuralism, and the consequential naturalization of capitalism, thereby reproducing the very bourgeois reifications Marx so chastised the classical political economists for.

Traditional Marxist explanations of the rise of capitalism have generally viewed it as a centuries-long process whereby capitalist relations *immanently* emerge within the *interstices* of feudal (or, more generally, pre-capitalist) societies. This was the result of the expansion of trade and exchange relations, quantitative accumulation of wealth and/or development of the productive forces. Yet, in assuming 'the operation of norms of capitalist rationality in a situation where capitalist social relations of production did not exist', such conventional explanations lapsed into a 'neo-Smithian' (that is, bourgeois) mode of theorizing (Brenner 1977, 45). Explaining the origins of capitalist development and modern economic growth in terms of *pre-capitalist* agents' responses to the spread of market exchange opportunities or new technologies take for granted precisely what needs to be explained: the existence of capitalist social relations (see Brenner 1986; Comninel 1987; Wood 1999; 1995, 49–75; Teschke 2003).[4] The 'neo-Smithian' model of capitalist development is thus charged with being inherently teleological; a philosophically idealist 'history-in-becoming' is no history at all.

In moving beyond the ahistoricism and techno-determinism associated with the basis/superstructure architecture, Political Marxists have developed Brenner's idea of social property relations. These identify the 'rules of reproduction' to which actors are subject within historically-bounded social systems. As Brenner (1986, 46) defines them, social property relations are conceived as specifying

> the relationships of possession and coercion among economic actors—the producers and producers, the exploiters and exploiters, the producers and exploiters—which make it possible for them to have the regular access to the means of production and/or the economic product which is necessary for their maintenance (reproduction) as they were.

Accordingly, these 'property relations will, to a large degree, determine the pattern of economic development of any society'. They set both the 'possibilities and limits for economic action by individuals and collectives' whilst inducing 'the adoption by these agents of specific strategies as the best way to pursue their interests' (Brenner 1986, 26; Harman and Brenner 2006, 137). The aggregate result of the carrying out of these strategies, or 'rules for reproduction', constitutes the historical 'logic of process' (as Wood terms it) unique to modes of production.

So far, these claims pose little challenge to the more traditional interpretations of Marx. However, Brenner cuts through the problem of basis and superstructure by making the *form of state itself constitutive of all modes of production*, whilst further severing this state-form from any relationship to the development of the productive forces. In pre-capitalist production modes, the direct producers (notably peasants) generally held full access to the means of subsistence—that is, they possessed the land, tools and labour-power necessary to maintain themselves *independently* of the market.[5] Consequently, the agrarian exploiting classes (or lords in European feudalism) necessarily relied on what Marx termed 'extra-economic coercion' to appropriate the surpluses necessary for their own reproduction. In almost every historical case, pre-capitalist ruling classes were 'thus obliged to construct, and maintain membership in, *political communities* ... that could maintain effective coercion and control' necessary to appropriate the product of the peasants. Crucially then, the capacity of the exploiting classes to reproduce themselves depended *not* on their participation in the production process—that is, by organizing and managing production through a specific labour process (or division of labour)—but in their ability to organize themselves *politically* (Brenner 2001, 178; see Brenner 1986). Hence, as Teschke avers: 'the economic process of production precedes the political process of exploitation, defined by rents in kind or in cash. The moment of exploitation is not economically built into the relations of production'. With some 'partial exceptions', he goes on, 'there is virtually no production relation between the lord and the dependent peasant' (Teschke 2003, 75fn9). Pre-capitalist social relations are, therefore, always (to use Brenner's term) 'politically constituted' forms of property relations.

The social property relations approach, therefore, dispenses with the idea of basis and superstructure. Modes of production are distinguished by the patterns and relations of distribution of access to the means of production. Only under capitalist property relations do we see the structured differentiation of the political and economic into distinct institutional spheres as methods of surplus-extraction become uncoupled from 'extra-economic' coercive means. In other words, under capitalism extra-economic coercion (that is, state power) and economic coercion (the compulsion to sell one's labour in order to access the means of production) are necessarily separate. 'As in every other exploitative system', Wood (2006, 15) writes, 'there are two "moments" of exploitation: the appropriation of surplus labour and the coercive power that sustains it. In capitalism, however these two "moments": are uniquely separate from each other'. This institutional differentiation of the political and economic is thus taken as the *differentia specifica* of capitalism. What are the implications of this analysis of capitalism and its origins for international relations?

Capitalism and the states system

For Brenner's students, the development of capitalism in England during the 17th century is taken as both the paradigmatic case of capitalism as well as its originating context.[6] Starting from this idea that capitalism first emerged as an entirely novel 'mode of exploitation' within post-1688 England, Hannes Lacher and Benno Teschke problematize conventional interpretations of the co-evolution of the modern international system of sovereign states and capitalism shared by most Marxists and IR theorists alike. Teschke (2003) declares the 1648 Treaty of Westphalia ending the Thirty Years' War—commonly described in mainstream IR as inaugurating *modern* international relations—as the foundational 'myth' of IR theory. A central corollary of this re-periodization of the origins of capitalism and the international states system is that the latter then preceded the former. How so?

According to the Political Marxists, the feudal social property relations gave neither peasant nor lord incentive to introduce more productive technological methods: Rather the lordly interest lay in extracting more surplus by directly coercive means. This could be done by pushing the peasants to the limit of subsistence or by seizing the demesnes of other lords. The latter course resulted in a process of 'political accumulation' amongst the lords themselves—a war-driven process of state formation. The lords left standing at the end of this process formed the basis for the absolutist state.[7] In contrast to classical Marxist conceptions of absolutism as a *transitional* or hybrid social formation—a transformed version of feudalism conducive to the development of capitalism—Lacher and Teschke (following Wood 1999 and Comninel 1987) view it as 'a *sui generis* social formation, displaying a specific mode of government and determinate pre–modern and pre–capitalist domestic and international "laws of motion"' (Teschke 2003, 191; Lacher 2005, 31–34).[8] Absolutism is thus conceived as a distinct 'mode of exploitation'. Unlike capitalism, the direct producers are subject to extra-economic coercion but, unlike feudalism, the coercive authorities are centralized. This conceptualization of the absolutist state follows from Lacher and Teschke's collapsing of the basis-superstructure relation into the social property relations concept and, their commitment to an almost 'platonic' conception of capitalism as a theoretical abstraction of which empirical reality must conform or remain something outside.

It is not at all clear, however, why a single economic structure (in this case, feudalism) cannot have varying 'corresponding' state forms, as Lacher and Teschke (2007, 571) allow for capitalism. In denying such co-variations between basis and superstructure, Lacher and Teschke tends towards the same fault for which Wood (1995) had so convincingly criticized structural Marxism: that is, an unnecessarily abstract and determinist conception of production modes which, among other things, results in a gnawing gap between the concrete-historical and abstract-theoretical.[9] For, what 'really existing' capitalist society corresponds to their abstract model of capitalism as defined by the differentiation of the political (state) and economic (surplus extraction/market) spheres?[10] What particularly concerns us here is the consequences of this restrictive conception of capitalism in Lacher and Teschke's theorization of its relationship with the states system and geopolitical rivalry.

From this historical analysis of the emergence of capitalism within the context of an antecedent states system, Lacher and Teschke claim that the 'interstate-ness of capitalism' cannot be derived from the nature of the capital relation itself. Rather, it must be 'regarded as a "historical legacy" of pre-capitalist development' (Lacher 2002, 148; 2006, 60; Teschke 2003, 145–46). 'Taking the international character of global capitalism to be a *contingent* aspect of capitalism', the states system is conceived as being structurally internalized within the totality of capitalist social relations through the spatio-temporally differentiated and geopolitically mediated development of capitalist social relations (Lacher 2006, 60, emphasis ours: see Lacher and Teschke

2007). For Lacher and Teschke then, there is neither any structural connection between capitalism and a multi-state system nor anything inherent to the nature of capitalism which would necessarily perpetuate it: the relationship is conceived as an entirely contingent one. As Teschke (2003, 144–45) puts it, 'there is no constitutive or genetic link between capitalism and a geopolitical universe'. 'Counterfactually', Lacher and Teschke (2007, 574) claim,

> it is perfectly possible to imagine that had capitalism emerged within an imperial formation—let us say, the Roman Empire—it would not have required its political break-up into multiple territorial units. Capitalism did not develop out of itself the system of territorial states that fragments capitalist world society; inversely, capitalism is structured by an international system because it was born in the context of a pre-existing system of territorial states.

Lacher and Teschke's main theoretical influence, Robert Brenner (2006a, 84), has arrived at a similar conclusion: 'Abstractly speaking, a single state governing global capital is perfectly conceivable and probably most appropriate from the standpoint of capital'.

Such reasoning is not universally shared by Political Marxists. Ellen Wood (1999; 2002; 2006) has, for example, persistently argued against the idea of global capital superseding the international system, insisting upon a necessarily systemic relationship between global capitalism and a multiplicity of states. Wood's position, however, seems theoretically tenuous: falling back on a 'soft functionalism' without specifying the precise mechanism(s) linking the requirements of capital to a multi-state system (Chibber 2005, 157; see Callinicos 2007). For the determinate relationship between capital and the states system is, according to Political Marxism, simply that economic and coercive power are separate. Since all states share the characteristic of separating economic from 'extra-economic' coercion, little can be said about the reasons for their multiplicity and competition in terms of that separation.

The social property relations approach therefore encounters a particular problem when dealing with multiple competitive states under capitalist relations. Despite Wood's resolve in claiming that 'the specific division of labour between political and economic power' constitutive of capitalism 'means that global capital needs the fragmentation of political space', she seems to acknowledge Political Marxism's difficulty in actually theorizing this relationship, conceding that it 'is not something that can be grasped entirely on the theoretical plane'. 'To a large extent', Wood continues, 'this proposition is a lower-level practical observation about the impossibility of sustaining on a large geographical scale the close regulation and predictability capital needs' (Wood 2006, 32, 26). The Political Marxists are led to this conclusion because of the enforced—if admirably rigorous—characterization of social property relations, from which the conceptual requirements of capital are to be derived like a problem in calculus. Yet, at what point do such dissociations between theory and 'empirical reality' become problematic for theoretical explanation?

Socially uneven and geopolitically combined development

To circumvent this empirical/theory disjunction, Lacher and Teschke (2007) turn to Trotsky's notion of U&CD, alternatively conceived as 'socially uneven and geopolitically combined development'. However, U&CD seems difficult to match with Lacher and Teschke's social property relations approach. The reason for this is that it depends upon the premise of 'development'. The underlying logic of Trotsky's position was that the developmental subject was the forces of production, 'the productivity of labour' (Trotsky 1977, 31), involving a dialectical relationship between the forces and relations of production. Yet, the overall thrust of social property relations is to deny explanatory weight to these forces, while rejecting the notion of their development in non-capitalist societies. Brenner argues that 'for the most part, new forces of production were readily assimilable by already existing social classes' (Harman and Brenner 2006, 138). This position seems at least partially contradictory with Teschke's argument, with which we agree:

> developmental potential of regionally differentiated sets of property régimes generates inter-regional unevenness, which translates into international pressures that spark sociopolitical crises in 'backward' polities. These crises activate and intensify the domestic fault lines in regionally pre-existing class constellations—processes that lead to power struggles within and between polities that renegotiate and transform class relations, territorial scales and state forms. These social conflicts result in highly specific combinations of the old and the new. The dynamics of domestic trajectories are thus accelerated, their sociological composition transformed, and their directionality deflected in unforeseen ways, while their results react back on the international scene.
>
> (Teschke 2005, 19)

Productive forces seem here to matter in the form of 'developmental potential' and the fact such potential inherent in one 'set of property regimes' exercises pressure on another implies some ranking amongst them. This claim suggests the kind of dialectical interaction between property regimes and forces of production Trotsky had in mind. It is the presence of these more advanced forces (emergent from the greater developmental potential of capitalist property relations)—*not in and of itself the balance of class relations*—that forces the adoption of the new property relations in the differentiated regions.[11]

Drawing out the implications of Teschke's accurate position above, however, we are led to a conception of U&CD rather different to his general use of 'socially uneven and geopolitically combined development'. The latter seems analogous to a 'mixed-actor' system such as that which prevailed in early modern Europe 'dominated by absolutist states which had a systemic need to accumulate geopolitically on an ever-expanding scale due to their precapitalist property relations' (Teschke 2005, 150). These claims are vital because it is this system whose 'historical legacy' Lacher and Teschke claims is responsible for the persistence of geopolitical multiplicity and competition under capitalism. The 'combination' occurs at the systemic level where absolutist states with different property relations interact with the Hanoverian British state in which capitalist property relations prevailed. This claim is different to the notion of 'highly specific combinations of the old and the new' inside states which then feed back into the international scene. Indeed, the latter characterization, which we support wholeheartedly, jars with the abstract definition of capitalism used by Lacher and Teschke. The very rigour and parsimony of that definition seems to rule out transitional or combined social formations—hence their rejection of Perry Anderson's (1974b) characterization of absolutism. In the face of continued inter-imperialist rivalries and the unevenness generated by capitalism, these are no mere theoretical objections.

For Lacher and Teschke, interstate rivalries and U&CD are part of the absolutist legacy bequeathed to capitalism—war is a nightmare from which capital is trying to awake. Their claims that there is then nothing inherent to capitalism which would have created multiple states in the first place leads to a degree of ambiguity regarding the possibility of contemporary processes of transnational state-formation. Here the property relations approach confronts empirical reality and comes off the worse. If, as Lacher and Teschke maintain, 'the concept of capital entails a global state', capital is seemingly unaware of its own conceptual requirements as 'the idea of a global state formation is hopelessly exaggerated'. Nevertheless, they admit, capitalist modernity remains 'characterized by certain elements of interstate competition' (Lacher and Teschke 2007, 566, 574–75; see also Teschke 2003, 267–68; Lacher 2006, 162).

This idea of some natural correspondence between capital and a hypothesized global state would seem to be based on an understanding of capitalist development as solely characterized by globalizing and equalizing tendencies. In critiquing Callinicos' explanation of the persistence of the territorial states system in terms of capitalism's tendency to uneven and combined development, Lacher and Teschke question to what degree U&CD is inherent to capitalism. 'If anything', they claim,

> capitalism developed unevenly not because it is in its nature—conceptually, of course (that is, abstracted from history and agency), it should even itself out inter-nationally through world-price formation and the long-term equalization of profit rates—but because its spatio-temporally differentiated historical origin and expan-sion was from the first suffused with non-capitalist (and often anti-capitalist) ele-ments that produced and kept reproducing unevenness, manifested in differential strategies of late development and catching-up.
>
> (Lacher and Teschke 2007, 579)

The concept of U&CD, they go on (2007, 579), is 'only meaningful only due to something that *lies outside the pure notion of capitalism* ... '. If this is to mean that *combined development* is only meaningful as lying outside any abstract conception of capitalism then this is clearly correct; combination, in Trotsky's sense, implies the fusion of different production modes within societies. But Lacher and Techke appear to be saying more than this when they claim that capitalism 'developed unevenly not because it is in its nature'. This suggests a view of *uneven development* as another historical hang-over from the feudal-absolutist eras.[12] Yet, this theoretically conflates the transhistorical fact of unevenness (in part accounting for political multiplicity) with the particulars of European feudalism/absolutism: Hence, Lacher and Teschke's conceptualization of the states system as a 'historical legacy'. But, if the states system is conceived as being internalized through capitalism's 'logic of process', whence does it cease to be simply a 'historical legacy'? And what of the unevenness of capitalism?

We may legitimately pose these questions on the basis of a rich and extensive body of Marxist and non-Marxist literature in the fields of human geography, economics, and development studies elucidating the many ways in which capitalism, *more than any other historical mode of production*, universalizes and systematizes the sources of unevenness (see, *inter alia,* Mandel 1970; Krugman 1981; Brett 1983; Agnew 1987; Weeks 2001; Rugman and Verbeke 2004; Kiely 2005; Harvey 2006). Many of these studies and others focus on the myriad ways capitalist industrialization is an inherently disequilibrating force, structuring and restructuring the uneven territoriality of social relations (see especially Storper and Walker 1989; Smith 1990; Harvey 2006; Ashman this volume). The problems with Lacher and Teschke's rejection of U&CD as a constitutive tendency of capitalism are illustrated in their accounts of contemporary geopolitics.

Teschke (2003, 256) for example, points to a Kautskian world on the horizon noting that since capitalism is not posited on a logic of domestic political accumulation, 'we should expect it to bring about the decline of external geopolitical accumulation that defined the war-driven international conduct of the feudal and absolutist ages'. He goes on to describe international organizations as a providing an 'arena of peaceful inter-capitalist conflict resolution', whilst concluding that 'the major lines of military conflict run between states that are locked out of the world market and those that reproduce the political conditions of the world market, backed up by the principle of collective security' (Teschke 2003, 267). This would seem the logical conclusion of any strict interpretation of the social property relations approach which conceives the separation of coercive power and economic relations as the *sine qua non* of capitalist modernity thus making any war-assisted mode of capital accumulation seemingly irrational (cf. Balakrishnan 2004, 157–58). From such a perspective, however, we cannot begin to understand, let alone respond politically to events such as the 2003 Anglo-American invasion of Iraq. For, again, how can historical legacies explain the persistence of geopolitical rivalry and war?

A common theme runs throughout Lacher and Teschke's work: the non-correspondence (or misrecognition) of conceptual abstractions ('capital') and empirical realities (a rivalrous states system). We might then ask when reality might begin to impede upon our conceptions of it? The social realm is certainly a messy, complex affair; full of accidents, contingencies and the untheorizable. A grand theory of everything is unlikely. Problems emerge, however, when the central objects of our theories (the modern states system, geopolitical rivalry, war) are considered pure contingencies in relation to the abstractions we seek to use in explaining them. Wood (1995, 55–56) criticized the Althusserians as viewing the relationship between the state and mode of production within actually existing social formations as having 'little to do' with capitalism's structural logic, thereby appearing 'almost accidental'. Might not the same be said of Lacher and

Teschke's conceptualization of the relationship between capitalism and the states system? Accidents may happen.

Despite our criticisms, Lacher and Teschke's work is illuminating in broaching the theoretical issue of the causal implications of geopolitical relations on social development. In doing so, they tackle the problematic status in Marxist theory of an apparently unified basis producing a multiplicity of competitive 'superstructural' entities. However, despite Lacher and Teschke's recognition of the distinctive properties of 'the international', they lack an adequate theorization of it and, further, with their emphasis on the 'pre-capitalist legacy' of the states system, a viable theoretical framework from which to explain contemporary patterns of *capitalist* geopolitical rivalry. To address this question, we move beyond the Political Marxist approach and examine Justin Rosenberg's reconceptualization of Trotsky's U&CD.

Uneven and combined development: from Trotsky to Rosenberg and back again

Extensions of uneven and combined development

Moving on from the Political Marxist influences of his earlier work, Justin Rosenberg has extended the analytical reach of Trotsky's concept of U&CD to propose a solution to the international problematique common to both social and IR theory. Rosenberg's argument begins from the claim that both theories suffer from a mutual misconception. International theory, particularly in its realist guise, conceptualizes the structure of international relations (anarchy) in abstraction from its underlying constitutive social relations, thus perpetuating a reified, ahistorical conception of the international (Rosenberg 2006, 312; Rosenberg 1994). Classical social theory, in turn, continually suffers from a unitary conception of society, theorizing the structure and dynamics of societies as if they developed in isolation. Consequently, the 'repressed' multi-linear and interactive nature of social development returns in the form of un-theorized exogenous factors (Callinicos and Rosenberg 2008, 17).

For Rosenberg, the answer to this dual problem facing social and IR theory is to reconceptualize social development in general as both uneven and combined thereby deriving the political multiplicity underlying the international problematic from the transhistorically multilinear and interactive nature of development. His formulation thus seeks to overcome the shared error of international and classical social theory by unifying their two logics in one, uneven and combined, social process. An important step in Rosenberg's argument is his extension of the concept of combined development. In Trotsky's original conception, combination sought to capture the interlacing or fusion of capitalist and pre-capitalist modes of production within a single social formation; the 'drawing together of the different stages of the journey, a combining of separate steps, an amalgam of archaic with more contemporary forms' (Trotsky 1977, 27). Rosenberg innovates by using the concept of 'combined development' in three distinct, but interconnected ways. First, combination refers to the co-existence and interactive development of all societies throughout history. Second, this interactivity integrates states and societies into 'regional political orders, cultural systems and material divisions of labour' (Rosenberg 2006, 324) resulting in novel amalgams of socio-political orders and cultural institutions. Finally, through this inter-societal development, there occurs 'combination' in Trotsky's original sociological sense noted above.

Rosenberg's threefold extension of combined development is both novel and useful: For it is only through the *process* of interactive inter-societal development that 'combined social formations' come into *effect* (see Barker 2006). In particular, it dispenses with any notion of societies as pre-formed discrete entities, only subsequently interacting in causally consequential ways. Rosenberg's approach seeks to provide a solution to the Marxist dilemma of why the same production basis could demonstrate such 'endless variations and gradations in appearance' as Marx (1981, 927) noted. If successful, it would then also overcome the problem of the non-correspondence between basis and superstructure, so central to Political Marxism. It seems no coincidence that Rosenberg began his investigations of the international problematique through the prism of a Political Marxist-influenced framework. For, if the state is viewed as constitutive of society's basis, as Rosenberg (1994, 54) claimed, it seems logically to follow that *interstate* relations (used interchangeably with the inter-societal) are also constitutive.

Capitalist and pre-capitalist forms of uneven and combined development

We accept Rosenberg's claim that unevenness and certain forms of combination appear to be transhistorical phenomena. The general historical condition of co-existing and interacting societies determining each other's development is not in dispute. Where we part company with Rosenberg is on the question of the nature of U&CD's transhistorical standing—the extent to which we can project back the *specificities* of the capitalist form of U&CD to pre-capitalist eras—and U&CD's development as a theory unto itself. The problem concerns the boundaries of operation of U&CD, which we characterized as only 'fully' operative under generalized commodity production—a usage in need of further specification (see Allinson and Anievas 2009).[13] If U&CD is a transhistorical phenomenon, to be used as a 'general abstraction' (Rosenberg 2006), much then hangs on the precise meaning of 'general abstraction', its functions in our theories, and how we conceive the qualitative differences in scale and scope between capitalist and pre-capitalist forms of U&CD and what accounts for these differences.

It is often assumed that transhistorical categories played no role in Marx's framework. This is, however, an incorrect view of Marx's method as numerous studies have convincingly demonstrated (see especially Fracchia 2004; Sayer 1979). Marx worked with a number of transhistorical categories: 'use-value', 'labour', and 'production in general'. Nevertheless, Marx's use of transhistorical categories is strikingly different from their employment within much traditional IR. For Realism, for example, a theoretical abstraction such as 'anarchy' or 'international system' takes the form of the primary *explanans* of the argument, from which all other relevant concepts (such as the balance of power) are to be deduced. From this perspective, the abstraction forms the theory itself. In contrast, for Marx the abstraction functions as an assumption which accounts for the existence of a concrete general condition whose historically specific form has to be accounted for by still further *explanans*. Marx was not seeking to build a transhistorical theory of labour or use-value, for example, but rather introduced these concepts as necessary presuppositions in his construction of a historically specific social theory of value. In like fashion, we argue that U&CD can be utilized in a similar (though not identical) way in filling out a distinctively historical materialist theory of 'the international'.[14] Hence, U&CD is *not a theory in itself*. It is rather a methodological fix in the larger research programme of historical materialism.

Rosenberg's own use of U&CD as a general abstraction, however, seemed to waver between these two very different conceptions (compare, for example, Rosenberg 2007, 455, 456–57 to Rosenberg 2006, 321, 322–23; 2008, 7–8, 20–21). At its strongest, U&CD is presented as a meta-theory; a paradigm rupture with all classical social theory (see especially Rosenberg 2006). Yet, for such a claim to be sustained, specifically in regards to Marxist theory, it would need to be demonstrated how historical materialism's abstractions are immune to the methodological incorporation of intersocietal determinations. Despite Marx's (1976) own employment of the 'pernicious postulate',[15] historical materialism's guiding abstraction ('modes of production') in no way logically presupposes society in the ontologically singular. As Eric Wolf (1997, 76) rightly claimed, one of the great benefits of the mode of production concept is that it 'allows us to visualize intersystemic and intrasystemic relationships'—the former representing 'interconnected systems in which societies are variously linked within wider "social fields"'.

To approach these issues from another angle, we are concerned here with the standing of U&CD within the apparatuses of historical materialism as a whole, which relates to the question of a fully operational U&CD. We base our claims on the core proposition that humans are embedded in a productive metabolism with their environment and that the development of this metabolism is the subject of historical materialism. That development is unevenly distributed, humans are consequently always dealing in some way with other 'stages' or forms of such development. Unevenness—and hence the potential or simple form of U&CD—extends in time and space beyond modes of production. However, it is only the capitalist form of the metabolism that contains essentially within it the impulse to transform all others. How is one to distinguish then, between U&CD in capitalist and pre-capitalist eras?

Notwithstanding our above criticisms of Political Marxism, we do accept Brenner's rigorous characterization of capitalist production relations. Unlike previous modes of production, every productive unit under capitalism is brought into '*coercive comparison*' with each other: The logic of capital is to bring these units into a relationship of universal equivalence (Barker 2006, 78; Ashman 2006). This follows from the inherently expansionary nature of capitalism's 'rules of reproduction'. As Brenner notes (2002), the capital relation is formed of two mutually constitutive dimensions: The 'vertical' antagonisms between capitalist and labourer and the 'horizontal' relations among individual competing capitals. This latter dimension functions as capitalism's inbuilt mechanism perpetuating and intensifying the tendential universalization and differentiation of development as described by Trotsky (see Ashman and Callinicos' essays in this volume). Hence, once capitalism emerges somewhere, the self-expanding and totalizing nature of capital locks 'all against all' in the battle to cheapen commodity production through an historically unprecedented development of the productive forces.

This inherently self-valorizing imperative of capital thus necessitates the ruling classes of all other modes to submit or face extinction. It does so via the enormous competitive gulf opened between capitalist and non-capitalist production units (Carling 2002, 110). The attempt to imitate this competitive dynamic of the capitalist mode provides the key inter-societal causal mechanism for the 'combinations' within social formations. Such 'combinations' then feed back into the system that first produced them, resulting in 'countless mini czarisms' (Rosenberg 1996, 12). This feedback loop is another distinguishing feature of modern forms of U&CD, again hinging on the specific nature of capitalist production relations. This form exerts a set of determinations in the international sphere that are neither purely 'social-internal' nor 'geopolitical-external' but greater than the sum of the two.

Our point is that we can pinpoint the specific dynamic of the capitalist mode that leads to the attempt to 'turn the foe into tutor'. This cannot be said of other modes. The uniqueness of capitalist U&CD lies in its ability to enforce its logic of societal reproduction through the abstract mechanism of market exchange mediated through economic and/or military-geopolitical relations. Such is the logic of the 'coercive comparison' which Barker speaks. By contrast, pre-capitalist instances of U&CD refer to pressures upon ruling classes within certain rules of reproduction given by particular modes of production. The pressures generated may be territorially expansionist ones, as in the example of 'political accumulation' by feudal lords (Brenner 1982). However, these pressures arise from the logics of production within the conflicting entities, not from the relations between them. *They do not force the wholesale transformation of those logics via abstract mechanisms as witnessed under capitalist rules of reproduction.* During the era of mercantile expansionism, for example, the transformation of less developed societies came through their direct military conquest, colonization and societal annihilation. While capitalism also expands and transforms societies through such direct means, it additionally does so through the abstract pressures and imperatives of the world capitalist market expressed in both military-geopolitical and economic forms of competition.

What are we to make of the very significant instances of the diffusion of productive techniques and ideas during the pre-capitalist era? The principles of mathematics, navigational inventions, arts of war, key military technologies, and even *haute cuisine*—all originated in the more advanced East eventually passing to the backward West predominately during the Christian Middle Ages (McNeil and McNeil 2003, 117–18; Abu-Lughod 1989, 112; Goody 2006). Around 1400AD, for example, European shipbuilders' began combining the lateen rig borrowed from the Arabs with the square rig of their own traditional model, thereby providing the key technological 'innovation' leading to the gun-bearing sailing ship—an invention instrumental to enabling the Portuguese and subsequent Europeans to expand into Asia (Wolf 1997, 235). Such examples demonstrate the advantages of historic 'backwardness,' (Hobson 2004, 192) accrued to the late-developing Europeans as a result of the transhistorical fact of unevenness, and given sufficient interaction ('combined development') between the uneven poles. In no way, therefore, would we want our argument to be construed as viewing these diffusionist processes (see below) as insignificant to European development: far from it. As John Hobson (2004, 301) notes, 'at every major turning point of European development, the assimilation of superior Eastern ideas, institutions and technologies played a major part'. Hence, the very categories of 'East' and 'West' are themselves problematized: The imperial encounter is constitutive of the imperial entity itself (Barkawi and Laffey 2002).

Nevertheless, it seems theoretically problematic to deny the massive qualitative differences between pre-capitalist and capitalist U&CD. The technical innovations imported into the West from the East affected the processes of production (and destruction) and were only put to full use by transformed relations of production. There was, in other words, a dialectical relationship between the forces and relations of production mediated through inter-societal interactions. Although conflict between Islamic states and Europe's feudal and later absolutist polities was a feature of Europe's entire history between the antique and capitalist epochs this did not result in imitative attempts at social re-organization by those polities—unless we are to take military pressure by the Ottoman Empire as a reason for the emergence of European absolutism. This relationship is the closest we can find to a thought experiment on the likely effects of a fully-formed pre-capitalist U&CD. The various medieval Islamic dynasties were more scientifically advanced than the Europeans with whom they were in close commercial and military contact but neither side of this relationship could be classified as capitalist.

To take this example further, the Ottoman state under Sulayman the Magnificent commanded tribute greater than any European absolutism. At its height, the Empire exerted great military pressures on the European (incipient) absolutist states in the 16th and 17th centuries. Yet those states were not compelled to adopt the Ottoman social structure in order to compete with it. The reverse was true. Once the capitalist ball was rolling, after the late 18th and early 19th centuries the Ottomans were forced to attempt to restructure along the lines of a 'rational' European state (Bromley 1994, 50). However, the Ottoman attempts to regularize administration and revenue necessarily clashed with the tax farming and tribute taking social structures on which the empire had hitherto relied (Tell 2000, 37; Bromley 1994, 51). The resulting crises and centrifugal pressures not only provided the opportunity for Western powers to grab parts of the Empire, but also created the conditions in which the 'Young Turks' of the Committee for Unity and Progress came to power in 1908. The Young Turks aspiration to 'turn the foe into tutor' fed back into international political crisis. 'In ... Turkey', Fred Halliday (1999, 197) argues, 'there was a direct link between the political upheaval, the Young Turk revolt and the subsequent world war. The new regime in Istanbul, espousing a more assertive Turkish nationalism, became embroiled in the Balkans war, the direct prelude to August 1914'. The case of the Ottoman Empire thus represents a particularly stark contrast between pre-capitalist and capitalist inter-societal relations.

Our argument here may seem to run the risk of the Eurocentrism associated with classical Marxism and so sharply criticized by John Hobson (2004; 2007) and other IR scholars (Barkawi and Laffey 2002). There is no denying that Trotsky often slipped into Eurocentric modes of analysis replete with the unfortunate clichés of his time such as 'Asiatic despotism' and 'Eastern barbarism'. Yet, the logic of his position need not lead in such directions. As noted, the diffusion of technical advances to Europe and their adoption was indeed crucial in the transition to capitalism. And, this was only possible because of Europe's 'privileges of historic backwardness' afforded in that period. Here again, we emphasize our agreement with the importance of analyzing the effects of diffusionism and its resulting cultural-political hybridity (see Shilliam 2009). Such emphasis is indeed necessary to avoid the essentializing, self-aggrandizing discourses of some internally-explained 'European miracle'. However, we also need to recognize the huge difference between the effects of pre-capitalist and capitalist 'combined development'.

What happens when we extend a fully-formed U&CD to pre-capitalist epochs? In a series of stimulating articles Kamran Matin (2006; 2007), a former student of Rosenberg, has attempted to do this by applying the 'theory' of U&CD in capturing the 'constitutiveness' of the inter-societal dimension of pre-modern Iran's state-formation process. In doing so, Matin draws a distinction between capitalist and pre-capitalist versions of U&CD: the expansionist logic of capitalism forces 'backward' polities to transform their fundamental social relations, whereas the pre-capitalist version results in political combination as it 'occurs within an uneven international space which has not yet been transformed into an organic totality under the unifying (but not homogenizing) impact of capitalist sociality' (2007, 428). As argued above, this distinction deserves far greater weight than Matin accords it.

This relates to the questions of the nature of the combined formations and the apparent abandonment of the notion of development (the progressive development of the productive forces) that we identified as problematic in the usage of U&CD by Political Marxists. In Matin's work we come full circle back to the Political Marxists, for he identifies amalgamations of pre-capitalist political forms as constitutive of U&CD. He describes pre-modern Iran as an example of an 'amalgamated state formation', meaning:

> a combination of different forms of authority (corresponding to different modes of socioeconomic organization) ruling over a particular geopolitical space within which they related to the (pre existing) social reproductive texture without (necessarily) transforming ... the actual process and organisation of labour and/or the basic forms and mechanism of surplus extraction.
>
> (Matin 2007, 429)

This extension of the concept of combination, however, cuts it loose from its explanatory foundation in modes of production and the consequences this has on societal developmental dynamics. As noted, combination denotes the interpenetration of different production modes within a single social formation in ways violating their hitherto assumed order of succession—that is, providing the possibility of skipping a 'whole series of intermediate stages' of development (Trotsky 1977, 26). Yet, by loosening the scope of the concept of 'combination' to incorporate *any* amalgamation of different political systems and cultural institutions, Matin seems to run the risk of triviality: For what society does not exhibit some type of combination in this much less specific sense?[16] Indeed, almost all state/societies consist of some mix of socio-political orders and cultural institutions which have been incorporated from abroad or 'survived' from the past. For example, the British state consists of a monarchy, an established Church of England and various other 'aristocratic' sociopolitical and cultural institutions, all of which are historical 'hang-overs'. But, to describe Britain as a 'combined' society would tell us very little. This in turn relates to a further problem.

Matin (2007, 429) argues that U&CD can refer to the political interpenetration of 'reproductively similar' non-capitalist societies. Yet, the essence of Trotsky's argument is quite the opposite; it is the yoking together of *reproductively dissimilar societies* so that one is compelled to adopt itself to the reproductive rules of the other. We see here again the affinity of this argument to a Political Marxist perspective replacing a sequence of modes of production with the concept of 'social property relations', the emergence of which is a contingent outcome of class struggle. On this basis, Matin reverses Trotsky's scheme of unevenness, in arguing that 'the almost unbroken geo-political pressure of Turkish tribal nomadism on the Iranian sedentary society' resulted in a particular amalgamated state formation (Matin 2007, 430). However, Trotsky is quite explicit (and for good reasons) in regarding Russia's Eastern nomadic neighbours as a less productively advanced formation, from which the Russian state did not experience the same pressure as from Western Europe. Trotsky could be wrong on this point of course. But, if so there seems little content left to his concept of U&CD. Matin's characterization of the pre-modern Iranian polity as an amalgam of tribal nomadic tax takers and settled taxpayers is surely correct. Yet would this insightful analysis not be better couched in the concept of 'articulation' rather than U&CD?

Diffusion, articulation, combination

Our question here leads us to sum up the preceding discussion by drawing a distinction between three concepts relating to inter-societal interaction: diffusion, articulation and combination. The first two of these hold for pre-capitalist epochs. The concept of diffusion simply refers to the spread of cultural traits and institutions—whether it be technologies, religious customs, political institutions, social habits etc.—from one social formation to another through migration, war, trade or any other means of inter-societal contact. The technological innovations we discussed above exemplify these diffusionist processes. However, the incorporation of these elements is not—in itself—enough to lead to the transformation of the mode of production in the recipient social formation. Often as a result of such diffusionist processes, two or more production modes can coexist and interconnect in a single social formation. Thus, following Nazih Ayubi's (1995, 28), 'modes of production ... are often not singular and uni-dimensional but rather are articulated'.[17] Ayubi uses the articulation concept in relation to the contemporary Middle East. However, there seems no reason why it cannot be characteristic of certain pre-capitalist social formations, as Matin's analysis well demonstrates.

In our reading of articulation, modes coexist and interlink with each other but do not necessarily impel the transformation of one by the other. Combination is a subset of articulation, but with the crucial difference that one of the modes—and only capitalism displays this characteristic—impels the transformation of the other. However, this transformation is never into an ideal type of capitalism but often of hybrid forms of 'countless mini-czarisms'. Neil Davidson is, therefore, correct to point out that an 'articulation' of two or more modes of production within a single social formation is not identical to a 'combined' society. Rather, '[t]he detonation of the process of U&CD requires sudden, intensive industrialization and urbanization, regardless of whether the pre-existing agrarian economy was based on feudal or capitalist relations' (Davidson 2009, 15). The result of uneven development, therefore, is that the logics of different modes of production interact with one another in consequential ways in 'backward' countries. Hence, the syntheticness of the notion of combination—itself flowing from the dialectical nature of the whole conceptual triplet (development + uneven + combined)—which seeks to capture the 'the real connections and consecutiveness of a living process' (Trotsky 1998, 77).

Conclusion: what's at stake in 'the international' debate?

A fellow traveller amongst Marxist circles—though not a Marxist himself—once asked us what was all the fuss about U&CD and 'the international'. In exasperation with the whole debate, he threw up his hands declaring: 'This uneven and combined shit is the dog's whistle that only Marxists can hear'! Hopefully, this chapter has clarified what's at theoretical stake in this debate over 'the international'.

If we have persisted, perhaps rather stubbornly, in stressing the qualitative differences between pre-capitalist and capitalist forms of U&CD, as well as the theoretical standing of the concept as a methodological fix *within* rather than paradigm shift *from* historical materialism, it is because much politically rests on such issues. For, if 'combination' in Trotsky's specific sense was a feature of all historical epochs and social formations, then very little remains of his strategic analysis of the Russian Revolution. Of course, this has much wider implications than the single case of Russia; rather, it is significant for the possibility and form of all radical democratic projects in any contemporary late-developing country, most especially in those regions at the receiving end of imperialism's whip.[18] Indeed, a significant lacuna within the recent IR literature on U&CD concerns the precise theoretical relationship between U&CD and a theory of capitalist imperialism: whether they are internally or only indirectly related. In our (tentative) view, a theoretical articulation of U&CD in the capitalist epoch would need to incorporate and sublate the classical Marxist conception of imperialism, providing a much richer and multi-dimensional understanding of imperialism. But, of course, this is much easier said than done and the difficult theoretical and empirical work still lies ahead.

Notes

1 This chapter builds on our article in the *Cambridge Review of International Affairs* (2009) section. We'd like to thank Colin Barker, John Hobson, Kamran Matin, Gonzo Pozo-Martin and Justin Rosenberg for their insightful comments.

2 'Political Marxism' is used here as shorthand for those basing their arguments on Brenner's notion of social property relations.

3 We employ the 'basis' rather than 'base' metaphor as Marx used the former when writing in English. Pointing this out, James Furner (2008, 4) further notes: 'Basis has the advantage over "base" in rarely being used to refer to the bottom of physical objects' the latter denoting 'that by which something else is sustained or supported'.

4 This neo-Smithian conception of modern economic development, according to Brenner (1989) and Wood (1995, 60fn13), is also symptomatic of the work of the 'young' Marx still developing under the baggage of classical bourgeois political economy and Hegelian idealism.

5 On the distinction between the means of subsistence and production, the former only being necessary for the emergence of capitalism see Brenner (2001, 178fn1).

6 In contrast, Brenner views capitalist property relations as developing earlier in such regions as Catalonia and the United Provinces in the late 15th and early 17th centuries, respectively (Brenner 1985, 49fn81; 2001).

7 This process is a complement to Brenner's (1982 and 1985) main thesis, that capitalism emerged in England because of the outcome of a class struggle in which the lords were too weak to re-impose serfdom, but the peasants not strong enough to maintain their independence from the market.

8 Lacher and Teschke's position here jars with Robert Brenner's (1982, 81) view of French absolutism as a 'transformed version of the old [feudal] system'—a perspective much closer to Anderson (1974b).

9 Such problems have also been a key concern of many scholars associated with the ideas of Tony Cliff; see particularly Barker (1997), Davidson (2005), Callinicos (2009) and Ashman (this volume). Their critique is tied to Cliff's theory of 'bureaucratic state capitalism' which holds that the Soviet bloc states represented a form of capitalism. *Irrespective* of whether one agrees with such theory, the Political Marxist conception of capitalism is unnecessarily restrictive.

10 Lacher and Teschke acknowledge the interventionist role of the state in maintaining and reproducing capitalist property relations (and thus, the economic/political separation). However, the possibility of state power functioning as a means of *surplus* or *tribute* extraction falls outside the scope of their conception. Not only does this fail to explain 'deviant' or 'unpure' forms of capitalism (such as antebellum slavery or heavily statist late-developing capitalisms), it also fails to recognize that the capitalist state itself appropriates a fraction of the surplus produced within society through taxation. The ability of the state apparatus to reproduce itself thus directly depends upon exploitation. In a fascinating piece, Colin Barker (1998) makes a case for developing the categories of tax and state tribute in theorizing the capitalist state.

11 An argument resembling Alan Carling's (1993) 'competitive primacy thesis'.

12 This argument is contradicted by earlier statements made by Lacher (2005, 43), as well by their key theoretical influences, Brenner and Wood, whom view unevenness as a constitutive feature of contemporary capitalism (see Brenner 2002; Wood 2002, 29, 32–33, 35–36; 2003, 136). For similar criticisms see Callinicos (2009, 95).

13 We are indebted to Kamran Matin for pushing us on this point.

14 We doubt Rosenberg would disagree with much said here regarding the interweaving of the general and particular in social theoretic explanation as his discussion of Marx's method of abstraction illustrates (Rosenberg 2000, 69–73).

15 As Charles Tilly (1984, 11) terms the singular society abstraction.

16 Matin is scarcely the first Marxist employing U&CD to run into this problem (see Trotsky 1972, 117; Novack 1972, 118–20).

17 For an excellent critical discussion of the notion of articulation which implicitly points to the international problematique see Foster-Carter (1978, especially 64–67, 71–73). We thank Justin Rosenberg for alerting us to this piece.

18 For an analysis stressing the contemporary relevance of 'Permanent Revolution' in the Middle East see Naguib (2007).

12 The geopolitics of passive revolution

Adam David Morton[1]

Introduction

'Just as medieval, feudal ideology forged a trans-temporal relationship between the person and god', argued Györg Lukács (2000, 53), 'bourgeois ... ideology constructs a trans-temporal "sociology"'. By contrast, it has been argued that 'historical sociology ... stands between the idiographic and the nomothetic in both history and sociology' to provide a *via media* between transhistorical generalizations and particularistic narrations (see Calhoun 2003, 386; Wallerstein 1991, 244; Lawson 2007, 356–60). Most recently, though, Justin Rosenberg has cast the condition of uneven and combined development (U&CD) as a transhistorical answer to questions posed by the multilinear and interactive dimension of social existence. As a consequence, it is argued that the term U&CD itself 'captures at a general level the sociological characteristics of *all* development' (Callinicos and Rosenberg 2008, 80 emphasis added).

This then raises the pitfall of a transhistorical sociological articulation of the theory of U&CD. One consequence is a relapse into transhistorical affirmations through the general abstraction of U&CD without exploring the actual modalities of historical and empirical unevenness and the combination of different stages of development within capitalism as a mode of production. As Alex Callinicos remarks when raising these objections, 'the work required to develop a Marxist theory of the geopolitical lies before us' (Callinicos and Rosenberg 2008, 106).

This chapter will dwell on such contentions by teasing out a neglected contribution to understanding the geopolitics of capitalism with specific reference to Antonio Gramsci's analysis of passive revolution (see also Morton 2007b). The argument advanced in this chapter is that Gramsci's theorizing of capitalist modernity through the conditions of passive revolution and his conceptualization of the states system therein offers a substantial contribution to present debates on uneven development. This is so because there is an appreciation within the theory of passive revolution of state forms that are relationally linked to the internalization of capitalist modernity. This *philosophy of internal relations*, specific to historical materialism, has much to contribute to understanding interstate geopolitics and uneven development (see Ollman 1976; Bieler and Morton 2008). Hence, there is a need to show how Gramsci can contribute to addressing two factors that John Hobson (2007, 587) holds as central to a non-reductionist theory of the geopolitical system, by indicating: 1) how the states system constitutes the reproduction of capitalism; and 2) how class relations are shaped by both capitalism as a mode of production and geopolitics. It is Gramsci's notion of passive revolution as an expression of the political rule of capital, emblematic in his focus on 'Americanism and Fordism', that promotes an understanding of the states system in its internal relation with capitalist modernity. The theory of passive revolution captures such dynamics whilst also highlighting the continued relevance of uneven development as a framing of social divisions within capitalism as a mode of production.

The specific structure of the argument falls as follows. The first section elaborates the theory of passive revolution as an expression of the political rule of capital, thereby focusing on the relationship between the states system and capitalist modernity to combine an appreciation of the world-historical context of uneven development and its connection to the formative influence of states. After all, in summing up such factors in a letter addressed to the Fourth World Congress of the Third International (20 November 1922), Gramsci (1978, 129) highlighted the conditions of passive revolution by stating that:

> The Italian bourgeoisie succeeded in organising its state not so much through its own intrinsic strength, as through being favoured in its victory over the feudal and semi-feudal classes by a whole series of circumstances of an international character (Napoleon III's policy in 1852–60; the Austro-Prussian War of 1866; France's defeat at Sedan and the development of the German Empire after this event).

It is therefore simply mistaken to assert that Gramsci's focus led him 'to refuse the international dimension any constitutive status in his guide to action' or that he 'rejected the international dimension' as a causal factor of social transformation' (Shilliam 2004, 72–73). It is equally remiss, in relation to Gramsci, to take for granted the claim that '[t]he historical nature of his concepts means that they receive their meaning and explanatory power primarily from their grounding in national social formations' within which 'they were used exclusively' (Germain and Kenny 1998, 20).

When approaching Gramsci, there is no need to concern ourselves with the task of 'scaling-up' his analysis of inter-societal relations, the conditions of unevenness within the states system, and thus how different relations of production become combined. A theorization of the geopolitics of capitalism through the conditions of passive revolution meant that such features were already a constitutive component of Gramsci's strategic thought and practice (see Morton 2007a). This argument will proceed here through an analysis of Gramsci's concern with the modern states system and its relation to the emerging hegemony of Anglo-Saxon capitalism and colonial exploitation linked to his analysis of the geopolitical and sociological aspects of 'Americanism and Fordism'. It will be argued that the theory of passive revolution provides a method of analysis that combines an appreciation of state geopolitical and capitalist dynamics.

Within this method also lies an appreciation of the nodal spatiality of capitalism, as well as how different scales between places relate to one another differentially over time within the conditions of uneven development (Agnew 2003, 13). 'Gramsci was extremely sensitive to issues of scale, scalar hierarchies of economic, political, intellectual and moral power', Bob Jessop (2006, 31–32) notes, 'and their territorial and non-territorial expression'. What is pivotal to this theory of passive revolution is the constitutive role granted to geopolitics and capitalism within an historical methodology that can account for specific contexts of state formation without succumbing to the problem of transhistorical categorizations.

The second section then turns to discuss how internalizing a methodological understanding of passive revolution might assist in tracing conditions of social development within post-colonial states; where the impasse of development has commonly been tied to state-led mechanisms that assisted in the emergence of capitalism to become the primary organ of primitive accumulation. The point here is that internalizing the method of multi-scalar articulation encapsulated in the theory of passive revolution can assist in appreciating the reciprocal influence of specific spatial scales in understanding the states system in its dynamic with global capitalism. The emphasis, though, is not one of theoretically relating instances of passive revolution as externalized relations to each other. Instead, instances of passive revolution can be understood through the method of *incorporated comparison*—elaborated by Philip McMichael (1990)—where the creation of the conditions for capitalist class consolidation in specific state formation processes are understood as relational moments within a self-forming whole that is the world context of capitalism. Rather than constructing an 'external' relationship between 'cases' of state formation, 'comparison becomes an "internal" rather than an "external" (formal) feature of inquiry, relating apparently separate processes (in time and/or space) as components of a broader, world-historical process' (McMichael 1990, 389). Rather than a transhistorical generalization, then, instances of passive revolution can be understood and analyzed as distinct, but multiple forms of mutually conditioning moments within a singular phenomenon that is the world-historical process of capitalism. The conclusion will then raise a set of reflections about uneven development, in general, within an overview of development sociology and the adequacy of the theorization of passive revolution, specifically.

Passive revolution and 'Americanism and Fordism'

'Capitalism is a world historical phenomenon and its uneven development', Gramsci (1977, 69) argued, 'means that individual nations cannot be at the same level of economic development at the same time'. Gramsci understood issues of U&CD across 18th and 19th century European history as a series of passive revolutions (see Morton 2005). To be precise, the theory of passive revolution refers to how 'restoration becomes the first policy whereby social struggles find sufficiently elastic frameworks to allow the bourgeoisie to gain power without dramatic upheavals' (Gramsci 1971: 115, Q10II§61).[2] As will be demonstrated in more detail with reference to 'Americanism and Fordism', the theory of passive revolution captures the *political rule of capital* in terms of the intertwined aspects of the geopolitics of the states system and global capitalism rather than as separate logics. Moreover, it does so without reducing the role of capital to a simplified social character, or 'ghost-walker', as *Monsieur le Capital*, or mere thing falsely separated from *Madame la*

Terre, thereby avoiding a mystification of capitalism as a mode of production (Marx 1984, 830).

Whilst the historical sociological implications of the theory of passive revolution, in tracing class struggles constitutive of processes of state formation have been developed in more detail elsewhere (Morton 2007b), the present discussion will tease out the key pointers of the concept in relation to furthering an understanding of the relationship of the geopolitics of the states system to capitalism. The primary feature here is the manner in which passive revolution is able to capture comparative conditions of class formation within specific state formation processes and how these impact on, and are themselves influenced by, geopolitics and capitalist expansion.

Initially developed to explain the Risorgimento, the movement for Italian national liberation that culminated in the political unification of the country in 1860–61, the notion of passive revolution was expanded to encompass a whole series of other historical phenomena. In the case of Italy, the 'passive' aspect refers to the restrictive form of hegemony that emerged out of the Risorgimento because of the failure of potential 'Jacobins' in the *Partito d'Azione* to establish a programme reflecting the demands of the popular masses and, significantly, the peasantry. Instead, challenges were thwarted and changes in property relations accommodated due to the 'Moderates', led by (Count) Camillo Benso Cavour, establishing alliances between big landowners in the Mezzogiorno and the northern bourgeoisie, whilst absorbing opposition in parliament through continually assimilated change (or *trasformismo*) within the current social formation. 'Indeed one might say', Gramsci (1971, 58, Q19§24) noted, 'that the entire state of Italy from 1848 onwards has been characterised by *trasformismo*'. The *Partito d'Azione* did not successfully emulate a Jacobin force, reflecting the relative weakness of the Italian bourgeoisie within the international states system of uneven development after 1815, so that,

> in Italy the struggle manifested itself as a struggle against old treaties and the existing international order, and against a foreign power—Austria—which represented these and upheld them in Italy, occupying a part of the peninsula and controlling the rest.
>
> (Gramsci 1971, 80–82, Q19§24)

The process is not literally 'passive' but refers to the attempt at 'revolution' through state intervention, or the inclusion of new social groups within the hegemony of a political order without an expansion of mass producer control over politics (Showstack Sassoon 1987, 210). Indicative here is the way the Moderates thought 'the national question required a bloc of all the right-wing forces—including the classes of the great landowners—around Piedmont as a state and as an army' (Gramsci 1971, 100, Q19§26). This left intact sedimentations of pre-capitalist social relations bequeathed by the parasitism of the rural southern bourgeoisie and the role of mercantile capital that shaped late medieval and early modern state formation in the Italian peninsula (see Morton 2007a, 51–63). The result was a process of fundamental social change but without an attempt to embrace the interests of subordinate classes and crucially the peasantry within a national state. That is why 'the concept of "passive revolution"', as Neil Davidson (2005, 19) has stated, 'is perhaps the most evocative one to describe the process of "revolution from above"', developed within the classical tradition of historical materialism.

Rooted in his writings on the crisis of the liberal state in Italy, Gramsci linked the notion of passive revolution to the spatial integration and transformation of national economies across Europe (Gramsci 1995, 330, Q10I§0; 348–50, Q10I§9). According to Gramsci, the French Revolution established a 'bourgeois' state on the basis of popular support and the elimination of old feudal classes. It was only in 1870–71 with the Third Republic that the 'new bourgeois class' defeated the old regime and demonstrated its vitality in the struggle for power so that 'all the germs of 1789 were finally historically exhausted' (Gramsci 1971, 179, Q13§17). However, across Europe, the institution of subsequent political forms suitable to the expansion of capitalism occurred differently. 'All revolutions, following the French Revolution', notes Kees van der Pijl (1996, 314), ' ... would then be compelled to reduce structurally freedoms and the "spaciousness" of social infrastructures in order to sustain the attempt to catch up'.

Following the post-Napoleonic restoration (1815–48), Gramsci (1994b, 230–33) regarded the tendency to establish 'bourgeois' social and political orders across Europe as mimetic processes of national unification. As Eric Hobsbawm (1975, 73, 166) puts it in a statement that resonates with the force of Leon Trotsky's (1936, 26) arguments on U&CD, 'countries seeking to break through modernity are normally derivative and unoriginal in their ideas, though necessarily not so in their practices'. It is this divergence in European historical processes of state formation within the conditions of U&CD that is captured by the notion of passive revolution. A passive revolution, therefore, *is* a revolution, marked by violent social upheaval, involving a relatively small elite engaging with 'the acceptance of certain demands from below' in order to restrict class struggle, whilst ensuring the creation of state power and an institutional framework consonant with capitalist property relations (Showstack Sassoon 1982, 133). The resultant dialectical combination of progressive and reactionary elements within conditions of passive revolution was described as 'revolution-restoration' or 'revolution without revolution' (Gramsci 1992, 137, Q1§44).

As a concept passive revolution thus reveals continuities and changes within the political rule of capital. It includes processes that exemplify the inability of a ruling class to fully integrate the producer classes through conditions of hegemony, when the leaders 'aiming at the creation of a modern state ... in fact produced a bastard' (Gramsci 1971, 90, Q19§28). Hence, a situation when 'more or less far-reaching modifications ... into the economic structure of the country' are made in a situation of '"domination without that of "leadership": dictatorship without hegemony' (Gramsci 1995, 350, Q10I§9; Gramsci 1971, 105–6, Q15§59). This might be because,

> the impetus of progress is not tightly linked to a vast local economic development ... but is instead the reflection of *international developments* which transmit their ideological currents to the periphery—currents born of the productive development of the more advanced countries. (Gramsci 1971, 116–17, Q10II§61 emphasis added)

A geopolitical expression of such international developments in the early twentieth century was the expansion of capitalism through 'Americanism and Fordism'.

Americanism and Fordism

Gramsci presented Americanism and Fordism as the outward expansion on a world scale of a particular mode of production supported by mechanisms of international organization. It was also intrinsically linked to aspects of modern culture and American 'civilization' related to the US capitalist industrial system (Gramsci 1992, 357–58, Q2§138; 1995, 256–57, Q15§30). The ideology of Americanism was therefore understood in its internal relation to the world of Fordist production as a material social product rather than as a separate set of cultural norms. This was manifest in both *sociological* and *geopolitical* dimensions.

At the *sociological level*, cultural features of Americanism conjoined with emergent patterns of Fordist production, which in turn marked the character and predominance of US geopolitics. As John Agnew (2005, 9 emphases added) has put it 'the *place* that comes to exercise hegemony [*Americanism*] matters, therefore, in the *content* and *form* that hegemony takes [*Fordism*]'. Gramsci's formulation at the time therefore recognized the 'transformation of the material bases of European civilization' induced by the 'repercussion of American super-power' that resulted in 'the superficial apish initiative' of emulative economic policies (Gramsci 1971, 317, Q22§15). Simultaneously, however, the role of high wages within the 'Fordian ideology' of mass production affects a 'tempering of compulsion (self-discipline) with persuasion' (Gramsci 1971, 310–12, Q22§13). The phenomenon of hegemony springing forth from the conditions of Fordism mixes 'coercion [that] has therefore to be ingeniously combined with persuasion and consent' (Gramsci 1971, 310, Q22§13). Americanism is an ideology manifested in 'café life' that 'can appear like a form of make-up, a superficial foreign fashion' whilst capitalism itself (expressed by the character and relationships between fundamental class relations) is not transformed, it simply acquires 'a new coating' in the climate of Americanism (Gramsci 1971, 317–18, Q22§15).

This equally led Gramsci to directly consider how new methods of discipline within the *labour process* were 1) linked to wider aspects of familial relations; 2) linked to the sexual division of labour; and 3) linked to changing norms of identity (see Morton 2007a, 102–5). What is key to unravelling Gramsci's sociological take on geopolitics, then, is that there is an overall growing analysis of the labour process inclusive of the economic function of reproduction linked to 'United States world expansionism' that he envisaged as causally significant on the world stage in struggles over the 'security of American capital' (Gramsci 1996, 56, Q3§55).

At the *geopolitical level*, Gramsci focused on moving beyond an account that simply offered a 'statesmen's manual' of geopolitics evident in the work of Rudolf Kjellén (a Swedish sociologist attributed with first coining the term geopolitics) and explicitly criticized his attempt to construct a science of the state and of politics on the basis of taking state territoriality as a given (Gramsci 1995, 195, Q2§39). The focus on Americanism and Fordism, instead, embraced a realization of the changing geography and spatiality of power emerging in the twentieth century. At the forefront here was inquiry into 'Fordism as the ultimate stage in the process of progressive attempts by industry to overcome the law of the tendency of the rate of profit to fall', or capital's contradictions (Gramsci 1971, 279, Q22§1). It could be said that Americanism and Fordism was 'one of the means immanent in capitalist production to check the fall of the rate of profit and hasten accumulation of capital-value through formation of new capital' (Marx 1984, 249).

Gramsci embedded the social conditions of the existing value of capital in Americanism and Fordism within a clear delineation of the geopolitics of the states system and the uneven development of capitalism by distinguishing between: 1) the group of capitalist states which formed the keystone of the international states system at that time (Britain, France, Germany, the United States), and: 2) those states which represented the immediate periphery of the capitalist world (Italy, Poland, Russia, Spain, Portugal) (Gramsci 1978, 408–10). Within the former, 'the global politico-economic system' was being more and more marked by Americanism and Fordism or what Gramsci explicitly referred to as 'Anglo-Saxon world hegemony' accompanied by the 'colonial subjection of the whole world to Anglo-Saxon capitalism' (Gramsci 1977, 81, 89). In Gramsci's view that is why the 'uneven development' of 'capitalism is a world historical phenomenon' within which 'the colonial populations become the foundation on which the whole edifice of capitalist exploitation is erected' (Gramsci 1977, 69–72, 302). Hence, the need to grant due regard to 'the class struggle of the coloured peoples against their white exploiters and murderers' producing 'cheap raw materials for industry … for the benefit of European civilisation' (Gramsci 1977, 60, 302).[3] Further, Gramsci also thought it possible that 'American expansionism [could] use American negroes as its agents in the conquest of the African market and the extension of American civilisation' (Gramsci 1971, 21, Q12§1).

Gramsci therefore traced specific contexts in the expansion of *both* the geopolitical system of states *and* capitalist uneven development. These insights are most compellingly combined in Gramsci's attempt to trace how 'the complex problem arises of the relation of internal forces in the country in question, of the relation of international forces, [and] of the country's geo-political position' (Gramsci 1971, 116, Q10II§61). This involved analyzing organic and conjunctural historical movements that were dealt with by the same concepts. Therefore, 'relations within society' (involving the development of productive forces, the level of coercion, or relations between political parties) that constitute 'hegemonic systems within the state', were inextricably linked to 'relations between international forces' (involving the requisites of great powers, sovereignty and independence) that constitute 'the combinations of states in hegemonic systems' (Gramsci 1971, 176, Q13§2; See Bieler and Morton 2003, 484–85).

Linking back to John Hobson's criteria outlined earlier in this chapter, such elements comprise a theory of geopolitics capable of relating: 1) the states system in constituting and reproducing capitalism; *and* 2) class relations in constituting both capitalism as a mode of production and geopolitics. This can be substantiated by, first, recognizing that historical materialism is marked by a philosophy of internal relations (see Ollman 1976, 47), meaning in this case that geopolitical relations linked to the states system are interiorized within the conditions of modernity as part of the make-up of capital. Put differently, in the modern epoch the geopolitical states system is internally related to capitalist relations of production. Second, for Gramsci, this meant that the states system, embedded in conditions of uneven development and linked to the differential position of states within that system, has to be internally related to the subsequent expression of capitalism as mode of production through the expansion of Americanism and Fordism. What this means is that through Americanism and Fordism, the extra-economic aspects of geopolitical competition are linked interactively to capitalism.

This was most starkly expressed in relation to Gramsci's analysis of US attempts to organize the world market to economically underpin its political hegemony:

> The world market, according to this tendency, would come to be made up of a series of markets—no longer national, but international (interstate)—which would have organised within their own borders a certain stability of essential economic activities, and which could enter into mutual relations on the basis of the same system.
>
> (Gramsci 1992, 351, Q2§125)

Additionally, developments such as colonialism, imperialism, nationalism, or fascism inhering within specific forms of state have to be related to the overall system of states, with the latter obtaining a certain sense of autonomy from the world market conditions of capitalism. This was most evocatively raised by Gramsci thus:

> Is the cultural hegemony by one nation over another still possible? Or is the world already so united in its economic and social structure that a country, if it can have 'chronologically' the initiative in an innovation, cannot keep its 'political' monopoly and so use such a monopoly as the basis of hegemony? What significance therefore can nationalism have today? Is this not possible as economico-financial imperialism but not as civil 'primacy' or politico-intellectual hegemony?
>
> (Gramsci 2001, Volume 5, 64–65, Q13§26, my translation).

Gramsci consequently highlights in Americanism and Fordism capital's attempt to mobilize effective responses to changing geopolitical developments within the states system whilst at the same time asserting that 'the whole economic activity of a country can only be judged in relationship to the international market ... and is to be evaluated in so far as it is inserted into an international unit' (Gramsci 1995, 233, Q9§32). Hence, the social relations of production inherent to Americanism and Fordism retain a determining influence in shaping the ideology of liberal internationalism due to the role of the 'decisive nucleus of economic activity' but without succumbing to expressions of economism (Gramsci 1971, 161, Q13§18). A *constitutive theory of geopolitics* is thus evident in the manner by which the states system is understood to reproduce capitalism through conditions of uneven development whilst the conditions of class struggle, through Americanism and Fordism, are linked to relations both *between* and *within* states (Gramsci 1975, 62). Therefore, 'in the international sphere, competition, the struggle to acquire private and national property, creates the same hierarchies and system of slavery as in the national sphere' (Gramsci 1977, 69).

Finally, the concept of passive revolution stands as a causative factor within the states system linking *both* the reproduction of capitalism on a global scale, through its outward expression as Americanism and Fordism, *and* responses within specific state forms. The most pertinent example from Gramsci's own time that sub-stantiates this linkage was the fascist phenomenon (see Morton 2007a, 71–72). As a consequence, the concept of passive revolution stands as a theory of the political rule of capital that, by extension, incorporates geopolitical competition within its frame of reference. This is what is meant when David Harvey (2003, 101) notes that 'the molecular processes of capital accumulation operating in space and time' generate passive revolutions in the geographical patterning of capital accumulation. State development strategies can therefore be seen as an attempt to secure the expansion of capital through the conditions of passive revolution. The contra-dictions of capitalism are therefore accommodated through changing space relations and geographical structures linked to the redefinition of territory and the state. Passive revolution is one expression of the shaping and reshaping of class struggle through the structured coherence (or 'spatial fix') of state power within conditions of U&CD (Harvey 2001, 324–25).

New 'north-south' questions of uneven development

Whilst strewn across diverse writings, Gramsci's underlying theory of the geopolitics of passive revolution offers a potential method of theory-construction in tracing how 'the international situation should be considered in its national aspect' (Gramsci 1971, 240, Q14§68; see Morton 2007b). Overall, Gramsci posed his approach to understanding the relation of the geopolitical circumstances of the states system and the role of capitalism in the following oft-cited question: 'Do international relations precede or follow (logically) fundamental social relations? There can be no doubt that they follow ... However, international relations react both passively and actively on political relations' (Gramsci 1971, 176, Q13§2). Once more there is little evidence of the need to 'scale-up' this analytical focus on the geographical position of states in relation to structural changes within the international.

The logic of the above theorizing is that there is an appreciation of the different scales between geography, territory, place, and space that may offer, through the theory of passive revolution, the lineaments of an approach to understanding post-colonial state formation and transformation. It reflects the need to identify a hierarchy of scales at which different policies might serve to anchor geopolitical priorities within specific spatial and geographical territorial forms (Jessop 2006). Similar to recent spatially-informed approaches to world politics, the argument sketched here is that there is an historical approach within the theory of passive revolution that can recognize the complex, intersecting effects of geographical representations and the spatial distribution of material conditions on political practices that has utility in understanding the post-colonial world (Agnew 2001). After all, that is why Gramsci indicated that the relations of production within state formation processes are 'further complicated by the existence *within every state* of several structurally diverse territorial sectors' (Gramsci 1971, 182, Q13§17, emphasis added).

To elaborate within the restrictions of this chapter, two themes will be briefly outlined within which the theory of passive revolution can link distinct processes of state formation within the post-colonial world and associated forms of geopolitics to capitalist expansion. It should be stressed, however, that no crude application of Gramsci's concepts and principles is advocated. The approach consists, rather, of internalizing a method of thinking about the geopolitics of the state system, the history of state formation, and the expansion of modern capitalism in order to capture the multi-scalar features of passive revolution (Morton 2007a, 35–38).

Post-colonial state formation has commonly emerged within a global division of labour shaped by the expansion of capitalism and the uneven tendencies of development. Following Ernest Mandel (1975, 46–81, 85–103), the condition of U&CD—involving uneven processes of primitive accumulation within combined capitalist and pre-capitalist modes production—has contributed greatly to shaping state sovereignty and economic development in post-colonial states. The uneven tendencies of development wrought by processes of primitive accumulation unfolded within the framework of an already existing world market and international states system. This means that the international growth and spread of capitalism in post-colonial states occurs through ongoing processes of primitive accumulation. The latter classically entails the displacement of 'politically' constituted property by 'economic' power involving a 'historical process of divorcing the producer from the means of production' generating propertyless individuals compelled to sell their labour (Marx 1996, 705–6). Yet, due to the presence of a territorialized state framework, processes of primitive accumulation in the post-colonial world became heavily reliant on the state as the locus of capital accumulation. 'Much has therefore depended on how the state has been constituted and by whom, and what the state was and is able or prepared to do in support of or in opposition to processes of capital accumulation' (Harvey 2003, 91).

Following Marx's reflections on state force within the colonial system as *itself* an economic power, Mandel pointedly notes that in these instances the state comes to act as the 'midwife of modern capitalism' (Marx 1996, 739; Mandel 1975, 54). It is within this context of U&CD and through the specific class conflicts ascribed to processes of capital accumulation that the theory of passive revolution can be related to geopolitical concerns in the following ways.

The state in Africa?

'Marxist analysis should always be slightly stretched', states Franz Fanon (1990, 31), 'every time we have to do with the colonial problem'. According to Mahmood Mamdani, following independence, the African post-colonial state comprised a bifurcated political structure in which the formal separation of the political and economic characteristics of modern capitalist states was compromised.

> The colonial state was a double-sided affair. Its one side, the state that governed a racially defined citizenry, was bounded by the rule of law and an associated

regime of rights. Its other side, the state that ruled over subjects, was a regime of extra-economic coercion and administratively driven justice.

(Mamdani 1996, 19)

The post-colonial state was therefore bifurcated due to the existence of a civil political form of rule similar to modern capitalist states, based on law, and concentrated in urban areas; and a customary form of power based on personalism, extra-economic compulsions, and exploitation centred in rural society and culture.

The age of imperialism suffocated the process of primitive accumulation so that the state became the prime channel of accumulation serving as a 'surrogate collective capitalist', for instance in Côte d'Ivoire, Gabon, Zaire, and Sierra Leone (Young 2004, 31). At the same time, 'the distortions of the state are not just the result of the external dependence of African political systems. They also arise from the evolution of their internal stratification' (Bayart 1986, 121). Hence, 'primitive accumulation ... entails appropriation and co-optation of pre-existing cultural and social achievements as well as confrontation and supersession' (Harvey 2003, 146). This is where Jean-François Bayart's (2000) notion of 'extraversion' gains purchase in appreciating the general trajectories of state formation shaped by historical patterns in the U&CD of capital accumulation alongside the predatory pursuit of power and wealth tied to particular state formation practices and social forms of organization in the post-colonial era.

Specific struggles within sub-Saharan African states (Liberia, Rwanda, Democratic Republic of Congo and Uganda) might then be interpreted as a mode of political production: a source of primitive accumulation that enables the seizure of the resources of the economy based on strategies of extraversion involving new claims to authority and redistribution (Bayart 1993, xiii–xiv). For instance, rebel groups in Sierra Leone in the 1990s such as Foday Sankoh's Revolutionary United Front (RUF) engaged in predatory forms of primitive accumulation through the seizure of resources such as conflict diamonds, or Charles Taylor's National Patriotic Front of Liberia (NPFL) funded warfare through the seizure of the timber, rubber, and diamond trades (Szeftel 2000; Reno 1998). Also, in the late-1990s, the rebel Alliance for the Liberation of Congo-Zaire, led by Laurent Kabila, played off the diamond cartel De Beers against one of its rivals, America Mineral Fields, concerning diamond mining contracts as well as contracts to mine copper, cobalt and zinc in a similar fashion. This arrangement is also somewhat mirrored by the intervention of the Ugandan Peoples' Defence Force (UPDF) in the ensuing Congo war through which some officers of the UPDF managed to institutionalize their private interests and benefit from the predatory pursuit of primitive accumulation whilst simultaneously underwriting the Ugandan state's compliance with debt obligations to creditors within the global political economy. Long-term aims of state building, however, remain thwarted by the volatile balance sustained by these competing factional interests in the Ugandan state (Reno 2002).

Throughout these conditions of extraversion—the predatory pursuit of wealth and power through primitive accumulation—there are connotations of the theory of passive revolution which can be related to specific state formation processes in

sub-Saharan Africa (Bayart 1993, 180–92). This focus might thus offer a more historically rich and nuanced approach to understanding post-colonial state formation
whilst any assiduous analysis would need to further engage history as process rather
than history as analogy, the latter meaning the exclusive privileging of European
historical experience as its touchstone (Mamdani 1996, 12).

Passive revolutions of capital in Latin America?

Within formal or informal Western imperialism, Eric Hobsbawm (2007b, 27) has
stated that,

> in the first instance, 'Westernisation' was the only form in which backward
> economies could be modernised and weak states strengthened. This provided
> Western empires with the built-in goodwill of such local elites as were inter-
> ested in overcoming local backwardness. This was so even when the indigenous
> modernisers eventually turned against foreign rule.

In Latin America, classic stratifications associated with uneven development have been
evident in terms of agrarian capitalism; the creation of a local bourgeoisie in the wake
of dominant foreign capital; and the tendency to assume statist forms of development
through Import Substitution Industrialization (ISI) induced by the demands of accelerated capitalist production for the world market (Amin 1974, 378–90). A formative
influence on the structures of specific state formation processes in Latin America has
thus been the geopolitical circumstances of the system of states. Additionally, the
impact of foreign capital and the gradual inclusion of such states within the world
market—or conditions of U&CD—meant that the state became the arbiter of class
struggle and the necessary precondition for the furtherance of capitalism.

Robert Cox (1987, 209–10) has directly noted how such conditions of uneven
development have shaped social relations of production and mechanisms of capital
accumulation within such social formations. The emergent state in Latin America
commonly reflected an impasse between social class forces, it was not itself hegemonic, and so 'initiated capitalist development as a passive revolution within an
authoritarian framework under state leadership for lack of any established bourgeois
hegemony' (Cox 1987, 218). Elsewhere, Michael Löwy (1981, 162–66) has characterized various passive revolutions (or 'semi-revolutions from above') in Latin
America that have driven the developmental catch-up process through planned
action, the mobilization of the social base, and populist-style national development,
for instance in Mexico under Lázaro Cárdenas (1934–40), in Brazil under Getúlio
Vargas (1937–45), and in Argentina under Juan Perón (1944–55) (see also van der
Pijl 2006b, 17–21, 177–80). The case of Brazil, according to Ronaldo Munck
(1979), during the administrations of Vargas, is clearly one where the strategy of
passive revolution opened up a new stage in the development of capitalism. At issue
here, as Carlos Nelson Coutinho states, is to 'embrace the Gramsci … who researched
the "nonclassical" forms of the transition to capitalist modernity (the problematic of
the "passive revolution")' (as quoted in Burgos 2002, 13–14).

This means that the political rule of capital through passive revolutions—or state-led attempts of developmental catch-up—often resulted in a 'bastard birth' of 'strikingly incomplete' achievements besides the construction of a modern state (Anderson 1992b, 115). Frequently in such cases, state formation literally became a process of *étatization* involving transplanted political structures introduced, sometimes by force, as an imported form of political centralization (Badie and Birnbaum 1983, 74, 97–99). The theory of passive revolution can therefore be linked to the extension of capitalism through the social form of the modern state as a historical precondition for its consolidation and expansion. 'To sharpen it', states Partha Chatterjee (1986, 30), 'one must examine several historical cases of "passive revolutions" in their economic, political and ideological aspects'.

One way of beginning this task in relation to Latin America is by analyzing the originality and peculiarity of 'national' differences within specific state formation processes while displaying an awareness of how local processes of capital accumulation shaping state forms are embedded in wider geopolitical circumstances. Illustrative here would be the outcome of the Mexican Revolution (1910–20) understood as a passive revolution, which gave capitalism there a particular form consistent with authoritarian dominance and hegemonic influence (see Morton 2010). This approach to situating state formation processes within the geopolitics of world order might not only represent the type of class strategy undertaken in establishing and maintaining the expansion of the state, but also the ways in which capitalism is forced to revolutionize itself *whenever* hegemony is weakened or a social formation cannot cope with the need to expand the forces of production.

Practices of passive revolution in the twentieth century in alternative conditions of development might then be traced whereby state mechanisms have been deployed to assist capitalist transformation. For instance, the manner in which the rise of neoliberalism as an accumulation strategy emerged in Mexico has been highlighted to trace the survival and reorganization of capitalism through periods of state crisis (Morton 2003; Soederberg 2001). Here, though, stress has been placed on the changing role of the state in relation to global restructuring. Uneven development is thus understood as consubstantial with the modern state through the *internalization* of neoliberalism (Bieler and Morton 2003, 485–89). How social class forces in Chile have sought to normalize a 'passive revolutionary' path to neoliberalism during the Augusto Pinochet era and then further neoliberal hegemony through the Chilean Socialist Party (PSCh) is a further pertinent example (Motta 2008). Overall, an opportunity is provided through these moves to situate the geopolitics of passive revolution within the uneven development of capitalism to expose the active political class agents in the construction and reproduction of 'modernization' as well as its contestation and resistance (see Morton 2007d).

Following pointers raised at the start of this chapter, though, it should be stressed that instances of passive revolution should not be posited as externalized expressions or 'cases' juxtaposed as contrasting patterns for comparative political analysis. Rather, instances of passive revolution can be regarded through the notion of incorporated comparison as historically connected and distinct but relational parts of a singular world-historical process. To expand, McMichael (1990) has delineated a historically-grounded approach that locates state formation processes within time and space relations to connect generative processes within the modern world. Specifically, the multiple form of incorporated comparison is regarded as expressive of differentiated but related instances of various state formation processes within a cumulative world-historical context (McMichael 1990, 392). Passive revolutions can therefore be regarded as particular instances of time/space relations of state formation within the uneven and combined process of capitalism. 'In other words, the instances and the combined process are not independent of one another, and cannot be adequately understood outside of the historical relations through which they form' (McMichael 2000, 672).

This method of inquiry may then assist in addressing parallel events in the emergence of the states system so that various passive revolutions could be regarded as ongoing, general processes manifested in particular settings that emerge within and interconnect with capitalism on a world scale. Recall here that the instance of passive revolution in Italy leading to the Risorgimento, as highlighted by Gramsci (1978, 129), involved 'a whole series of circumstances of an international character (Napoleon III's policy in 1852–60; the Austro-Prussian War of 1866; France's defeat at Sedan and the development of the German Empire after this event)'. What would the method of incorporated comparison offer in inquiring into similar instances of passive revolution? What would be distinguished as significant when addressing parallel factors within the emergence of the state system?

It instructive to note here, for example, that in Latin America the relations of state formation in Mexico were similarly marked by 'a whole series of circumstances of an international character' that were coeval in their temporality. The United States' annexation and war in 1846–48, the occupation of Veracruz by Spanish, British and French forces in 1861, the installation by the French of Emperor Maximillian in 1863, the occupation by us troops in Veracruz in 1914 and the development of the 'American Century' after this event would all be interrelated instances shaping the conditions of passive revolution within the history of state formation in Mexico (see Morton 2010). That these instances of state formation in Italy and Mexico are temporally coincident may thus be addressed through a focus on the incorporated comparison of passive revolutions in an attempt to highlight how such interrelations are integral to, and define, the general historical process of transitions to capitalist modernity. Theory and history is therefore seen as internally related rather than opposed through the separation of cases.

Conclusion: capitalism as a universal concept with specific geographical seats

It has been argued in this chapter that the theory of passive revolution as the political rule of capital provides an approach to theorizing state geopolitics and global capitalism. A focus on the geopolitics of passive revolution captures, 1) the uneven insertion of different territories into the capitalist world market, 2) the geographical reproduction of class and productive relations across spatial scales and, 3) the persistence of geopolitical competition within conditions of global capitalism. Moreover,

through its focus on the class strategies of capitalist consolidation within state formation processes, the theory of passive revolution is also attentive to the restoration
and reconstitution of class power so central to capital accumulation and the states
system. It should thus be obvious that there is no need to 'scale-up' the focus of
passive revolution from the 'national' to 'the international'; it was always-already
multi-scalar in its appreciation.

The argument is therefore that there is a constitutive theory of capitalism within
the theorizing of the geopolitics of passive revolution that can reveal the spatial role
of the state within the project of modernity across various scales. Undoubtedly, these
spatial practices of passive revolution require further attention in terms of the relationship of local to global and how the modern state domesticates geopolitical space.
What the geopolitics of passive revolution links to, though, is the recognition that,

> the violence of the state must not be viewed in isolation: it cannot be separated
> either from the accumulation of capital or from the rational and political prin-
> ciple of *unification*, which subordinates and totalises the various aspects of social
> practice—legislation, culture, knowledge, education—within a determinate
> space; namely the space of the ruling class's hegemony over its people and over
> the nationhood that it has arrogated. (Lefebvre 1991, 280–81)

Yet, the theory of passive revolution and its focus on uneven development is
nevertheless faced with the meta-theoretical critique that Marxist concepts have
proved incapable of consistent application to the subject matter of development studies. Most controversially, this has been encapsulated in David Booth's (1985) overview of development sociology in arguing that the complex and challenging issues of
development in post-colonial social formations cannot be sufficiently grasped in terms
of the dynamics and differential spread of capitalism through U&CD. The problem of
'picking off and lumping together' specific structures within 'national' state forms
that are pitched within the generality of laws of uneven development, it is argued,
results in contorting state specificities to international causal factors of world capitalism (Booth 1985, 774). The same argument about the suppression of different types
and stages of development within post-colonial state forms—outside 'core' states of
the global economy—could also be extrapolated to those considerations of U&CD
that similarly accord priority to international causal factors (for example, Rosenberg
2005; 2006). The unfulfilled promise of theorizations on U&CD, then, is to combine
an appreciation of the generality of capitalism with a historical sociology of transformations *within* specific forms of state (Kiely 2005, 33).

At issue here is whether the theorization of passive revolutions of uneven development can capture the common and the distinct conditions that have faced the post-
colonial state on a world scale. Yet, it should be clear from the preceding argument
that one cannot presume uniform developments either within, or across, different
regional state formation processes. On the contrary, the pressures of uneven development are clearly mediated through different *forms of state* as nodal points of nationally
specific configurations of class fractions and struggles over hegemony and/or passive
revolution within accumulation conditions on a world scale. This is the challenge,

after all, of the internal relation between theory and history where *incorporated comparison* becomes an internal rather than an external feature of inquiry so that passive revolutions within the states system are part of an ongoing, general process manifested in particular national settings that emerge within the world-historical process of capitalism (McMichael 1990, 391–92). Or, as Gramsci put it, the task is one of analyzing 'universal concepts', such as capitalism, 'with "geographical seats"' (Gramsci 1971, 117, Q10II§61). Theorizing the geopolitics of passive revolution therefore entails appreciating the multi-scalar trajectory of specific emergent and ongoing state spatialization strategies within the general tendencies of capitalism, thus encouraging a diligent empirical account of U&CD across historical and contemporary cases.

Notes

1 I would like to thank Chris Hesketh for our ongoing conversations on spatiality and the state and for his feedback on this chapter.
2 Throughout this chapter, a specific convention associated with citing the *Prison Notebooks* is adopted. In addition to giving the reference to the selected anthologies, the notebook number (Q) and section (§) accompanies all citations to enable the reader to trace the specific collocation of the citations.
3 This quotation is referred to in Slater's (2004, 160) study of the geopolitical unevenness of development intrinsic to colonial and post-colonial power relations.

13 Politics and the international

Simon Bromley

Introduction

Both in mainstream International Relations (IR) theory and in recent critical and Marxist discussions the *international* is taken as a distinct object of analysis and most commentators agree that the basic or primary reference of the concept of the international is to the fact of political multiplicity. The political is defined and explained in a variety of ways but what sets the international apart as a distinct object of study—constituting the basis for a distinct discipline of IR—is the fact that many politically organized societies interact with one another. But why do political boundaries serve to individuate one society from another in the way that, say, economic or cultural differentiation need not? What is in need of further elaboration, I believe, is an explanation of the generic features of political life in the production of social order. What is the distinct contribution of politics to the production of social order?

If we can clarify the place or role of politics in social order more generally, then this might cast some light on why political multiplicity is the defining feature of the international—or, to use a less historically contingent term, the inter-societal. I want to suggest that one way of making sense of the international is by investigating the character of political order. What follows is divided into five sections. In Section 1, I outline a general notion of political order which is sufficiently precise to capture the contribution of politics to social order more generally yet open enough to allow for the diversity of known societies. Sections 2, 3 and 4 then develop three very stylized accounts of different routes to achieving political order—three different ways of doing the politics of force. Section 5 briefly discusses questions of territory and collective action in relation to political order and I conclude with some thoughts about the status of the argument.

There is a sense, then, in which this investigation is of a different kind to those pursued either in mainstream IR or in the critical and Marxist literature to date. To a very large extent, these discussions take for granted the question of political order in the sense of bracketing the question of how, as an ongoing accomplishment of social life, it is routinely achieved or instantiated. For mainstream IR it is the *consequences* of political multiplicity which are the focus of interest; and for Marxism at least it is, more or less, the *relations between* states and the states system, on the one side, and societies, on the other, that are the object of attention. Neither mainstream IR nor Marxism has very much to say about what politics is and how political order is accomplished in those circumstances where it obtains—or so I claim.

Political order

So what, then, is political order? Politics is a distinct kind or moment of social activity concerned with reaching and giving effect to collectively-binding decisions and rules in circumstances where there is (potential) disagreement over alternative courses of action. Political power is simply the ability to effect favoured political outcomes in competition with other social actors. As such, there is a political moment to large areas of social life, distributed across a wide range of organizations and institutions, and (the competition for) political power is a ubiquitous component of social interaction. But there is an important sense in which collectively-binding rules about the use of *force* play a basic and defining role in political life, or at least in the workings of any given political order. What distinguishes the most basic political activity from other social practices, and the powers they generate, is its purpose: namely, the provision of those (public goods) elements of social order that relate to individual and collective security in relation to the potential use of force. I will call this, following Bernard Williams (2005), the 'first' or 'Hobbesian' political question.[1] The need for this kind of political activity arises because people are social beings whose agency can be erased by force: they must live together if they are to live recognizably human lives at all; if they are to live together, there must be some minimal level of social order; and a key component of social order is the need for individual and collective security, including security of property and promises, in the presence of the (potential) use of force.

Understood in the context of strategic interaction, guarantees of the security of persons, property and promises, and the ability to make and enforce collectively-binding decisions to that end, are, to some degree, public goods insofar as these outcomes are very largely non-rival and, to a more variable extent, non-excludable. Given this, how can people bind themselves and others so that cooperative undertakings do not founder on the disruptive logic of independent self-interest?[2] It is an essential feature of any satisfactory answer to this question that, in the final analysis, (some) people (at least) cannot be coerced: if a political order is reached, at least some sub-group of the society concerned—that is, those with political power—must be capable of cooperating among themselves, rather than being coerced by others. To be sure, any given group can be bound by the coercive power of another, but the collective, social process of cooperation must apply at least to the most powerful groups.

The question of force is basic because the social use of force is quite different from other exercises of power. Force operates by changing the options in an agent's environment so far as to deny the agent's ability to act, thereby treating the agent as (literally) a merely physical object. Force constrains, or destroys, agency in the way that no other source of social power seeks to do and for that reason it can never be self-legitimating: might is never right. In all other cases, the exercise of social power always presupposes a capacity for agency, however limited, on the part of its subordinate targets. Consider the case of coercion.[3] In circumstances of more or less unequal strategic interaction, coercive power may be exercised by control over (some combination of) the means of reproduction, the means of production and subsistence, the means of violence, and the means of persuasion.

There are, then, two differences between force and coercion: first, although coercion depends on the threat of one party to worsen the position of another unless the target changes its course of action, it may, by virtue of its capacity to mobilize the agency of subordinates, be materially productive in a way that force can never be.[4] In this respect, it is important to see that even '[w]hen the possibility of the use of force grounds an agent's attempt to avoid its exercise, the action takes place in the logical space of coercive power rather than force' (Wartenberg 1990, 101). And secondly, precisely because coercion is potentially productive of overall gains, it may become self-enforcing. In this case, those who are coerced are only exploited relevant to some notion of a 'fair' division of the gains or by virtue of a remediable defect in the process of interaction itself.[5]

Despite these differences between force and coercive power, it is also important to see that *all* social power, including the use of force, presupposes a degree of coordinated collective action on the part of those who would wield that power. For it is axiomatic that *social* power is always 'situated': even where it takes the form of one party exercising force against another, it is constituted by the presence and agency of peripheral agents who are both oriented to the actions of the principal parties concerned and coordinated in their responses to those actions. A capacity for power is never a mere physical possession of resources that can be used to forcibly constrain (and thence also coerce) others: it is always also a socially recognized and coordinated set of rules geared to the use of those resources. And it is a basic feature of conventions that solve coordination problems that they produce benefits for those involved, *ex nihilo*, by lifting the possibilities of social interaction onto a higher plane. So, at the root of all organized—that is, social power—there is an element of more or less conventional coordination. That is, there is an element of social cooperation in all organized forms of social power. A capacity to exercise power by any given social actor presupposes an ability to draw upon rules and resources of a more or less institutionalized kind. Some form of coordinated collective action lies at the basis of all enduring exercises of power, however limited the cooperating sub-group and however much domination is involved in its relationships with others.

It therefore follows that the fundamental problem of political order is one of aligning or coordinating people's actions and expectations on a set of rules or institutions that can govern interactions involving force so as to cope with the facts that force is neither productive nor self-legitimating. As such, political order answers to a particular set of human vulnerabilities in the face of force which are ontologically and existentially central to human existence.[6] Politics constitutes and (to a greater or lesser extent) authorizes force. But force, unlike coercion, exchange or consensus, depends for its routine exercise on physical co-presence. So, the answer to the first political question resolves a question among those who are physically co-present with one another—that is, broadly speaking those who are not just socially but also *territorially* in proximity with one another.[7] Political order is, then, always an order for a particular segment of the human population, organized as a group in a given, perhaps shifting, territory. The creation of political order necessarily creates an 'inside' and an 'outside' in the way that economic and cultural forms of social order need not.

Political order, by virtue of what it orders (that is, physically co-present force), necessarily has a determinate location: it must serve to define territorial boundaries or borders. Of course, economic and cultural activity is always also located in historical time and social space but it is not intrinsic to these activities that they demarcate and fragment space and people in particular ways. We live together politically, if we live under a political order at all, in a qualitatively different way to the ways in which we might live together economically or culturally. The corollary of this is that we also live *apart* politically in ways that are different to our economic and cultural differences.

Nevertheless, Carl Schmitt had it the wrong way around: it is not that politics presupposes a distinction between 'friend' and 'enemy', understood as pre-political groups that may confront one another as violent antagonists, but rather that the establishment of political order forges a distinction and a difference between those who are on the inside and those who on the outside. The result is, as Schmitt says, that the political world is necessarily a 'pluriverse' but this is so for essentially Hobbesian or, as we shall see, Humean reasons.

Once force has been constituted as a social power, there is a further question as to how far those empowered by force rule over others primarily by means of coercion or through additional coordination. We will see that there are, in principle, three possible solutions to the need for political order: 'community governance' in simple societies based on reciprocity where the means of force are widely distributed; coercive rule based on the domination of the governed by the rulers; and legitimate authority founded on extensive coordination among rulers and ruled. Because I want to focus on some key questions involved in the analysis and explanation of politics, I will present these as three ideal-typical routes to achieving political order. Historically, most actual societies involve more or less complex mixtures of these analytically distinct mechanisms of rule. With that proviso in mind, let us now consider these in turn.

Distributed force

Community governance is found in forms of social anarchy in which there is a limited or even minimal concentration of force among the members of society and a relative absence of political specialization. In these societies, there is extensive participation in political activities and the component elements of the society (families, lineages, tribes, etc.) owe their protection and obligations not to a political body that is permanently and institutionally separated from society but to each other. How does this work? In the course of his excoriation of social contract theories of government (in 'Of the Original Contract'), David Hume speculated about the origins of government 'in the woods and the desarts', noting that since the 'natural force' of people is 'nearly equal', a 'man's natural force ... could never subject multitudes to the command of one. Nothing but their own consent, and their sense of the advantages from peace and order, could have had that influence' (Hume 1994, 188).

Although it is located ambiguously somewhere between historical speculation and thought-experiment,[8] Hume's observation is nonetheless well founded. Even the simplest known societies distinguish individual acts of murder from the murder of many. While individual acts of murder may be 'private' offences against the deceased and his or her family, acts which may be redressed by kin, the murder of many is an offence against the community and is typically addressed by someone or some special group sanctioned by the community. Tribes without chiefs, compounds of lineages interlinked by marriage and sharing a common ecological habitat of pastoral nomadism, for example, recognize some among themselves as legitimate arbiters of disputes. If we consider hunter-gatherer societies, in which accumulated social power is extremely limited, or the big-man systems or chiefdoms based on horticulture or primitive agriculture, in which small accumulations of social power are possible but are either dissipated (for example, by big-men to their lineages or by tribal leaders to their tribesmen) or shared (typically among adult male heads of households), we find that political power does indeed rest upon consent, or at least acquiescence,[9] in the 'advantages of peace and order'.

This is because where a society's power resides very largely in its people and their mobile property, and where fission from the larger society is a real option for a disgruntled minority, it is virtually impossible to institutionalize coercive power based on a credible threat of the use of force—without effecting the transition to statehood. To be sure, these societies contain subordinates—clients, kinsmen or slaves—and the dominant may reproduce themselves across the generations. But while the dominant group may, collectively, monopolize coercive power, no one member of that group 'can aspire to a role to which there attaches a more than marginally or temporarily larger share of the power available to it' (Runciman 1989, 151).

In these small-scale, stateless societies, characterized by a rough equality of condition and direct and many-sided relations among their members, the threat of self-help retaliation, combined with the offer and threat of reciprocity,[10] as well as practices such as the shaming and exile of those who break local conventions or norms, can achieve sufficient political order for the reproduction of social life. As Michael Taylor (1982, 10) says, all these societies

> use social controls of some kind to maintain social order; they redistribute resources amongst their members; and they make collective decisions; nearly all ... also defend or make preparations to defend themselves against actual or imagined external enemies and competitors.

What holds these societies together, politically speaking, are the practices of conditional cooperation, operating in dense networks of interaction, which serve to sustain conventions of reciprocity.

The first kind of political order, then, is the coordinated authority created by conventions of reciprocity in the social anarchies, that is, in pre-state examples of community governance.[11] Community governance of this kind can only be sustained if the consequences of deviation from the conditionally cooperative practices that sustain conventions of reciprocity are relatively high, 'which requires worse outcomes from dealing with people outside the group'. In social anarchies, there 'is a trade-off: better within-group cooperation may require worse cross-group relations' (Dixit 2004, 40).

This is because any transactions that serve to undermine the rough equality among the members—or favourable opportunities to diversify away from direct and many-sided patterns of interrelations with 'insiders', or both—threaten the delicate balance of self-help and reciprocity on which the coordinated reproduction of political order in these societies depends. The stability of these political systems is, therefore, directly dependent on their ability to negotiate or manage their boundaries. These boundaries may be ecological or they may derive from the relations established with neighbouring societies but the point is that the political stability of these systems is always contingent on the management of the boundary. Small changes in the nature of the boundaries, and hence changes in the interactions across them, can have major implications for the ability of these societies to reproduce themselves in their existing form.[12]

Put the other way around, the nature of the inter-societal coexistence of these societies directly impinges on their ability to reproduce themselves as the distinctive kind of political order that they are. Or, more accurately, in this distinctive political form, these societies have no stable existence outside of a particular (im)balance of interactions between their 'insides' and 'outsides'. The point to emphasize here is one about the resilience or otherwise of these societies; it concerns the conditions for their *stability*. The point is that no account of the logic of process of these societies makes any sense outside a careful specification of their boundaries and their transactions with their neighbours. They simply do not have a logic of process, a typical pattern of reproduction and transformation—in short, a pattern of development—that can be specified in abstraction from their insertion into a wider configuration.

It is, in fact, a moot point as to when an acephalous society may be said to have a political order. For while it may be true that even the simplest societies are territorially organized and have rules for the use of force, it is also often the case that the very unit of political order itself—what is 'inside' and 'outside'—is highly fragile and mobile in these societies, ranging from family, through lineage, to tribes and federations of the same as circumstances and the occasion demand. To the extent that the boundaries of political order are fragile, shifting and complex entanglements of different units, the very idea of the inter-societal becomes problematic.

Coercive rule

Are these observations of any more than historical or anthropological significance? Does anything of this carry over to the world of settled agriculture and statehood proper? Hume, notoriously, ridiculed the idea of tacit consent (his explicit antagonist was the John Locke of the *Two Treaties of Government*):

> Should it be said, that, by living under the dominion of a prince, which one might leave, every individual has given a *tacit* consent to his authority; it may be answered, that such an implied consent can only have a place, where a man imagines, that the matter depends on his choice. Can we seriously say, that a poor peasant or artisan has a free choice to leave his country, when he knows no foreign language or manners, and lives from day to day, by the small wages he

acquires? We may as well assert, that a man, by remaining in a vessel, freely consents to the dominion of the master; though he was carried on board while asleep, and must leap into the ocean, and perish, the moment he leaves her.

(Hume 1994, 193)

Nevertheless, Hume held that acquiescence in the advantages of peace and order was a key component of political order in more developed polities. And it is by following his reasoning along this path that we will begin to appreciate the significance of the nature of political power under third-party enforcement.

Reflecting on the question of why 'the many are governed by the few' (in 'Of the First Principles of Government'), Hume says that:

as FORCE is always on the side of the governed, the governors have nothing to support them but opinion. It is therefore, on opinion only that government is founded; and this maxim extends to the most despotic and military governments, as well as to the most free and most popular. The soldan of EGYPT, or the emperor of ROME, might drive his harmless subjects, like brute beasts, against their sentiments and inclinations: but he must, at least, have led his *mamalukes*, or *praetorian bands*, like men, by their opinion.

(Hume 1994, 16)

Now, clearly, the historical examples indicate that we are in the world of settled agriculture, writing, cities and states—in short, civilization. Hume's point—and it is now an instance of empirical analysis—is both simple and far-reaching. Political power in these societies, even when it is most dependent on the exercise of force, presupposes opinion, which he defines as: first, 'opinion of interest', that is, 'the general advantage which is reaped from government', and; secondly, 'opinion of right', by which he means the more or less spontaneously evolved conventions about appropriate rules of property and power.[13] Hume is arguing that even when force is the means of exercising political power something more is involved because political order (*at least among the rulers and their agents*) rests on a convention to coordinate on a structure of rule—that is, to grant and recognize authority, on condition that others do likewise.

Recall that in circumstances of coordination actors align their intentions and expectations of one another on a single course of action, such that each serves their own and the mutual benefit, because the coordinated outcome produces gains over the un-coordinated *status quo ante*. It is a form of conditional cooperation in which each prefers to coordinate provided others do likewise and it is self-enforcing because, once they are coordinated, nobody has an interest in deviating from it, even if many would have preferred to have coordinated differently. It is, therefore, both a historical and analytical truth to say that social cooperation, more precisely, social coordination precedes government. At least for one of the collective actors in dyadic power relations of domination (even ones that rest ultimately on monopolization of force), what was true in the forests and deserts of antiquity survives the transition to statehood and civilization.

To be sure, states can exercise their rule over *subordinate* classes through force and domination. In this case, relations between the rulers (here understood as the state personnel and the ruling class, who together control access to the means of production and violence) and the governed may be, in the final analysis, coercively, even forcefully, imposed. This aspect of politics might centre on conflicts of interests in which one party gains and another loses, relative to a relevant baseline condition, and political order might be the outcome of constraint, the domination of some by others. In interactions involving conflicts of interest the parties either go their separate ways, in which case they cease to have a social and, *a fortiori*, political existence, or one party coerces the other to follow a particular course of action: Political order is then fundamentally about the collective domination of one group of people over another and the competitive struggle for power is the essence of social life.

Consider, for example, Robert Brenner's account of the world or pre-capitalist, settled agriculture. In this world, political power 'was made possible by the self-organization of exploiters (lords) precisely so as to mobilize and monopolize the means of force', such that 'the structures of property rights behind unequal appropriation have been *about*—have been constituted in order to make possible—the economic reproduction of some collectivities at the expense or exclusion of others' (Brenner 2006b, 208). Rule was always *ipso facto* a form of coercive domination over peasants and other subordinate groups, where economic exploitation was ultimately backed up by the use of force. Yet, are we to suppose that politics is somehow bimodal? Is it the case that political order is either a relatively pure form of coordination among political equals or else an arrangement in which one class coordinates amongst itself in order to dominate another? This would give us, on the one side, the forms of community governance in social anarchies that practised a very limited division of labour. And, on the other side, we would have the pre-capitalist, class-divided world of settled agriculture, as described by Brenner.

For what it is worth, I don't think Brenner's formulation captures Marx's view. The Marxist anthropologist, Maurice Godelier, hypothesizes that '*for relations of domination and exploitation to be formed and reproduced in a lasting fashion, they must be presented as an exchange, and as exchange of services*', He further argues that 'not all the services provided by those who were dominant were purely imaginary or illusory. Otherwise the movement which engendered estates, castes, classes and the state, when that emerged in certain class societies … would not have forged ahead' (Godelier 1986, 160, 166). Similarly, a Marxist historian, John Haldon (2006, 178), suggests that 'a crucial element in the longer-term success of a state formation is a degree of acceptance of that state as normatively desirable, especially by elites, but even by the broader populace from which it draws its resources'. And if we ask of Marx, 'why does the successful class succeed?', as GA Cohen rightly observes:

> *Marx finds the answer in the character of the productive forces.* "The conditions under which definite productive forces can be applied are the conditions of the rule of a definite class of society". The class which rules through a period, or emerges triumphant after epochal conflict, is the class best suited, most able and disposed, to preside over the development of the productive forces at the given time. Hence

> Marx frequently allows that a dominant class promotes not only its own interests but, in so doing, those of humanity at large—until its rule becomes outmoded, and it becomes reactionary—and he gives no explanation of class supremacy which is not founded on the productive needs of the relevant age.
>
> (Cohen 2000, 149)

Surely, it is more accurate to see pure social anarchy and Brenner's view of the feudal order as the outer boundaries of political life—Rousseau and Thrasymachus, respectively—rather than adequate characterizations of the pre-industrial historical record.

Politics is always about much more than class domination and exploitation.[14] In addition, class domination and exploitation can rarely be reckoned in zero-sum terms. Because the authority of the state cannot be external to the coordination of powerful social groups, and because that authority lies behind the ability of the state to deploy force and exercise coercion, it is in general a deep mistake to think of states as protection rackets writ-large. The point about criminal gangs, roving bandits and the like is, precisely, that they are—or at least aim to be—external to the societies on which they are predators. But even stationary bandits (for example, feudal lords on Brenner's account) have an incentive to reduce their theft from society to the point where their gains (from a lower rate of extortion on a higher output) are just offset by their losses (from a smaller share of the output) and to invest a share of their own resources in public goods up to the point where the increase in output is equal to the reciprocal of their share of total output.

In fact, it is important to see that, as well as authorizing the use of force and other forms of coercive sanctions, the creation of political authority makes possible further coordination, such that it becomes itself one of the mechanisms by which rulers can order their relations with the rest of society. For not only does the creation of durable, institutionalized political authority represent a major increase in political power over and above community forms of governance, it also makes possible further advances in social coordination mobilized through the agency of the state. Coordination can be imposed from the 'outside' and still be productive: people can coordinate and they can be coordinated by others.

Legitimate authority

In order to get a sense of this, let us stay with some of Hume's examples a little longer—here are three more of them. In the first (in 'That Politics may be reduced to a Science'), Hume claimed that the success of a state that imposed its power upon society (an 'absolute government') was dependent on the qualities of the people who administered it. By contrast, states that institutionalized their power in cooperation with elements of civil society ('republican and free' governments) were capable of making 'even bad men ... act for the public good' (Hume 1994, 5). Similarly (in 'Of the Origin of Government'), Hume (1994, 23) says that 'men, once raised to that station, though often led astray by private passions, find, in ordinary cases, a visible interest in the impartial administration of justice'. Secondly, adopting a characteristic trope of enlightenment thought (which he, in turn, attributed to Machiavelli), Hume stated that:

> a monarch may govern his subjects in two different ways. He may either follow the maxims of the eastern princes, and stretch his authority so far as to leave no distinction of rank among his subjects, but what proceeds immediately from himself ... Or a monarch may exert his power after a milder manner, like our EUROPEAN princes; and leave other sources of honour, beside his smile and favour; Birth, title, possessions, valour, integrity, knowledge, or great or fortunate achievements. ... a gentle government is preferable, and gives the greatest security to the sovereign as well as to the subject. Legislators, therefore, ought not to trust the future government of a state entirely to chance, but ought to provide a system of laws to regulate the administration of public affairs to the latest posterity.
>
> (Hume 1994, 9–11)

Finally, Hume (1994, 23) says that:

> The sultan is master of the life and fortune of any individual; but will not be permitted to impose new taxes on his subjects: a French monarch can impose taxes at pleasure; but would find it dangerous to attempt the lives and fortunes of individuals.

The social development at work in each of these examples, according to Hume (and the entire tradition that descends from the Scottish Enlightenment), was the development of commercial, or capitalist society, and the linked ideas of the separation of powers and the rule of law as applied to the institutions of the state. Hume's examples register the importance of the creation of an indirect relation between the constitutional authorization of force, on the one hand, and the economic power of the ruling classes, on the other. Hume is describing the early capitalist regime in which a bureaucratic state is effectively controlled by a merchant and capitalist class that gains its surplus, at least in the first instance, through economic mechanisms.

In the capitalist or bourgeois regime, those who are authorized to use force are institutionally separate from those who control access to the means of production and subsistence. To be sure, the outright fusion of control over the means of force and production in pre-capitalist societies does not indicate that politics was simply about the domination of one class over another; the question of the extent to which control over the use of force served a wider purpose and was, to that extent, authorized by subordinate classes remains to be answered. But agrarian and later industrial capitalism is a clear instance where the institutional separation of function was clearly a case of more or less explicitly codified constitutional authority. Whatever sense we attribute to the idea of a constitution in the pre-capitalist world, the constitutional settlement in England after 1688 is clear enough. Moreover, later and after much struggle, subordinate classes gained some power in the constitutional order as well.

Now, one does not need to accept Hume's liberal understanding of capitalist society and rule to distil the analytical point that it is important to distinguish rule that is simply a form of externally imposed coercive domination from that which also involves a degree of authority that is authorized by those over whom it is exercised. As David Beetham (1991, 49) says:

> in the case of [political] authority, it is the *relationship* between the dominant and the subordinate itself that is specified by the rules. ... [A]uthority constitutes both an aspect of power relations *and* a means of power in its own right (power deriving from positions of command).

Political power, accordingly, is legitimate to the extent that it is authorized by the members of society, that is, to the extent that it serves 'ends that are recognized as socially necessary' and 'interests that are general' (Beetham 1991, 149). Force, coercion and legitimate authority are very different ways of producing social order and authority is the least costly and most effective of these, since it is the one most able productively to mobilize the agency of subordinates. Force, coercion and authority, accordingly, are not simply three interchangeable forms of political power but an ascending series of modalities of rule located on a trajectory of increasing productivity or efficiency.[15]

Of course, all political orders have a degree of legitimacy, for without some degree of acquiescence to authority occasioned by the gains produced by conditional cooperation to achieve a degree of coordination in relation to the use of force, neither the social organization of force itself nor the coercive power deriving from it can be established. But to the extent that a political order is founded on socially encompassing coordination between rulers and governed on a source of authoritative rule, it serves not only to constitute might but also to turn might into right: the state is *authorized* to use force on behalf of the governed. This, as Hobbes (1996) explained, creates a form of legitimate third-party enforcement. But, as Hobbes also insisted, insofar as the basis of rule rests upon coordination among those of more or less equal political power, this is a *self-enforced* form of mutually binding rule: the covenant Hobbes's citizens make is to *each other* in order to establish a sovereign authority for and set over them all.

The outer limit of this process, far beyond what Hobbes had in mind (since his citizens were male and propertied) would be what might be called a rule of law state in which *all* the citizens effectively control a state that uses force to enforce the rules. Under such an arrangement, there would be a mutual subjection of both state and society to the rule of law. In principle, it is possible to reconcile forcible enforcement of the rules by an outside party—that is, 'third-party enforcement'—with the rule of law because specialization, in which states develop a comparative advantage in enforcement (while the direct use of force is extruded from social relations elsewhere in society), makes possible 'nesting third-party enforcement *within* self-enforced relationships'. The critical point, Yoram Barzel (2002, 121) explains, is that:

> the protector [the state] has a *comparative advantage* in the use of violence. In the aggregate, his clients have more power than he does. Because the clients'

comparative advantage is in activities other than the use of violence, it is expensive for them to mobilize their power. If they are willing to incur the cost, however, they can have an *absolute advantage* in power.

With this division of labour between the 'protector' and the 'clients', the state and the citizens can coordinate rule on institutions such as the constitutional protection of certain rights, the separation of powers and the rule of law, and a key role for elected representatives in passing legislation and supervising the affairs of the executive, in order to subordinate the state to the interests and powers of the citizens. The state thus becomes a particular kind of third-party enforcement mechanism, in which a single enforcer monopolizes the role for a given population and where the power of the enforcer is internal to the society concerned, self-enforced by the mutual gain of those who recognize and thereby constitute its authority.[16]

To be sure, such mechanisms—even the most encompassing, legitimate ones—have to accommodate to a distribution of power of property and other resources *which they can neither create not control*. And these resources and the interests associated with them serve, in part, to define the ends that are recognized as socially necessary and the interests that are general. Thus, for example, the most legitimate, liberal-democratic capitalist states are still *capitalist* states. Accordingly, even the most legitimate states are selective about the issues and institutions over which they attempt to enforce collectively-binding rules. Thus, not only is the territorial domain of the state—that is, the spatial reach of the enforcer's power—limited but so also is its scope, as measured by the ratio of state-enforced interactions to the totality of societal interactions. This is simply the other side of the coin of authority: attempts to extend the power of the state into areas that are not recognized as socially necessary or which do not comprise general interests simply serve to undermine its legitimacy. Authority, that is to say, operates *both* to empower *and* to limit the capacities of the state—states are authorized to do some things, say, protect property, and not others, perhaps, redistribute it too widely.

It is time to take stock. In cases of distributed force in the social anarchies, conditional cooperation serves to coordinate people or groups of roughly equal political power on conventions of reciprocity, even if, collectively, they dominate others. Coercive rule, the domination (and exploitation) of one group by another, can arise as a result of class-divided coordination in which the ruling class cooperates among itself while preventing subordinate classes from doing likewise. And legitimate political authority is constituted to the extent that encompassing social coordination serves socially necessary ends and general interests. In each instance, however, the creation of political order involves conditional cooperation to provide for individual and collective security in which successful coordination both constitutes force (including lethal force) as an organized form of social power and legitimates the exercise of that power in the eyes of those who are thus coordinated.

We have also seen that the extent of authoritative coordination is a separate question from the reach of the coercive power that is, thereby, enabled. The question of how far a process of authoritative coordination extends beyond the rulers to the relations between the rulers and the governed is a question that answers to the strategic circumstances in which these actors find themselves. Nothing that has been said this far implies that because conditional cooperation works by producing gains over an un-coordinated *status quo ante* there is anything optimal about the creation of political order. Many opportunities for coordination to mutual advantage, including the advantage of the powerful, are simply missed.[17] Coordination is conventional not optimal. By parity of reasoning, however, the mere fact that there is a difference in power between rulers and governed tells us nothing about whether the outcome of their interaction will be one of mutual gain, the gain of one party at the expense of another, or even the mutual ruin of the contending parties.

Au fond coordination is self-enforcing, but the specialization and nesting of relationships, one within another, allows plenty of scope for coercive domination from the outside. Agents of different power may act collectively by coordinating further to establish (expanded) authority among themselves or one agent (or sub-set of agents) may use its power advantage to benefit at the expense of another (or others)—that is, to establish a relationship of *domination*. Rule of law states and dictatorships can both serve as coordination equilibria for capitalist societies. In fine, authoritative coordination around the fundamental aspects of physical force is the fount and origin of political order and power but the coincidence or otherwise of that authority and the coercive power that it establishes is mutable, depending, in part, on the strategic circumstances of interaction among the parties concerned. In short, political order is but one component or aspect of social order more generally, but it is distinctive in that it is an outcome of coordination on a structure of more or less legitimate authority that both constitutes force as a social power and, to a greater or lesser extent, turns might into right for those who are thus coordinated and might into domination for those who are not.

Territory and collective action

Whatever may be said for acephalous, pre-state societies, political order is necessarily territorial. In fact, Robert David Sack (1986) says that it is generally agreed that even 'primitive' societies—that is, essentially classless and pre-state communities—use territoriality for classification, communication of boundaries and enforcement of access. That may be so, but the transition to statehood represents a very substantial augmentation of the level of human social development insofar as it represents the emergence of a set of institutions and relations of rule that are durable and separate from the rest of society, to which are channelled sufficient economic resources to enable state personnel to specialize in their new roles—roles which are acknowledged as legitimate by at least the most powerful elements of the society. With the possible exception of feudalism during some of its history, statehood involves rule over a territory and its people—or, more precisely, a territorially-ordered people.[18] Certainly, pre-modern states were only able to exercise third-party enforcement over a limited range of issues and few institutions, rather than the generality of a territory and its people. And different enforcement agencies have overlapped and competed with one another in any given territory. But chiefdoms, city-states, generic or national states and empires all aimed to be paramount in the rule of their territories and its people.

Moreover, there are very powerful pressures towards monopolization of rule for any given territory. On the side of enforcers: if the cost of defection from an enforcer of rules is low, then the power of that enforcer over potential subjects is limited and it will have little incentive to form agreements with them. So unless they differ significantly in their functions, rivalry between enforcers for a given population undercuts their power. And, further, competition between enforcers gives rise to an incentive to create a demand for their services, thereby potentially extorting more from society than the benefits provided. Therefore, there are clear efficiency gains—for both states and subjects—to the monopolization of enforcement in a single organization. Multiple enforcers could, in principle, coordinate so as to overcome these liabilities but the costs of coordination rise exponentially with the number of jurisdictions. That said, all states coexist, to a greater or lesser extent, with rival sources of third-party enforcement.

Territoriality is a general strategy which, according Sack, is

> best understood as a spatial strategy to affect, influence, or control resources and people, by controlling area ... [and it] must provide a form of classification by area, a form of communication by boundary, and a form of enforcement or control.
>
> (Sack 1986, 1, 28)

While many institutions and organizations deploy territorial strategies, it is a defining feature of states that they use territoriality to effect their coordinated use of force, coercion and authority. Except insofar as they are mediated by the political order, territorial strategies are not, typically, defining features of economic or cultural interaction (for much of its history, the Christian Church is a major qualification to this, quite unlike the world of Islam, for example). Trade *qua* trade between societies, for example, is not categorically or causally distinct from trade within a given society: the gains from trade, to take just one central instance, apply to specialization and exchange both between agents within a given economy as much as they do between collectivities of agents in one economy and another. But the exceptions in this case are (potentially) the rule because, for any given society, the political order is in a unique position to regulate interactions of an economic nature, thereby subjecting their 'anarchical' order to a degree of, more or less effective, collective regulation. To the extent that this happens, economic interactions between societies are, to a greater or lesser extent, politically mediated; and this very fact changes the nature of those interactions in ways that cannot be explained in terms of determinations found solely at the economic level.

Sack remarks that, for social groups in general, territoriality is a strategy that can be 'turned on and off'. Not so for political order, still less for states. Political order, then, answers to distinctive ontological and existential needs and concerns; it is irreducibly territorial and focused on physical co-presence in respect of the regulation of force; it authorizes the social use of force; and it is inevitably particular, creating an inside and an outside. It is also, by virtue of these properties, the principal vehicle and target of collective action in society, both for domestic and inter-societal interaction. The creation and maintenance of political order creates the conditions for cooperative collective action on behalf of a territory and its people. We need to tread carefully at this point for it is not the case that coordination on collectively-binding conventions can only emerge as a result of political activity. On the contrary, most such conventions in social life emerge spontaneously.[19] The crucial point is that once a political order is in place it provides an authoritative resource for further collective action; it is able to regulate and order other interactions and exercise more or less binding constraints over those interactions; and, therefore, it becomes the principal means by which the most powerful groups in society can orient themselves both to subordinates within and to their engagements and transactions with other societies. It is for these reasons that it is primarily through or by means of the political order that societies collectively manage the terms of their inter-societal coexistence.

Conclusion

If the arguments set out here are reasonably robust, then one important conclusion follows: by virtue of ordering force among those who are routinely physically co-present political order answers a distinctive set of ontological and existential needs on a territorial basis in ways which inevitably fragments and divides peoples. (The diversity of human history, on the one side, and the eventual diseconomies of scale, on the other, are two straightforward reasons why there has never been any prospect of a singular political order). The political world is a pluriverse, as Schmitt insisted, but for essentially Hobbesian and Humean reasons. In respect of political order, at least, I'm tempted to agree with Quine's quip that the Humean predicament is the human predicament.

Notes

1 It is 'Hobbesian' not only because this concern lay at the centre of his thinking about politics but also because of the enduring insight into the character of political order in general that can be distilled from Hobbes's unsurpassed reflections on the conditions of possibility for authorizing rule.
2 Providing public goods in circumstances where the gains (or losses) of each depends not only on their actions but also the actions of others, so that each person's best strategy depends on the strategies of all others, involves resolving a collective action problem in which solutions are not automatically reached on the basis of independent, self-interested decision-making.
3 Standardly, coercive power refers to the ability to change the costs and benefits associated with various courses of action in a subordinate's social environment such that unless the target acts in a prescribed manner it will incur costs, relative to some relevant baseline condition. See, for example, Wertheimer (1987).
4 To be sure, force can allow one group to gain at the expense or exclusion of another but coercion can produce gains overall: force is zero- or even negative-sum; coercion is potentially positive-sum.
5 Liberal notions of exploitation tend to emphasize the former, Marxist ones the latter. For the difficulty of making precise the notion of exploitation in a non question-begging way, see Wertheimer (1996).
6 It is, I think, a transhistorical fact that the fear and suffering of physical vulnerability occasions a degree of disruption to social life that is of a different order of magnitude to that brought about by economic deprivation or cultural impoverishment. It is when the

disruptions occasioned by economic and cultural stress cross over into political conflict that they have their most devastating effects.

7 This is true even in those societies that are, at times, always socially organized times, physically mobile; for it is the society that is mobile, or at least coherent segments of it, not its individual members considered as a physically random agglomeration.

8 Hume (1994, 188) says: 'In vain, are we asked in what records this charter of our liberties is registered. It was not writ on parchment, nor yet on leaves or barks of trees. It preceded the use of writing and all the other civilized arts of life. But we trace it plainly in the nature of man, and in the equality, or something approaching equality, which we find in all the individuals of that species.'

9 Acquiescence merely involves a recognition that the outcome is better than the *status quo ante*, even if one would have preferred a different outcome, whereas the requirements of consensus are more demanding, since consent involves a situation in which the freely chosen action of each party shares in the responsibility for the outcome. Taken as a whole, it is clear that Hume's argument is one about acquiescence not consent *sensu stricto*.

10 Reciprocity involves what is sometimes called a 'throffer' (a combination of a threat and an offer): that is, practitioners meet friendly, cooperative relations and hostile failures of cooperation in kind.

11 Clearly, forms of community governance over certain issues and institutions survive the transition to statehood, and continue to underpin key aspects of state power; here I am concerned with community governance for a people and their (often shifting) territory as a whole: that is, community governance of political order as defined above.

12 The instability may lead, on one side, towards state formation or, on another, to political subordination to outside polities.

13 Hume is not the first to say this, of course. It is the core of Hobbes's analysis of the conditions for sovereign authority and it is implicit in Socrates reply to Thrasymachus in the *Republic* that even thieves must cooperate if they are to achieve a common purpose. But Hume's presentation of the argument is much more precise than Socrates's reply and does not have the liabilities of the social contract idiom that Hobbes tended to favour.

14 Brenner does not make it clear whether or not he sees feudal exploitation as purely redistributive, though his claim that peasant communities were 'fully capable of self-government' and his description of lordly 'protection' as an offer peasants couldn't refuse suggests that he does see it in these terms. I'm not sure how to reconcile this claim about peasant self-government with Brenner's admission elsewhere that peasant organization was pretty much confined to the village level. But let that pass. The reason why Brenner needs to insist on the self-governing capacity of the peasantry (and to deny that lordship represented anything other than a protection racket, 'an offer that [the peasants] could not refuse') is that otherwise his claim that pre-capitalist rule and property relations are about the economic reproduction of one group at the expense or exclusion of another cannot be sustained. If the peasantry was not capable of self-government, at its given level of economic well-being, then coercive rule may nonetheless have served some common interests (Brenner 2006b, 209).

15 Suitably elaborated this can provide the basis for a non-teleological notion of political *development*.

16 So the answer to the question, *quis custodiet ipsos custodes?* (Who will guard the guards themselves?), is the collective power of those to whom the authorities are answerable.

17 Indeed, the very fact that a constituted political authority cannot credibly commit itself not to renege on certain commitments means that some opportunities for mutual gain are inevitably foregone. Some constitutions may be better at mitigating this circumstance than others but none can entirely avoid it.

18 It is very likely the case that our understanding of states, rather than some of the specific features of the European, capitalist forms of state—specifically, its impersonal, corporate character—has been clouded by a historiography obsessed with the origins of the modern state in early modern Europe. For a valuable corrective, see Finer (1997), who notes of the non-territorial state that 'the only type of this to be found in this *History* [of government

from Sumer to industrial Europe of the 19th century] is the purest form of feudal state'. It is perhaps not coincidental that during this epoch the Church was a territorial organization in some respects.

19 There are, to be sure, many other forms of coordination in social life that are not directly political—driving on the left/right-hand side of the road, using a particular money for economic transactions, speaking a natural language, adopting a set of weights and measures, etc. Though it is interesting, and not accidental, that polities often seek to standardize these within their territories.

References

Abu-Lughod, Janet L (1989) *Before European Hegemony: The World System* AD *1250–1350* (Oxford: Oxford University Press).

Agnew, John (1987) *The United States in the World-Economy: A Regional Geography* (Cambridge: Cambridge University Press).

—— (2000) *Reinventing Geopolitics: Geographies of Modern Statehood* (Heidelberg: University of Heidelberg).

—— (2003) *Geopolitics: Re-visioning World Politics*, 2nd edition (London: Routledge).

—— (2005) *Hegemony: The New Shape of Global Power* (Philadelphia: Temple University Press).

Alic, John A *et al.* (1992) *Beyond Spin-off: Military and Commercial Technologies in a Changing World* (Cambridge, MA: Harvard Business School Press).

Alker, Hayward R Jr. and Thomas J Biersteker (1984) 'The Dialectics of World Order: Notes for a Future Archaeologist of International Savoir Faire', *International Studies Quarterly*, 28:2, 121–42.

Allinson, Jamie C and Alexander Anievas (2009) 'The Uses and Misuses of Uneven and Combined Development: An Anatomy of a Concept', *Cambridge Review of International Affairs*, 22:1, 47–67.

Althusser, Louis (1969) *For Marx* (London: Allen Lane).

Amelio, William, J (2007) 'Worldsource or Perish', *Forbes*, on-line edition, 8 August <http://www.forbes.com/2007/08/16/lenovo-world-sourcing-oped-cx_wja_0817lenovo.html>, accessed 26 March 2007.

Amin, Samir (1974) *Accumulation on a World Scale: A Critique of the Theory of Underdevelopment*, transl by Brian Pearce (New York: Monthly Review Press).

Anievas, Alexander (2005) Review of Alex Callinicos's *The New Mandarins of American Power* and David Harvey's *The New Imperialism*, *Cambridge Review of International Affairs*, 18:2, 303–6.

—— (2008) 'Theories of a Global State: A Critique, *Historical Materialism*, 16:2, 190–206.

Anderson, Benedict (1993), 'The New World Disorder', *New Left Review*, I:193, 3–13.

Anderson, Perry (1974a) *Passages from Antiquity to Feudalism* (London: Verso).

—— (1974b) *Lineage of the Absolutist State* (London: New Left Books).

—— (1992a) *A Zone of Engagement* (London: Verso).

—— (1992b) *English Questions* (London: Verso).

Appelbaum, Richard, and William I Robinson (2005) *Critical Globalization Studies* (New York: Routledge).

Arrighi, Giovanni (1994) *The Long Twentieth Century: Money, Power and the Origins of Our Times* (London: Verso).

—— (2005a) 'Hegemony Unravelling—1', *New Left Review*, II:32, 23–80.

—— (2005b) 'Hegemony Unravelling—2', *New Left Review*, II:33, 83–116.

—— (2007) *Adam Smith in Beijing: Lineages of the Twenty-first Century* (London: Verso).

Arthur, Christopher J (2002) 'Capital, Competition and Many Capitals' in Martha Campbell and Geert Reuten (eds) *The Culmination of Capital* (Basingstoke: Palgrave), 128–48.

Ashley, Richard K (1986) 'The Poverty of Neo-realism' in Robert O. Keohane (ed.) *Neo-realism and Its Critics* (New York: Columbia University Press), 255–300.

Ashman, Sam (2006) 'Globalization as Uneven Development', PhD thesis, University of Birmingham.

—— (2009) 'Capitalism, Uneven and Combined Development and the Transhistoric', *Cambridge Review of International Affairs*, 22:1, 29–46.

Ashman, Sam and Alex Callinicos (2006) 'Capital Accumulation and the State System', *Historical Materialism*, 14:4, 107–31.

Augelli, Enrico and Craig N Murphy (1988) *America's Quest for Supremacy* (London: Pinter).

Ayubi, Nazih (1995) *Overstating The Arab State: Politics and Society in The Middle East* (New York: St Martin's Press).

Bacevich, Andrew (2005) *The New American Militarism* (Oxford: Oxford University Press).

—— (2008) *The Limits of Power: The End of American Exceptionalism* (New York: Metropolitan Books).

Badie, Bertrand and Pierre Birnbaum (1983) *The Sociology of the State*, transl by Arthur Goldhammer (Chicago: University of Chicago Press).

Baker, Kevin (2006) 'Stabbed in the Back! The Past and Future of a Right-wing Myth', *Harper's Magazine* (June), < http://www.harpers.org/archive/2006/06/0081080 >, accessed 13 March 2009.

Balakrishnan, Gopal (2004) 'The Age of Warring States', *New Left Review*, II:26, 148–60.

Banaji, Jairus (1977) 'Modes of Production in a Materialist Conception of History', *Capital & Class*, 3, 1–44.

—— (2003) 'The Fictions of Free Labour: Contract, Coercion, and So-called Unfree Labour', *Historical Materialism*, 11:3, 69–95.

Barkawi, Tarak and Mark Laffey (2002) 'Retrieving the Imperial: *Empire* and International Relations', *Millennium: Journal of International Studies*, 31:1, 109–27.

Barker, Colin (1978a) 'A Note on the Theory of Capitalist States', *Capital & Class*, 4, 118–29.

—— (1978b) 'The State as Capital', *International Socialism*, 2:1, 16–42.

—— (1997) 'Some Reflections on Two Books by Ellen Wood', *Historical Materialism*, 1:1, 22–65.

—— (1998) 'Industrialism, Capitalism, Value, Force and States: Some Theoretical Remarks', Anglo-Bulgarian Comparative History Seminar, Wolverhampton University, June.

—— (2006) 'Extending Combined and Uneven Development' in Bill Dunn and Hugo Radice (eds) *100 Years of Permanent Revolution: Results and Prospects* (London: Pluto Press), 72–87.

Bartlett, Robert (1993) *The Making of Europe* (London: Allen Lane).

Barzel, Yoram (2002) *A Theory of the State* (Cambridge: Cambridge University Press).

Bayard, Thomas O and Kimberly Ann Elliott (1994) *Reciprocity and Retaliation in US Trade Policy* (Washington, DC: Institute for International Economics).

Bayart, Jean-François (1986) 'Civil Society in Africa' in Patrick Chabal (ed.) *Political Domination in Africa: Reflections on the Limits of Power* (Cambridge: Cambridge University Press), 109–25.

—— (1993) *The State in Africa: The Politics of the Belly*, transl by Mary Harper, Christopher Harrison and Elizabeth Harrison (London: Longman).

—— (2000) 'Africa in the World: A History of Extraversion', *African Affairs*, 99:396, 217–67.

Beetham, David (1991) *The Legitimation of Power* (London: Macmillan).

Bernstein, Henry (1988) 'Capitalism and Petty-Bourgeois Production: Class Relations and the Division of Labour', *Journal of Peasant Studies*, 15:2, 258–71.

—— (1992) 'Poverty and the Poor' in Henry Bernstein, Ben Crow and Hazel Johnson (eds) *Rural Livelihoods: Crises and Responses* (Oxford: Oxford University Press and the Open University), 13–26.

—— (2000) 'Colonialism, Capitalism, Development' in Tim Allen and Alan Thomas (eds) *Poverty and Development into the 21st Century* (Oxford: Oxford University Press), 241–70.

—— (2007) 'Capitalism and Moral Economy: Land Questions in Sub-Saharan Africa', paper presented at the conference *Poverty and Capital* organized by the Global Poverty Research Group and the Brooks World Poverty Institute, University of Manchester, 2–4 July.

Beik, William (2005) 'The Absolutism of Louis XIV as Social Collaboration', *Past & Present*, 188, 195–224.

Bell, Duncan (ed.) (2008) *Political Thought and International Relations: Variations on a Realist Theme* (Oxford: Oxford University Press).

Bello, Walden (2005) *Dilemmas of Domination: The Unmaking of the American Empire* (New York: Henry Holt).

Berki, Robert N (1971) 'On Marxian Thought and the Problem of International Relations', *World Politics*, 24:1, 80–105.

Bhagwati, Jagdish (1990) 'Aggressive Unilateralism: An Overview' in Jagdish Bhagwati and Hugh T Patrick (eds) *Aggressive Unilateralism: America's 301 Trade Policy and the World Trading System* (Ann Arbor: University of Michigan Press), 1–45.

Bidet, Jacques (2000) *Que faire du Capital?* (Paris: Presses Universitaires de France).

—— (2007) *Exploring Marx's 'Capital': Philosophical, Economic and Political Dimensions*, transl by David Fernbach and foreword by Alex Callinicos (Leiden: Brill Academic Press).

Bieler, Andreas and Adam David Morton (2003) 'Globalisation, the State and Class Struggle: A "Critical Economy" Engagement with Open Marxism', *British Journal of Politics and International Relations*, 5:4, 467–99.

—— (eds) (2006) *Images of Gramsci: Connections and Contentions in Political Theory and International Relations* (London: Routledge).

—— (2008) 'The Deficits of Discourse in IPE: Turning Base Metal into Gold?', *International Studies Quarterly*, 52:1, 103–28.

Bilderberg.org (2007), <http://www.bilderberg.org/2007.htm#tbbr>, accessed 28 June 2008.

Bin Laden, Osama (1998) 'Fatwa Declaring Jihad against Jews and Crusaders', *PBS* Newshour, <http://www.pbs.org/newshour/terrorism/international/fatwa_1998.html>, accessed 13 March 2009.

Blatty, William Peter (1972) *The Exorcist* (London: Corgi Books).

Block, Fred (1980) 'Beyond Relative Autonomy: State Managers as Historical Subjects' in Ralph Milliband and John Saville (eds) *The Socialist Register* (London: Merlin Press), 227–42.

—— (1987) *Revising State Theory* (Philadelphia: Temple University Press).

Bloomberg (2005) 'US-EU Aircraft Talks Stalled over Airbus Aid Push, People Say', 22 March <http://www.bloomberg.com/apps/news?pid=10000087&sid=aHOt6GRXlfdk&refer = top_world_news>, accessed 12 March 2009.

Blum, William (1995) *Killing Hope: US Military and CIA Interventions since World War II* (Monroe: Common Courage Press).

Boltuck, Richard and Robert E Litan (1991) 'America's "Unfair" Trade Laws' in Richard Boltuck and Robert E Litan (ed.) *Down in the Dumps: Administration of the Unfair Trade Laws* (Washington, DC: Brookings), 1–22.

Bonney, Richard (1991) The European Dynastic States, *1494–1660* (Oxford: Oxford University Press).

Booth, David (1985) 'Marxism and Development Sociology: Interpreting the Impasse', *World Development*, 13:7, 761–78.

Borochov, Ber (1972 [1937]) *Nationalism and the Class Struggle: A Marxian Approach to the Jewish Problem* (Westport: Greenwood Press).

Boron, Atilio (2005) *Empire and Imperialism* (London: Zed).

Bratsis, Peter (2006) *Everyday Life and the State* (Boulder, CO: Paradigm).

Braudel, Fernand (1985) *Civilization and Capitalism, 15th–18th Century: The Wheels of Commerce*, Volime II (London: Fontana Press).

Brecher, Jeremy, Tim Costello, and Brenda Smith (2008) 'The G-20 vs. The G-6 Billion', *Znet*, 20 Nov, < http://www.zmag.org/znet/viewArticle/19707 >, accessed 26 March 2009.

Brennan, Teresa (2000) *Exhausting Modernity: Grounds for a New Economy* (London: Routledge).

Brenner, Robert (1977) 'The Origins of Capitalist Development: A Critique of neo-Smithian Marxism', *New Left Review*, I:104, 25–92.

—— (1982) 'The Agrarian Roots of European Capitalism', *Past & Present*, 97, 16–113.

—— (1985) 'Agrarian Class Structure and Economic Development in Pre-Industrial Europe' in Trevor H Aston and Charles HE Philpin (eds) *The Brenner Debate: Agrarian Class Structure and Economic Development in Pre-Industrial Europe* (Cambridge: Cambridge University Press), 10–63.

—— (1986) 'The Social Basis of Economic Development' in John Roemer (ed.) *Analytical Marxism* (Cambridge: Cambridge University Press), 23–53.

—— (1987) 'Feudalism' in John Eatwell, Murry Milgate, and Peter Newman (eds) *The New Palgrave Dictionary of Economics: Marxian Economics* (London: Macmillan), 170–85.

—— (1993) *Merchants and Revolution: Commercial Change, Political Conflict, and London's Overseas Traders, 1550–1653* (Cambridge: Cambridge University Press).

—— (1998) 'The Economics of Global Turbulence', *New Left Review*, I:229, 1–265.

—— (2001) 'The Low Countries in the Transition to Capitalism', *Journal of Agrarian Change*, 1:2, 169–241.

—— (2002) *The Boom and the Bubble* (London: Verso).

—— (2006a) 'What Is, and What Is Not, Imperialism?', *Historical Materialism*, 14:4, 79–105.

—— (2006b) 'From Theory to History' in John A Hall and Ralph Schroeder (eds) *An Anatomy of Power: Essays on the Work of Michael Mann* (Cambridge: Cambridge University Press), 189–232.

—— (2007) 'Structure versus Conjuncture', *New Left Review*, II:43, 33–59.

Brenner, Robert and Christopher Isett (2002) 'England's Divergence from the Yangzi Delta: Property Relations, Microeconomics, and Patterns of Development', *Journal of Asian Studies*, 61:2, 609–63.

Brett, EA (1983) *International Money and Capitalist Crisis: The Anatomy of Global Disintegration* (London: Heinemann).

Brewer, Anthony (1990) *Marxist Theories of Imperialism: A Critical Survey*, 2nd edition (London: Routledge).

Brewer, John (1989) *The Sinews of Power* (London: Routledge).

Bruff, Ian (2008) *Culture and Consensus in European Varieties of Capitalism* (Houndmills: Palgrave Macmillan).

Brunhoff, Suzanne de (1976) *Etat et capital: Recherches sur la politique économique* (Grenoble: Presses Universitaires de Grenoble).

Bromley, Simon (1991) *American Hegemony and World Oil* (University Park: Pennsylvania University Press).

—— (1994) *Rethinking Middle East Politics: State Formation and Development* (Cambridge: Polity Press).

Buci-Glucksmann, Christine (1979) 'State, Transition and Passive Revolution' in Chantal Mouffe (ed.) *Gramsci and Marxist theory* (London: Routledge), 207–36.

Bukharin, Nikolai Ivanovich (1972 [1915]) *Imperialism and World Economy* (London: Merlin).

—— (1979 [1920]) *The Politics and Economics of the Transition Period* (London: Routledge and Kegan Paul).

Bull, Hedley (1966) 'Society and Anarchy in International Relations' in Herbert Butterfield and Martin Wight (eds) *Diplomatic Investigations* (London: Allen and Unwin), 35–50.

Burnham, Peter (2000) 'Globalization, Depoliticization and "Modern" Economic Management' in Werner Bonefeld and Kosmas Psychopedis (eds) *The Politics of Change: Globalization, Ideology and Critique* (Basingstoke: Palgrave), 9–30.

Burgos, Raul (2002) 'The Gramscian Intervention in the Theoretical and Political Production of the Latin American Left', *Latin American Perspectives*, 29:1, 9–37.

Buroway, Michael (1989) 'Two Methods in Social Science: Skocpol versus Trotsky', *Theory & Science,* 18:6, 759–805.

Butterfield, Herbert (1951) *History and Human Relations* (London: Collins).

Buzan, Barry (2004) *The United States and the Great Powers* (Cambridge: Polity).

Buzan, Barry and Richard Little (2000) *International Systems in World History* (Oxford: Oxford University Press).

—— (2001) 'Why International Relations Has Failed as an Intellectual Project and What to Do about It', *Millennium: Journal of International Studies*, 30:1, 19–39.

Byres, Terence (2005) 'Neoliberalism and Primitive Accumulation in Less Developed Countries' in Alfredo Said-Filho and Deborah Johnston (eds) *Neoliberalism: A Critical Reader* (London: Pluto), 83–90.

Callinicos, Alex (1982) *Is There a Future for Marxism?* (London: Macmillan).

—— (1987) 'Imperialism, Capitalism, and the State Today', *International Socialism*, 2:35, 71–115.

—— (1991) 'Marxism and Imperialism Today', *International Socialism*, 2:50, 3–48.

—— (2000) *Equality* (Cambridge: Polity).

—— (2001a) 'Periodizing Capitalism and Analysing Imperialism' in Robert Albritton, Makoto Ito, Richard Westra and Richard Westra (eds) *Phases of Capitalist Development* (Basingstoke: Palgrave), 230–45.

—— (2001b), 'Plumbing the Depths: Marxism and the Holocaust', *Yale Journal of Criticism*, 14:2, 385–414.

—— (2002) 'Marxism and Global Governance' in David Held and Anthony McGrew (eds) *Governing Globalization* (Cambridge: Polity), 249–66.

—— (2003) *The New Mandarins of American Power: The Bush administration's Plans for the World* (Cambridge: Polity).

—— (2004a) *Making History*, 2nd edition (Leiden: Brill).

—— (2004b) 'Marxism and the International', *British Journal of Politics and International Relations*, 6, 426–33.

—— (2005a) 'Against the New Dialectic', *Historical Materialism*, 13:2, 41–59.

—— (2005b) 'Iraq: Fulcrum of World Politics', *Third World Quarterly*, 26, 593–608.

—— (2005c) 'Imperialism and Global Political Economy', *International Socialism*, 2:108, 109–27.

—— (2005d) 'Epoch and Conjuncture in Marxist Political Economy', *International Politics*, 42:3, 353–63.

—— (2006) 'Making Sense of Imperialism: A Reply to Leo Panitch and Sam Gindin', *International Socialism*, 2:110, 196–203.

—— (2007) 'Does Capitalism Need the State System?', *Cambridge Review of International Affairs*, 20:4, 533–49.

—— (2009) 'How to Solve the Many-State Problem: A Reply to the Debate', *Cambridge Review of International Affairs*, 22:1, 89–105.

Callinicos, Alex and Justin Rosenberg (2008) 'Uneven and Combined Development: The Social-relational Substratum of "the International"? An Exchange of Letters', *Cambridge Review of International Affairs*, 21:1, 77–112.

Callinicos, Alex *et al.* (1994) *Marxism and the New Imperialism* (London: Bookmarks).

Cammack, Paul (2007) 'Forget the Transnational State', Papers in the Politics of Global Competitiveness, No. 3, Institute for Global Studies, Manchester Metropolitan University, <http://hdl.handle.net/2173/6759>, accessed 15 March 2009.

Carling, Alan (1992) *Social Division* (London: Verso).

—— (1993) 'Analytical Marxism and Historical Materialism', *Science & Society*, 57:1, 31–65.

—— (2002) 'Analytical Marxism and the Debate on Social Evolution' in Paul Blackledge and Graeme Kirkpatrick (eds) *Historical Materialism and Social Evolution* (Basingstoke: Palgrave Macmillan), 98–128.

Carr, Edward H (1946) *The Twenty Years' Crisis 1919–1939*, 2nd edition (Basingstoke: Macmillan).

Carroll, William K and Colin Carson (2003a) 'Forging a New Hegemony? The Role of Transnational Policy Groups in the Network and Discourses of Global Corporate Governance', *Journal of World-Systems Research*, 9:1, 67–102.

—— (2003b) 'The Network of Global Corporations and Elite Policy Groups: A Structure for Transnational Capitalist Class Formation?', *Global Networks*, 3:1, 29–57.

Carroll, William, K and Meindert Fennema (2002) 'Is There a Transnational Business Community?', *International Sociology*, 17:3, 393–419.

Castells, Manuel (1996) *The Rise of the Network Society: The Information Age: Economy, Society, Culture*, Volume I (Oxford: Blackwell).

—— (1998) *The Information Age: Economy, Society and Culture—End of Millennium*, Volume III (Malden: Blackwell).

Castoriadis, Cornelius (1988 [1949]), 'Socialism or Barbarism' in David Ames Curtis (ed.) *Political and Social Writings: From the Critique of Bureaucracy to the Positive Content of Socialism*, Volume 1, 1946–55 (Minneapolis: University of Minnesota Press), 76–106.

Chandler, Alfred (1990) *Scale and Scope: The Dynamics of Industrial Capitalism* (Cambridge, MA: Harvard University Press).

Chang, Ha-Joon (2007) *Bad Samaritans: Rich Nations, Poor Policies and the Threat to the Developing World* (New York: Random House).

Chase, Kerry A (2004) 'Imperial Protection and Strategic Trade Policy in the Interwar Period', *Review of International Political Economy,* 11:1, 177–203.

Chase-Dunn, Christopher K (1981) 'Interstate System and Capitalist World-economy: One Logic or Two?', *International Studies Quarterly*, 25:1, 19–42.

Chatterjee, Partha (1986) *Nationalist Thought and the Colonial World* (London: Zed Books).

Chibber, Vivek (2005) 'Capital Outbound', *New Left Review,* II:36, 151–58.

Clarke, Simon (1991) *The State Debate* (London: Palgrave Mcmillan).

Cliff, Tony (2003 [1948]) 'The Nature of Stalinist Russia' in *Marxist Theory after Trotsky, Selected Writings*, Volume 3 (London: Bookmarks), 1–138.

Cohen, Gerry (1978) *A Defence of Karl Marx's Theory of History* (Oxford: Clarendon).

Cohen, Gerry (2000) *A Defence of Karl Marx's Theory of History*, expanded edition (Oxford: Oxford University Press).

Coll, Steve (2004) *Ghost Wars* (New York: Penguin).

Collier, Paul (2007) *The Bottom Billion: Why the Poorest Countries Are Failing and What Can Be Done about It* (Oxford: Oxford University Press).

Comninel, George (1987) *Rethinking the French Revolution* (London: Verso).

Cooper, Robert (2003) *The Breaking of Nations: Order and Chaos in the Twenty-first Century* (London: Atlantic Books).

Cox, Michael (2002) 'The Search for Relevance: Historical Materialism after the Cold War' in Mark Rupert and Hazel Smith (eds), *Historical Materialism and Globalization* (London: Routledge), 59–74.

Cox, Robert W (1983) 'Gramsci, Hegemony and International Relations: An Essay in Method', *Millennium: Journal of International Studies*, 12:2, 162–75.

—— (1986) 'Social forces, States and World Orders: Beyond International Relations Theory' in Robert O Keohane (ed.) *Neo-realism and its Critics* (New York: Columbia University Press), 204–54.

—— (1987) *Production, Power and World Order: Social Forces in the Making of History* (New York: Columbia University Press).

—— (1996) *Approaches to World Order* (Cambridge: Cambridge University Press).

Davidson, Neil (2000) *The Origins of Scottish Nationhood* (London: Pluto).

—— (2005) 'How Revolutionary Were the Bourgeois Revolutions?—2', *Historical Materialism*, 13:4, 3–54.

—— (2006) 'Enlightenment and Anti-Capitalism', *International Socialism*, 2:110, 85–112.

—— (2009) 'Putting the Nation back into "the International"', *Cambridge Review of International Affairs*, 22:1, 9–28.

Davis, Bob (1993) 'Economy: Clinton Team to Suggest Import Goals for Japan as Trade Talks Approach', *Wall Street Journal*, 20 May, A2, A11.

Davis, Mike (2007) *In Praise of Barbarians: Essays against Empire* (Chicago: Haymarket).

de Goede, Marieke (2003) 'Beyond Economism in International Political Economy', *Review of International Studies,* 29, 79–97.

DelForge, Isabelle (2004) 'Thailand: The World's Kitchen', *Le Monde Diplomatique*, 5 July..

Denemark, Robert, Jonathan Friedman, Barry K Gills and George Modelski (eds) (2000) *World System History* (New York: Routledge).

Dicken, Peter (2003) *Global Shift*, 4th edition (New York: Guilford).

Dixit, Avinash (2004) *Lawlessness and Economics* (Princeton: Princeton University Press).

Draper, Hal (1978) *Karl Marx's Theory of Revolution: State and Bureaucracy*, Volume 1 (New York: Monthly Review).

Dufour, Frédérick (2008) 'Historical Materialism and International Relations' in Jacques Bidet and Stathis Kouvelakis (eds) *Contemporary Marxism: A Critical Companion* (Leiden: Brill), 453–70.

Duménil, Gérard (1978) *Le concept de loi économique dans 'Le Capital'* [The Concept of Economic Law in *Kapital*] (Paris: Maspéro).

Dussel, Enrique (2001) 'The Four Drafts of *Capital*', *Rethinking Marxism*, 13:1, 10–26.

Engels, Friedrich (1962 [1880]) *Socialism, Utopian and Scientific* in Karl Marx and Fredrich Engels, *Selected Works*, Volume 3 (Moscow: Foreign Languages Publishing House), 95–151.

—— (1970 [1884]) 'The Origins of the Family, Private Property and the State' in Karl Marx and Friedrich Engels, *Selected Works*, Volume 3 (Moscow: Progress Publishers), 449–583.

Estulin, Daniel (2007) 'Bilderberg 2007: Towards a One World Empire', *Nexus Magazine*, August-September, 19–25.

European Commission (2004) *EU–US Agreement on Large Civil Aircraft 1992: Key Facts and Figures*', MEMO/04/232, Brussels, 6 October < http://trade.ec.europa.eu/doclib/docs/2007/april/tradoc_134256.pdf >, accessed 12 March 2009.

Evans, Richard (2003) *The Coming of the Third Reich* (London: Allen Lane).

Evenett, Simon *et al.* (2000) 'Antitrust Policy in an Evolving Global Marketplace' in Simon J Evenett, Alexander Lehmann and Benn Steil (eds) *Antitrust Goes Global: What Future for Transatlantic Cooperation* (Washington DC: Brookings), 1–28.

Feenstra, Robert C, Gene M Grossman and Douglas A Irvin (eds) (1996) *The Political Economy of Trade Policy: Papers in Honour of Jagdish Bhagwati* (Cambridge, MA: MIT Press).

Fennema, Meindert (1982) *International Networks of Banks and Industry* (The Hague: Nijhoff).

Ferguson, Niall (2004) *Colossus: The Rise and Fall of the American Empire* (London: Allen Lane).

Fine, Ben (1978) 'On the Origins of Capitalist Development', *New Left Review*, I:109, 88–95.

—— (1994) 'Coal, Diamonds and Oil: Towards a Comparative Theory of Mining', *Review of Political Economy*, 6:3, 279–302.

—— (2004) 'Addressing the Critical and the Real in Critical Realism' in Paul Lewis (ed.) *Transforming Economics: Perspectives on the Critical Realist Project* (London: Routledge), 222–26.

Fine, Ben and Lawrence Harris (1979) *Rereading 'Capital'* (London: Macmillan).

Fine, Ben and Andy Murfin (1984) *Macroeconomics and Monopoly Capitalism* (Brighton: Wheatsheaf).

Fine, Ben and Costas Lapavitsas and Dimitris Milonakis (2000) 'Dialectics and Crisis Theory: A Response to Tony Smith', *Historical Materialism*, 6:1, 133–37.

Finer, Sam (1997) *The History of Government from the Earliest Times*, 3 Volumes (Oxford: Oxford University Press).

Flamm, Kenneth (1996) *Mismanaged Trade? Strategic Policy and the Semi-Conductor Industry* (Washington, DC: Brookings).

Foster, John Bellamy (2003) 'The New Age of Imperialism', *Monthly Review*, 55:3, 1–14.

—— (2006) *Naked Imperialism: US Pursuit of Global Dominance* (New York: Monthly Review).

Foster-Carter, Aidan (1978) 'The Modes of Production Controversy', *New Left Review*, I:107, 47–77.

Ford, Peter (2002) 'Is America the "Good Guy"? Many Now Say "No"', *Christian Science Monitor*, 11 September, <http://www.csmonitor.com/2002/0911/p02s03-wogi.html>, accessed 13 March 2009.

Fracchia, Joseph (2004) 'On Transhistorical Abstractions and the Intersection of Historical Theory and Social Critique', *Historical Materialism*, 12:3, 125–46.

Frank, Andre Gunder and Barry K Gills eds (1996) *The World System: Five Hundred or Five Thousand Years?* (London: Routledge).

Frank, Thomas (2004) *What's the Matter with America? The Resistible Rise of the American Right* (London: Secker and Warburg).

Franklin, H Bruce (1992) *MIA or Mythmaking in America* (New York: Lawrence Hill Books).

Friedman, Thomas (2006) 'Contending with China', *New York Times* weekly selection with *Le Monde*, 18 November.

Fukuyama, Francis (1992) *The End of History and the Last Man* (Harmondsworth: Penguin).

Furner, James (2008) 'Marx's Conception of Basis and Superstructure', PhD Dissertation, University of Sussex.

Gaddis, John L (1982) *Strategies of Containment* (Oxford: Oxford University Press).

Gamble, Andrew (1988) *The Free Economy and the Strong State: The Politics of Thatcherism* (Houndmills: Macmillan).

Garten, Jeffrey E (2005) 'The Big Blowout: Why the Airbus-Boeing Case Could Wreck the WTO, and How to Stop It', *Newsweek International*, 27 March.

Gerschenkron, Alexander (1966) *Economic Backwardness in Historical Perspective: A Book of Essays* (Cambridge: Harvard University Press).

Gerstenberger, Heide (2006 [1990]) *Die subjektlose gewalt: theorie der Entstehung Bürgerlicher Staatsgewalt {Impersonal Power: History and Theory of the Bourgeois State}*, 2nd edition (Münster: Westfälisches Dampfboot).

Gibson, James (1994) *Warrior Dreams: Paramilitary Culture in Post-Vietnam America* (New York: Hill and Wang).

Giddens, Anthony (1985) *The Nation-State and Violence* (Cambridge: Polity).

—— (1990) *The Consequences of Modernity* (Cambridge: Polity).

Gill, Stephen (1990) *American Hegemony and the Trilateral Commission* (Cambridge: Cambridge University Press).

—— (ed.) (1993) *Gramsci, Historical Materialism and International Relations* (Cambridge: Cambridge University Press).

Gilpin, Robert (1981) *War and Change in World Politics* (Cambridge: Cambridge University Press).

Godelier, Maurice (1986) *The Mental and the Material* (London: Verso).

Goody, Jack (2006) 'Gordon Childe, the Urban Revolution, and the Haute Cuisine: An Anthropo-archaeological View of Modern History, *Comparative Studies in Society and History*, 48:3, 503–19.

Gough, Ian (1979) *The Political Economy of the Welfare State* (London: Macmillan).

Gowan, Peter (1999) *The Global Gamble: Washington's Faustian Bid for World Dominance* (London: Verso).

—— (2003) 'US Hegemony Today', *Monthly Review*, 55:3, 30–50.

Graham, Edward M (2000) 'Economic Considerations in Merger Review' in Simon J Evenett, Alexander Lehmann and Benn Steil (eds) *Antitrust Goes Global: What Future for Transatlantic Cooperation* (Washington, DC: Brookings), 57–78.

Gramsci, Antonio (1971) *Selections from the Prison Notebooks*, edited and transl by Q Hoare and G Nowell-Smith (London: Lawrence and Wishart).

—— (1975) *History, Philosophy and Culture in the Young Gramsci*, edited by Pedro Cavalcanti and Paul Piccone (Saint Louis: Telos Press).

—— (1977) *Selections from Political Writings, 1910–1920*, edited by Quintin Hoare, transl by John Matthews (London: Lawrence and Wishart).

—— (1978) *Selections from Political Writings, 1921–1926*, edited and transl by Quintin Hoare (London: Lawrence and Wishart).

—— (1988) *A Gramsci Reader: Selected Writings, 1916–1935*, edited by David Forgacs (London: Lawrence and Wishart).

—— (1992) *The Prison Notebooks*, Volume 1, edited by Joseph A Buttigieg, transl by Joseph A Buttigieg and Antonio Callari (New York: Columbia University Press).

—— (1994a) *Letters from Prison*, Volume 1, edited by Frank Rosengarten, transl by Raymond Rosenthal (New York: Columbia University Press).

—— (1994b) *Pre-prison Writings*, edited by Richard Bellamy, transl by Virginia Cox (Cambridge: Cambridge University Press).

—— (1995) *Further Selections from the Prison Notebooks*, edited and transl by D Boothman (London: Lawrence and Wishart).

—— (1996) *The Prison Notebooks*, Volume 2, edited and transl by Joseph A Buttigieg (New York: Columbia University Press).

—— (2001) *Cuadernos de la cárcel* [*Prison Notebooks*] (Mexico City: Ediciones Era).

Gray, John (1995) *Isaiah Berlin* (London: HarperCollins).

Graz, Jean-Christophe (2003) 'How powerful are Transnational Elite Clubs? The Social Myth of the World Economic Forum', *New Political Economy*, 8:3, 321–40.

Greenfield, Liah (2001) *The Spirit of Capitalism: Nationalism and Economic Growth* (Cambridge, MA: Harvard University Press).

Greenspan, Alan (2008) *The Age of Turbulence: Adventures in a New World* (London: Penguin Books).

Grossman, Henryk (1943) 'The Evolutionist Revolt against Classical Economics: II. In England— James Steuart, Richard Jones, Karl Marx', *Journal of Political Economy*, 51:6, 506–22.

Grove, Samuel (2008) 'The Bottom of the Barrel: A Review of Paul Collier', *MR Zine*, <http://mrzine.monthlyreview.org/grove150808.html>, accessed 1 November 2008.

Gruffydd Jones, Branwen (ed.) (2006) *Decolonizing International Relations* (Landham: Rowman and Littlefield).

Halbfinger, David A and Holmes, Steven A (2003) 'The Troops: Military Mirrors a Working Class America', *New York Times*, 30 March, < http://query.nytimes.com/gst/fullpage.html?res=9F0DEFDD1539F933A05750C0A9659C8B63 >.

Haldon, John (2006) 'Review of The Paths of History by Igor M. Diakonoff', *Historical Materialism*, 14:2, 169–201.

Hall, Martin and John M Hobson (2010) 'Liberal International Theory: Eurocentric but not always Imperialist?', *International Theory* 2(1): forthcoming.

Hall, Stuart (1986) 'Gramsci's Relevance for the Study of Race and Ethnicity', *Journal of Communication Inquiry*, 10:2, 5–27.

Halliday, Fred (1994) *Rethinking International Relations* (Houndmills: Macmillan).

—— (1999) *Revolution and World Politics: The Rise and Fall of the Sixth Great Power* (London: Macmillan Press).

—— (2002a) 'The Persistence of Imperialism' in Mark Rupert and Hazel Smith (eds) *Historical Materialism and Globalization* (London: Routledge), 75–89.

—— (2002b) 'For an International Sociology' in Stephen Hobden and John Hobson (eds) *Historical Sociology of International Relations* (Cambridge: Cambridge University Press), 244–64.

Halperin, Sandra (2004) *War and Social Change in Modern Europe: The Great Transformation Revisited* (Cambridge: Cambridge University Press).

Hardt, Michael, and Antonio Negri (2000) *Empire* (Cambridge: Harvard University Press).

—— (2004) *Multitude* (New York: Penguin).

Harman, Chris (1984) *Explaining the Crisis: A Marxist Reappraisal* (London: Bookmarks).

—— (1989) 'From Feudalism to Capitalism', *International Socialism*, 2:45, 35–87.

—— (1991) 'The State and Capitalism Today', *International Socialism*, 2:51, 3–54.

—— (2003) 'Analysing Imperialism', *International Socialism*, 2:99, 3–81.

—— (2004) 'The Rise of Capitalism', *International Socialism*, 2:102, 53–86.

Harman, Chris and Robert Brenner (2006) 'The Origins of Capitalism', *International Socialism,* 2:111, 127–62.

Harvey, David (1990) *The Condition of Postmodernity* (London: Blackwell).

—— (2001 [1985]) 'The Geopolitics of Capitalism' in David Harvey *Spaces of Capital: Towards a Critical Geography* (New York: Routledge), 312–44.

—— (2003) *The New Imperialism* (Oxford: Oxford University Press).

—— (2005) *A Brief History of Neoliberalism* (Oxford: Oxford University Press).

—— (2006 [1982]) *The Limits to Capital* (Oxford: Blackwell).

Hausmann, Ricardo and Dani Rodrik (2006) 'Doomed to Choose: Industrial Policy as Predicament', Paper Presented at the Blue Sky Seminar, Center for International Development at Harvard University, 9 September, <http://www.cid.harvard.edu/bluesky/papers/hausmann_-doomed_0609.pdf>, accessed 12 March 2009.

Held, David, Anthony McGrew, David Goldblatt, and Jonathan Perraton (1999) *Global Transformations* (Cambridge: Polity).

Hegel, G W F (1923 [1817]) *Encyclopädie der philosophischen Wissenschaften im Grundrisse* 3rd edition, edited by G. Lasson (Leipzig: Felix Meiner).

Heider, Ulrike (1994) *Anarchism: Left, Right and Green* (San Francisco: City Lights).

Hennessy, Peter (2006) *Having It So Good: Britain in the Fifties* (London: Allen Lane).

Henwood, Doug (2003) *After the New Economy* (New York: The New Press).

—— (2005) 'The "Business Community"' in Leo Panitch and Colin Leys (eds) *The Socialist Register 2006* (London: Merlin), 59–77.

Hersh, Seymour (1997) *The Dark Side of Camelot* (New York: Little Brown).

Hickel, Rudolf (1975) 'Kapitalfraktionen: Thesen zur Analyse der herrschenden Klasse', *Kursbuch* 42, 141–54.

Hicks, John R (1939) *Value and Capital: An Inquiry into Some Fundamental Principles of Economic Theory* (Oxford: Clarendon).

Hilferding, Rudolf (1981 [1910]) *Finance Capital: A Study of the Latest Phase of Capitalist Development*, (London: Routledge).

Hirsch, Joachim (1978) 'The State Apparatus and Social Reproduction: Elements of a Theory of the Bourgeois State' in John Holloway and Sol Picciotto (eds) *State and Capital: A Marxist debate* (London: Edward Arnold), 57–107.

Historical Materialism (2006) 'Symposium on David Harvey's *The New Imperialism*', 14:4.

Hobbes, Thomas (1996 [1651]) *Leviathan* (Cambridge: Cambridge University Press).

Hobden, Stephen (1998) *International Relations and Historical Sociology: Breaking Down Boundaries* (London: Routledge).

Hobden, Stephen and Richard Wyn Jones (2005) 'Marxist Theories of International Relations' in John Baylis and Steve Smith (ed.) *The Globalization of World Politics,* 4th edition (New York: Oxford University Press), 225–49.

Hobsbawm, Eric (1975) *The Age of Capital, 1848–1875* (London: Weidenfeld & Nicolson).

—— (1987) *The Age of Empire* (London: Weidenfeld & Nicolson).

—— (2007a) *Globalisation, Democracy and Terrorism* (London: Little, Brown).

—— (2007b) 'Who Controls the World Now That the Age of Empire Is Dead?', *The Observer*, 3 June, 27.

Hobson, John M (2000) *The State and International Relations* (Cambridge: Cambridge University Press).

—— (2004) *The Eastern Origins of Western Civilisation* (Cambridge: Cambridge University Press).

—— (2006) 'Mann, the State and War' in John A Hall and Ralph Schroeder (eds) *An Anatomy of Power: Essays on the Work of Michael Mann* (Cambridge: Cambridge University Press), 150–66.

—— (2007) 'Back to the Future of "One Logic or Two?" or Forward to the Past of "Anarchy versus Hierarchy?"', *Cambridge Review of International Affairs*, 20:4, 581–97.

Hochschild, Arlie (2004) 'Let Them Eat War', *AlterNet*, 15 January, <http://www.alternet.org/story/16885>, accessed 13 March 2009.

Holman, Otto and Kees Van der Pijl, (2003) 'Structure and Process in Transnational European Business' in Alan W Cafruny and Magnus Ryner (eds) *A Ruined Fortress: Neoliberal Hegemony and Transformation in Europe* (Lanham: Rowman & Littlefield), 71–94.

Holloway, John (1995) 'Global Capital and the National State' in Werner Bonefeld and John Holloway (eds) *Global Capital, National State and the Politics of Money* (London: Macmillan), 116–40.

Holloway, John and Sol Picciotto (1991) 'Capital, Crisis, and the State' in Simon Clarke (ed.) *The State Debate* (Basingstoke: Macmillan), 109–41.

Holsti, Kal J (1985) *The Dividing Discipline: Hegemony and Diversity in International Theory* (Winchester: Allen and Unwin).

Homer, Sydney (1963) *A History of Interest Rates* (New Brunswick: Rutgers University Press).

Horlick, Gary N (1989) 'The United States Antidumping System' in John H Jackson and Edwin A Vermlost (eds) *Antidumping Law and Practice: A Comparative Study* (Ann Arbor: University of Michigan Press), 99–166.

Hume, David (1994 [1741]) 'That Politics May Be Reduced to a Science' in Knud Haakonssen (ed.) *Hume: Political Essays* (Cambridge: Cambridge University Press), 4–15.

—— (1994 [1741]) 'Of the First Principles of Government' in Knud Haakonssen (ed.) *Hume: Political Essays* (Cambridge: Cambridge University Press), 16–19.

—— (1994 [1748]) 'Of the Original Contract' in Knud Haakonssen (ed.) *Hume: Political Essays* (Cambridge: Cambridge University Press), 186–201.

—— (1994 [1777]) 'Of the Origin of Government' in Knud Haakonssen (ed.) *Hume: Political Essays* (Cambridge: Cambridge University Press), 20–23.

Hunt, Michael (1988) *Ideology and US Foreign Policy* (New Haven: Yale University Press).

Huntington, Samuel P (1999) 'The Lonely Superpower', *Foreign Affairs*, 78:2, 35–49.

International Monetary Fund (2004) 'Independent Evaluation Office (IEO) of the IMF, Report on the Evaluation of the Role of the IMF in Argentina, 1999–2001', 30 June, <http://www. imf.org/external/np/ieo/2004/arg/eng/index.htm>, accessed 26 March 2009.

Israel, Jonathan (1998) *The Dutch Republic: Its Rise, Greatness, and Fall, 1477–1806* (Oxford: Clarendon Press).

James, Oliver (2007) *Affluenza {ae flu enza}: How to Be Successful and Stay Sane* (London: Vermillion).

Jameson, Fredric (1981) *The Political Unconscious* (London: Methuen).

Jarvis, Anthony (1989) 'Societies, States and Geopolitics: Challenges from Historical Sociology', *Review of International Studies*, 19:3, 281–93.

Jeffords, Susan (1989) *The Remasculinization of America: Gender and the Vietnam War* (Bloomington: Indiana University Press).

Jessop, Bob (2006a) 'Gramsci as a Spatial Theorist' in Andreas Bieler and Adam David Morton (eds) *Images of Gramsci* (London: Routledge).

Jha, Prem Shankar (2006) *The Twilight of the Nation State: Globalisation, Chaos and War*, (London: Pluto).

Johnson, Chalmers (1982) *MITI and the Japanese Miracle: The Growth of Industrial Policy, 1925–1975* (Stanford: Stanford University Press).

—— (1995) *Japan: Who Governs? The Rise of the Developmental State* (New York: WW Norton & Co).

Jordan, Robert S (1971) 'The Influence of the British Secretariat Tradition on the Formation of the League of Nations' in Robert S Jordan (ed.) *International Administration* (New York: Oxford University Press), 27–50.

Kandal, Terry (1989) 'Marx and Engels on International Relations, Revolution, and Counter-revolution' in Michael T Martin and Terry R Kandal (eds) *Studies of Development and Change in the Modern World* (Oxford: Oxford University Press), 25–76.

Kaplinsky, Raphael (2005) *Globalization, Poverty and Inequality: Between a Rock and a Hard Place* (Cambridge: Polity).

Kagarlitsky, Boris (2004) 'From Global Crisis to Neo-Imperialism: the Case for a Radical Alternative' in Alan Freeman and Boris Kagarlitsky (eds) *The Politics of Empire: Globalisation in Crisis* (London: Pluto in association with Transnational Institute), 241–74.

Kautsky, Karl (1914) 'Ultra-Imperialism,' *Die Neue Zeit*, transl by *Marxist Writers Archive, Kautsky Internet Archive*, <http://www.marxists.org/archive/kautsky/1914/09/ultra-imp.htm>, accessed 26 March 2009.

Kentor, Jeffrey (2005) 'The Growth of Transnational Corporate Networks, 1962 to 1998', *Journal of World-Systems Research*, 11:2, 262–86.

Kentor, Jeffrey and Yong Suk Jang (2004) 'Yes, There Is a (Growing) Transnational Business Community', *International Sociology*, 19:3, 355–68.

Kershaw, Ian (2000) *Hitler, 1936–1945: Nemesis* (London: Allen Lane).

—— (2007) *Fateful Choices: Ten Decisions that Changed the World, 1940–1941* (London: Allen Lane).

Kidron, Michael (1974) *Capitalism and Theory* (London: Pluto).

Kiely, Ray (1995) 'Marxism, Post-Marxism and Development Fetishism', *Capital & Class*, 55, 73–101.

—— (2005) 'Capitalist Expansion and the Imperialism-Globalization Debate: Contemporary Marxist Explanations', *Journal of International Relations and Development*, 8:1, 27–57.

—— (2006) 'United States Hegemony and Globalisation: What Role for Theories of Imperialism?', *Cambridge Review of International Affairs*, 19:2, 205–21.

Kinzer, Stephen (2003) *All the Shah's Men* (New York: Wiley).

—— (2006) *Overthrow: America's Century of Regime Change from Hawaii to Iraq* (New York: Times Books).

Klare, Michael T (2001) *Resource Wars: The New Landscape of Global Conflict* (New York: Henry Holt Metropolitan Books).

—— (2003) 'The New Geopolitics', *Monthly Review*, 55:3, 51–56.

—— (2004) *Blood and Oil* (New York: Metropolitan Books).

Knei-Paz, Baruch (1978) *The Social and Political Thought of Leon Trotsky* (Oxford: Oxford University Press).

Kolko, Gabriel (1970) *The Politics of War* (New York: Vintage).

—— (1988) *Confronting the Third World* (New York: Pantheon).

Krasner, Stephen D (1982) 'Structural Causes and Regime Consequences: Regimes as Intervening Variables', *International Organisation,* 36:2, 185–205.

—— (1999) 'State Power and the Structure of International Trade' in Jeffrey A Frieden and David A Lake (eds) *International Political Economy: Perspectives on Global Power and Wealth* (London: Routledge), 19–36.

Krugman, Paul (1981) 'Trade, Accumulation, and Uneven Development', *Journal of Development Economics* 8, 149–61.

Kubalkova, Vendulka and Albert Cruickshank (1980) *Marxism-Leninism and Theory of International Relations* (London: Routledge).

—— (1989) *Marxism and International Relations* (Oxford: Oxford University Press).

Kull, Steven (2004) 'The Separate Realities of Bush and Kerry Supporters', *Program on International Policy Attitudes*, University of Maryland, 21 Oct, <http://www.pipa.org/OnlineReports/Iraq/IraqRealities_Oct04/IraqRealitiesOct04rpt.pdf>, accessed 13 March 2009.

Kuruvilla, Benny (2006) 'Services Industry Drives Indian GATS Negotiations', *Focus on Trade*, 121, June, <http://focusweb.org/services-industry-drives-india-gats-negotiations.html>, accessed 26 March 2009.

Lacher, Hannes (2002) 'Making Sense of the International System: Promises and Pitfalls of Contemporary Marxist Theories of International Relations' in Mark Rupert and Hazel Smith (eds) *Historical Materialism and Globalization* (London: Routledge), 147–64.

—— (2005) 'International Transformation and the Persistence of Territoriality: Toward a New Political Geography of Capitalism', *Review of International Political Economy*, 12:1, 26–52.

—— (2006) *Beyond Globalization: Capitalism, Territoriality and the International Relations of Modernity* (London: Routledge).

—— (2008) 'Good-bye Lenin: Interstate Competition and Cooperation in Capitalist Modernity', unpublished manuscript.

Lacher, Hannes and Benno Teschke (2007) 'The Changing "Logics" of Capitalist Competition', *Cambridge Review of International Affairs*, 20:4, 565–80.

LaFeber, Walter (1989) *The American Age: United States Foreign Policy at Home and Abroad, 1750 to the Present* (New York: Norton).

Laffey, Mark and Kathryn Dean (2002) 'A Flexible Marxism for Flexible Times' in Mark Rupert and Helen Smith (eds) *Historical Materialism and Globalization* (London: Routledge), 90–109.

Layne, Christopher (2006) *The Peace of Illusions: American Grand Strategy from 1940 to the Present* (Ithaca: Cornell University Press).

Lefebvre, Henri (1991) *The Production of Space* (Oxford: Blackwell).

Lembke, Jerry (1998) *The Spitting Image: Myth, Memory, and the Legacy of Vietnam* (New York: New York University Press).

Lenin, Vladimir Ilich *Collected Works*, 39 Vols. (Moscow: Progress Publishers).

—— (1964 [1916]) 'Imperialism, the Highest Stage of Capitalism' in *Collected Works*, Volume 22 (Moscow: Progress Publishers), 185–304.

—— (1973 [1916]) *Imperialism, the Highest Stage of Capitalism: A Popular Outline* (London: Merlin Press).

Leys, Colin (2001) *Market-driven Politics: Neoliberal Democracy and the Public Interest* (London: Verso).

Lieven, Anatole (2004) 'Demon in the Cellar', *Prospect Magazine*, March, <http://www.prospect-magazine.co.uk>, accessed 13 March 2009.

Linklater, Andrew (1990) *Beyond Realism and Marxism: Critical Theory and International Relations* (Basingstoke: Macmillan).

Lonsdale, John and Bruce Berman (1979) 'Coping with the Contradictions: The Development of the Colonial State in Kenya, 1895–1914', *Journal of African History*, 20:4, 487–505.

Löwy, Michael (1981) *The Politics of Combined and Uneven Development: The Theory of Permanent Revolution* (London: Verso).

Lukács, Györg (1971 [1923]) *History and Class Consciousness: Studies in Marxist Dialectics* (London: Merlin).

—— (1972 [1926]) 'Mosses Hess and the Problem of Idealist Dialectics' in *Tactics and Ethics: Political Writings, 1919–1929*, edited by Rodney Livingstone (London: New Left Books), 181–223.

Luttwak, Edward (1998) *Turbo-Capitalism: Winners and Losers in the Global Economy* (London: Weidenfeld and Nicolson).

Luxemburg, Rosa (2003 [1913]) *The Accumulation of Capital* (London: Routledge).

Luxemburg, Rosa and Nikolai Bukharin (1972 [25–26]) *Imperialism and the Accumulation of Capital* (London: Allen Lane).

Mabey, Nick (1999) 'Defending the Legacy of Rio: the Civil Society Campaign against the MAI' in Sol Picciotto and Ruth Mayne (eds) *Regulating International Business: Beyond Liberalization* (Basingstoke: Macmillan), 60–81.

MacIntyre, Alasdair (2008 [1958–59]) 'Notes from the Moral Wilderness' in *Alasdair MacIntyre's Engagement with Marxism: Selected Writings, 1953–1974*, edited with an introduction by Paul Blackledge and Neil Davidson (Leiden: Brill), 45–68.

Maclean, John (1977) [1919]) 'The Coming War with America' in *In the Rapids of Revolution: Essays Articles and Letters, 1902–1903*, edited with an introduction by Nan Milton (London: Alison and Busby), 182–90.

Mamdani, Mahmood (1996) *Citizen and Subject: Contemporary Africa and the Legacy of Late Colonialism* (London: James Currey).

Mandel, Ernest (1970) 'The Laws of Uneven Development', *New Left Review* I:59, 19–38.

—— (1973) [1969]) 'The Inconsistencies of State Capitalism' in *Readings on 'State Capitalism'* (London: International Marxist Group Publications), 7–26.

—— (1975) *Late Capitalism*, transl by Joris De Bres (London: Verso).

Mann, Michael (1986) *The Sources of Social Power: A History of Power from the Beginning to AD 1760* Volume I (Cambridge: Cambridge University Press).

—— (1993) *The Sources of Social Power: The Rise of Classes and Nation-States, 1760–1914* Volume II (Cambridge: Cambridge University Press).

—— (2003) *Incoherent Empire* (London: Verso).

Marglin, Stephen (1982) 'What Do the Bosses Do? The Origins and Functions of Hierarchy in Capitalist Production' in Anthony Giddens and David Held (eds) *Classes, Power and Conflict: Classical and Contemporary Debates* (Berkeley and Los Angeles: University of California Press), 285–98.

Marshall, Alfred (1925) *Principles of Economics* (London: Macmillan).

Marx, Karl (1954 [1867]) *Capital*, Volume I (London: Lawrence & Wishart).

—— (1959 [1894]) *Capital*, Volume III (London: Lawrence & Wishart).

—— (1962) 'Critique of the Gotha Programme' in *Marx-Engels Selected Works*, Volume II (Moscow: Foreign Languages Publishing House), 13–30.

—— (1965) *Capital,* Volume 1 *(1887 English Translation)* (Moscow: Foreign Languages Publishing House).

—— (1958 [1851–2]) 'The Eighteenth Brumaire of Louis Bonaparte' in *Marx-Engels Selected Works*, Volume 1 (Moscow: Progress Publishers). 243–344.

—— (1970 [1859]) *A Contribution to the Critique of Political Economy* (Moscow: Progress Publishers).

—— (1972 [1863]) *Theories of Surplus-Value*, Volume III (London: Lawrence & Wishart).

—— (1973 [1857–58]) *Grundrisse: Introduction to the Critique of Political Economy (Rough Draft)*, transl and edited by Martin Nicolaus (London: Penguin).

—— (1975 [1843]) *'Letter to* Arnold Ruge, September 1843' in *Marx–Engels Collected Works,* Volume 3 (Moscow: Progress), 141–45.

—— (1976 [1859]) *A Contribution to the Critique of Political Economy* (Beijing: Foreign Languages Publishing House).

—— (1976 [1867]) *Capital*, Volume I (Harmondsworth: Penguin).

—— (1981 [1894]) *Capital* Volume 3, introduced by Ernst Mandel, transl by David Fernbach (London: Penguin/NLR).

—— (1983 [1858]) 'Letter to Frederick Engels' in *Marx-Engels Collected Works*, Volume 40 (London: Lawrence and Wishart), 248.

—— (1983 [1858]) 'Letter to Friedrich Engels, 2 April 1858' in *Marx-Engels Collected Works*, Volume XL (Moscow: Progress), 296–304.

—— (1984 [1894]) *Capital*, Volume 3 (London: Lawrence and Wishart).

—— (1986 [1893]) *Capital*, Volume II (London: Lawrence and Wishart).

—— (1996 [1867]) *Capital*, Volume I, in Karl Marx and Friedrich Engels, *Collected works*, Volume 35 (London: Lawrence and Wishart).

Marx, Karl and Friedrich Engels (1976 [1845–46]) 'The German Ideology' in *Marx-Engels Collected Works*, Volume 5 (Progress Publishers: Moscow), 19–539.

—— (2002 [1848]) *The Communist Manifesto* (Harmondsworth: Penguin).

Mason, Tim (1995) *Nazism, Fascism and the Working Class*, edited with introduction by Jane Caplan (Cambridge: Cambridge University Press).

Matin, Kamran (2006) 'Uneven and Combined Development and "Revolution of Backwardness": The Iranian Constitutional Revolution, 1906–11' in Bill Dunn and Hugo Radice (ed.) *100 Years of Permanent Revolution: Results and Prospects* (London: Pluto Press), 119–32.

—— (2007) 'Uneven and Combined Development in World History: The International Relations of State-formation in Premodern Iran', *European Journal of International Relations*, 13:3, 419–47.

May, Christopher (2000) *A Global Political Economy of Intellectual Property Rights: The New Enclosures?* (London: Routledge).

May, Ernest R (ed.) (1993) *American Cold War Strategy: Interpreting NSC-68* (Boston: Bedford Books).

Mayer, Arno J (1981) *The Persistence of the Anción Regime* (New York: Pantheon).

McManus, Doyle (2003) 'The World Casts a Critical Eye on Bush's Style of Diplomacy', *Los Angeles Times*, 3 March, <http://www.commondreams.org/headlines03/0303–7.htm>, accessed 13 March 2009.

McMichael, Phillip (1990) 'Incorporating Comparison within a World-Historical Perspective: An Alternative Comparative Method', *American Sociological Review*, 55:3, 385–97.

McNeill, William H (1982) *The Pursuit of Power* (Oxford: Blackwell).

McNeill, JR and McNeill, WH (2003) *The Human Web: A Bird's Eye View of World History* (New York and London: Norton).

Mearsheimer, John (1994–95) 'The False Promise of International Institutions', *International Security*, 19:3, 5–49.

—— (2001) *The Tragedy of Great Power Politics* (New York: WW Norton & Co).

Merk, Jeroen (2004) 'Regulating the Global Athletic Footwear Industry: The Collective Worker in the Product Chain' in Kees van der Pijl, Libby Assassi, and Duncan Wigan (eds) *Global Regulation: Managing Crises after the Imperial Turn* (Basingstoke: Palgrave Macmillan), 128–41.

MEW: Marx-Engels *Werke*. Berlin: Dietz Verlag, 43 volumes.

Miéville, China (2005) *Between Equal Rights: A Marxist Theory of International Law* (Leiden: Brill).

Miliband, Ralph (1983) 'State Power and Class Interests', *New Left Review*, I:138, 57–68.

Mitchell, Timothy (2007) 'Dreamland' in Mike Davis and Daniel Bertrand Monk (eds) *Evil Paradises: Deamworlds of Neoliberalism* (New York: The New Press), 1–33.

Moe, Nelson (2002) *The View from Vesuvius: Italian Culture and the Southern Question* (Berkeley: University of California Press).

Monthly Review (2003) 'Imperialism Now', Special Issue, 55:3.

—— (2004) 'Note from the Editors', November, 64–65.

Moore, Phoebe (2007) *Globalization and Labour Struggle in Asia* (Houndmills: Palgrave Macmillan).

Moravcsik, Andrew (2005) 'Dream on America', *MSNBC/Newsweek*, 31 January, <http://http://www.newsweek.com/id/48345>, accessed 13 March 2009.

Morgenthau, Hans J (1946) *Scientific Man versus Power Politics* (Chicago: University of Chicago Press).

—— (1955) *Politics among Nations* (New York: Alfred Knopf).

Morton, Adam David (2003) 'Structural Change and Neoliberalism in Mexico: "Passive Revolution" in the Global Political Economy', *Third World Quarterly*, 24:4, 631–53.

—— (2005) 'The Age of Absolutism: Capitalism, the Modern States-System and International Relations', *Review of International Studies*, 31:3, 495–517.

—— (2007a) *Unravelling Gramsci: Hegemony and Passive Revolution in the Global Political Economy* (London: Pluto Press).

—— (2007b) 'Waiting for Gramsci: State Formation, Passive Revolution and the International', *Millennium: Journal of International Studies*, 35:3, 597–621.

—— (2007c) 'Disputing the Geopolitics of the States System and Gobal Capitalism', *Cambridge Review of International Affairs*, 20:4, 599–617.

—— (2007d) 'Global Capitalism and the Peasantry in Latin America: The Recomposition of Class Struggle', *Journal of Peasant Studies*, 34:3–4, 44–73.

—— (2010) 'Reflections on Uneven Development: Mexican Revolution, Primitive Accumulation, Passive Revolution', *Latin American Perspectives*, 37:1, 7–34.

Mosley, Fred (2002) 'Hostile Brothers: Marx's Theory of the Distribution of Surplus-Value in Volume III of *Capital*' in Martha Campbell and Geert Reuten (eds) *The Culmination of Capital* (Basingstoke: Palgrave), 65–101.

Motta, Sara C (2008) 'The Chilean Socialist Party (PSch): Constructing Consent and Disarticulating Dissent to Neoliberal Hegemony in Chile', *British Journal of Politics and International Relations*, 10:2, 303–27(25).

Murakami, Yasusuke (1996) *An Anticlassical Political-Economic Analysis* (Stanford: Stanford University Press).

Murray, Patrick (1988) *Marx's Theory of Scientific Knowledge* (New Jersey: Humanities Press International).

Naguib, Sameh (2007) 'Interview: Egypt's Strike Wave', *International Socialism,* II:116, <http://www.isj.org.uk>, accessed 9 May 2009.

National Security Council (1975) [1950]) 'NCS-68: United States Objectives and Programs for National Security', *Naval College Review* 27, 51–108.

Neocosmos, Michael (1986) ©Marx's Third Class: Capitalist Landed Property and Capitalist Development', *Journal of Peasant Studies*, 13:3, 5–44.

Nesvetailova, Anastasia (2007) *Fragile Finance: Debt, Speculation and Crisis in the Age of Global Credit* (Basingstoke: Palgrave Macmillan).

Nivola, Pietro (1990) 'Trade Policy: Refereeing the Playing Field' in Thomas E Mann (ed.) *A Question of Balance: The President, the Congress and Foreign Policy* (Washington, DC: Brookings), 201–55.

Novack, George (1972) *Understanding History: Marxist Essays* (New York: Pathfinder).

Oborne, Peter (2007) *The Triumph of the Political Class* (London: Simon and Schuster).

Offe, Claus (1984) *Contradictions of the Welfare State* (London: Hutchinson).

Offe, Claus and Volker Ronge (1982) 'Theses on the Theory of the State' in Anthony Giddens and David Held (eds) *Classes, Power, and Conflict* (Berkeley/Los Angeles: University of California Press), 249–56.

Ohmae, Kenichi (1996) *The End of the Nation State: The Rise of Regional Economies* (New York: Free Press).

Ollman, Bertell (1976) *Alienation*, 2nd edition (Cambridge: Cambridge University Press).

—— (1979) 'Marxism and Political Science: Prolegomenon to a Debate on Marx's Method' in *Social and Sexual Revolution: Essays on Marx and Reich* (London: Pluto), 99–156.

Owen, John M (1994) 'How Liberalism Produces Democratic Peace', *International Security*, 19:2, 87–125.

Padfield, Peter (2000) *Maritime Supremacy and the Opening of the Western Mind: Naval Campaigns that Shaped the Modern World, 1588–1782* (London: Pimlico).

Palmisano, Samuel (2006) 'Multinationals Have Been Superseded', *Financial Times*, 12 June, 19.

Panitch, Leo and Sam Gindin (2003) 'Global Capitalism and American empire' in Leo Panitch and Colin Leys (eds) *The New imperial Challenge: Socialist Register 2004* (London: Merlin), 1–42.

—— (2004) 'Finance and American Empire' in Leo Panitch and Colin Leys (eds) *The Empire Reloaded: Socialist Register 2005* (London: Merlin), 46–81.

—— (2005) 'Superintending Global Capital', *New Left Review*, II:35, 101–23.

—— (2006) '"Imperialism and Global Political Economy": A Reply to Alex Callinicos', *International Socialism*, 2:109, 194–99.

Pape, Robert A (2005) 'Soft Balancing against the United States', *International Security*, 20:1, 7–45.

Pasha, Mustapha Kamal (2006) 'Islam, "Soft Orientalism" and Hegemony: A Gramscian Rereading' in Andreas Bieler and Adam D Morton (eds) *Images of Gramsci* (London: Routledge), 149–64.

Pashukanis, Evgeny (1978) [1924]) *Law and Marxism: A General Theory—Towards a Critique of the Fundamental Juridical Concepts*, edited and introduced by Chris Arthur (London: Ink Links).

Paul, TV (2005) 'Soft Balancing in the Age of US Primacy', *International Security*, 30:1, 46–71.

Payne, Anthony J (2005) *The Global Politics of Unequal Development* (Houndmills: Palgrave Macmillan).

Phillips, Kevin (2006) *American Theocracy: The Peril and Politics of Radical Religion, Oil, and Borrowed Money in the 21st Century* (New York: Viking Penguin).

Phinney, David (2005) 'Blood, Sweat and Tears: Asia's Poor Build US Bases in Iraq', *Corp-Watch*, 3 October, < http://www.corpwatch.org/article.php?id=12675 >, accessed 26 March 2009.

Pollard, Robert (1987) *Economic Security and the Origins of the Cold War* (New York: Columbia University Press).

Pomeranz, Kenneth (2000) *The Great Divergence: China, Europe and the Making of the Modern World Economy* (Princeton: Princeton University Press).

Poulantzas, Nicos (1973) *Political Power and Social Classes*, transl Timothy O'Hagan (London: New Left Books).

Pozo-Martin, Gonzalo (2006) 'A Tougher Gordian Knot: Globalization, Imperialism and the Problem of the State', *Cambridge Review of International Affairs*, 19:2, 223–42.

—— (2007) 'Autonomous or Materialist Geopolitics?', *Cambridge Review of International Affairs*, 20:4, 551–63.

Rai, Saritha (2006) 'I.B.M. India', *New York Times*, 5 June, A1.

Rees, John (1998) *The Algebra of Revolution: The Dialectic and the Classical Marxist Tradition* (London: Routledge).

—— (2006) *Imperialism and Resistance* (London: Routledge).

Reinert, Erik S (ed.) (2004) *Globalization, Economic Development and Inequality* (Cheltenham: Edward Elgar).

Reno, William (1998) *Warlord Politics and African States* (Boulder: Lynne Rienner).

—— (2002) 'Uganda's Politics of War and Debt Relief', *Review of International Political Economy*, 9:3, 415–35.

Ritsert, Jürgen (1973) *Probleme politisch-ökonomischer Theoriebildung* (Frankfurt: Athenäum).

Robinson, William I (1996) *Promoting Polyarchy: Globalization, US Intervention, and Hegemony* (Cambridge: Cambridge University Press).

—— (2001) 'Social Theory and Globalization: The Rise of a Transnational State', *Theory and Society*, 30:2, 157–200.

—— (2002) 'Global Capitalism and Nation-State Centric Thinking: What We Don't See When We Do See Nation-States. Response to Arrighi, Mann, Moore, van der Pijl, and Went', *Science & Society*, 65:4, 500–508.

—— (2003) *Transnational Conflicts: Central America, Social Change, and Globalization* (London: Verso).

—— (2004) *A Theory of Global Capitalism: Production, Class and State in a Transnational World* (Baltimore: Johns Hopkins University Press).

—— (2005a) 'Gramsci and Globalization: From Nation-State to Transnational Hegemony', *Critical Review of International Social and Political Philosophy*, 8:4, 1–16.

—— (2005b) 'Global Capitalism: The New Transnationalism and the Folly of Conventional Thinking', *Science & Society*, 69:3, 316–28.

—— (2006a) 'Reification and Theoreticism in the Study of Globalization, Imperialism, and Hegemony: A Comment on Kiely, Pozo, and Valladao', *Cambridge Review of International Affairs*, 19:3, 529–33.

—— (2006b) 'Aqui Estamos y No Nos Vamos!: Global Capitalism and The Struggle for Immigrant Rights', *Race and Class*, 48:2, 77–91.

—— (2007) 'The Pitfall of Realist Analysis of Global Capitalism: A Critique of Ellen Meiksins Wood's *Empire of Capital*', *Historical Materialism*, 15:3, 71–93.

—— (2008) *Latin America and Global Capitalism: A Critical Globalization Perspective* (Baltimore: Johns Hopkins University Press).

—— (2009) 'Saskia Sassen and the Sociology of Globalization', *Sociological Analysis*, 3:1, 5–29.

Robinson, William I and Jerry Harris (2000) 'Towards a Global Ruling Class? Globalization and the Transnational Capitalist Class', *Science & Society*, 64:1, 11–54.

Rosdolsky, Roman (1977) *The Making of Marx's 'Capital'* (London: Pluto).

Rose, Charlie (2003) Interview with Thomas Friedman, video excerpt on line at <http://www.youtube.com/watch?v=HOF6ZeUvgXs>, accessed 13 March 2009.

Rosenberg, Justin (1994) *Empire of Civil Society: A Critique of the Realist Theory of International Relations* (London: Verso).

—— (1996) 'Isaac Deutscher and the Lost History of International Relations', *New Left Review*, 1:215, 3–15.

—— (2000) *The Follies of Globalization Theory: Polemical Essays* (London: Verso).

—— (2005) 'Globalization Theory: A Post-mortem', *International Politics*, 42:1, 2–74.

—— (2006) 'Why Is There No International Historical Sociology?', *European Journal of International Relations*, 12:3, 307–40.

—— (2007) 'International Relations—the "Higher Bullshit": A Response to the Globalization Theory Debate', *International Politics*, 44:4, 450–82.

—— (2008) 'Anarchy in the Mirror of Uneven and Combined Development: An Open Letter to Kenneth Waltz', paper presented at *The British German IR Conference BISA/DVPW*, 16–18 May, Arnoldshain, Germany.

Rosengarten, Frank (1984–85) 'The Gramsci-Trotsky Question (1922–32)', *Social Text*, 11, 65–95.

Ross, Dorothy (1991) *The Origins of American Social Science* (Cambridge: Cambridge University Press).

Rugman, Alan M and Alain Verbeke (2004) 'A Perspective on Regional and Global Strategies of Multinational Enterprises', *Journal of International Business Studies*, 35:1, 3–18.

Runciman, WG (1989) *A Treatise on Social Theory*, Volume II (Cambridge: Cambridge University Press).

Rupert, Mark (1995) *Producing Hegemony: The Politics of Mass Production and US Global Power* (Cambridge: Cambridge University Press).

—— (2000) *Ideologies of Globalization* (London: Routledge).

—— (2005) 'Reading Gramsci in an Era of Globalizing Capitalism', *Critical Review of International Social and Political Philosophy*, 8:4, 483–97.

—— (2009) 'Reflections on Academia and the Culture of Militarism in the US' in Anthony Nocella, Steven Best, and Peter McLaren (eds) *Academic Repression: Reflections from the Academic Industrial Complex* (Oakland: AK Press), forthcoming.

Rupert, Mark and Hazel Smith (eds) (2002) *Historical Materialism and Globalization* (London: Routledge).

Ryner, Magnus J (2002) *Capitalist Restructuring, Globalization and the Third Way* (London: Routledge).

Sack, Robert David (1986) *Human Territoriality* (Cambridge: Cambridge University Press).

Sassen, Saskia (2001) *The Global Cities: New York, London, Tokyo*, 2nd edition (Princeton: Princeton University Press).

—— (2007) *A Sociology of Globalization* (New York: Norton).

Saull, Richard (2007) *The Cold War and After: Capitalism, Revolution and Superpower Politics* (London: Pluto).

Sayer, Derek (1979) *Marx's Method: Ideology, Science and Critique in Capital* (Brighton: Harvester).

Schmitt, Eric (2003) 'Soft Economy Aids Recruiting Effort, Army Leaders Say,' *New York Times*, 22 September, < http://www.nytimes.com >, accessed 13 March 2009.

Seidman, Steven (1983) *Liberalism and the Origins of European Social Theory* (Berkeley: University of California Press).

Serfati, Claude (2004) *Impérialisme et militarisme* [Imperialism and Militarism] (Lausanne: Editions Page deux).

Schlesinger, Arthur M (1965) *A Thousand Days: John F Kennedy in the White House* (New York: Maringer).

Schumpeter, Joseph (1972) *History of Economic Analysis* (London: George Allen & Unwin).

Shields, Stuart (2009) *The International Political Economy of Transition* (London: Routledge).

Shilliam, Robbie (2006a) 'Marcus Garvey, Race and Sovereignty', *Review of International Studies*, 32:3, 379–400.

—— (2006b) 'Marx's Path to "Capital": The International Dimension of an Intellectual Journey', *History of Political Thought*, XXVII:2, 349–37.

—— (2009) 'The Atlantic as a Vector of Uneven and Combined Development', *Cambridge Review of International Affairs*, 22:1, 69–88.

Shirokogorov, Sergeĭ Mikhaĭlovich (1970 [1931]) *Ethnological and Linguistical Aspects of the Ural-Altaic Hypothesis* (Oosterhout: Anthropological Publications).

Sinclair, Tim (2005) *The New Masters of Capital* (Ithaca: Cornell University Press).

Sklair, Leslie (2001) *The Transnational Capitalist Class* (Oxford: Blackwell).

—— (2002) *Globalization: Capitalism and Its Alternatives* (New York: Oxford University Press).

Sifry, Micah and Christopher Cerf (eds) (2003) *The Iraq War Reader* (New York: Simon and Schuster).

Skarstein, Rune (2005) 'Economic Development by Means of Free Trade?' in G Chaloupek *et al.* (eds) *Sisyphus als Optimist* (Hamburg: VSA Verlag), 352–66.

Skocpol, Theda (1979) *States and Social Revolutions: A Comparative Analysis of France, Russia and China* (Cambridge: Cambridge University Press).

Slater, David (2004) *Geopolitics and the Post-Colonial: Rethinking North-South Relations* (Oxford: Blackwell Publishing).

Smith, Hazel (1994) 'Marxism and International Relations Theory' in AJR Groom and Margot Light (eds) *Contemporary International Relations: A Guide to Theory* (London: Frances Pinter), 142–55.

Smith, Neil (1990) *Uneven Development: Nature, Capital and the Production of Space* (Oxford: Blackwell).

Smith, Steve (2002) 'Historical Sociology and International Relations Theory' in Stephen Hobden and John Hobson (eds) *Historical Sociology of International Relations* (Cambridge: Cambridge University Press), 223–43.

Soederberg, Susanne (2001) 'From Neoliberalism to Social Liberalism: Situating the National Solidarity Program within Mexico's Passive Revolutions', *Latin American Perspectives*, 28:3, 102–23.

Sorenson, Ted (1965) *Kennedy* (New York: HarperCollins).

Spence, Michael L (1981) 'The Learning Curve and Competition', *Bell Journal of Economics*, 12, 49–70.

Stedman Jones, Gareth (1970) 'The Specificity of US Imperialism', *New Left Review* I:60, 59–86.

Storper, Michael and Richard Walker (1989) *The Capitalist Imperative: Territory, Technology and Industrial Growth* (Oxford: Oxford University Press).

Sutcliffe, Bob (2002) 'How Many Capitalisms? Historical Materialism in the Debates about Imperialism and Globalization' in Mark Rupert and Hazel Smith (eds) *Historical Materialism and Globalization* (London: Routledge), 40–58.

Sweezy, Paul M (1968) *The Theory of Capitalist Development* (New Yortk: Monthly Review Press).

Szeftel, Morris (2000) 'Between Governance and Underdevelopment: Accumulation and Africa's "Catastrophic Corruption"', *Review of African Political Economy*, 27:84, 287–306.

Taylor, Michael (1982) *Community, Anarchy and Liberty* (Cambridge: Cambridge University Press).

Tell, Tariq (2000) 'Guns, Gold, and Grain: War and Food Supply in the Making of Transjordan' in Steven Heydemann (ed.) *War, Institutions and Social Change in the Middle East* (Berkeley/Los Angeles: University of California Press), 33–59.

Tempest, Rone (2005) 'Who's Dying in Our War?', *Los Angeles Times*, 30 January, <http://www.latimes.com>, accessed 13 March 2009.

Tenbruck, Friedrich (1994) 'Internal History or Universal History?', *Theory, Culture & Society*, 11, 75–93.

Teschke, Benno (1998) 'Geopolitical Relations in the European Middle Ages: History and Theory', *International Organization*, 52:2, 325–58.

—— (2002) 'Theorising the Westphalian System of States: International Relations from Absolutism to Capitalism', *European Journal of International Relations*, 8:1, 5–48.

—— (2003) *The Myth of 1648: Class, Geopolitics and the Making of Modern International Relations* (London: Verso).

—— (2005) 'Bourgeois Revolution, State-formation and the Absence of the International', *Historical Materialism*, 13:2, 3–26.

—— (2006) 'Debating "The Myth of 1648": State-formation, the Interstate System and the Rise of Capitalism—A Rejoinder', *International Politics*, 43:5, 531–73.

—— (2008) 'Marxism and International Relations' in Christian Reus-Smit and Duncan Snidal (eds) *The Oxford Handbook of International Relations* (Oxford: Oxford University Press), 163–87.

Therborn, Goran (1978) *What Does the Ruling Class Do When it Rules? State Apparatuses and State Power under Feudalism, Capitalism and Socialism* (London: New Left Books).

—— (1985) *Science, Class and Society: On the Formation of Sociology and Historical Materialism* (London: Verso).

—— (1999) *The Power of Ideology and the Ideology of Power* (London: Verso).

Thompson, William R (1988) *On Global War: Historical-Structural Approaches to World Politics* (Columbia: University of South Carolina Press).

Thucydides (1972) *History of the Peloponnesian War*, transl by Rex Warner (Harmondsworth: Penguin).

Tilly, Charles (1975) 'Reflections on the History of European State-Making' in Charles Tilly (ed.) *The Formation of National States in Western Europe* (Princeton, NJ: Princeton University Press), 3–83.

—— (1984) *Big Structures, Large Processes, Huge Comparisons* (New York: Russell Sage Foundation).

—— (1990) *Coercion, Capital and European States, AD 990–1990* (Oxford: Blackwell).

Tönnies, Ferdinand (1957) [1887]) *Community and Society*, transl and edited by Charles P. Loomis (East Lansing: The Michigan State University Press).

Trotsky, Leon (1936 [1930]) *The History of the Russian Revolution*, Volume 1 (London: Victor Gollancz Ltd).

—— (1932) *What Next? Vital Questions for the German Proletariat*, transl by Joseph Vanzler (New York: Pioneer Publishers).

—— (1962 [1930]) *The Permanent Revolution and Results and Prospects*, transl by John G Wright and Brian Pearce (London: New Park Publications).

—— (1971) [1924]) 'Perspectives of World Development' in *Europe and America: Two Speeches on Imperialism* (New York: Pathfinder), 3–43.

—— (1972 [1933]) 'Uneven and Combined Development and the Role of American Imperialism: Minutes of a Discussion' in *Writings of Leon Trotsky (1932–33)* (New York: Pathfinder), 116–20.

—— (1977 [1930]) *The History of the Russian Revolution*: transl by Max Eastman (London: Pluto).

—— (1980 [1930]) *The History of the Russian Revolution*, 3 Volumes, transl by Max Eastman (New York: Pathfinder).

—— (1970 [1929]) *The Third International after Lenin*, transl by John G Wright (New York: Pathfinder).

—— (1998) *Trotsky's Notebooks, 1933–1935: Writings on Lenin, Dialectics and Evolutionism*, edited by Philip Pomper (New York: Columbia UP).

United Nations Conference on Trade and Development (UNCTAD) *World Investment Report* (Geneva: United Nations).

Van der Linden, Marcel (2007) 'The "Law" of Uneven and Combined Development: Some Underdeveloped Thoughts', *Historical Materialism*, 15:1, 145–65.

Van der Linden, Marcel (2009) *Western Marxism and the Soviet Union* (London: Haymarket).

Van der Pijl, Kees (1984) *The Making of an Atlantic Ruling Class* (London: Verso).

—— (1996) 'A Theory of Transnational Revolution: Universal History according to Eugen Rosenstock-Huessy and its Implications', *Review of International Political Economy*, 3:2, 287–318.

—— (1998) *Transnational Classes and International Relations* (London: Routledge).

—— (2006a) 'A Lockean Europe?', *New Left Review*, II:37, 9–37.

—— (2006b) *Global Rivalries from the Cold War to Iraq* (London: Pluto).

—— (2007) *Nomads, Empires, States: Modes of Foreign Relations and Political Economy*, Volume I (London: Pluto).

Van der Pijl, Kees and Or Raviv (2007) 'European Integration and Redistribution: Changes in the Structure of Interlocking Directorates since German Reunification', paper presented at the *Political Science Association* Annual Conference, Bath, United Kingdom, 11–13 April.

Vernon, Raymond (1973) *Sovereignty at Bay: The Multinational Spread of US Enterprises* (Harmondsworth: Penguin).

von Braunmuhl, Claudia (1978) 'On the Analysis of the Bourgeois Nation State within the World Market Context: An Attempt to Develop a Methodological and Theoretical Approach' in John Holloway and Sol Picciotto (eds) *State and Capital: A Marxist debate* (London: Edward Arnold), 160–77.

Walker, Richard and Daniel Buck (2007) 'The Chinese Road: Cities in the Transition to Capitalism', *New Left Review*, II:46, 39–66.

Wallerstein, Immanuel (1974) *The Modern World System*, Volume I (London: Academic Press).

—— (2006a) 'An American Dilemma of the 21st Century?', *Societies Without Borders*, 1:1, 7–20.

—— (2006b) 'The Curve of US Power', *New Left Review*, II:40, 77–94.

Walras, Leon (1954) *Elements of Pure Economics*, transl by William Jaffe (London: Routledge).

Waltz, Kenneth N (1959) *Man, the State and War: A Theoretical Analysis* (New York: Columbia University Press).

—— (1979) *Theory of International Politics* (New York: McGraw Hill).

—— (1993) 'The Emerging Structure of International Politics', *International Security*, 18:2, 44–79.

—— (2000) 'Structural Realism after the Cold War', *International Security*, 25:1, 5–41.

Wartenberg, Thomas (1990) *The Forms of Power* (Philadelphia: Temple University Press).

Weber, Max (1994 [1919]) 'The Profession and Vocation of Politics' in *Political Writings*, edited and introduced by Peter Lassman and Ronald Speirs (Cambridge: Cambridge University Press), 309–69.

—— (1995) *The Russian Revolutions* (Cambridge: Polity).

Weeks, John (2001) 'The Expansion of Capital and Uneven Development on a World Scale', *Capital & Class*, 74, 9–30.

Wendt, Alexander (1999) *Social Theory of International Politics* (Cambridge: Cambridge University Press).

—— (2003) 'Why a World State Is Inevitable', *European Journal of International Relations*, 9:4, 491–542.

Werner, Richard (2003) *Princes of the Yen: Japan's Central Bankers and the Transformation of the Economy* (New York: M.E. Sharpe).

Wertheimer, Alan (1987) *Coercion* (Princeton: Princeton University Press).

—— (1996) *Exploitation* (Princeton: Princeton University Press).

White House (2002) *National Security Strategy of the United States*, <http://www.whitehouse.gov/nsc/print/nssall.html>, accessed 13 March 2009.

Williams, Bernard (2005) 'Realism and Moralism in Political Theory' in Bernard Williams *In the Beginning Was the Deed* (Princeton: Princeton University Press), 1–17.

Williams, William Appleman (1991) *The Tragedy of American Diplomacy* (New York: WW Norton & Co).

Wilpert, Gregory (2007) 'Chávez Dimisses International Disapproval of Venezuela's Media Policy', 4 June, <www.venezuelanalysis.com>, accessed 13 June 2007.

Wohlforth, William C (1999) 'The Stability of a Unipolar World', *International Security*, 24:1, 5–41.

Wolf, Eric (1997[1982]) *Europe and the People without History* (Berkeley and Los Angeles: University of California Press).

Wood, Ellen Meiksins (1981) 'The Separation of the Economic and the Political in Capitalism', *New Left Review*, I:127, 66–95.

—— (1991) *The Pristine Culture of Capitalism: An Essay on Old Regimes and Modern States* (London: Verso).

—— (1995) *Democracy against Capitalism: Renewing Historical Materialism* (Cambridge: Cambridge University Press).

—— (2002) 'Global Capital, National States' in Mark Rupert and Hazel Smith (eds) *Historical Materialism and Globalization* (London: Routledge), 17–39.

—— (2003) *Empire of Capital* (London: Verso).

—— (2006) 'Logics of Power: A Conversation with David Harvey', *Historical Materialism*, 14:4, 9–34.

Yergin, Daniel (1991) *The Prize* (New York: Simon and Schuster).

Young, Crawford (2004) 'The End of the Post-colonial State in Africa? Reflections on Changing Africa Political Dynamics', *African Affairs*, 103:410, 23–49.

Zeitlin, Irving, M. (2000) *Ideology and the Development of Sociological Theory*, 7th edition (Englewood Cliffs: Prentice Hall).

Index

absolutism 33, 34, 96, 201
abstract labour 192
abstraction 6, 39, 83, 193; general 8, 9, 149, 152–53, 156–58, 159, 168, 207; Marx's method 8, 47–48, 160, 173, 192, 207–8; sociological 149; theoretical 23–24, 158, 201, 207; transhistorical 169–1, 183, 184, 185
Abu Ghraib scandal 108
'advantages of backwardness' 190–91
Afghanistan 58, 90, 101
Africa: state and passive revolution 224–26
African National Congress 76
Agnew, J. 220
Airbus 137
al-Qaeda 100, 101, 104, 105
Alliance for the Liberation of Congo-Zaire 225
Allinson, J.C. 111; and Anievas, A. 9, 197–214
Althusser, L. 80, 118, 205
Americanism, Fordism and passive revolution 217, 220–23
anarcho-capitalist thought 78
anarchy: geopolitical 32; international 110, 206; logic of 4, 32, 116; social 234, 239
Anderson, P. 32–33, 117–18, 158, 178
Anglo-Boer War 91
Anglo-Iranian Oil Company 101
Anievas, A. 1–9, 73, 74, 111; and Allinson, J.C. 9, 197–214
anti-capitalism 40, 204
anti-dumping policy 132–33
anti-trust regulation 133–34
Arabian-American Oil Company (ARAMCO) 100
Argentina 226
Aristotle 161, 173

Arrighi, G. 80, 90
articulation: combination and diffusion 212–13
Ashley, R. 43
Ashman, S. 8, 22, 111, 183–96; and Callinicos, A. 86
Asia: and globalization 23, 39, 178; imperialism 209; markets 131
Association of Southeast Asian Nations (ASEAN) 138
Austria (and Austria-Hungarian Empire) 45, 46, 53, 191, 218
Ayubi, N. 212

Ba'ath regime 100
Bacevich, A. 98
balance of power 2, 18, 27, 102, 104, 207
Balkans 210
Barkawi, Tarak 210
Barker, C. 21, 29
Bartlett, R. 170
Barzel, Y. 241–42
base/superstructure metaphor 5, 9, 111, 113, 114–15, 117, 122, 198–200
Bayart, F. 225
Bechtel 72
Beetham, D. 241
Bello, W. 15
Bernstein, H. 190
Bhagwati, J. 133
Bidet, J. 21
Bilderberg Istanbul Conference (2007) 51–60; Afghanistan 58; agenda 58–59; China 59; Iran 58; participant list 54–58; Russia 59; World Bank 59
Bin Laden, O. 100
Blair, T. 49, 177
Block, F. 22, 83

Boeing 136–37
Bolshevik Revolution 7
Bonney, R. 34
Booth, D. 229
Bourgeoisie 3, 34, 71, 83, 84, 86, 112, 113,
    141, 216, 217, 218
Bratsis, P. 50
Braudel, F. 88
Brazil 226
Brenner, R. 4, 8, 19–20, 117, 153–54,
    170, 185, 187–88, 198–200, 209, 238,
    239
Brewer, A. 29
Bromley, S. 9, 100, 231–47
Brown, G. 70
Bukharin, N. 14, 20, 28, 29, 36, 37, 38,
    89–90, 91
bureaucracy 85
Buroway, M. 8
Bush, G.W. 14, 15, 45, 104, 105, 106–7,
    125, 133, 177; National Security Strategy
    (2002) 102
Buzan, B. 179

Calhoun, J. 78
Callinicos, A. 4, 5, 8, 13–26, 27–28, 31, 68,
    80, 85, 110, 115–17, 119, 183–84, 188,
    192, 193, 194, 204, 215; and Ashman, S.
    86; Rosenberg letter exchange 149–82
capital accumulation 22, 30, 32, 43, 48, 68,
    74, 75, 80, 86, 95, 96, 97, 109, 138, 145,
    188, 195, 223, 224
capital circuits 82
Capital (Marx) 3, 19, 20–21, 81, 118, 154,
    155, 160, 161, 165, 168, 171, 172, 173,
    174, 175, 192
capital-in-general 44–45
capitalism: and absolutism 33–35;
    competitive accumulation 88–91;
    economic/political separation 82–83
    185–89, 201–2; and geopolitics 95–98;
    industrial development 125–46;
    international political conflict 4, 5, 15,
    16, 28, 31, 36, 38, 39, 61, 68, 73, 93,
    125–46, 201, 205; interstateness 4; late
    development 35; and state system 13–26,
    28–36; and uneven and combined
    development 6, 7, 22, 36, 37–38, 40, 73,
    115, 149–82, 183–96, 197, 204, 206–13,
    215
capitalist competition: and perpetual peace
    89–91
capitalist political forms 185–89
capitalist social relations 185–89

capitalist state system 29, 38, 193;
    multiplicity and diversity 189–91
Cárdenas, L. 226
Carlyle Group 72
Carr, E.H. 176
Carroll, W.: and Carson, C. 52
Carter Doctrine 101
Carver, T. 117
Case-Dunn, C. 110
Castells, M. 67
Central Intelligence Agency (CIA) 101
Chatterjee, P. 227
Cheney, D. 90
Chibber, V. 17, 79, 83, 113, 202
Chile 227
Chilean Socialist Party 227
China 51, 142; Bilderberg Istanbul
    Conference (2007) 59
Chirac, J. 137
Churchill, W. 99
civil society 88
civilian aircraft production 136–37
class-equilibrium theory 112
Clinton, B. 49
coercive rule: and political order 236–39
Cohen, G.A. 123, 198, 238–39
Cold War 92, 100, 150
collapsed base/superstructuralism 117–21
collective action: political order 243–45
combined development 6, 7, 22, 36, 37–38,
    40, 73, 115, 149–82, 183–96, 197, 204,
    206–13, 215
combination: diffusion and articulation
    212–13
commodity fetishism 114, 173, 175
competitive accumulation 88–91
communism 126
communitarianism 167
'community governance' 9, 234
comparative advantage 241–42
'competitive primacy' thesis (Carling) 26,
    214
consciousness 48, 84, 85, 112, 155
constructivism (IR theory) 2, 26, 123
contender states: China 51; vassals 45, 51;
    and Western hegemony 42–45
contradictory unity: and differential
    development 47–49
Cooper, R. 140
core-periphery framework 75
Côte d'Ivoire 225
Council on Foreign Relations 53
Coutinho, C.N. 226
Cox, R. 44, 98, 121–22, 226

crises: capitalist/capitalism 19, 21, 25, 35, 66, 97, 168, 186, 193, 194, 203, 210
Cuba 98

Davis, M 96
Davidson, N. 5, 77–93, 111, 213, 219
deep structure: capital and world politics 43, 47
democracy 7, 51, 98, 102, 104, 105
Democratic Party (US) 106
Democratic Peace 43
Dependency Theory 151
Deterritorialization 67
Dialectics 2, 8, 97; Hegel 26, 46, 47, 48, 81; Marx 3, 111, 114, 122; and reductionism 3, 19, 95, 123
differential development: and contradictory unity 47–49
diffusion: articulation and combination 212–13
distributed force: and political order 234–36, 242
division of labour 82
'domestic analogy' 151, 156, 157, 163, 179
domination 17, 30, 31, 34, 65, 70, 71, 76, 79, 92, 96, 98, 100, 103–5, 144, 189, 238
Draper, H. 77, 79, 82
Duménil, E. 173
dumping: and anti-dumping policy 132–33

East Asian Co-Prosperity Area 131
economies of scale 5, 127, 128, 129, 130, 131, 136, 138, 139, 142, 144, 145, 146
economism 3, 46, 110, 111, 112, 118; and Marxist anti-economism 121–23
Eisenhower, D. 92
Egypt 237
emancipation 3
empire: British 43; Ottoman 9, 210; Roman 36, 202; *see also* informal empire
Engels, F. 129, 176; class-equilibrium theory 112
England 20, 34, 41, 91, 96, 170, 188, 189, 193, 200, 214, 240
English Civil War and Glorious Revolution 43–44
Environment 80, 98, 99, 102, 106, 107, 131, 208, 232
equality 50, 52, 154, 172, 177, 235
essentialism 153, 154, 156, 158, 170, 177
Estulin, D. 58, 59
'ethical realism' 178, 182; *see also* realism

ethics: and international relations 27, 166; and Marxism 3, 122; and Realism 178; Weber on 166, 182
Eurocentrism 210–11
European Commission Competition Directorate (DGIV) 133
European Union (EU) 43; anti-trust regulation 133–34; Constitution 59; Single Market 131; transnational capitalism 68–69
Evenett, S.: *et al* 134
exchange relations 66, 162, 174, 188, 199
exchange rates 187, 191
exchange-value 48, 140, 181, 192
expressive totality: capitalism 80

fair value 132
Fanon, F. 224
fascism 98, 222
feminism 108
feudalism 118
finance capital 20, 33, 35, 36, 37, 50, 51, 78, 112, 143, 186, 190
Finland 53
Flamm, K. 132
flexible accumulation 32
force and political order 234–36, 242
Fordism 98–99, 106; Americanism and passive revolution 217, 220–23
foreign investment 51,
foreign policymaking: and capitalism 45, 68, 69, 70, 84–85, 98–99; and ideology 36
Foster, J.B. 68
France: capitalist transition 33–34
free trade agreements (FTAs) 135
free trade 5, 28, 36, 70, 102, 132, 143, 144; and imperialism 131
French Revolution 219
Friedman, T. 51, 108
functionalism 17, 18

G8 24
Gabon 225
Gamble, Andrew 87
Gemienschaft und Gesellschaft (Tönnies) 78
gender: and gendered narratives 108; and globalizing capital 105–6; and Iraq War 108; and War on Terror 108
general abstractions: danger 153, 156–58, 165, 169, 185, 192, 195
General Agreement on Tariffs and Trade (GATT) 125, 132

geopolitical competition 16–17, 27, 38, 39, 62, 89, 114, 116, 150, 193; and logic of capital 19–23
geopolitics 13, 15, 16, 162–63, 164, 221, 222; and capitalism 95–98
German State Debate 191
Germany 91, 191: as late developer 22; and Nazism 87–88; and WWII 87–88 99, 146
Gerschenkron, A. 35, 190–91
Gerstenberger, H. 31
Giddens, A. 16, 67
Gindin, S.: and Panitch, L. 15, 16, 24, 78
global capitalism: crisis and US state 70–73; transnational state apparatus 68–70
global governance: class format 49–51
global state 77–79, 89
globalization 4, 5, 13, 27, 63, 75, 137–38; and class 66–67; Globalization theory 36, 38, 47, 138, 153; and imperialism 4, 14, 144
Godelier, M. 238
Gowan, P. 5, 15, 24, 125–46
Graham, E. 133–34
Gramsci, A. 9, 46, 51, 52, 191, 215–30
Greater East-Asian Co-Prosperity Sphere 39
Greenspan, A. 78
Grossman, H. 88
Grundrisse (Marx) 79, 81, 154, 168
Grupo Carso 75
Gulf War 108

Haldon, J. 238
Halliburton 72
Halliday, F. 78, 210
Halperin, S. 141
Hardt, M. 15, 17, 28, 37; and Negri, A. 78, 113, 151
Harman, C. 15, 23, 90
Harvey, D. 4, 15, 16, 18, 19, 21, 23, 29, 31, 64–68, 74, 80, 88–89, 223
Hayek, Friedrich 154
Heckscher-Ohlin Model 145
Hegel, G.W. 46, 47, 81
hegemony: Western 43–60
hegemonic stability theory 25
Herodotus 181
Hicks, Sir J. 128–29
high tech economic warfare 135–37; civilian aircraft production 136–37; semi-conductor production 135–36
Hilferding, R. 14, 40, 61
historical materialism 46; renaissance 1–9
historicism (historicity) 2, 4, 46, 48, 74

historical sociology 149, 152, 171, 179, 215, 229
History of the Russian Revolution (Trotsky) 7
Hobbes, T. 241
Hobsbawm, E. 219, 226
Hobson, J.A. 73
Hobson, J.M. 5, 110–24, 209–10, 215, 221
Hochschild, A. 106–7
Holland 20, 85, 188, 189, 193
Holloway, J. 188
Holocaust 87–88
humanitarian intervention 49
Hungary 46
Hume, D. 234, 237, 239–41
Hundred Years War 90
Huntington, S. 13
Hussein, Saddam 100, 104

Iceland 91
idealism 27
identity: national 63; and culture 13, 48, 106; and norms 220
ideology 1, 3, 9, 62, 87, 88, 92, 106, 135, 154, 160, 161, 165, 171, 178, 215, 220, 222
imperialism 4, 48, 73, 92, 143, 151, 225, 226; enlargement of capitalism 73–76; Lenin-Bukharin theory 14–15, 16, 27–28, 36, 38, 40; new imperialism 64–68, 69, 70; renewed debate 14–19; USA global power 6, 61–62, 70–73, 94–109
India 51, 66, 71
Indonesia 71
industrial competition: increasing returns to scale 126–29; learning economies 129–30, 131; and political tensions 126–31
industrial development: capitalism 125–46; industrial mercantilist school 125; neoclassical school 125
Industrial Revolution 35, 188
informal empire 15, 24, 39
Information and Communication Technologies (ICT) 141
inter-imperialist rivalries 16–17, 36, 39
internal relations: philosophy 275
'the international': beyond political Marxism 6–9, 197–214; and politics 231–47
international division of labour: power hierarchy/process 139–40
international institutions 17, 70
international law 27
International Monetary Fund (IMF) 69, 70
international political conflict: capitalism 125–46

International Relations (IR) 27; and Marxism 2–4
inter-societal relations: diffusionism 209–10, 212–13; problem in Marxist theory 3; and uneven and combined development 6
Internet 46–47
Iran 100, 101
Iranian Revolution (1979) 101
Iraq 72, 90, 100, 104–5, 109, 205
Ireland 170
Islam 100–101, 104, 210, 244
Israel 47, 58, 85, 177
Italy: passive revolution 218

Jacobins 218
James, O. 85
Jameson, F. 2
Japan 131, 140, 141; semi-conductor production 136; and transnational capitalist class 53
Jessop, B. 217

Kabila, L. 225
Kagarlitsky, B. 91
Kant, I. 154
Kautsky, K. 14–15, 22, 37, 63, 113
Kennedy, J.F. 176
Keynes, J.M. 154
Keynesianism 72, 106
Kidron, M. 85–86
Kiely, R. 14, 15, 18, 75
Kissinger, H. 58, 59, 176
Kjellén, R. 220
Klare, M. 62, 98
Krasner, Stephen 145
Kuwait 100

labour: abstract 21, 161, 172, 192; division of 74, 75, 82, 135, 139–40, 142, 184, 187, 190; and globalization 23, 48, 69, 141, 224; as movement 83; resistance to capital 70, 79; unfree 83
labour-power 19, 89, 95, 154, 173, 174, 186, 187, 188, 200
Lacher, H. 20, 80, 96–97, 111, 115, 117–18, 198, 200, 201, 202, 203–5; and Teschke, B. 4–5, 17, 27–41, 94, 118–21
Laffey, Mark 50, 210
landed property 20
late development 35, 40, 190, 194, 204
Latin America: passive revolution 226–28
law of value 172
learning economies: industrial competition 129–30, 131

Lebanon 177
Lebensraum 39
Lefebvre, H. 72, 229
legitimate authority: and political order 239–43
Lenin, V. 14, 22–23, 28, 29, 36, 48, 61
Lenin-Bukharin theory 27–28, 36, 38, 40; capitalism 14–15, 16
liberalism 159–60, 165, 166, 176, 177, 178
Liberia 225
Lieven, A. 105
Locke, J. 236
Lockean Heartland: defining characteristics 43; and Western hegemony 6, 43–60
Löwy, M. 226
Lukács, G. 2, 5, 80, 81, 215
Luttwak, E. 86
Luxemburg, R. 40
Lynch, J. 108

Machiavelli, Niccolò 240
McCain, J. 109
McCulloch, J.R. 126
MacIntyre, A. 79
McMichael, P. 217, 227–28
Mamdani, M. 224
Mandel, E. 85, 224
Mann, M. 16, 17, 18, 19, 115, 119, 120, 171, 178–79
Marginalism 126
Marshall, A. 126–27
Marxist imperialism theory: 4, 15, 18, 28, 91, 149, 150, 164; poverty 36–38
Marxist International Relations Theory (MIRT) 110–24; collapsed base-superstructuralism 117–21; relative autonomy approach 112–13, 121; two logics pluralism 113–17
Marxist state theory 29, 112, 175
masculinity: and militarism 95, 106, 108; and geopolitics 95, 98; and working class 106; 'masculinized militarism' 95, 106 108
Matin, K. 111, 211–12
Mayer, A. 24
Mearsheimer, J. 21, 154, 175
Melian Dialogue 162–63
Mercantilism 5, 33, 125,126, 131, 132–37, 138, 188, 218
Mexican Revolution 227
Mexico 75, 226, 228
Mezzogiorno 218
microfoundations 21–22
Miéville, China 83

militarism 86, 108, 118
Milosevic, S. 49
Mitchell, T. 83
Mitteleuropa 39
A Modern Utopia (Wells) 77
mode of production; 6, 8, 21, 64, 153, 154,
    158–59, 183, 193; forces of production
    82; and international/inter-societal/foreign
    relations 23–24, 79, 88, 92, 93, 116, 118,
    123, 151, 212; and Marx 16, 19, 81, 112,
    157; and uneven and combined
    development 195
'mode of foreign relations' (Van der Pijl)
    42, 52
monopoly capitalism 48–49
Monroe Doctrine 43, 98
Morgenthau, H. 176–77
Morton, A.D. 9, 73, 215–30
Mossadegh, M. 101
Multilateral Agreement on Investment 47
Multilateralism 47, 99, 135
multinational enterprise (MNE) 138, 145;
    classification 139; distribution 139
Munck, R. 226

Napoleon I 44
'national interest' 18, 19, 38, 63, 86, 87,
    166; and capitalist class 29
nation states and transnational capital 69–70
national economies: myth 62–63
nationalism 35, 59, 87, 88, 93, 105, 167,
    191, 210, 222
National Patriotic Front of Liberia 225
Native Americans 98
Navigation Act 43
Nazism: and capitalism 87–88; and
    holocaust 87
Negri, A. 15, 17, 28, 37; and Hardt, M. 78,
    113, 151
neo-classical economics 125, 128–29; and
    Other Canon 126, 130–31
neo-conservatism 90
neo-Gramscian theory: post-Fordism and
    imperial power 94–109
neo-liberalism 71–72
neo-realism 116–17
New Deal 106
new imperialism 15–16, 62–63; reification
    and theoreticism 64–68
The New Imperialism (Harvey) 16, 21, 64–68
New International Economic Order 49
New Left Review 15
Nietzsche, F. 154, 165, 178
non-reductionist Marxism 110–24

norms 3, 106, 125, 133, 144, 180, 187,
    191, 199, 220, 235
North Atlantic Treaty Organization
    (NATO) 91
North-South framework 75
North-South relations 125
NSC-(68) 92, 98–100

Obama, B. 109
Oborne, P. 84–85
oil: and USA foreign policy 99, 100
Ollman, B. 81
'Open Door' 98
Ottoman Empire 210
organic intellectual 52
overaccumulation 66, 71, 73

Pacific Rim Union 59
Paine, T. 103
Pakistan 101
Palestine 58
Panitch, L.: and Gindin, S. 15, 16, 24, 78
Parsons, T. 177
Partito d'Azione 218
Passages from Antiquity to Feudalism
    (Anderson) 158
passive revolution: and the African state
    224–26; Americanism and Fordism 217,
    220–23; geopolitics 215–30; Latin
    America 226–28
pastoral nomadism 235
Pentagon 72, 101, 107
Perle, R. 59
Perón, J. 226
permanent revolution 7, 214
Persian Gulf: geopolitics of 98, 101
Philippines 98
Piedmont 218
Pinochet, A. 227
Poland 221
Polanyi, Karl 64
political accumulation 19, 22, 153–54, 158,
    170, 188, 209
political Marxism 9, 31, 40, 41, 111, 118,
    122; and 'the international' 197–214
political order 232–36; coercive rule 233,
    236–39; community governance 235; and
    distributed force 234–36; force 232; and
    legitimate authority 239–43; territory and
    collective action 243–45
Political Power and Social Classes (Poulantzas)
    112
politicians: state managers and capitalists
    83–88

Politics as a Vocation (Weber) 178
Polybius 178, 181
Portugal 188, 221
post-Fordist capitalism: and blue-collar
    patriotism 105–9; and imperial
    power 94–109
post-colonial states 217, 224
post-Napoleonic restoration 219
post-Washington consensus 71
Poulantzas, N. 80, 112, 113, 118, 193
Poverty 85, 102, 159, 184, 190
Pozo-Martin, G. 14, 18, 21, 82, 89, 113–14,
    175, 194
primitive accumulation 76, 225
Principles of Economics (Marshall) 126–27
privatization 72, 95, 187
production: capitalist relations 140–42;
    feudal 8, 19, 33, 82, 158, 170, 188; forces
    of 140–42
productive forces: and social relations 46–47
property rights 33
protectionism 94, 131, 132, 146, 234, 239,
    242, 246
Prussia 45, 216, 228; *see also* Germany
public goods 24, 25, 232, 239, 245
public sector 129–30
public sphere 43
Puerto Rico 98

Quebec 43
Quine, W.V.O. 245

race 46
Rand, A. 78
rate of profit 20, 192; tendency to fall 21,
    127, 192, 221
Raviv, Or 53
Rawls, John 154
realism 116–17, 152, 153, 154, 155, 158,
    159–69, 171, 175–79, 205
real subsumption of labour 184, 188, 189
Reagan, Ronald 108
Rees, J. 15
Reinert, E.S. 125–26, 144
relative autonomy 5, 111, 112–13, 115, 121,
    122, 124
Results and Prospects (Trotsky) 6
returns to scale: industrial competition
    126–29
revolution: 'from above' 35; passive 9, 51,
    60, 191, 215–30
Revolutionary United Front: Sierra Leone
    225
Ricardo, D. 145

Rice, Condoleezza 45
Risorgimento 218, 228
Robinson, W. 5, 15, 28, 61–76, 79, 113
Rodrik, D. 130
Roosevelt Corollary 98
Rosenberg, J. 8, 95, 111, 183–85, 191–93,
    194, 197, 206–8, 211, 215; Callinicos
    letter exchange 149–82
Rothbard, M. 78
Rousseau, J.-J. 239
rules of reproduction 19, 32
Rupert, M. 6, 94–109
Russia 7–8, 50–51; Bilderberg Istanbul
    Conference (2007) 59
Russo-Japanese War 91
Rwanda 225

Sack, R.D. 243–44
Sanctions 78, 239
Sankoh, F. 225
Sassen, S. 74
Saudi Arabia 100
Sayer, D. 81
Schlesinger, A. 176
Schmitt, C. 234
Schumpeter, J. 126, 127, 128, 129
Scientific Man versus Power Politics
    (Morgenthau) 176–77
Scotland 43
Scottish Enlightenment 240
Second International 7, 46
Second World War 15, 92
semi-conductor production: economic warfare
    135–36
Semi-Conductor Trade Agreement
    (STA) 136
September 11th attacks 102, 104
Serfati, C. 15
Sierra Leone 225
Singapore 61
Sklair, L. 52
Skocpol, T. 16, 19, 33, 115, 119
Slavery 214, 222
Smith, A. 126
Smith, H. 151
social contract 234, 258
social property relations 201, 202; and base/
    superstructure problem 198–200
social relations: and productive forces 46–47
social theory of value 3
Socialism 46, 48, 77
Socrates 246
South Africa 66, 71, 76
South Korea 138

Sovereignty 13, 17, 23, 29, 31, 34, 35,
    38, 47, 79, 82, 96, 103, 120, 159,
    221, 224
Soviet Union 83; state managers 85
space and globalization 66–67
spatio-temporal fixes 66
Spain 170, 188, 221
Stalinism 85
state building 19, 153, 170, 180, 188,
    189, 225
state capitalism 78, 85, 91, 214
state class 35, 42, 45, 51
state managers: politicians and
    capitalists 83–88
states system: and capitalism 4, 9, 13–26,
    28–36, 39, 80, 89, 110, 200–202, 218,
    222
state theory 195; Marxist 112; Weberian
    17, 83
Stirner, M. 78
structuralism 199
sub-Saharan Africa 225, 226
Subjectivity 41, 141
Suez Crisis 92
Sulayman The Magnificent 210
Sumer 247
Superstructure *see* base/superstructure
    metaphor
surplus-labour 170, 186
surplus value 161–62, 171–75, 187, 188
Sutherland, P. 58
Switzerland 61

Taliban 106
taxation 35, 44, 78, 84, 112, 191, 214
Taylor, C. 225
Taylor, M. 235
Ten Hours Act (1847) 112
territoriality 29, 34, 35, 43, 67, 80, 82, 97,
    114, 205, 220, 243, 244
territory: and political order 243–45
Teschke, B. 80, 82, 83, 111, 115, 198, 200,
    201, 202, 203–5; and Lacher, H. 4–5, 17,
    27–41, 94, 118–21
Thatcher government 87
'theoreticism' 5, 64–68
Third International 25, 77, 123, 216
'Thirty Years' War 200–201
Thrasymachus 239
Thucydides 162–63
Tillman, P. 108
time-space distanciation 67
Tocqueville, Alexis de 154
Tönnies, F. 78

totality 2, 5, 44, 48, 64, 75, 80–88, 160,
    165, 171, 192, 211; expressive 80
Toyotism 130
trade: liberalization 28, 36, 39, 59, 70, 99,
    102, 131, 135, 143; policy 133, 143
trade unions 106
transhistorical: uses 169–71, 183–99, 207
transnational capital 62–63; and Western
    hegemony 43–60
transnational capitalist class 62, 70, 71;
    Bilderburg Conference (2007) 51–60; class
    strategists 52; interlocking directorates
    52–53; and Japan 53
transnational state: and global capitalism
    61–76; USA state and global capitalism
    crisis 70–73
transnational state apparatus 5, 23, 28, 79;
    and global capitalism 61–76; USA state
    and global capitalism crisis 70–73
Trasformismo 218
Treaty of Rome (1957) 133, 146
Treaty of Westphalia (1648) 200–201
Trilateral Commission 58
Trinity Formula 162
Trotsky, L. 6–7, 22, 40, 73, 149, 155–58,
    164, 169, 170, 190–91, 194, 207, 208,
    212, 213, 219
Trotskyism 124
Truman, H. 92
Turkey 210
The Twenty Years' Crisis (Carr) 176
two logics pluralism 113–17

Uganda 225
Ugandan Peoples' Defence Force 225
ultra-imperialism 14–15, 22, 37, 38, 63,
    113
underdevelopment 131, 184, 190
unequal development 29, 75, 115
uneven and combined development 6–9, 23,
    115, 149–82, 225, 226, 229, 230;
    articulation 212–13; capitalist forms
    205–12; capitalist political forms 185–89;
    capitalist social relations 185–89; danger
    of general abstractions 156–58; diffusion
    212–13; extensions 206–7; mode
    of production approach 158–59; pre-
    capitalist forms 207–8; realism 159–69;
    theoretical status 191–94; and the
    transhistorical 169–71, 183–96
unilateralism 102, 133
United Kingdom (UK) 100, 180
United Nations (UN) 49
United Netherlands 85

United States of America (USA):
Americanism and Fordism 217, 220–23;
anti-dumping policy 132–33; anti-trust
regulation 133–34; blue-collar patriotism
105–9; exceptionalism ideologies 103–5;
Fordist geopolitics 98–103; global
capitalism crisis and US state 70–73;
Global War on Terror 100, 102, 104,
105, 108; Gulf geopolitical project
100–103; hegemony 24, 78–79;
imperialism and global power 94–109;
and Iran 100, 101; National Security
Council document (NSC-68) 92, 98–100
Uruguay Round 132
Universalism 166, 176, 177
use-value 21, 48, 140, 172, 173, 175, 192,
207, 208

value 3, 161–62, 164, 171–75
value theory 175
Van der Pijl, K. 6, 43–60, 219
Vargas, G. 226
Veblen, T. 49
Vernon, R. 47
Vietnam 107, 108
Vietnam War 107–8
violence 83

wage labour 20, 173, 186, 187
Wallerstein, I. 110
Walras, L. 128
Waltz, K. 13, 21, 154, 157, 166
war: and capitalism 4
War on Iraq 1, 15, 58, 72, 90, 100–101,
105, 108–9, 205

War on Terror 72, 83, 100, 101, 102, 105, 108
Washington consensus 71, 72
Weber, M. 31, 50, 154, 165, 166, 178
Weberians 29–30, 114, 120
welfare policy 112
welfare state 72
Wells, H.G. 77
Wendt, A. 26
Western hegemony: Bilderberg Conference
(2007) 51–60; and China 51; contender
states 42–45, 46; global governance
49–51; and Russia 50–51; and
transnational capital 43–60; vassals 45, 51
Williams, B. 232
Wilsonianism 182
Wolf, E. 3, 208
Wood, E.M. 4, 8, 29, 63, 67–69, 79, 80, 82,
95, 185, 186, 198–99, 200, 201, 202,
205–6
Workers Party: Brazil 76
working class *see* proletariat
World Bank 59
World Economic Forum 53
World Systems theory 110, 151, 198
World Trade Organization (WTO) 69, 131,
132, 137, 141, 142
World War One 91
World War Two 92

'Young Turks' 210
Yugoslavia 91

Zaire 225
zero-sum games 90, 99, 239
Zoellick, R. 59